THE SIGNET CLASSIC
POETRY SERIES is under the
general editorship of poet, lecturer,
and teacher JOHN HOLLANDER.
Mr. Hollander's first volume
of poetry, *A Crackling of Thorns*,
won the Yale Series of Younger Poet
Awards for 1958. He was a recipient of a
National Institute of Arts and Letters
grant (1963) and has been a member of
the Wesleyan University Press Poetry
Board and the Bollinger Poetry
Translation Prize Board. Mr. Hollander is
Professor of English at Hunter College.

SIGNET CLASSIC POETS OF THE
17th CENTURY, VOLUMES
ONE AND TWO, are edited by
John Broadbent, formerly of
King's College, Cambridge, and
currently Professor of English
Literature, School of English and
American Studies, University of East
Anglia, Norwich, England.

SIGNET CLASSIC POETS
OF THE 17th CENTURY
VOLUME TWO

*An anthology of
about 250 poems and extracts
by 100 poets
of the 17th century*

———◆◆———

EDITED BY

John Broadbent

THE SIGNET CLASSIC POETRY SERIES
GENERAL EDITOR:
John Hollander

A SIGNET CLASSIC
NEW AMERICAN LIBRARY
TIMES MIRROR
NEW YORK AND SCARBOROUGH, ONTARIO
THE NEW ENGLISH LIBRARY LIMITED, LONDON

Library of Congress Catalog Card Number: 74–79805

ACKNOWLEDGMENTS

EDWARD TAYLOR: "I, kenning through astronomy." Originally published in *New England Quarterly*, #10, 1937. Reprinted by permission of *New England Quarterly* and Thomas H. Johnson. "Upon a wasp chilled with cold." Originally published in *New England Quarterly*, #16, 1943. Reprinted by permission of *New England Quarterly* and Thomas H. Johnson. "Meditation. Can. I. 12" (beginning "Lord, dub my tongue . . ."). Reprinted by permission from the *Yale University Library Gazette*, Vol. XXIX, No. 1 (July 1954).

SIGNET, SIGNET CLASSICS, MENTOR, PLUME and
MERIDIAN BOOKS are published *in the United States* by
The New American Library, Inc., 1301 Avenue of the Americas,
New York, New York 10019, *in Canada* by
The New American Library of Canada Limited,
81 Mack Avenue, Scarborough, 704, Ontario, *in the
United Kingdom* by The New English Library Limited,
Barnard's Inn, Holborn, London, E.C.1, England

First Printing, December, 1974

1 2 3 4 5 6 7 8 9

PRINTED IN THE UNITED STATES OF AMERICA

PREFACE

I have modernised the spelling and punctuation of all texts. They have been drawn from a variety of British and American sources, and they carry no textual authority. The table of contents doubles as an index to first lines and titles.

I am grateful to the publishers and to the general editor John Hollander for giving me the opportunity to compile this anthology; and to King's College, Cambridge, and the Universities of Cambridge and East Anglia for maintaining me and giving me leave while I started the work.

J. B. B.

CONTENTS

[vii]

COMMENTARY 3   108

James I
1603–1625

Religion: Scripture and Emblems

COMMENTARY 5   176

King Charles I
1625–1649

Pre-War Poets

ANONYMOUS 183

THE REVEREND WILLIAM STRODE (1602–1645) 184

ROBERT BARON (fl 1645) 191

WILLIAM HABINGTON (1605–1654) 192

THE REVEREND CLEMENT BARKSDALE (1609–1687) 198

COMMENTARY 7   270

*Civil War and
Commonwealth
1642–1660*

Baroque Religion

COMMENTARY 8   314

*Civil War and
Commonwealth
1642–1660*

Friendship and Marriage

COMMENTARY 9   351

*Commonwealth
and Restoration
1649–1685*

Satire and Panegyric

COMMENTARY 10   396

*Restoration
and Revolution
1660–1688*

Sentiment and Burlesque

COMMENTARY 11   439

*Restoration
and Revolution
1660–1688*

Religion: Hymns and Visions

INTRODUCTION

This is an anthology of about 250 extracts from the work of 100 poets writing between 1600 and 1688. It excludes Ben Jonson, George Herbert, Milton, Crashaw, Vaughan, Marvell and Dryden because they are represented in Volume One of *Signet Classic Poets of the 17th Century*; and most of them are represented again, on a fuller scale, in the volumes devoted to individuals of the period in the Signet Classic Poetry series. Each volume can be used independently but they fit into this design: (1) Volume One introduces the great poets of the century. (2) The individual volumes represent most of them again more fully and with more elaborate apparatus. (3) This volume, Volume Two, provides the setting for the great poets, and offers a history of 17th-century poetry which is meant to speak for itself.

But the chief function of this volume is to put forward a number of writers and poems in their own right. They may be unfamiliar; and so when considered against the arrangement of this volume, they may suggest a new canon—or at least an independent canon—of 17th-century poetry; and hence, perhaps, of poetry in general, for us.

Many histories of 17th-century poetry have been written, and many interpretations and classifications imposed on it. It is divided into spheres of influence—Jonson and Donne, Miltonic and Metaphysical, Cavalier and Roundhead; it is split by the civil war, or by a dissociation of sensibility, or by the Chinese Wall of Milton's verse; it deteriorates with the change in the nature of 'wit', or the loss of religious faith. Each pattern is the herald of an ideology which the critic or historian wants to promote *now*—naturally enough; but, that being so, you might as well compose your own account, on the basis of the poems here and in other volumes, and of the reading-lists at the end of this volume.

Of course this volume too is biassed. The choice of which poets to include in it, and which to promote to the companion volume of (major) poets, would be different at the margins for every editor; but it is not an entirely personal choice: the economics of publishing, the physique of books, the design of syllabuses, affect it powerfully. What *is* personal is the choice of poets and poems inside this volume. You can check my prejudices against somebody else's anthology and against your own. In general, I think my selection differs from others now popular in the following ways:

Prejudice against: The lighter 'lyric' element in Jonson, the 'cavalier' in Suckling. Laborious elegance in Campion, Drummond. The notion of there being something called 'metaphysical poetry'. Decayed wit of the metaphysical sort as in Cowley and Waller, who both seem to me at their best when dotty. The canonical Restoration poets: Shadwell seems to me superior to Dryden as a satirist, and Otway as a dramatist; Flatman superior to Rochester.

Prejudice for: Various poets, mostly minor in the sense of having not written much or not often rung the bell, who nevertheless achieve something extraordinary or eccentric or bizarre, in diction (e.g. Dekker, Benlowes, Joseph Beaumont), or in rhythm (Barksdale, Cleveland, Davenant, Heyrick, Anne Killigrew), or in sentiment (Marston, Latham, Strode, Habington, Cartwright, Jane Barker). A few who have original intellects—Chapman, Butler, the Duchess of Newcastle. Several, again, in the Restoration period, who are known to the ordinary reader merely as figures of fun but who strike me as special people—Nahum Tate, Flecknoe; Traherne and Edward Taylor, who have still not been written in to the history of 17th-century religious poetry. Women poets. Documentary poets such as Rowlands, Corbet, Quarles, in whom you hear the authentic voice of the time, and poetry going into dark corners. Bawdy and anonymous more-or-less-folk poetry. The special notes of verse written for masque and drama. Mad poets, or writers of what amounts to mad poetry, e.g. John Taylor the Water Poet, Burton, Duffett.

I have included one or two poets because they are significant in history *and* have rich personalities showing in their work—Fanshawe, Montrose, Ann Bradstreet; but nearly all the poets here belong to a network of relationship which can be traced through the entire volume. For example, to be local—I am writing in Norwich—Ralph Knevet (Section 7) was chaplain to a Norfolk family, and active in Norwich, at the period when Sir Thomas Browne was a physician here and Richard Corbet (Section 2) was bishop of Norwich; Corbet was acquainted with Fulke Greville (Section 1) and Jonson (Vol. I); and when he was Dean of Christ Church his chaplain had been William Strode (Section 5), whose play for Charles I and Queen Henrietta-Maria had music by Lawes; Lawes wrote the music for *Comus,* and acted in it; and Milton wrote a sonnet to him—so back to Vol. I again.

The poems themselves, and what you make of them, are the only worthwhile flesh of any introduction to 17th-century poetry. I have however provided a skeleton, in the series of periods and themes under which I arrange the poems. Here it is, contracted from the contents pages and showing where I would place the poets of Vol. I.

James I   1603–1625
 1. Melancholy
 2. Pastoral
 3. Religion: scripture and emblems
   George Herbert 1593–1633
 4. Courtly sex
   Ben Jonson 1572–1637
   John Donne 1572–1631

Charles I   1625–1649
 5. Pre-war poets
   Robert Herrick 1591–1674

Civil War and Commonwealth 1642–1660
 6. Casualties and survivors
 7. Baroque religion
   John Milton 1608–1674
   Richard Crashaw 1612–1650
   Henry Vaughan 1622–1695
 8. Friendship and marriage
   Andrew Marvell 1621–1678

Commonwealth and Restoration 1649–1685
 9. Satire and panegyric
   John Dryden 1642–1692

Restoration and Revolution 1660–1688
 10. Sentiment and Burlesque
 11. Religion: hymns and visions

The skeleton is original, arbitrary, expendable; but I believe its articulations represent some useful ways of arranging the material. Of course there was satire and panegyric under James I as well as under Charles II; my Section 9 indicates merely that during the Commonwealth and Restoration period it emerged as one of the dominant modes. I realise that 'pre-war poets' is not an adequate classification; but I believe it points to a more profitable way of thinking about Randolph, Suckling and Godolphin, say, than the usual Caroline or Cavalier.

Each poet is represented in only one section, so there is a good deal of squeezing. Which section a poet is squeezed into depends partly on his dates but also on how I use him to represent a particular tradition or motif in the century. I have used a few poems as cement: e.g. Harding's elegy on the great dead which ends Section 5 could as well open Section 6. I often push elegiac poems towards the end of sections, and funny ones towards the beginning.

Within each poet, I have tried to make the poems run in some sort of order, usually thematic. For example, in Section 4, Carew, a tiresomely various writer, starts with a poem, *Love's force*, which moves from a primitivistic to a Platonic position; then we have two fetish poems (Celia's mole and Celia's blood); then, in *Ask me no more*, a poem packed with little fetishes or conceits, the centre of Carew's work and indeed a centre of 17th-century verse; then a pastoral poem, a pastoral dialogue, and a nuptial dialogue; and two epitaphs. The epitaphs lead into the next poet, Henry King.

The skeleton itself proposes relations between the poetry and history. Each of the eleven sections also has its own introduction. These sectional introductions are concerned with the poetry more than with history or pattern; but they suggest ways in which the material of that section might be worked on in order to produce an account of the state of sensibility at that time; quite often, the introductions are concerned with specific historical processes such as change in the status of women, superstition, attitudes to kingship.

Those are only suggestions for further work. In the footnotes, however, I have been as full as possible because there is a shortage of annotation that answers the questions that readers actually ask. In some cases I don't know the answers.

It will be seen that I am sceptical about the value of literary history as at present written, and eclectic about criticism; for, as Butler says in Section 9, 'All pheonomenás May be expounded several ways'. So in the case of each poet I offer hardly more than an indication of where to start work for oneself. But I am not sceptical about private initiatives, or about criticism conducted in small groups. This volume is designed on the assumption that the reader will use it as a starter for work of his own, or as material for group activities. To pretend to more is to deny the virtue of poetry as messages from the interior:

The heart's land's unknown, wherein what monsters make
Their hides and dens, few yet have understood. . . .

—DANIEL CUDMORE Section 7

ADVERTISEMENT

Dekker
: Then, clapping their obstreperous squallid wings,
Each of them on the frozen Russian dings.

Quarles
: One rubs his itchless elbow, shrugs, and laughs,
The other bends his beetle brows, and chafes.

Strode
: When Westwell Downs I 'gan to tread,
  Where cleanly winds the grass did sweep,
Methought a landscape there was spread,
  Here a bush and there a sheep.

Habington
: Then in the language of the drum
  I will instruct my yet affrighted ear:
All women shall in me be dumb
  If I but with my Araphil be there.

Davenant
: There from sick mirth neglected feasters reel,
  Who cares of want in wine's false Lethe steep;
There anxious empty gamblers homeward steal
  And fear to wake ere they begin to sleep.

Cleveland
: I saw a vision yesternight
Enough to sate a Seeker's sight—
I wished myself a Shaker there
And her quick pants my trembling sphere.

Benlowes
: As nature's prime confectioner, the bee,
  By her flower-nibbling chemistry
Turns vert to or: so, verse gross prose does
  rarefy.

Joseph Beaumont
: Home's home, although it reachèd be
  Through wet and dirt and night.

Duke of Newcastle
: Love, forty years ago, served Dr. Donne,
But we're beyond it far: our wise delight
Is what we know, not know that's infinite.

Duchess of Newcastle
: Their eyes did stare, their lids were open wide,
For the small nerves were shrunk on every side.
In some again those glassy balls hung by

[7]

Small slender strings, as chains to tie the eye,
Which strings when broke, the eyes fell trundling
round
And then the film was broke upon the ground.

Thomas
Heyrick

Through devious ways are without Pole Star led
And upon barren desolate isles
They stupidly unto the care
Of hatching sands their shelly brood commend,
Or to the sun's auspicious smiles.

Cotton

See how like twilight slumber falls
To obscure the glory of those balls.

Anne
Killigrew

Sea-monsters there abide
The coming of the tide;
No noise is there
To make them fear;
God-sleep might there reside.

Durfey

Then murmurs in a soft complaint, and cries,
Alas! and thus in soft convulsions dies.

Edward
Taylor

Take earth's brightest darlings, in whose mouths
all flakes
Of luscious sweets she hath do crowd their
head:
Their spicèd cups, sweetmeats and sugar-cakes
Are but dry sawdust to this living bread.

COMMENTARY 1

James I
1603–1625

Melancholy

'Fair summer droops,' Nashe wrote in 1592 . . . 'Brightness falls from the air; Queens have died young and fair.' But the Elizabethan period had not been all summer. The Queen was 60 then, and died at 70, carrying the syphilis of Henry VIII. Essex, the young favourite of her old age, had concocted a futile rebellion against her and been executed. His sister, Sir Philip Sidney's Stella, had been married to another; Sidney had died at Arnhem.

But the agonies of living do not go in historical phases. These continued into the new century. Essex's son was married at the age of 14 to Lady Frances Howard; after a few years of unhappiness she divorced him to marry Robert Carr, ruling favourite of the homosexual James I; they murdered a jealous friend on the side, and were unmasked; their disgrace was the scandal of 1616, and occasion for a lot of poetry. Later, the young Essex remarried, again unhappily; he commanded the parliamentary army in the civil war, without perhaps adequate élan. The Carrs' grandson was executed in 1683 for plotting against Charles II.

Cowley complained that the English climate is bad enough for poetry at the best of times but that his century was 'a long and a sharp winter . . . a warlike, various, and a tragical age', specially difficult for writing in (preface to *Poems* 1656). Milton too complained about the weather (invocation at *Paradise lost* IX). Yet the century was not all wintry. Milton had been confident of his time and place: 'Lords and commons of England, consider what nation it is whereof ye are, and whereof ye are the governors: a nation not slow and dull but of a quick, ingenious and piercing spirit; acute to invent, subtle and sinewy to discourse' (*Areopagitica*). He was right: the nation was extraordinarily inventive—religions, political constitutions, New England, British India, logarithms, the decimal point, the circulation of the blood. Milton's adjectives define the poetry of the Commonwealth, as represented

[9]

here in sections 6–8. It has never been acknowledged because it is independent of the canonical 'great'. It contains some of the most viable poetry, as well as some of the oddest, in English.

In literature it was an age of expansion. Printing had been available for over 100 years; popular literature was being printed and sold in the streets (broadside ballads etc); literacy seems to have spread upwards from the middle class to be complete among the nobility and gentry (not the case at all in Henry VIII's time) and downwards to some extent as well. The production of books was accelerating: 1500, 45; 1630, 460; 1640, 550+.

The population was expanding too but much of the literary expansion is real because the population rise was much slower. The population of England in 1600 was about 4 or 4½ m, nearly all in small parishes and south of Yorkshire; by 1700 it was at most 6 m. But it was in our period that London achieved its dominance: the population of greater London doubled between 1600 and 1660, to perhaps ½ m.

All this means an increase in the rate of ideological and emotional metabolism. 'All coherence gone,' says Donne; 'crumbled out again to atomies.' But why does he say it? Marvell's age was much more crumbled but his poetry coheres, and is coherent; Laud was not confused, or Cromwell; Hobbes and Locke, and the founders of the Royal Society, had faith, in reason if not in God, in their own acuity of scepticism if not in reason. We take Donne's *Anniversaries* as we take *Lear* or *Troilus*, too literally, like advertisements we sneakingly believe. In reality, the medium overrides the message: the power to write *Lear*, to stage it and to understand it, denies the pessimism of its content. That power derived largely from the crumbling of the medieval castle; but it was an active crumbling, an anatomy, an investigation—not a loss of faith, or surrender to a *coup d'état*. For the first time in England the materials of the medieval world became available for analysis, and hence for re-synthesis. It is the 17th, not any earlier century, that is famous for making poetical use of the Christian cosmos—Samson as Christ, Christ as Apollo, the harmony of the spheres, tears frozen into diamonds, diamonds sovereign among gems as lions among beasts, and pure as virgin lilies. For the first time it became possible to *play upon* the co-ordinates of an item within the cosmic framework— the relationship, say, of the vital fluid called blood with blood as it stands for pedigree, breeding, and thence with blood as metaphor for lust, redeemable only by the blood of Christ— and so playing, as on strings, to elicit statements which were not there before; to find what there is to be said by trying to say it.

That was new. It accounts for the surprise—even if merely epigrammatic—of reading 17th-century poetry. Perhaps its lack also accounts for one's sense in reading 16th-century poetry that the ending is known—the stanza will conclude with an alexandrine, the feet will fit, the rhymes chime; and that the items brought into the poem will stay as they are and not turn into other things. Here is Spenser mourning *The ruins of time* in 1591:

> Where my high steeple whilom used to stand
> On which the lordly falcon wont to tower
> There now is but an heap of lime and sand
>   For the screech-owl to build her baleful
>   bower;
> And where the nightingale wont forth to pour
> Her restless plaint to comfort wakeful lovers
> There now haunt yelling mews and whining
>   plovers.
>
> And where the crystal Thamis wont to slide
> In silver channel down along the lea,
> About whose flowery banks on either side
> A thousand nymphs with mirthful jollity
>   Were wont to play, from all annoyance free,
> There now no river's course is to be seen
> But moorish fens and marshes ever green.

The stanzas, like a magic lantern, show us a succession of pictures which slide from one to the other—steeple with hawk, rubble with owl, and so on. Elizabethan love poetry is about beauty rather than love; in the same way, this lament points to sad objects rather than sadness.

Raleigh was the same age as Spenser but survived him for nearly 20 years until execution in 1618. I think his unfinished *Poem entreating of sorrow* will be found to accord with Spenser's mode. I have not included him here, but I have included Fulke Greville. He was Sidney's companion but lived till 1628. He sees that melancholy is not in the objects, but internal; the devils of the night 'expressions be of inward evils'. Yet he expresses his gloom with a Tudor stateliness, a solid list of items. One of his sonnets starts:

> Whenas man's life, the light of human lust,
> In socket of his earthly lantern burns,

> That all this glory unto ashes must
> And generation to corruption turns . . .

A full 17th-century poet would have elaborated that conceit
in detail—candle = phallus, lantern = body lit from within
by soul; and he would have at least implied possibilities arising
from that analysis—perhaps life *is* desire? Greville's concern
is not speculative; it is ethical:

> Then living men ask how he left his breath
> That, while he livèd, never thought of death.

With what manner did he die? and in what state, of grace, or
sin? That is Christian humanism. Its humanist element has
to do with man's dignity as a rational being rather than with
anything more familiarly, as we say, 'human'. L. G. Salingar
puts it in the *Pelican guide* to the age of Shakespeare:

> The main achievement of Elizabeth's age in poetry
> was to find a style of measured grandiloquence that
> answered to the renaissance ideals of civility and the
> active life. The rhetoric of the Jacobeans is more
> accomplished, more supple and condensed, with
> 'words perpetually juxtaposed in new and sudden
> combinations' [Eliot, essay on Massinger] . . . There
> is unbroken development from the 1590s . . . But
> . . . The crowded subtleties of the Jacobeans denotes
> a quicker sense of the ambiguities of humanism, its
> uncertainties and contradictions.

See Haydn, *The counter-renaissance*. Bacon's poem in this
section indicates that shift, statesman and polymath though
he was. Instead of overbearing mutability and grief with
stateliness, he clutches death and examines corruption on the
mind's tongue. He makes a wry face at the taste. He has
learned a Jacobean contempt for regal state, a contempt later
than *Tamburlaine* and Shakespeare's history plays: 'Courts
are but only superficial schools To dandle fools.' His last
couplet echoes Lear:

> What then remains, but that we still should cry
> Not to be born, or, being born, to die?

Even more clearly, Bacon's contemporary Chapman can be
seen bending Tudor language to more practical, plain, scepti-

cal but also more inward concerns. It is a puritan effort. Chapman has the rational sententiousness of Christian human-ism: 'Reason being ground, structure and ornament To all inventions grave and permanent.' Then he struggles with the priorities of soul and body—a typically Jacobean anxiety. He still uses kingly imagery but is pushing his way towards something more personal, like a puritan talking about the Holy Ghost:

> our bodies, that are traitors born
> To their own crowns, their souls; betrayed to
>   scorn,
> To gaudy insolence and ignorance
> By their base flesh's frailties; that most dance
> Profane attendance at their states and birth,
> That are mere servants to this servile earth—
> These must have other crowns for meeds than
>   merits,
> Or starve themselves and quench their fiery
>   spirits.

For the Elizabethans, body and soul were more easily, more catholically separable; for most poets of the 17th century, the tension between body and soul, the habit of each to drag the other with it, was a motive force; but except for Chapman and Donne it mostly took effect later, in the 1620s.

I have included Chapman because the shadow of night lies over his work; he is grave; he is wry—even when Corinna undresses, with a characteristically Elizabethan crackle of tinsel, he gets involved in a series of comparisons in which 'the brightest day Is but a black and melancholy shroud'. It was more common, though, for the Jacobeans' wryness to come out in two other tones, less thought-packed, less clutch-ing than Chapman's. There is the neat poise of Horace and Ben Jonson, represented here by Wotton: a beginning of the Cavalier cool. And there is the shouting as they stand under cataracts of grief and chaos, refusing to come out, of the tragic heroes and heroines.

Jacobean tragedy no longer celebrates the dignity of man as he suffers the terrible: it celebrates the terrible itself. The terrible had not altered but it was more articulately recognised as such (rather as, with improved communications, we also now recognize torture as part of war, instead of labelling it 'atrocity'). Perhaps this extravagant acceptance of the terrible acts of men was hoped to neutralise them. You meet vicious cruelty with stubborn agnosticism:

'Tis weakness
Too much to think what should have been done.
I go
I know not whither.   (*Malfi* V.ii)

But why do the excerpts from Jacobean tragedy seem so old-fashioned, so out of touch with the work of many of the poets who saw the plays? How is that losing of touch related to the change in 1625 from James's court to Charles I's slightly less extravagant, more stately, more feminine régime? And how to the consequent rise of masque? (Certainly the first 20 years of the century are rather bare of published verse; it floods out after 1625.) I think the loss of touch is not so much to do with extravagance of themes as with the dramatists' inability to match it. The themes were realistic: conspiracy, vengeance, murder, political execution were facts of life; adultery, homosexuality and edgy honour were endemic at court, incest in the country. But these are only the forms that motives take; the writers of the 17th century, other than these early dramatists, were increasingly concerned with the motives, so they discarded the sensational forms, or replaced them with more artificial ones such as Platonism. So the passion of Ford's brother and sister is less intense than that in the pastoral dialogues of Edward Herbert and Carew; the implicit violence of Davenant and Marvell, the implicit lesbianism of the matchless Orinda, are more satisfying than their obvious versions in Webster.

The drama shares with all the poetry of its time another quality: ordinariness. It is particularly ordinary at the point of death: 'I am i' the way to study a long silence. To prate were idle. I remember nothing' (*White devil*). Elizabethan heroes died with lips that were stiff but by no means shut. This taciturnity is Jacobean; so is the flattening of the enormous: 'I have caught An everlasting cold;' or, tied to a post and being stabbed, 'O, what blade is it? a Toledo, or an English fox?' (*White devil*). You can see from Marston's blank verse how close these dry histrionics are to the incipient prose of fiction and reportage: 'She fumbled out, Thanks, good. And so she died'. Sometimes it shifts into actual prose: 'What's this flesh? a little crudded milk, fantastical puff-paste' (*Malfi*). It is a prose of prancing vigour but every bit of it quotidian, like some American idiom to unfamiliar English ears, or Cockney before broadcasting.

More mainline is the *documentary* ordinariness of Dekker, Heywood, Nashe, Rowlands. Though older and using Elizabethan diction, they were more of the future than the sensational dramatists, perhaps because they were really journalists. Dekker's vocabulary is a vigorous Germanic laced with half-cooked polysyllables and impatiently chucked-in conceits— 'clapping their obstreperous squallid wings'. Added to that mixture is the mixture of folk life with the gods of Olympus —'sparrowbills to clout Pan's shoon'; and the raconteur's chatter in cosmic situations, such as hell—'I bellowed to the ferryman, methought'. In these points Dekker resembles Milton, as well as Du Bartas and Sylvester. It was the century that domesticated kings and God.

Jacobean literature seems all a mixture. I don't see any decorum of genres in it really. Heywood's *Lucrece*, a play about the rape of a Roman matron, contains both a Christian dirge and a bawdy catch. The catch was still being sung in another form when I was a boy, and it was mass-popularised later on the basis of a Negro spritual version with the refrain 'Hear the word of the Lord' (see *Did he take fair Lucrece by the toe man?*). The other way round, anonymous popular literature of this time is remarkable for its classical allusions— *The witch* and *Mad Tom* are about the most heavily anno-tated poems in this anthology. Perhaps this was more normal than we assume, even before the time of the Beatles and Simon and Garfunkle: Gilbert and Sullivan is highly allusive, Cole Porter's *Night and day* quotes *Tintern Abbey*; but I suspect that it *began* about 1600. The most significant case for us is John Taylor the water poet. He claims to have had 'no learning but the book of nature' yet as an adult read widely and wrote voluminously; his enthusiasm as a writer seems tinged with contempt for what he is doing, like a weightlifter singing; so I have represented him with a couple of anti-sonnets.

Taylor's nonsense sonnets—indeed, his entire life of mis-cellaneous exhibitionism—were one defence against madness. Madness was very evident—in the lunatics and vagrants, in the many who, like Burton himself, were psychiatrically ill but lived in the world; and on the stage. 'Surely we are all mad people' says Tourneur's revenger; 'This isle is a mere bedlam and therein We all lie raving, mad in every sin,' declares Drayton. Madness then was a form taken by other pressures of the time—by incoherence, violent change, evil, and of course by melancholy itself. Burton's treatise might as well have been called an anatomy of madness, or on the other hand an anatomy of psychology. The concern with melancholy, and with madness, was a concern with the more extreme cases of what people 'feel'.

For further independent work I would recommend Chapman, Dekker and Heywood: they seem to have been neglected at the expense of the more exciting but to my mind dead-end Webster, Tourneur, Ford. Start with verse analysis, especially for Chapman. Some useful smaller projects could be done on such topics as: treatments of Lucrece, including Shakespeare's and painting; melancholy; when did the vogue start for poems that mourn children? the earliest masques; the Somerset scandal; the Essex family; Turkey (starting with Greville's *Mustapha*) in the 17th century. Go back to Southwell and Constable: is their exclusion from this anthology justifiable? Consider the range of a miscellaneous writer at this time, e.g. Brathwaite, Taylor, Wither, and how an uneducated one like Taylor compares with a Nashe or Dekker; Marston other than as a playwright; handlings of the death of Prince Henry; versions of *Tom of Bedlam* (see ed. by J. Lindsay, n.d.); nonsense poetry; the prose of some of these poets.

THOMAS HEYWOOD

Dramatist of domestic realism and sentiment, e.g. *A woman killed with kindness*, tragedy of middle-class adultery c.1603. Lord Mayor's shows till they were stopped in 1640; *Hierarchy of the blessed angels*, a didactic poem, 1635. Friend of Cartwright, Jordan, Marmion. Start with selection ed. Verity 1888 and Swinburne's essay in *Age of Shakespeare* 1908; see Eliot in *Selected essays*, L. C. Knights in *Drama and society in the age of Jonson*. *Rape* ed. Holaday, Urbana 1950.

from The Rape of Lucrece

Dirge

Come, list and hark! the bell doth toll
For some but new-departing soul;
And was not that some ominous fowl—
The bat, the night-crow or screech-owl?
To these I hear the wild wolf howl   5
In this black night that seems to scowl.
All these my black book shall enroll
For, hark! still, still the bell doth toll
For some but now departing soul.

Catch

[Publius Valerius; Horatius; Clown]

Publius Valerius	Did he take fair Lucrece by the toe man?
Horatius	Toe man.
Publius Valerius	Aye man.
Clown	Ha ha ha ha man.
Horatius	And further did he strive to go man? 5
Clown	Go man.

[17]

Horatius	Aye man.
Clown	Ha ha ha ha man, fa derry derry down, ha ha derry dino.
Publius Valerius	Did he take fair Lucrece by the heel man?
Clown	Heel man.
Publius Valerius	Aye man.
Clown	Ha ha ha ha man.
Horatius	And did he further strive to feel man? etc. . . .
Publius Valerius	Did he take the lady by the shin man? . . .
Horatius	Further too would he have been man? . . .
Publius Valerius	Did he take the lady by the knee man? . . .
Horatius	Further than that would he be man? . . .
Publius Valerius	Did he take the lady by the thigh man? . . .
Horatius	And now he came it somewhat nigh man . . .
Publius Valerius	But did he do the tother thing man? . . .
Horatius	And at the same time had he a fling man?
Clown	Fling man.
Horatius	Aye man.
Clown	Ha ha ha ha man, ha fa derry derry down, ha fa derry dino.

1608

ANONYMOUS

from The song of the death of Mr. Thewlis
(to the tune of Dainty, come thou to me)

Then did he friendly leave
  Of all his brethren take,
Saying, Do you not grieve
  Nor mourn not for my sake;

For it is God's blessèd will   5
  That I must lead the way;
But be you constant still
  And I will for you pray.

And then with watery cheeks
  They parted mournfully;   10
His gesture little shrank,
  Such was his constancy.

Another constant wight,
  Which I had near forgot,
Was constant day and night   15
  And thankful for his lot:

One Wrennal was he called,
  A layman happy he.
They both prepared themselves
  On hurdle for to lie;   20

To the execution place
  They being thither drawn,
Present before their face
  Was fire one cruel flame.

Then did they them attempt   25
  Their faith for to deny,
Saying they must be hanged
  And buried cruelly.

Then, smiling, Thewlis said:
   If that the worst may be,   30
Our Saviour Christ hath paid
   Far greater pains for me.

Then mildly they prepared
   To the execution place.
Three felons they did see   35
   Hangèd before their face.

And at the ladder foot,
   Where many people stood,
He held them with dispute
   While ever they would abide.   40

Then did they proffer them
   Part of the oath to take
And they should not be slain
   Such friendship they would make.

But all could not prevail   45
   Their minds for to remove;
Nor once their courage quail
   So constant was their love.

With cross and signs so meek
   The ladder he did take,   50
Where many a watery eye
   Appearèd for his sake.

A hundred pounds was there
   For his life offered free
If he would yet consent   55
   A Protestant to be.

Then smilingly he said,
   That ransom I deny:
That may no way be paid
   But by death eternally.   60

I thank you for your loves,
   Your good will all I see;
But I must take the cross
   That Christ hath left for me.

Then willingly he did   65
   Himself most ready make;
He proffered to unbare
   And his clothe off to take.

A cap as white as snow
  Over his face pulled he;   70
His hat he threw him fro
  And purse away gave he.

The hangman played his part
  As he did him command:
Three strokes upon his breast   75
  He gave with his right hand.

          •   •   •

When that the rope was cut,
  And quartered he should be,
The hangman did deny
  And then away went he.   80

The sherrif did him oppress
  With great extremity
And said, Either thou or I
  Must do this butchery.

When Thewlis was unbared,   85
  A vision there was seen:
Out of his mouth appeared
  A colour bright and sheen

Most like the glorious sun
  Shining in clearest sky,   90
Down over his body run
  And vanish from their eye.

The butcher played his part,
  His body he did gore;
And sure the hardest heart   95
  Did much his death deplore.

A hundred handkerchieves
  With his sweet blood was dight
As relics for to wear
  For this said blessèd wight.   100

Then were his quarters set
  Upon the castle high,
Where happed as strange a thing
  As ever man did see:

A flight of ravens came   105
  And pickèd flesh from bones;
In the churchyard they did light
  And scrapèd there deep holes.

O Christian hearts, relent,
   Prepare your souls to save,   110
When feathered fowls shall help
   For us to make a grave!

O happy martyred saints,
   To you I call and cry
To help us in our wants   115
   And beg for us mercy!

O Christ, that suffered death
   Thy spouse for to defend,
Like constancy till death
   And in heaven be our end.   120

° **Thewlis**   a recusant priest, executed 1616. This is a ballad made up at
the time and sold in broadsheet form. Execution normally consisted of
being hanged, cut down while alive, genitals amputated, abdomen ripped
open and intestines burnt, body beheaded and carved into four quarters.
Beheading without these tortures was reserved for high political victims
such as Laud, Strafford, Charles I. Cf. Montrose *On himself.*

from The Masque of Flowers°

[Girls costumed as flowers are transformed into girls again.]

Thrice happy flowers!
   Your leaves are turned into fine hair,
   Your stalks to bodies straight and fair,
   Your sprigs to limbs, as once they were,
   Your verdure to fresh blood, your smell   5
   To breath; your bloom, your seedy cell,
   All have a lovely parallel.

Chorus   The nymphs that on their heads did wear you
           Henceforth in their hearts will bear you.

° **Masque**   celebrating the marriage of Robert Carr or Ker, 1st Earl of
Somerset, to Frances Howard, Countess of Essex. Bacon paid for it; the
law students of Gray's Inn performed it at Whitehall on Twelfth Night
1614. Somerset came from Scotland as page to James I and had been
his lover. Frances was a member of a pro-Spanish and Roman Catholic
family. She was married to the 3rd Earl of Essex (son of Elizabeth I's
favourite, executed for treason 1601) in 1606 when both were 14. Essex
went abroad, Frances and Somerset fell in love and on Essex's return
had the marriage annulled and were married to each other on Boxing
Day 1613. (Essex married again, unsuccessfully, and fought for Parliament in the Civil War.) Sir Thomas Overbury, probably jealous of

Frances, had protested against the annulment; he was put in the Tower of London, allegedly fed with poisoned tarts, and died. In 1614 King James took a new favourite, George Villiers, and created him 1st Duke of Buckingham. In 1616 the murder of Overbury was revealed and the Somersets were imprisoned. They were released in 1622; she died in 1632, he in 1645. Their daughter Anne married the 1st Duke of Bedford, who fought for Parliament at the battle of Edgehill and for Charles I at Newbury. A son of that marriage, Lord William Russell, was executed in 1683 for plotting against Charles II to avoid a catholic succession to the throne. See next 3 poems and Davenant.

from *A satire entitled The Witch supposed to be made against the Lady Frances, Countess of Somerset*°

She with whom troops of bustuary° slaves
Like legion sojourned still amongst the graves
And there laid plots which made the silver moon
To fall in labour° many times too soon;
    Canidia° now draws on.   5

She that in every vice did so excel
That she could read new principles to hell
And show the fiends recorded in her looks
Such deeds as were not in their blackest books; Canidia . . .

She that by spells could make a frozen stone   10
Melt and dissolve with soft affectïon
And in an instant strike the factors° dead
That should pay duties to the marriage-bed; *etc.*

      •   •

She that could reek within the sheets of lust,   15
And there be searched, yet pass without mistrust;
She that could surfle up the ways of sin
And make strait posterns where wide gates had been; *etc.*

She that could cheat the matrimonial bed
With a false-stamped, adulterate maidenhead   20
And made the husband think those kisses chaste
Which were stale pandars to his spouse's waste;° *etc.*

Whose breast was that Acéldama° of blood,
Whose virtues still became the canker's° food,
Whose closet might a Golgotha be styled   25
Or else a charnel where dead bones are piled; *etc.*

Whose waxen pictures made by incantation,
Whose philtres, potions for love's propagation,
Count Circe° but a novice in the trade
And scorn all drugs that Calchos° ever made; *etc.*   30

O let no bells be ever heard to ring,
Let not a chime the nightly hoùrs sing,
Let not the lyric lark salute the day
Nor Philoméla° tune the sad dark away;
Canidia still draws on.   35

Let croaking ravens and death-boding owls,
Let groaning mandrakes° and the ghastly howls
Of men unburied be the fatal knell
To ring Canidia down from earth to hell; *etc.*

Let wolves and tigers howl, let serpents cry,   40
Let basilisks° bedew their poisoning eye,
Let Pluto's dog° stretch high his barking note
And chant her dirges with his triple throat;
   Canidia still draws on . . .

° **Title** See previous and next poems. This ballad c.1616. 1 **bustuary**
funereal. 4 **labour** be eclipsed, by the witchcraft. 5 **Canidia** a prosti-
tute whom Horace loved; when she rejected him he accused her of
being a sorceress. 12 **factors** doers. 22 **waste** promiscuity. 23 **Acél-
dama** the field of blood, land bought with Judas' 30 pieces of silver, to
bury strangers in. 24 **canker** parasite that eats rosebuds. 29 **Circe**
classical witch who turned men into swine. 30 **Calchos** soothsayer in
Trojan war. 34 **Philomela** nightingale. 37 **mandrakes** the root of the
mandrake, or mandragora, looks like a human figure and was supposed
to shriek when pulled up. Whoever uprooted it died. Preparations of the
root could send one mad, or act as an aphrodisiac. The root was supposed to be engendered under the earth by the leakage of semen from
executed murderers. See Heyrick. 41 **basilisks** fabulous serpents which
could kill by looking. 42 **dog** Cerberus, the 3-headed dog which
guarded the underworld over which Pluto reigned.

SIR HENRY WOTTON

Intelligence agent and diplomat for 35 years, mostly in Italy. On retirement became provost of Eton. Chronically short of money. Interested in architecture and science: saw Kepler's experiments in Linz, corresponded with Bacon. Friendly with Izaak Walton and himself fished in the Thames near Eton at a bend called Black Pots. Approved of *Comus* and gave Milton letters of introduction for his continental tour. Miscellaneous writings published posthumously as *Reliquiae Wottoniae, or a collection of lives, letters, poems, with characters of sundry personages* ed. with a life by Walton 1651, posthumously.

Upon the sudden restraint of the Earl of Somerset,° then falling out of favour

Dazzled thus with height of place,
   Whilst our hopes our wits beguile
No man marks the narrow space
   'Twixt a prison and a smile.

Then, since Fortune's favours fade,   5
   You that in her arms do sleep,
Learn to swim and not to wade:
   For the hearts of kings are deep.

But if greatness be so blind
   As to trust in towers of air,   10
Let it be with goodness lined
   That at least the fall be fair.

Then, though darkened, you shall say,
   When friends fail and princes frown,
Virtue is the roughest way   15
   But proves at night a bed of down.

° **Somerset**   see previous two poems.

FRANCIS BACON, 1ST BARON VERULAM AND VISCOUNT ST. ALBAN'S

Son of a statesman; courtier; homosexual; favoured by Earl of Essex, testified against him in his trial for treason, 1601. Married. Promoted by James I: Lord Chancellor 1618. Dubiously convicted of bribery and disgraced 1621. Great philosopher of science: *Essays* 1597, *Advancement of learning* 1605, *Novum organum* 1620. Friend of Fulke Greville, Herbert of Cherbury, George Herbert, Donne, Jonson, Wotton.

The world's a bubble

The world's a bubble; and the life of man
   Less than a span:
In his conception wretched, from the womb
   So to the tomb;
Cursed from his cradle, and brought up to years   5
   With cares and fears.
Who then to frail mortality shall trust
But limns° the water or but writes in dust.
Yet, since with sorrow here we live oppressed,
   What life is best?   10
Courts are but only superficial schools
   To dandle fools;
The rural parts are turned into a den
   Of savage men;
And where's a city from all vice so free   15
But may be termed the worst of all the three?

Domestic cares afflict the husband's bed,
   Or pains his head;
Those that live single take it for a curse
   Or do things worse;   20
Some would have children; those that have them, moan
   Or wish them gone:
What is it, then, to have or have no wife
But single thraldom or a double strife?

[26]

Our own affections still at home to please   25
      Is a disease;
To cross the seas to any foreign soil,
      Perils and toil;
Wars with their noise affright us; when they cease,
      We're worse in peace.   30
What then remains, but that we still should cry
Not to be born, or, being born, to die?

° **limns**   paints.

SIR FULKE GREVILLE, 1ST
BARON BROOKE

Family enriched with monastery land by Henry VIII.
School with Philip Sidney, to court with him, wrote his biography. Much favoured by Queen Elizabeth. Formed literary
society with Sidney and others; gave patronage and friendship
to Bacon; Camden and Speed the antiquaries, Coke the
lawyer; and poets including Spenser and Daniel, Corbet,
Davenant. Became chancellor of the exchequer under James I.
Stabbed by a servant whom he had left out of his will; the
servant then stabbed himself, Greville died 4 weeks later.
Mustapha, a Senecan tragedy, 1609; *Caelica*, lyrics written
in earlier life, published posthumously in *Certain learned and
elegant works* 1633. *Poems and dramas* ed. G. Bullough,
Edinburgh 1939; *Remains . . . poems of monarchy and religion* ed. G. A. Wilkes, Oxford 1965.

Whenas man's life, the light of human lust

Whenas man's life, the light of human lust,
In socket° of his earthly lantern burns,
That all this glory unto ashes must
And generation to corruption turns:
   Then fond desires that only fear their end   5
   Do vainly wish for life but to amend.
But when this life is from the body fled
To see itself in that eternal glass
Where time doth end and thoughts accuse the dead,
Where all to come is one with all that was: 10
   Then living men ask how he left his breath
   That, while he livèd, never thought of death.

2 **socket** when the candle in the lantern burns down to the socket it
gutters and goes out.

from Mustapha

Fall none but angels suddenly to hell?
Are kind° and order grown precipitate?
Did ever any other man but he
In instant lose the use of doing well?
Sir, these be mists of greatness: look again: 5
For kings that, in their fearful icy state,°
Behold their children as their winding-sheet,
Do easily doubt; and what they doubt they hate.

2 **kind**   nature. 6 **state**   majesty.

GEORGE CHAPMAN

Earned a living by writing for the stage, under the patronage of Essex, Prince Henry and Somerset (see previous
poems)—notably *Bussy D'Ambois* 1607 and its revenge sequel.
Imprisoned with Marston and Jonson for libelling the Scots in
Eastward ho! Formed with Raleigh, Marlowe, Harriot the
astronomer and a mathematician a secret intellectual society
called 'the school of night'; cf. a pair of early poems, *The
shadow of night*. Completed Marlowe's *Hero and Leander*.
Like many others trans. Petrarch's seven penitential psalms
(cf. Wyatt, Sidney, etc.); large-scale translator of classics into
verse; completed Homer's *Iliad* and *Odyssey* c.1612. Latest ed.
of his Homer by A. Nicoll, 2 vols. 1956; *Poems* ed. P. B.
Bartlett 1941. Chapman needs slow annotated reading—he
has to be chewed; but see Swinburne in *Age of Shakespeare*
1908; J. Smith in *Scrutiny* IV (1935); M. MacLure, *G. C.: a
critical study* Toronto 1966.

from To my admired and soul-loved friend, master of all essentials and true knowledge, Mr. Harriots°

To you, whose depth of soul measures the height
And all dimensions of all works of weight
(Reason being ground, structure and ornament
To all inventions grave and permanent,
And your clear eyes the sphere° where reason moves):   5
This artisan, this god of rational loves,
Blind Homer, in this shield° and in the rest
Of his seven books which my hard hand hath dressed
In rough integuments, I send for censure,
That my long time and labour's deep extensure   10
Spent to conduct him to our envious light,
In your allowance may receive some right

To their endeavours; and take virtuous heart
From your applause, crowned with their own desert.
Such crowns suffice the free and royal mind,　　　　　15
But these subject hang-byes of our kind,°
These children that will never stand alone
But must be nourished with corruptiön,
Which are our bodies; that are traitors born
To their own crowns, their souls; betrayed to scorn,　　20
To gaudy insolence and ignorance
By their base flesh's frailties; that most dance
Profane attendance at their states° and birth,
That are mere servants to this servile earth—
These must have other crowns for meeds° than merits,　25
Or starve themselves and quench their fiery spirits.
Thus, as the soul upon the flesh depends,
Virtue must wait on wealth; we must make friends
Of the unrighteous mammon, and our sleights
Must bear the forms of fools or parasites.　　　　　30
　　Rich mine of knowledge! O that my strange muse
Without this body's nourishment could use
Her zealous faculties only to aspire,°
Instructive light, from your whole sphere of fire.
But woe is me! what zeal or power soever　　　　　35
My free soul hath, my body will be never
Able to attend; never shall I enjoy
The end of my hapless birth; never employ
That smothered fervour that in loathed embers
Lies swept from light and no clear hour remembers.　　40
O had your perfect eye organs to pierce
Into that chaos whence this stifled verse
By violence breaks! where, glow-worm-like, doth shine
In nights of sorrow this hid soul of mine;
And how her genuine forms struggle for birth　　　　45
Under the claws of this foul panther° earth:
Then under all those forms you should discern
My love to you, in my desire to learn.
　　Skill and the love of skill do ever kiss;
No band of love so strong as knowledge is;　　　　　50
Which who is he that may not learn of you
Whom Learning doth with his light's throne endow?
What learnèd fields pay not their flowers to adorn
Your odorous wreath?—compact, put on and worn
By apt and adamantine industry,　　　　　　　55
Proposing still demónstrate verity
For your great object, far from plodding gain

Or thirst of glory; when, absurd and vain,
Most students in their whole instruction are
But in traditions more particular,   60
Leaning like rotten houses out on beams;
And with true light fade in themselves like dreams.
True learning hath a body absolute
That in apparent sense itself can suit,
Not hid in airy terms as if it were   65
Like spirits fantastic that put men in fear
And are but bugs formed in their foul conceits,
Nor made for sale, glazed° with sophistic sleights,
But wrought for all times proof, strong to bid prease°
And shiver ignorants, like Hercules,   70
On their own dunghills. But our formal clerks,°
Blown for profession, spend their souls in sparks,
Framed of dismembered parts that make most show,
And like to broken limbs of knowledge go—
When thy true wisdom by thy learning won   75
Shall honour learning while there shines a sun;
And thine own name, in merit far above
Their tympanies of state that arms or love,
Fortune or blood shall lift to dignity;
Whom though your reverence, and your empery   80
Of spirit and soul, be servitude they think,
And but a beam of light broke through a chink
To all their waterish splendour, and much more
To the great sun and all things they adore
In staring ignorance: yet your self shall shine   85
Above all this in knowledge most divine
And all shall homage to your true worth owe,
Your comprehending all, that all, not you.
     And when thy writings, that now error's night
Chokes earth with mists, break forth like eastern light,   90
Showing to every comprehensive eye
High sectious° brawls becalmed by unity,
Nature made all transparent and her heart
Gripped in thy hand, crushing digested art
In flames unmeasured, measured out of it,   95
On whose head for a crown thy soul shall sit
Crowned with heaven's inward brightness, showing clear
What true man is and how like gnats appear,
O fortune-glossèd pompists and proud misers
That are of arts such impudent despisers!   100
Then past anticipating dooms and scorns
Which for self-grace each ignorant suborns,
Their glowing and amazèd eyes shall see

How short of thy soul's strength my weak words be;
And that I do not, like our poets, prefer   105
For profit, praise, and keep a squeaking stir
With called-on muses to unchild their brains
Of wind and vapour, lying still in pains
Of worthy issue: but as one professed
In nought but truth's dear love, the soul's true rest . . . 110

° **Harriots** member of Sir Walter Raleigh's household; distinguished astronomer, one of the first to use telescope; see Cowley *Ecstasy*. 5 **sphere** transparent sphere for each planet, guided by angel or muse; hence the astronomer's eyeball guided by reason. See E. Herbert *Platonic love*. 7 **shield** this letter prefaces an extract called *Achilles' shield* from *Iliad* xviii which Chapman published 1598 as prospectus for his translation of Homer; cf. Auden's poem. 16 **subject . . . kind** subjects and dependents of our nature, i.e. bodies as opposed to 'the free and royal mind' or soul. The paragraph is moving towards an excuse for the need for praise, and patronage. 23 **states** ceremonies. 25 **meeds** rewards. 33 **aspire** inspire. 46 **panther** emblem of lust, corruption, noted for its dangerously sweet smell. 68 **glazed** with sugar. 69 **prease** press. 71 **clerks** clerics, scholars. 92 **sectious** factious.

from Ovid's banquet of sense°

In a loose robe of tinsel forth she came,
Nothing but it betwixt her nakedness
And envious light. The downward-burning flame
Of her rich hair did threaten new accéss
    Of venturous Phaëton° to scorch the fields.   5
And thus to bathing came our poet's goddess,°
    Her handmaids bearing all things pleasure yields
To such a service: odours most delighted
And purest linen which her looks had whited.

Then cast she off her robe and stood upright   10
As lightning breaks out of a labouring cloud,
Or as the morning heaven casts off the night,
Or as that heaven cast off itself and showed
    Heaven's upper light, to which the brightest day
Is but a black and melancholy shroud;   15
    Or as when Venus° strived for sovereign sway
Of charmful beauty in young Troy's desire:
So stood Corinna, vanishing her tire.°

° **Title** a fantasy on the Roman poet Ovid and his mistress Corinna, designed to study the relation between wisdom and excess. 5 **Phaëton** son of Phoebus the sun-god, borrowed his father's chariot and by driving it badly burnt up parts of Africa into desert. 6 **goddess** mistress. 16 **Venus** goddess of love, one of the 3 goddesses exposed to 'the judgment of Paris'. Paris, who was son of the king of Troy, gave the prize to Venus. Cf. Tennyson, *Oenone*. 18 **tire** attire.

[WILLIAM SHAKESPEARE]

THOMAS DEKKER

Wrote for stage in collaboration or competition with Drayton, Jonson, Ford, Webster, etc.; and much documentary work. Most notable play, partly with Massinger, *The honest whore* 1604–05: courtlings versus bourgeoisie. In prison for debt for 6 years. Known for sunny disposition. For all the dramatists in this section see Swinburne in *Age of Shakespeare* (1908), Eliot in *Selected essays* and L. C. Knights, *Drama and society in the age of Jonson;* and editions of single plays in one of the well-annotated and introduced series now available. But for work of your own on them it is worth trying a masque or documentary because there has been little study of their minor works, usually, and too much said about a few big plays.

from The Noble Soldier

O Sorrow, Sorrow, say where dost thou dwell?
   In the lowest room of hell.
Art thou born of human race?
   No, no, I have a furier face.
Art thou in city, town or court?   5
   I to every place resort.
O why into the world is sorrow sent?
   Men afflicted best repent.
What dost thou feed on?
   Broken sleep.   10
What tak'st thou pleasure in?
    To weep,
    To sigh, to sob, to pine, to groan,
    To wring my hands, to sit alone.
O when, O when shall Sorrow quiet have?   15
  Never, never, never, never,
  Never till she finds a grave.

[35]

from Dekker his Dream

Death terrible in countenance

I bellowed to the ferryman, methought,
And with a stretched voice cried, A boat! a boat!
He came at first call and when near he drew,
That of his face and form I had full view,
My blood congealed to ice and with a cold fear   5
To see a shape so horribly appear:
His eyes flashed fire, grizzled and shagged his hair,
Snarled all in feltlocks; terror and despair
Lay in his wrinkled cheeks; his voice was hoarse
And grumbling; he looked ghastlier than a corse . . .   10

The extremities of cold in hell

The Hyperborean° wind, whose rough hand flings
Mountains for snowballs and on his marble wings
Bears rocks of ice fetched from the frigid zone
Which, stuck in the north seas (seas and shores were one),
Ten thousand wild waves hardened in the air,   5
Rattling like icicles on his grizzly hair,
And in his drivelling beard snow ten times more
Than e'er the bald-pate alps in periwigs° wore,
When from his caves of brass (bound there in gyves
Of adamant) out he whorries and 'fore him drives   10
In whirlwinds, hail, frosts, sleet and storms; and meets
With rugged Winter, whom he roaring greets;
Then, clapping their obstreperous squallid wings,
Each of them on the frozen Russian dings
Such bitter blasts down that they fly in droves   15
(Though swaddled all in furs) to sweltering stoves—
The Muss,° the Scythian° nor the Freezeland boor°
Nor the Laplandian witch° once peeping o'er
A threshold, lest their noses, cheeks and eyes,
Pinched off by his clumsy nails, be made a prize   20
To snarling Boreas. O yet, all this cold,
Were it piled up in heaps an hundredfold
In stiffened clouds to freeze ten thousand year,
Is a warm thaw to the piercing horrors here.
Hell's cold so biting, so invincible,   25
That from all cold else the sharp nips doth steal;

Should fire come near it, it would fire congeal
Till flames turn icy flakes and force fire leese°
His virtue so that coals red-hot will freeze . . .

1 **Hyperborean** arctic. 8 **bald . . . wigs** conceit quoted from Sylvester's
Du Bartas. 17 **Muss** Muscovite. **Scythian** Russian. **Freezeland boor**
Dutch peasant (Friesland). 18 **witch** Lapland was supposed to be the
home of witches. 28 **leese** lose.

Thwick-a-thwack

Brave iron! brave hammer! from your sound
The art of music has her ground;
On the anvil thou keep'st time,
Thy knick-a-knock is smith's best chime:
    Yet thwick-a-thwack,   5
    Thwick, thwack-a-thwack, thwack,
    Make our brawny sinews crack,
    Then pit-a-pat, pit-a-pat, pat,
    Till thickest bars be beaten flat.

We shoe the horses of the sun,°   10
Harness the dragons of the moon,
Forge Cupid's quiver, bow and arrows,
And our dame's coach° that's drawn with sparrows:
    Till thwick-a-thwack, *etc.*

Jove's roaring cannons and his rammers   15
We beat out with our Lemnian° hammers;
Mars his gauntlet, helm and spear,
And Gorgon° shield, are all made here: *etc.*

The grate which, shut, the day outbars,
Those golden studs which nail the stars,   20
The globe's case° and the axle-tree,
Who can hammer these but we? *etc.*

A warming-pan to heat earth's bed,
Lying in the frozen zone half-dead;
Hobnails to serve the man in the moon   25
And sparrowbills to clout Pan's shoon,°
    Whose work but ours? *etc.*

Venus' kettles, pots and pans
We make or else she brawls and bans;°
Tongs, shovels and irons have their places   30
Else she scratches all our faces:

Till thwick-a-thwack,
Thwick, thwack-a-thwack, thwack,
Make our brawny sinews crack,
Then pit-a-pat, pit-a-pat, pat   35
Till thickest bars be beaten flat.

London's Tempe 1629

10 **Sun**   see Chapman *Ovid.* 13 **coach**   of Venus, treated as a fairy god-mother. Sparrows are emblems of lust. 16 **Lemnian**   when Hephaestos the god of metalsmiths was thrown out of heaven, he fell onto the island of Lemnos and set up a workshop there. 18 **Gorgon**   serpent-haired witch so ugly that sight of her turned you to stone. Her head was cut off and fixed in a shield. 21 **case**   frame. 26 **sparrowbills . . . shoon**   nails to patch or stud the shoes of Pan, goatfooted god of shepherds. 29 **bans**   chides.

THOMAS MIDDLETON

Son of a London bricklayer originally of good family. Queen's College, Oxford. Notable for documentary comedy (e.g. *A trick to catch the old one* 1608, revised by Massinger as *A new way to pay old debts* 1626) and psychological tragedy in the early 1620s (*Changeling; Game at chess*, source of that section of *The Waste Land*, etc.); also wrote masques, and pageants for the City. See Dekker.

from *Women Beware Women: a tragedy*

prithee forgive me,
I did but chide in jest: the best loves use it
Sometimes; it sets an edge upon affection.
When we invite our best friends to a feast,
'Tis not all sweetmeats that we set before 'em;   5
There's something sharp and salt, both to whet appetite,
And make 'em taste their wine well: so, methinks,
After a friendly sharp and savoury chiding,
A kiss tastes wondrous well, and full o' the grape.

THE REVEREND JOHN MARSTON

Father a lawyer, mother Italian. Oxford, studied law but
wrote satires early in life which were burnt for obscenity by
order of the Archbishop of Canterbury. Dramatist, notably
The malcontent, a revenge tragedy, 1604. In 1607 he left the
theatre, took holy orders, became rector of a parish in
Hampshire and married a priest's daughter. See Dekker.

from *What You Will: a comedy*

Now is Albano's marriage-bed new hung
With fresh rich curtains; now are my valance° up,
Embossed with orient pearl, my grandsire's gift;
Now are the lawn sheets fumed with violets
To fresh the palled lascivious appetite;   5
Now work the cooks, the pastry sweats with slaves,
The marchpanes° glitter; now, now the musicians
Hover with nimble sticks o'er squeaking crowds,°
Tickling the dried guts of a mewing cat;
The tailors, starchers, semsters, butchers, poulterers,   10
Mercers, all, all—none think on me.

2 **valance** valances, borders hung round the canopy of a 4-poster bed.
7 **marchpanes** sweetmeats, marzipan. 8 **crowds** fiddles.

from *Antonio's Revenge*

[The Duchess of Genoa describes the death of her daughter-
in-law.]

Being laid upon her bed she grasped my hand
And, kissing it, spake thus: Thou very poor,
Why dost not weep? the jewel of thy brow,

The rich adornment that enchased thy breast,
Is lost: thy son, my love, is lost, is dead.   5
And have I lived to see his virtues blurred
With guiltless blots? O world! thou art too subtle
For honest natures to converse withal:
Therefore I'll leave thee. Farewell, mart of woe!
I fly to clip my love, Antonio.   10
With that, her head sunk down upon her breast,
Her cheek changed earth, her senses slept in rest:
Until my fool, that crept unto the bed,
Screeched out so loud that he brought back her soul,
Called her again, that her bright eyes 'gan ope   15
And stared upon him. He, audacious fool,
Dared kiss her hand, wished her soft rest, loved bride.
She fumbled out, Thanks, good. And so she died.

CYRIL TOURNEUR

Little known. *The revenger's tragedy* (possibly not his) published in 1607, *The atheist's tragedy* 1611. Then on government service in the Netherlands, and disastrous expedition against Cadiz on which he fell ill; was disembarked in Ireland and died there. See Dekker.

from The Revenger's Tragedy

[Vendice, the avenger, disguised as a ponce; Hippolito his brother.]

Ven. And now methinks I could e'en chide myself
For doting on her beauty, though her death
Shall be revenged after no common action.
Does the silkworm expend her yellow labours
For thee? for thee does she undo herself? 5
Are lordships sold to maintain ladyships
For the poor benefit of a bewildering minute?
Why does yon fellow falsify highways
And put his life between the judge's lips
To refine such a thing—keep horse and men 10
To beat their valours for her?
Surely we are all mad people, and they
Whom we think are, are not: we mistake those—
'Tis we are mad in sense, they but in clothes.
Hip. Faith, and in clothes too we, give us our due! 15
Ven. Does every proud and self-affecting dame
Camphire° her face for this, and grieve her Maker
In sinful baths of milk, when many an infant starves
For her superfluous outside—all for this?
Who now bids twenty pounds a night? prepares 20
Music, perfumes and sweetmeats? All are hushed.
Thou may'st lie chaste now! It were fine, methinks,
To have thee seen at revels, forgetful feasts

And unclean brothels: sure, 'twould fright the sinner
And make him a good coward: put a reveller   25
Out of his antic amble
And cloy an epicure with empty dishes.
Here might a scornful and ambitious woman
Look through and through herself. See, ladies, with
    false forms
You deceive men, but cannot deceive worms.   30

---

17 **camphire**   apply camphor as a cosmetic.

JOHN WEBSTER

Son of a London tailor. Playwright, collaborating with Dekker, Drayton, Middleton and others. Joined with Heywood and Tourneur in volume of elegies for Prince Henry, 1613, dedicating his part to Somerset (see Wotton, Wither). *The white devil* 1612 and *Duchess of Malfi* (c.1616) attracted the best actors and actresses throughout the century. Admired by Lamb, revived by Swinburne, often quoted by Eliot in *The Waste Land*. See Dekker. See Rupert Brooke's essay on him, published 1916.

from The White Devil

[Cornelia, at the bier of her murdered son; Flamineo, her other son; attendants.]

Cor.   Do you hear, sir?
        I'll give you a saying which my grandmother
        Was wont, when she heard the bell toll, to sing o'er
        Under her lute.
Fla.   Do, an' you will, do.
Cor.   Call for the robin redbreast and the wren,   5
        Since o'er shady groves they hover
        And with leaves and flowers do cover
        The friendless bodies of unburied men.
        Call unto his funeral dole
        The ant, the field-mouse and the mole   10
        To rear him hillocks that shall keep him warm
        And, when gay tombs are robbed, sustain no harm.
        But keep the wolf far thence, that's foe to men,
        For with his nails he'll dig them up again.
                They would not bury him 'cause he died in a
                    quarrel   15
        But I have an answer for them:
                Let holy church receive him duly

Since he paid the church-tithes truly.
    His wealth is summed and this is all his store—
This poor men get and great men get no more.   20
Now the wares are gone, we may shut up shop.
Bless you all, good people.   [*Exit*

Fla. I have a strange thing in me to the which
I cannot give a name, without it be
Compassion. I pray, leave me.   25

from The Duchess of Malfi

[The Duchess, guilty of romantic love for her steward, is
locked up to break her nerve with lunatics—a mad Astrologer,
Lawyer, Priest, Doctor; Cariola her waiting-woman; Bosola,
her treacherous captain of horse and cynical malcontent.]

[*Enter Madmen. Here this song is sung to a dismal kind of
music by a madman.*]

    O let us howl some heavy note,
      Some deadly doggèd howl,
    Sounding as from the threatening throat
      Of beasts and fatal fowl.
    As ravens, screech-owls, bulls and bears   5
      We'll bell and bawl our parts
    Till irksome noise have cloyed your ears
      And corrosíved your hearts.
    At last, whenas our choir wants breath,
      Our bodies being blest,   10
    We'll sing like swans to welcome death
      And die in love and rest.

Ast. Doomsday not come yet? I'll draw it nearer by a
perspective,° or make a glass that shall set all
the world on fire upon an instant. I cannot sleep: 15
my pillow is stuffed with a litter of porcupines.
Law. Hell is a mere glass-house,° where the devils are
continually blowing up women's souls on hollow
irons, and the fire never goes out.
Pri. I will lie with every woman in my parish the tenth   20
night; I will tithe° them over like haycocks.
Doc. Shall my 'pothecary outgo me because I am a
cuckold?
    I have found out his roguery: he makes alum of his

wife's urine and sells it to puritans that have sore
throats with over-straining.   25

     •   •   •

[*Here a dance of 8 Madmen, with music answerable
thereto; after which Bosola, like an Old Man, enters.*]

Duch. Is he mad too?
Serv.   Pray, question him. I'll leave you.

[*Exeunt Servant and Madmen.*]

Bos. I am come to make thy tomb.
Duch.   Ha! my tomb?
    Thou speak'st as if I lay upon my deathbed
    Gasping for breath: dost thou perceive me sick?
Bos.   Yes, and the more dangerously, since thy sickness   30
is insensible.°
Duch. Thou art not mad, sure. Dost know me?
Bos. Yes.
Duch. Who am I?
Bos.   Thou art a box of worm-seed,° at best but a   35
salvatory of green mummy.° What's this flesh? A little
crudded milk, fantastical puff-paste. Our bodies are
weaker than those paper prisons boys use to keep flies in;
more contemptible, since ours is to preserve earthworms.
Didst thou ever see a lark in a cage? Such is the soul in   40
the body: this world is like her little turf of grass; and
the heaven o'er our heads, like her looking-glass, only
gives us a miserable knowledge of the small compass of
our prison.
Duch. Am not I thy duchess?   45
Bos.   Thou art some great woman, sure, for riot° begins
to sit on thy forehead (clad in grey hairs) twenty years
sooner than on a merry milkmaid's. Thou sleepest worse
than if a mouse should be forced to take up her lodging
in a cat's ear; a little infant that breeds its teeth, should it   50
lie with thee, would cry out as if thou wert the more
unquiet bedfellow.
Duch. I am Duchess of Malfi still.
Bos.   That makes thy sleep so broken:
Glories, like glow-worms, afar off shine bright,   55
But looked to near, have neither heat nor light.
Duch. Thou art very plain.
Bos.   My trade is to flatter the dead, not the living:
I am a tomb-maker.

Duch. And thou comest to make my tomb?   60
Bos. Yes.
Duch.   Let me be a little merry.

          •   •   •

Bos. Hark! now everything is still,
The screech-owl and the whistler shrill
Call upon our dame aloud   65
And bid her quickly don her shroud.
Much you had of land and rent:
Your length in clay's now competent;
A long war disturbed your mind:
Here your perfect peace is signed.   70
Of what is't fools make such vain keeping?
Sin their conception, their birth weeping,
Their life a general mist of error,
Their death a hideous storm of terror.
Strew your hair with powders sweet,   75
Don clean linen, bathe your feet,
And (the foul fiend more to check)
A crucifix let bless your neck.
'Tis now full tide 'tween night and day;
End your groan and come away.   80
Car. Hence, villains, tyrants, murderers! alas!
What will you do with my lady? Call for help!
Duch. To whom? to our next neighbours? they are mad-
folks.
Bos. Remove that noise. [*Executioners seize Car.*]
Duch.   Farewell, Cariola.
In my last will I have not much to give: 85
A many hungry guests have fed upon me;
There will be a poor reversion.
Car.   I will die with her.
Duch. I pray thee, look thou giv'st my little boy
Some syrup for his cold, and let the girl
Say her prayers ere she sleep.   90

          [*Car. forced out by Executioners.*]

                              Now what you please:
What death?
Bos. Strangling; here are your executioners.
Duch. I forgive them:
The apoplexy, catarrh,° or cough o' the lungs,
Would do as much as they do.   95
Bos. Doth not death fright you?
Duch.   Who would be afraid on't,

Knowing to meet such excellent company
In the other world?
Bos.   Yet, methinks,
The manner of your death should much afflict you:
This cord should terrify you.   100
Duch.   Not a whit:
What would it pleasure me to have my throat cut
With diamonds? or to be smothered
With cassia?° or to be shot to death with pearls?
I know death hath ten thousand several doors
For men to take their exits; and 'tis found   105
They go on such strange geometrical hinges,
You may open them both ways—any way, for
   heaven sake,
So I were out of your whispering. Tell my brothers
That I perceive death, now I am well awake,
Best gift is they can give or I can take.   110
I would fain put off my last woman's fault—
I'd not be tedious to you.
1 Ex.   We are ready . . .

31 **insensible** can't be felt. 35 **worm-seed** to feed worms. 36 **salvatory** **. . . mummy** box of ointment made from Egyptian mummy. 47 **riot** debauchery, and tumult. 94 **catarrh** cerebral haemorrhage. 103 **cassia** cinnamon.

JOHN FORD

Born in Devon. Oxford, law student. Dramatist of frustrated love, 1625–33. *The broken heart* claims Platonic authority for illicit love; cf. poets in sections 4, 5, 8. *'Tis pity* may be based on Sir Philip Sidney, Stella and her husband. See G. F. Sensabagh *The tragic muse of J.F.* Palo Alto 1944.

from The Broken Heart

[Orgilus, in love with Penthea; Ithocles, tyrannical brother of Penthea who marries her to an old man. They hear her singing.]

Orgilus . . . List! what sad sounds are these? extremely sad ones.
Ithocles Sure, from Penthea's lodgings.
                Hark! a voice too.

[*Song within*]

O no more, no more! too late
   Sighs are spent; the burning tapers
Of a life as chaste as fair—   5
   Pure as are unwritten papers—
Are burnt out; no heat, no light
Now remains; 'tis ever night.

Love is dead. Let lovers' eyes,
   Locked in endless dreams,   10
   The extremes of all extremes,
Ope no more, for now love dies,
   Now love dies—implying,
   Love's martyrs must be ever, ever dying.

Ithocles O my misgiving heart!
Orgilus   A horrid stillness   15
Succeeds this deathful air. Let's know the reason.
Tread softly: there is mystery in mourning.

RICHARD BRATHWAITE

Born Westmorland; Oriel College, Oxford at 16. Officer in militia, J.P. Poet, pamphleteer, novelist. See M. W. Black *R. Brathwait Philadelphia* 1928 (spellings of his name vary).

I am not as I wish

Jug-jug!° Fair fall° the nightingale
  Whose tender breast
Chants out her merry madrigal,
  With hawthorn pressed:
Te'u, te'u! thus sings she even by even   5
And represents the melody in heaven:
    'Tis, 'tis,
  I am not as I wish.

Rape-defilèd Philomel
  In her sad mischance   10
Tells what she is forced to tell
  While the satyrs dance:
Unhappy I! quoth she, unhappy I!
That am betrayed by Tereus' treachery:
    'Tis, 'tis,   15
  I am not as I wish.

Chaste-unchaste, deflowered yet
  Spotless in heart;
Lust was all that he could get
  For all his art: 20
For I ne'er attention lent
To his suit, nor gave consent;
    'Tis, 'tis,
  I am not as I wish.

Thus hath faithless Tereus made   25
  Heartless Philomele

Moan her in her fórlorn shade
   Where grief I feel—
Grief that wounds me to the heart,
Which though gone hath left her smart: 30
    'Tis, 'tis,
   I am not as I wish.

Nature's embassy, or the wild man's measures,
danced naked by 12 satyrs 1621

1 **Jug-jug and tereu** represents sounds made by the nightingale. It is supposed to sing leaning its breast on a thorn. Tereus went to fetch his wife's sister, Philomela, to stay with them. On the journey he raped her and cut out her tongue so that she could not betray him; but she wove pictures of the rape into a garment and sent it to his wife, Procne. In revenge, Procne chopped up her son, cooked him and served the dish to Tereus. When he realised what he had eaten he pursued Procne; she fled to Philomela but the gods changed them all into birds—Tereus into a hawk, Procne a swallow and Philomela a nightingale. **fall** befall.

ANONYMOUS

Fara diddle dyno

Ha-ha! ha-ha! this world doth pass
   Most merrily, I'll be sworn,
For many an honest Indian ass°
   Goes for a unicorn.
           Fara diddle dyno,   5
           This is idle fyno.

Tee-hee! tee-hee! O sweet delight!
   He tickles this age that can
Call Tullia's ape° a marmasyte
   And Leda's goose° a swan. *etc.*   10

So so! so so! fine English days!
   For false play is no reproach,
For he that doth the coachman praise
   May safely use the coach.
           Fara diddle dyno,   15
           This is idle fyno.

T. Weelkes ed. *Airs of fantastic spirits*
1608

3 **Indian ass** donkey? mule? 9 **Tullia's ape** don't know. Tullia was the much-married daughter of Cicero; apes were emblems of lust; to lead apes in hell was the fate of women who died virgin—see Campion *Hark*. A marmoset is a small monkey of the kind kept as pets. 10 **Leda's goose** Zeus turned himself into a swan to seduce Leda. All your geese are swans = you overrate.

Mad Tom of Bedlam°

Forth from the dark and dismal cell
And deep abyss of hell
Poor Tom° is come to view the world again
To see if he can cure his distempered brain.

Fears and cares oppress my soul   5
And hark how the angry Furies° howl
Pluto laughs and Proserpine° is glad
To see poor Tom of Bedlam mad.

Through the world I wander night and day
To seek my straggled senses;   10
In an angry mood I meet old Time
With his pentarchy° of tenses.

When he me spied
Away he hied
For Time will stay for no man   15
In vain with cries
I rend the skies
For pity is not common

Cold and comfortless I lie
Help O help for charity.   20

Hark I hear Apollo's team°
The carman 'gins to whistle
Chaste Diana° has bent her bow
And the boar begins to bristle

Come Vulcan° with tools and with tackles   25
Come knock off these troublesome shackles
Bid Charles° make ready his wain
To bring me my senses again

Last night I heard the Dog-star° bark
Mars met with Venus in the dark   30
Limping Vulcan het° an iron bar
And furiously ran at the god of war

Mars with his weapon laid about
But limping Vulcan had the gout
His broad horns did hang so in's light   35
He could not see to aim his blow aright

Mercury the nimble post° of heaven
Stood still to see the quarrel
Gorbellied Bacchus° giant-like
Bestrid a great beer-barrel   40

To me he drank
I did him thank
But I could get no cider
He drank whole butts

And split his guts   45
But mine were ne'er the wider

Poor Tom is very dry
A little drink for charity
Hark! I hear Actaeon's horn°
The Huntsman whoops and holloas   50
Bowman, Ringwood, Royster, Jowler, ho ho
At the chase now follows
The man in the moon drinks claret
Eats powdered beef, turnip and carrot
But a glass of old Malaga sack   55
Will fire the Bush at his back.

° **Mad Tom of Bedlam** printed in various forms in miscellanies throughout the century; also one about Mad Bess. Bedlam means madhouse,
from St. Mary of Bethlehem, a London religious house converted into
the first British and the second European asylum, 1403. In the 16th
century it could not contain all its patients and they began to roam
about on parole, begging, singing and wearing fantastic garb. Others pretended to be mad in order to beg—Abram men, from the Abraham ward
in Bedlam where the parole patients lived. When the hospital moved to
Moorfields in 1676 it became a popular resort for making fun, meeting
whores, stealing, etc. Bethlehem psychiatric hospital is now in Kent.
3 **Poor Tom** the Fool calls himself this in *Lear*. 6 **Furies** the 3-winged
avengers. 7 **Pluto . . . Proserpine** god of the underworld and his queen.
12 **pentarchy** government by 5 rulers. Fingers? Past, present, future
etc.? 21 **Apollo's team** horses of the sun, here confused with carthorses
and their driver. 23 **Diana** goddess of the moon, and of hunting and
chastity. She sent a boar to ravage the lands of a king who forgot to
sacrifice to her. 25 **Vulcan** = Haephestus, god of blacksmiths; see Dekker
Thwick-a-thwack. Lame from being thrown out of heaven (perhaps
prehistoric smiths were crippled to keep them in the tribe?). He was the
husband of Venus, goddess of love. She was in bed with Mars, god of
war, when Vulcan caught them in a net and displayed them to all the
gods. Vulcan thus became also the patron of cuckolds. 27 **Charles**
Charles' Wain was a name for the constellation of the Plough or Great
Bear. 29 **Dog-star** Sirius, a star of unfavourable influence. 31 **het**
heated, or hefted? 37 **post** messenger. 39 **Bacchus** god of wine. 49
Actaeon's horn Actaeon was a great huntsman. Diana changed him
into a stag and had him chased and eaten by 50 hounds. Some say they
represent the debilitating effect of the dog-days. Cf. *Waste Land*. 51
Bowman . . . Jowler hounds' names. 56 **Bush** sometimes the name of
an inn from the bush of ivy (sacred to Bacchus) displayed outside.

JOHN TAYLOR THE WATER-POET

Born in Gloucester, local grammar-school but bad at Latin
so apprenticed to a London waterman (the Thames being then
the city's chief highway). Press-ganged into the navy, at siege
of Cadiz under Essex in 1596, at Flores in the Azores under
Grenville and Howard, 1597. Retired in 1603 with a lame
leg and became a waterman, famous for repartee, impromptu
verses and wagering journeys. Friendly with Jonson, Dekker
and other writers. In 1613 arranged the water-pageant to
celebrate the marriage of Princess Elizabeth and in 1620 he
visited her in Prague. In 1618 he walked to Edinburgh under
a wager not to buy or beg for money, food or shelter. He got
far beyond, to Braemar in the highlands where he stayed at a
hunting-lodge with the Earl of Mar. On his return he met
Ben Jonson, also walking to Scotland. For another wager
he rowed to Kent in a brown-paper boat with oarblades of
dead fish. In 1622 he sailed from London to York, had to
land in Norfolk in bad weather and was arrested as a pirate.
In 1625 the plague drove him to Oxford where he stayed for
a while at Oriel College. When the civil war broke out in
1642 he returned to Oxford to keep a pub and write lampoons
against parliament; Charles I made him a yeoman of the guard.
Published numerous prolix works.

Dick Swash°

Dick Swash drew out his three-piled° blunted blade
And slashed in twain the equinoctial line;
Tom Thumb° did through the Arabian deserts wade,
Where Castor and his brother Pollux shine;
The threadbare flapjacks° of the Western Isles°   5
Exasperate the marble Scythian° snow;
Dame Venus travelled fifty thousand miles
To see the bounds of Nilus ebb and flow;
The gormandising quagmires of the east
Ingurgitate the Erymanthean bull;°   10

And rude rebounding Sagittarius ceased
To pipe levaltos to Gonzaga's trull;°
The Adriatic polecats sat carousing
And hidebound Gogmagog° his shirt was losing,

Sweet semi-circled Cynthia° played at maw°   15
The whilst Endymion ran the wild goose-chase;
Great Bacchus with his crossbow killed a daw
And sullen Saturn° smiled with pleasant face.
The ninefold bugbears of the Caspian lake°
Sat whistling ebon hornpipes to their ducks;   20
Madge-owlet° straight for joy her girdle brake
And rugged satyrs frisked like stags and bucks.
The untamed tumbling fifteen-footed Goat,°
With promulgation of the Lesbian shores,
Confronted Hydra° in a sculler boat,   25
At which the mighty mountain Taurus° roars;
   Meantime great Sultan Solyman° was born
   And Atlas blew his rustic rumbling horn.

° **Swash**   pigswill; sewage; crash; splash; swashbuckler, i.e. a braggart,
one who goes about banging his sword on his buckler (shield). From a
series of burlesque sonnets. **three-piled** 3-pointed or 3-bladed. 3 **Tom
Thumb** tiny man in a fairy tale. 5 **flapjacks** sort of pancake, especially
in Scotland. **Western Isles** Outer Hebrides. 6 **Scythian** Russian. 10
Erymanthian bull Erymanthos is a Greek mountain famous for legendary boar and bear. 12 **Gonzaga's trull** trull = whore. Gonzaga may
refer to Louis de G., Duke of Nevers, a French general who married in
Spain, died 1595. 14 **Gogmagog** Gog, king of Magog; usually Gog and
Magog. Giant devils of Biblical and English legend. Statues of them
stood at the Guildhall in London but were burnt in the fires of 1666
and 1940; wickerwork models were carried about in Lord Mayors'
shows. There are a pair in Norwich (called Samson and Hercules) and
some hills east of Cambridge are called after them. Cf. Corbet *Iter
boreale*. 15 **Cynthia** moon goddess. She was in love with the shepherd
Endymion. **maw** card-game. 18 **Saturn** god of melancholy. 19 **ninefold . . . lake** presumably an allusion to demons inhabiting the
Caspian Sea. 21 **Madge-owlet** don't know. 23 **Goat** probably Capri-
corn, sign of the zodiac next to Sagittarius the archer. 25 **Hydra** fabulous 9-headed snake. 26 **Taurus** another sign of the zodiac. 27 **Solyman**
king of the Turks; appears in Tasso's *Jerusalem delivered* trans. Fairfax
1600.

THE REVEREND
ROBERT BURTON

Brasenose and Christ Church Colleges, Oxford; holy orders; academic life. A wry depressive; unmarried; died in Oxford, perhaps suicide. *Anatomy of melancholy* 1621 et seq. In this verse preface, melancholy includes pensiveness, as in Milton's *Il penseroso*. See L. Babb *The Elizabethan malady* East Lansing 1951; and Martin Lluelyn *Elegy on the death of R. B.* in his *Men-miracles* Oxford 1646.

from The author's abstract of melancholy

When I go musing all alone,
Thinking of diverse things foreknown,
When I build castles in the air
Void of sorrow and void of fear,
Pleasing my self with phantasms sweet,   5
Methinks the time runs very fleet:
   All my joys to this are folly,
   Naught so sweet as melancholy.
When I lie waking all alone,
Recounting what I have ill done,   10
My thoughts on me then tyrannise,
Fear and sorrow me surprise;
Whether I tarry still or go,
Methinks the time goes very slow:
   All my griefs to this are jolly,   15
   Naught so sad as melancholy.

Methinks I hear, methinks I see
Sweet music, wondrous melody,
Towns, palaces and cities fine
Here now, then there—the world is mine—   20
Rare beauties, gallant ladies shine,
What e'er is lovely or divine:

All other joys to this are folly,
None so sweet as melancholy.
Methinks I hear, methinks I see   25
Ghosts, goblins, fiends—my fantasy
Presents a thousand ugly shapes—
Headless bears, black men and apes,
Doleful outcries and fearful sights
My sad and dismal soul affrights;   30
    All my griefs to this are jolly,
    None so damned as melancholy.
Methinks I court, methinks I kiss,
Methinks I now embrace my mistress.
O blessèd days, O sweet content,   35
In paradise my time is spent;
Such thoughts may still my fancy move,
So may I ever be in love:
    All my joys to this are folly,
    Naught so sweet as melancholy.   40

                    .   .

'Tis my sole plague to be alone,
I am a beast, a monster grown,
I will no light nor company,
I find it now my misery;
The scene is turned, my joys are gone,   45
Fear, discontent and sorrows come:
    All my griefs to this are jolly,
    Naught so fierce as melancholy . . .

JOHN HAGTHORPE

Dissertation on colonial economics and *Divine meditations and elegies* 1622 dedicated to James I: 'Pardon, mighty Prince, my boldness, thus presuming into your presence with so lame an oblation. Having a suit to your Majesty (which is not for money but a few good words), and having no friend in court, I thought a petition might miscarry, and this therefore the safer kind of begging, to make truth speak for herself. Whereas therefore I am much impoverished through suits of law, wherein I have been ten years forbidden from mine own by the malice of a stronger adversary and many other bad debtors, who by their ill dealing compel me to transport myself and family into Virginia, or New England: my suit is, that your gracious Majesty would be pleased to speak a good word for me, that I may obtain the benefit of Master Sutton's Charity for a little son of mine, whom I would gladly leave behind me to increase an ancient (and not ignoble) name again in your Majesty's dominions, wherein there is not a man living of that name beside myself and mine. For which your gracious clemency, I shall not fail daily to pray for your Majesty's health and prosperity in this world, and eternal happiness in the world to come'. S. E. Brydges ed. *Hagthorpe revived* Lee Priory, Kent 1817.

from An elegy upon the death of the most illustrious Prince Henry°

I do not grieve when some unwholesome air
Mildews rich fields; nor when the clusters fair
Of claret rot through too abundant showers;
I grieve not when some gay unsavoury flowers
Are nipped and withered by the untimely frost.   5
Only herein my patience suffers most,
When the sweet harvest and expected gain
Of virtue's vintage, ere full ripe, is slain;

When Time the wheat with cruel scythe cuts down
But leaves such vulgar weeds as are unmown,   10
Darnel and vetches; when these mortal lights
Extinguished be should guide our dimmer sights:
Then, then I weep and wish the watery clouds
Would furnish me with tears to weep whole floods;
Then wish I Boreas (whose killing breath   15
Is ne'er perfúmed with sweets of Indian° earth)
To lend me sighs; I wish the culver's° groans,
The pelican's shrill shrieks, to express my moans;
I wish myself those Daedaléan° wings
To search the glorious courts of the eastern kings   20
And a strong patent° sealed from powerful love
Freely to take all that my thoughts approve.
First would I then in Indian forests slit
The weeping plant with ivory knife to get
Such precious liquor uncorrupted clear   25
As might embalm heroic Henry here;
Then would I next to Pauris' gardens pierce
For rarest flowers to strew upon his hearse;
The Indies should yield us diamonds; China, gold;
Peru, that silver that her lap doth hold;   30
Ceylon and Ormus,° all their pearls should send,
The Congian slaves from secret caves should rend
The Chian marble, white cassídony,
Green lacedemon and red porphyry,
The pure white marble got in Palestine   35
And rare Numidian, spotted serpentine . . .

° **Prince Henry** eldest son of James I and heir-apparent to the throne,
died 1612 and was the subject of copious elegies by Donne, Heywood,
Tourneur, Webster, Wither, etc. 16 **Indian** Boreas, the north wind,
supposed not to blow in India—probably meaning the East Indies. 17
culver wood-pigeon. 19 **Daedalean** Daedalus was a legendary inventor who made himself wings. 21 **patent** license granting a monopoly.
27 **Pauris** don't know. 31 **Ormus** near Kuwait.

GEORGE WITHER

Squire's son, Oxford, law student, spent most of his life in London. Friend of William Browne and Drayton. Published volume of elegies on Prince Henry (see preceding poem) and another of epithalamions for Princess Elizabeth (visited her in Bohemia 1629). Imprisoned for 6 months for a satire and wrote some of his best verse in jail—he had another sentence in 1621 for a satire called *Wither's motto,* which John Taylor the water poet parodied. In the 1620s his work became pious and puritan. Friends of this period included Christopher Brooke (a friend of Donne), John Davies of Hereford, Brathwaite; but he was disliked by and quarrelled with Jonson and his circle. In 1625 he wrote an account of that year's serious outbreak of plague in London. A London publisher, having bought the plates of a series of emblems with foreign mottoes, employed Wither to write English verses for them and his *Emblems* appeared 1635. Soon afterwards he retired to country near Farnham to study theology but in 1639 he served as a captain of horse for Charles I against the Scots, and in 1642 sold some of his estate to raise a troop of horse for parliament. He was appointed commander of Farnham Castle but withdrew (without, apparently, being attacked). The royalists captured him but his life was saved by Sir John Denham who said that so long as Wither lived there would be one worse poet in England than himself. Married, 6 children. Life by Aubrey.

from Rhomboidal dirge°

But why,
O fatal Time,
Dost thou constrain that I
Should perish in my youth's sweet prime?
I but a while ago, you cruel powers,   5
In spite of fortune, cropped contentment's sweetest
flowers
And, yet unscornèd, serve a gentle nymph, the fairest she
That ever was beloved of man or eyes did ever see!
Yea, one whose tender heart would rue for my distress:
Yet I, poor I, must perish ne'ertheless;   10
And (which much more augments my care)
Unmoanèd, I must die
And no man e'er
Know why.

Fair Virtue
1622

° **dirge** . an example of 17th-century concrete poetry; cf. Herbert's *Altar*,
Easter-wings etc. and their gardens, title-pages. See chap. on the poem as
hieroglyph by J. H. Summers in his *G. Herbert, his religion and art* 1954
repr. in Keast ed. *17th-century English poetry* 1962.

COMMENTARY 2

James I
1603–1625

Pastoral

I quoted Nashe to introduce melancholy; now he opens the pastoral section. He was an urban journalist. These are not really paradoxes. I use 'pastoral' to label material which ranges from the primitive to the highly artificial so long as it has to do with the country; but there need not be sheep, sometimes not even scenery, but often country matters: for pastoral was a standard environment for fictional sex. Where we use detectives or space travellers they used shepherds (hence, presumably, Nashe's rustic diction round about line 90 of *Valentines*).

There is little 'nature poetry' in the 17th century. That was to become a genre in its own right in the 18th. It developed from the philosophical, delineative view of such Restoration writers as Milton, Denham, the Duchess of Newcastle, Cotton, the Countess of Winchilsea. There was more of it even in the 16th century: the heroic narrative so largely practised then—*Fairy Queen, Hero and Leander, Venus and Adonis, Complaint of Rosamund, Mirror for magistrates*—required large landscapes, topographia. Drayton went on with this in the 17th century; but wouldn't it be fair to say that *Gondibert, Davideis*, even *Paradise lost* do not present so assuredly complete and immense scenery as their subjects demand? The towns—Davenant's Verona, Dryden's London in *Annus mirabilis*, Milton's Pandemonium—are fitter.

Drayton's *Endymion and Phoebe*, written about 1595, exemplifies the older mode. The moon goddess, in love with the shepherd boy, disguises herself as a country girl—but as one dressed up as queen of the may: 'Embosted rainbows did appear in silk, With wavy streams as white as morning's milk.' The pastoral stuff is all there, including sheep, and sensuality; but it is not simple; it is glamorised in a way parallel to the shiny art of Giulio Romano, Bronzino, Varga:

> About her neck a chain twice twentyfold,
> Of rubies set in lozenges of gold,

> Trussed up in trammels and in curious pleats
> With sphery circles falling on her teats.

It includes a commercial realism, a sense of what is touchable
and rich.

In the 17th century formal pastoral became chaster—see
Drayton's own *Eclogues*, Chapman's sequel to *Hero and
Leander*. Attention shifts from lustre to music, and to detail.
Pastoral is the frame for the most exquisite rhythms of
language (as well as of sound) at this time—in Campion
obviously but also in anonymous contemporaries for whom
Dowland and others wrote the music:

> Melt not in weeping
> While she lies sleeping
> Softly, now softly lies
> Sleeping.

See the last 50 pages of the *Oxford book of 17th-century verse*
or *A poetical rhapsody* ed. Francis Davison 1602 et seq.

The detail I refer to is a plainness or normality which re-
places the Tudor decor. It is found in all our poets in this
section, especially William Browne. His lucid facts—'the cattle
chewed the cud Low levelled on the grass'—go on in Milton's
most modern style:

> others on the grass
> Couched, and now filled with pasture gazing sat,
> Or bedward ruminating.
>
> —*PL* IV.350

And so to Thomson, Wordsworth, Keats (who was particularly fond of Browne). Browne contributes to what is simple
in the great pastorals, those that transcend their genre: 'His
coffin tossed by fish and surges fell' is for *Lycidas*; this for
Hyperion:

> Only the curlèd streams soft chidings kept,
> And little gales, that from the green leaf swept
> Dry summer's dust, in fearful whisperings stirred,
> As loath to waken any singing bird.

Indeed it is for Tennyson. That bit of Browne's is a fine ob-
jective correlative; he also made mythology relate effectively
to emotion. This is unusual but Beaumont and Fletcher are
comparable.

Jacobean detailing could run to complex microscopy as in Drayton's *Nymphidia*—'The walls of spiders' legs are made.' The interest in fairies, prevalent in this section, was part of a nostalgia for merrie England: that is, as Corbet and the Christmas ballad admit, for Roman catholic England; Mary's, not Elizabeth's. In Herrick the fairies become major; the nostalgia ripens to a scholarly possession of folklore (anthropology began in the 17th century). The detail is delicately obsessional: 'He with his pretty finger pressed The ruby niplet of her breast'. Eventually Marvell was to turn the pretty details upside down and get inside them:

> Who of his great design in pain
> Did for a model vault his brain,
> Whose columns should so high be raised
> To arch the brows that on them gazed.
> *Appleton House*

Surrealism needs a cold eye. Horace provided it. Perfectly cultivated, his father's model son, the emperor's friend, wifeless and childless, Horace expressed in occasional odes another pastoral tone. English squires were climbing out of the mud and taking their daughters to London for husbands; Horace's tone suited that aspiration to refinement: it treated the country not as where most people made their living but where gentlemen retired to from the town—quiet, simple, leisured, clean. I have represented the Horatian tone by Ashmore. It was not (at least until after Herrick) more central than that, though it was more extensive. However, being a donnish attitude, it has been over-rated.

I have tried to redress it with bawdy—another donnish interest but less familiar in the textbooks. This is where Nashe helps. *The choice of valentines, or the merry ballad of Nashe his dildo* is pornography in the literal sense of writing about whores. It is not therefore really pastoral: whores are urban. But Nashe was writing within a general move (regretted by the authorities of the time) to use printing for erotic purposes. We probably find his whorehouse erotics weaker than the rural in some ways; closer perhaps to the Restoration, obsessed with performance. But the effect of printing was not merely to weaken-cheapen: the erotic itself could gain from literacy. Lines 101–14 of our excerpt about the interchange of looks—'On him her eyes continually were fixed'—are a rough model for a relation that is crucial in 17th-century love poetry at all levels: see Donne *Ecstasy* and Commentary 4.

If Nashe makes his brothel share that spiritual imagery, those more serious poems of love are in their turn environed by his physical documentation. His girl's jumps and cries, followed by a couplet of such realistic sentimentality it might come from Beaumont and Fletcher, provide an actuality that validates the later Platonism.

The merry haymakers is fully rural. It resounds to buttocks being treated as hindquarters. But that country talk, getting printed and so lodging in city minds, made it possible to retain in print some of the qualities of oral publishing: speed, audience participation, laughter, and an idiom which is both unabashed and exact. It may even have been possible to produce new statements from a combination of that popular style with the highbrow. Nashe applies heraldry to bottoms—'A lofty buttock barred with azure veins'—and so, while making fun of both, by association makes both more acceptable and beautiful; unites nature and art, tart and chivalry, in a way that was the special genius of the century. (*Haymakers* was revised as *The country wake* by Durfey. For the syndrome folk-bawdy-burlesque see him and others in Section 10, anonymous pieces passim, Taylor the water poet, Rowlands. Contrast the courtliness of 4–6; see Commentary 9.)

For further work on this section see Nashe's journalism (cf. Dekker, Rowlands) and his novel (cf. Fielding). See Walton's angling book which leads to Cotton and, via the Peak district, back to Drayton. See Christmas in a textbook of folklore. See the music section in the reading list. Fairies (back to *Midsummer night's dream*, on to Herrick, the masque, Fuseli, Christina Rossetti, Lewis Carroll, Barrie, Andrew Lang, Arthur Rackham and the catholic nostalgia of the 1950s in C. S. Lewis, Charles Williams and Tolkein). Horace. Milton can be started with a comparison of his diction in *Comus* and *Lycidas* with that of Browne and Drayton. Corbet introduces literary travelogues, and Norwich, then second city (cf. Sir Thomas Browne, Knevet, the Pastons), and leads on to his chaplain, Strode. What justification is there for separating Strode, Herrick and Randolph from this section?

For major independent work, Drayton, Beaumont and Fletcher, William Browne seem still to need at any rate critical attention. Drayton deliberately tried to turn himself from an Elizabethan into a Jacobean. Did he succeed? Of all three I would want to ask, What has he got to say? E.g. Drayton's *attitude* to the heroes of Agincourt or the colonists of Virginia seems to have meaning; so does Browne's method of using mythology. Drayton leads out in many directions suitable for limited work—the poetry of America (Hagthorpe,

Bradstreet, Edward Taylor, Sandys); patronage (the Countess of Bedford, and Donne); the effect (see *Of his lady*) of mechanical watches and clocks on the concepts of time and mutability (cf. Baron, Suckling *Of thee*, Vaughan *Man*, Philips *Friendship*, Anon. *Christ Church*, Wanley *Divorce*).

Pastoral itself can be pursued in the following directions: (1) Creation as primal pastoral: Sylvester, Psalm xix, *Paradise lost* VII, *Job* xxxix etc.; consider also mystical landscape in Vaughan and Traherne and allegorical landscape in *Pilgrim's progress*. (2) Pastoral as erotic environment: *Solomon's song*, Herbert *Ode*, Carew *Pastoral dialogues*, Herrick, Randolph, Cleveland, Lovelace *Aramantha*, much in the Restoration, paintings, *Paradise lost* IV. (3) Nature poetry of various sorts, in Strode, occasionally in Davenant, bizarre in Duchess of Newcastle; Cotton. (4) Randolph *To Stafford*, Lovelace *Grasshopper* and (not printed here) Herrick *Country life* are quasi-Horatian advertisements for the country as a place for friendship. (5) Joseph Beaumont's *Garden* indicates Marvell's, and then the great house poem—Marvell's *Appleton*, Jonson's *Penshurst*, with its antithesis in Pope on Timon's villa (*Moral essays* iv); there is also the curiously urban park-pastoral of Waller; and where in these categories do *L'allegro* and *Il penseroso* and Denham *Cooper's Hill* belong?

I close this section with laments for old superstitions and old religion: pastoral is nostalgic. The next section shows the beginning of modern religious feeling.

THOMAS NASHE

Son of a minister; St John's College, Cambridge; travel in
France and Italy; to London in 1588 (year of the Spanish
Armada) to become miscellaneous professional writer. Satir-
ised the puritans, and social abuses (imprisoned for political
satire 1597). In 1594 produced *The unfortunate traveller or
the life of Jack Wilton*, first picaresque novel in England.
Summer's last will and testament is a pastoral comedy but his
main work was in documentary and satire. See *Works* ed. R.
B. McKerrow 5 vols. 1904–10 repr. 1958; G. R. Hibbard
T. N. a critical introduction 1962.

from Summer's Last Will and Testament

*Enter Summer, leaning on Autumn's and Winter's shoul-
ders, and attended on with a train of satyrs and wood-
nymphs, singing; Vertumnus also following him.*

Summer   Fair Summer droops, droop men and beast
        therefore:
  So fair a summer look for nevermore.
  All good things vanish less than in a day;
  Peace, plenty, pleasure suddenly decay.
    Go not yet away, bright soul of the sad year: 5
    The earth is hell when thou leavest to
      appear.

  What, shall these flowers that decked thy gar-
    land erst
  Upon thy grave be wastefully dispersed?
  O trees, consume your sap in sorrow's source;
  Streams, turn to tears your tributary course.   10
    Go not yet away, bright soul of the sad year:
    The earth is hell when thou leavest to
      appear.

Enter Ver with his train overlaid with suits of green moss,
representing short grass, singing.

Ver°   Spring, the sweet spring, is the year's pleasant
               king,
             Then blooms each thing, then maids dance in a
               ring,
             Cold doth not sting, the pretty birds do sing,   15
             Cuckoo, jug-jug, pu-wee, tu-witta-whoo!

             The palm and may make country houses gay,
             Lambs frisk and play, the shepherds pipe all
               day
             And we hear aye birds tune this merry lay,
             Cuckoo, jug-jug, pu-wee, tu-witta-whoo!   20

             The fields breathe sweet, the daisies kiss our
               feet,
             Young lovers meet, old wives a-sunning sit,
             In every street these tunes our ears do greet,
             Cuckoo, jug-jug, pu-wee, tu-witta-whoo!
               Spring, the sweet spring!   25

         •   •   •

Summer   This is the last stroke my tongue's clock must
               strike,
             My last will, which I will that you perform.
               My crown I have disposed already of.
               Item, I give my withered flowers and herbs
             Unto dead corses for to deck them with;   30
             My shady walks to great men's servitors
             Who in their masters' shadows walk secure;
             My pleasant open air and fragrant smells
             To Croydon and the ground abutting round;
             My heat and warmth to toiling labourers,   35
             My long days to bondmen and prisoners,
             My short nights to young married souls,
             My drought and thirst to drunkards' quenchless
               throats;
             My fruits to Autumn, my adopted heir;
             My murmuring springs, musicians of sweet   40
               sleep,
             To murmuring malcontents who with their
               well-tuned cares
             Channelled in a sweet falling quatorzain°
             Do lull their ears asleep, listening themselves.
               And finally—O words, now cleanse your
               course—

Unto Eliza,° that most sacred dame   45
Whom none but saints and angels ought to
    name,
All my fair days remaining I bequeathe,
To wait upon her till she be returned.
Autumn, I charge thee, when that I am dead
Be pressed and serviceable at her beck,   50
Present her with thy goodliest ripened fruits,
Unclothe no arbours where she ever sat,
Touch not a tree thou think'st she may pass by.
And Winter with thy writhen frosty face,
Smooth up thy visage when thou look'st on her: 55
Thou never look'st on such bright majesty;
A charmèd circle draw about her court
Wherein warm days may dance and no cold
    come;
On seas let winds make war, not vex her rest,
Quiet enclose her bed, thought fly her breast.   60
Ah, gracious Queen! though Summer pine away
Yet let thy flourishing stand at a stay:
First droop this universal's agèd frame
E'er any malady thy strength should tame;
Heaven raise up pillars to uphold thy hand,   65
Peace may have still his temple in thy land.
    Lo, I have said: this is the total sum.
Autumn and Winter, on your faithfulness
For the performance I do firmly build.
Farewell, my friends. Summer bids you fare-   70
    well,
Archers and bowlers, all my followers,
Adieu! and dwell with desolatïon.
Silence must be your master's mansïon;
Slow marching thus descend I to the fiends.
Weep, heavens; mourn, earth: here Summer   75
    ends.

*Here the satyrs and wood-nymphs carry him out, singing,
as he came in.*

Autumn hath all the Summer's fruitful treasure;
Gone is our sport, fled is poor Croydon's pleas-
    ure;
Short days, sharp days, long nights come on
    apace—
Ah, who shall hide us from the Winter's face?
Cold doth increase, the sickness will not cease 80
And here we lie, God knows, with little ease.

> From winter, plague and pestilence, good
>   Lord deliver us.

> London doth mourn, Lambeth is quite forlorn,
> Trades cry woe worth that ever they were born;
> The want of term° is town and city's harm;   85
> Close chambers we do want to keep us warm;
> Long banishèd must we live from our friends;
> This low-built house will bring us to our ends.
>   From winter, plague and pestilence, good
>   Lord deliver us.

written c.1592; published 1600

13 **Ver** Spring. 42 **quatorzain** 14-lined poem. 45 **Eliza** the queen.
85 **term** sitting of law courts.

from *The choice of valentines, or the merry ballad of Nashe his dildo*

. . . By blind meanders and by crankled ways
She° leads me onward (as my author says)
Until we come within a shady loft
Where Venus' bouncing vestals skirmish oft;
And there she sat me in a leather chair   5
And brought me forth of pretty trulls a pair,
To choose of them which might content mine eye;
But her I sought I could nowhere espy.
I spake them fair and wished them well to fare,
Yet so it is, I must have fresher fare.   10
    Wherefore, dame bawd, as dainty as you be,
Fetch gentlest mistress Frances forth to me.
    By halidom!° quoth she, and God's own Mother,
I well perceive you are a wily brother!
For if there be a morsel of more price   15
You'll smell it out though I be ne'er so nice.
As you desire, so shall you swive° with her—
But think your purse-strings shall abide it dear:
For he that will eat quails must lavish crowns,
And mistress Frances in her velvet gowns   20
And ruffs and periwigs as fresh as May
Cannot be kept with half-a-crown a day.

     •   •   •

Sweeping she comes, as she would brush the ground;

Her rattling silks my senses do confound:
   O I am ravished! Void the chamber straight,   25
For I must needs upon her with my weight.
   My Tomalin! quoth she, and then she smiled.
   Aye, aye, quoth I, so more men are beguiled
With smiles, with flattering words and feignèd cheer
When in their deeds their falsehood doth appear.   30
   As how, my lambkin? blushing she replied:
Because I in this dancing-school abide?
If that be it that breeds this discontent,
We will remove the camp incontinent.°
For shelter only, sweetheart, came I hither,   35
And to avoid the troublous stormy weather.°
But now the coast is clear we will be gone,
Since but thyself true lover have I none.
   With that she sprung full lightly to my lips
And fast about the neck me culls and clips;   40
She wanton faints and falls upon the bed
And often tosseth to and fro her head,
She shuts her eyes and waggles with her tongue—
O who is able to abstain so long?
I come, I come! Sweet linen, by thy leave!   45
Softly my fingers up this curtain heave
And make me happy stealing by degrees—
First bare her legs, then creep up to her knees;
From thence ascend unto her manly thigh—
A pox on lingering when I am so nigh—   50
Smock, climb apace that I may see my joys.
O! heaven and paradise are all but toys
Comparèd with this sight I now behold,
Which well might keep a man from being old:
A pretty rising womb without a weam°   55
That shone as bright as any silver stream
And bare out like the bending of an hill,
At whose decline a fountain dwelleth still
That hath his mouth beset with ugly briars
Resembling much a dusky net of wires;   60
A lofty buttock barred with azure veins
Whose comely swelling when my hand distrains
Or wanton checketh with a harmless stripe—
It makes the fruits of love eftsoons be ripe
And pleasure, plucked too timely from the stem,   65
To die ere it hath seen Jerusalem:
O gods! that ever anything so sweet
So suddenly should fade away and fleet!
Her arms are spread and I am all unarmed:

Like one with Ovid's cursèd hemlock° charmed,   70
So are my limbs unwieldy for the fight
That spend their strength in thought of their delight.
What shall I do to show myself a man?
It will not be for aught that beauty can:
I kiss, I clap, I feel, I view at will,   75
Yet dead he lies, not thinking good or ill.
    Unhappy me! quoth she, and will't not stand?
Come, let me rub and chafe it with my hand:
Perhaps the silly worm is laboured sore
And wearièd that it can do no more;   80
If that be so (as I am great adread)
I wish ten thousand times that I were dead.
Howe'er it is, no means shall want in me
That may avail to his recovery.
    Which said, she took and rolled it on her thigh   85
And when she looked on't she would weep and sigh,
And dandled it and danced it up and down,
Not ceasing till she raised it from his swoun;
And then he flew on her as he were wood°
And on her breech did thack and foin° a-good: 90
He rubbed and pricked and pierced her to the bones,
Digging as far as eath° he might for stones;
Now high, now low, now striking short and thick,
Now diving deep he touched her to the quick;
Now with a gird he would his course rebate,   95
Straight would he take him to a stately gait.
    Play while him list and thrust he ne'er so hard,
Poor patient Grisel lieth at her ward
And gives and takes as blithe and free as May
And e'ermore meets him in the middle way.   100
On him her eyes continually were fixed,
With her eyebeams his melting looks were mixed,
Which like the sun that 'twixt two glasses plays
From one to the other casts rebounding rays.°
He, like a star that to regild his beams   105
Sucks in the influence of Phoebus' streams,°
Embathes the lines of his descending light
In the bright fountains of his clearest sight;
She, fair as fairest planet in the sky,
His purity to no man doth deny;   110
The very chamber that enclouds her shine
Looks like the palace of that god divine°
Who leads the day about the zodiac
And every even descends to the ocean lake.
So fierce and fervent is her radiance,   115

Such fiery stakes she darts at every glance
As might inflame the icy limbs of age
And make pale death his surquedry° assuage,
To stand and gaze upon her orient lamps
Where Cupid all his chiefest joys encamps   120
And sits and plays with every atomy
That in her sunbeams swarm abundantly.

   Thus gazing and thus striving we persevere;
But what so firm that may continue ever?
O not so fast! my ravished mistress cries,   125
Lest my content, that on thy life relies,
Be brought too soon from his delightful seat
And me unwares of hopèd bliss defeat.
Together let our equal motions stir,
Together let us live and die, my dear;   130
Together let us march unto content
And be consumèd with one blandishment.

   As she prescribed, so kept we crotchet-time,
And every stroke in order like a chime,
Whilst she, that had preserved me by her pity,   135
Unto our music° framed a groaning ditty.

   Alas! alas! that love should be a sin—
Even now my bliss and sorrow doth begin:
Hold wide thy lap, my lovely Danaë,°
And entertain the golden shower so free   140
That trilling falls into thy treasury!
As April drops not half so pleasant be,
Nor Nilus' overflow to Egypt plains,
As this sweet streams that all her loins embains.°
With O! and O! she itching moves her hips   145
And to and fro full lightly starts and skips,
She jerks her legs and sprawleth with her heels—
No tongue may tell the solace that she feels.

   I faint! I yield! O death, rock me asleep!
Sleep, sleep, desire, entombèd in the deep!   150

   Not so, my dear! my dearest saint replied,
For from us yet thy spirit may not glide
Until the sinewy channels of our blood
Withold their source from this imprisoned flood;
And then will we (that then will come too soon)   155
Dissolvèd lie as though our days were done.

   The whilst I speak my soul is fleeting hence
And life forsakes his fleshy residence.

   Stay! stay! sweet joy, and leave me not forlorn:
Why shouldst thou fade that art but newly born?   160
Stay but an hour, an hour is not so much—

But half an hour if that thy haste be such?
Nay, but a quarter! I will ask no more
That thy departure, which torments me sore,
May be alightened with a little pause   165
And take away this passion's sudden cause.
He hears me not, hard-hearted as he is:
He is a son of time and hates my bliss;
Time ne'er looks back, the rivers ne'er return—
A second spring must help me or I burn!   170
No no: the well is dry that should refresh me,
The glass is run of all my destiny.
Nature of winter learneth niggardise,
Who, as he overbears the stream with ice
That man nor beast may of their pleasance taste,   175
So shuts she up her conduit all in haste
And will not let her nectar overflow
Lest mortal men immortal joys should know.
Adieu, inconstant love, to thy disport!
Adieu, false mirth, and melody too short!   180
Adieu, fainthearted instrument of lust,
That falsely hast betrayed our equal trust!
Henceforth no more will I implore thine aid,
Or thee or men of cowardice upbraid:
My little dildo shall supply their kind—   185
A knave that moves as light as leaves by wind,
That bendeth not nor foldeth any deal
But stands as stiff as he were made of steel
And plays at peacock 'twixt my legs right blithe
And doth my tickling 'suage with many a sigh;   190
For, by St. Runnion,° he'll refresh me well,
And never make my tender belly swell . . .

2 **She** the bawd. 13 **By halidom!** by all that's holy! 17 **swive** fuck.
Like most of the archaic words in this poem, swive is of Anglo-Saxon
origin; but it continued into the Restoration as slang while the others
died out. Cf. Rochester. 34 **remove . . . incontinent** leave the place at
once. 36 **stormy weather** presumably the same phrase as in the blues.
55 **womb . . . weam** belly without a blemish. 70 **hemlock** opiate and
poison; don't know why Ovid's. 89 **wood** mad. 90 **thack and foin**
thatch (slap? lay?) and thrust. 92 **eath** easily. 104 **Which like . . . rays**
The similes in this paragraph were common in serious love poetry. 106
Phoebus' streams sunbeams. Stars were thought to absorb sunshine and
store it up; cf. P. Fletcher *To my soul*. 112 **that god divine** Phoebus,
the sun. 118 **surquedry** arrogance. 136 **music** slang for copulation, as
in the nursery-rhyme of *Ride a cockhorse*: 'She shall have music wher-
ever she goes.' 139 **Danaë** to seduce her, Zeus turned himself into a
shower of gold; she spread her lap to catch it. See Rembrandt, Klimt.
144 **embains** embathes. 191 **St. Runnion** runnion was slang for whore
and for penis.

SAMUEL ROWLANDS

Prolific journalist. All his volumes are rare. Complete works [except *Theatre of delightful recreation* 1605 and *The bride* 1617] ed. E. Gosse and S. J. Herrtage 1880; *Night-raven* 1620 etc. ed. E. V. Utterson 1880; *Bride* ed. A. C. Porter, Boston 1905. Not worth pursuing as a poet.

Like mistress, like maid

Susan would meet with Richard and with Ned
As soon as e'er her mistress was a-bed,
For a sack-posset they agreed to eat—
And she besides would have a bit of meat—
And so be merry that they would° in sadness.   5
But even about the time of mirth and gladness,
When both the young men were bestowed within,
One that had long her mistress' lover been
Knocks at the door; whereat herself came down
(As loose of body as she was of gown)   10
And in the dark put Lecher in the room
Where both the youths attend till Susan come—
Who in the meantime to light a candle went;
So did her mistress for the same intent,
And meeting with her maid, O, strange! quoth she, 15
What cause have you at this time here to be?
Mistress, quoth she, unto you I'll be true:
There's two as honest youths as ere I knew
Came late to see me. Pray you be content!
Wench, this may be, said she, and no harm meant: 20
For there's an honest man to make them three
That came in kindness for to visit me.
Good Susan, be as secret as you can—
Your master is a foolish jealous man.
Though thou and I do mean no hurt or ill,   25
Yet men take women in the worst sense still,

And fear of horns more grief in hearts hath bred
Than wearing horns doth hurt a cuckold's head.

The night-raven 1620

5 would meaning? that they would otherwise?

ANONYMOUS

A well-wishing to a place of pleasure

See that building which, when my mistress living,
    Was pleasure's essence:
See how it droopeth, and how nakedly it looketh
    Without her presence;
Hark! how the hollow wind doth blow   5
    And seems to murmur
    In every corner
For her being absent, from which doth chiefly grow
The cause that I do now this grief and sorrow show.

See that garden where oft I had reward in   10
    For my true love;
See the places where I enjoyed those graces
    The gods might move;
Oft in that arbour, while that she
    With melting kisses   15
    Distilling blisses
From her free lips, for joy did ravish me,
The pretty nightingale did sing melodiously.

Hail to those groves where we enjoyed our loves
    So many days!   20
May trees there be springing and the pretty birds be singing
    Their roundelays.
O may the grass grow ever green
    On which we lying
    Have oft been trying   25
More several ways of pleasure than that queen°
Which once in bed with Mars by all the gods was seen.

                British Museum MS. before 1627

26 that queen   Venus.

The merry haymakers, or pleasant pastime between the young men and maids in the pleasant meadows

In our country, in our country,
　Where ruffelers° was a-raking°
And the rarest pastime that ever you see
　Was when haycocks they were a-making, to be.°

There's Timmy and Tommy with bottle and bag—　　　5
　As soon as the lasses beheld them,
Because they did not give them what they did lack,
　Adzuggers° they swore they would geld 'em, to be.

And did you not know one Vulking° the smith
　And Mary that went to the dairy?　　　　　　10
O give me, quoth she, a thing that is stiff
　And make me look buxom° and airy, to be.

And down in a dale was tumbledown Dick
　With Mary and Sarah and Susan;
They being in haste for to play the old trick　　　15
　They leapt into bed with their shoes on, to be.

And some they fork and some they will rake
　When merrily they were a-quaffing;
And if you had seen how Joan's buttocks did wag
　'Twould broke a man's side out of laughing, to be.　20

Young Bridget came next and, plaguily vexed,
　With fury she fell upon Robin;
His clater-de-vengeance° adzuggers she clawed
　'Cause he with young Kate had been bobbing, to be.

With that he made bold with speed to take hold　　25
　Of Bridget's young chitter-de-widgeon,°
He threw her along but did it no wrong
　Because it was just upon fledging, to be.

Her mother came by and as she drew nigh
　The sight put her into a laughter,　　　　　30
His buttocks she banged and bid him be hanged
　For playing the fool with her daughter, to be.

The men and the maids they love their comrades
　Above any paltry riches:
Quoth Nancy to Dick, Adzuggers I'm sick　　　35
　For something thou hast in thy breeches, to be.

What say'st thou me so, then to it we'll go,
   Thou shalt have thy earnest desire,
For thou art the lass, I swear by the mass,
   Which I above all do admire, to be.   40

At making of hay they frolic and play
   As you may observe by this ditty
And when they are cracked away they are packed
   For virgins away to the city, to be.

Ballad, Bodleian Library, Oxford

2 **ruffelers** a ruffler was a vagabond or a professional beggar, but it may mean just the wild lads of the village. **a-raking** making hay; and raising hell. 4 **to be** the refrain seems to be meaningless. 8 **Adzuggers** God's secrets? 9 **Vulking** conventional name for a blacksmith, from Vulcan, the Roman god. 12 **buxom** has come to mean, especially, plump; but had the more general sense of amenable and lighthearted—'the lineaments of gratified desire'. 23 **clater-de-vengeance** possibly from cleat=wedge or pin. The French phrasing gives it the air of a chivalric weapon. 26 **chitter-de-widgeon** bird's tail? Chitterling, a butcher's word for the intestines of a pig, was slang for bowels or belly; a widgeon is a duck. Chitterling also came to mean girl.

Weep you no more, sad fountains

Weep you no more, sad fountains:
   What need you flow so fast?
Look how the snowy mountains
   Heaven's sun doth gently waste;
   But my sun's heavenly eyes   5
     View not your weeping,
     That now lie sleeping
  Softly, now softly lies
      Sleeping.

Sleep is a reconciling,   10
   A rest that peace begets.
Doth not the sun rise smiling
   When fair at even he sets?
   Rest you then, rest, sad eyes,
     Melt not in weeping   15
     While she lies sleeping
  Softly, now softly lies
      Sleeping.

John Dowland set *Third and last book
of songs or airs of four parts with
tablature for lute* 1603

DR. THOMAS CAMPION

Son of a squire. Peterhouse, Cambridge; Gray's Inn; neither course completed but took medical degree on continent. Wrote all the words and with Philip Rosseter half the music for *A book of airs*—solo songs to the lute—1601. Words and music for two further volumes c.1613 and c.1617. Wrote an essay championing unrhymed syllabic verse. The only writer to combine important work in music and verse. *Works* ed. Walter R. Davis 1967.

So tired are all my thoughts

So tired are all my thoughts that sense and spirits fail:
Mourning I pine, and know not what I ail.
O what can yield ease to a mind
   Joy in nothing that can find?

How are my powers fore-spoke? What strange distaste is   5
  this?
Hence, cruel hate of that which sweetest is!
Come, come, delight! make my dull brain
   Feel once heat of joy again.

The lover's tears are sweet, their mover makes them so;
Proud of a wound the bleeding soldiers grow;   10
Poor I alone, dreaming, endure
   Grief that knows nor cause nor cure.

And whence can all this grow? even from an idle mind,
That no delight in any good can find;
Action alone makes the soul blest: 15
   Virtue dies with too much rest.

Kind are her answers

Kind are her answers
   But her performance keeps no day,
Breaks time, as dancers
   From their own music when they stray.
    All her free favors   5
And smooth words wing my hopes in vain.
O did ever voice so sweet but only feign?
   Can true love yield such delay,
   Converting joy to pain?

Lost is our freedom   10
   When we submit to women so.
Why do we need them
   When in their best they work our woe?
    There is no wisdom
Can alter ends by fate prefixed.   15
O why is the good of man with evil mixed?
   Never were days yet call'd two
   But one night went betwixt.

Hark, all you ladies

Hark, all you ladies that do sleep!
   The fairy queen Prosérpina°
Bids you awake and pity them that weep.
   You may do in the dark
    What the day doth forbid;   5
Fear not the dogs that bark,
   Night will have all hid.

But if you let your lovers moan,
   The fairy queen Prosérpina
Will send abroad her fairies every one   10
   That shall pinch black and blue
    Your white hands and fair arms
   That did not kindly rue
    Your paramours' harms.

In myrtle° arbours on the downs   15
   The fairy queen Prosérpina,
This night by moonshine leading merry rounds,

Holds a watch with sweet love,
   Down the dale, up the hill;
No plaints or groans may move   20
   Their holy vigil.

All you that will hold watch with love,
   The fairy queen Prosérpina
Will make you fairer than Diónë's° dove;
   Roses red, lilies white   25
     And the clear damask hue°
   Shall on your cheeks alight:
     Love will adorn you.

All you that love, or loved before,
   The fairy queen Prosérpina   30
Bids you increase that loving humor more;
   They that yet have not fed
     On delight amorous,
   She vows that they shall lead
     Apes in Avernus.°   35

2 **Prosérpina** Persephone, abducted by Pluto, god of the underworld, to be his queen. Later became goddess of sleep. 15 **myrtle** emblem of love, sacred to Aphrodite. 24 **Dione** Aphrodite (actually her mother). The dove, sacred to her, is an emblem of love. 26 **damask hue** silkiness; from kinds of silk and linen woven at Damascus. 35 **Avernus** hell. It was said that old maids would be punished in hell by having to lead apes about—emblems of lust.

MICHAEL DRAYTON

Son of prosperous Warwickshire tanner; by age of 10 was page to Sir Henry Goodere who was a friend of Sidney and father of a friend of Donne. Goodere passed him to the patronage of Lucy, Countess of Bedford (see Donne's verse epistles). He spent his life in concentrated literary activity, producing work on almost every genre and repeatedly bringing it up to date with changing fashions. Specially popular with bourgeois readers. Some early religious verse (he knew Quarles and Sandys); *Idea,* Spenserian pastorals praising Queen Elizabeth and mourning Sidney, 1591 (revised 1605, 1619); *Idea's mirror* 1594, a sonnet sequence rather in the manner of Shakespeare (whom he knew; he was also at one time treated by Shakespeare's doctor son-in-law, John Hall): the sonnets, colloquial in tone, were addressed to Goodere's daughter and although she married soon afterwards, and Drayton remained a bachelor, it seems they had enjoyed a youthful love, and they remained friends. About 1595 he wrote *Endymion and Phoebe,* a glittering mythological pastoral, for Lady Bedford; then a period of epic and historical verse—*The barons' wars* 1596; *England's heroical epistles*—for 200 years his most popular work—1597; and then till 1602 a dramatic period, mostly in collaboration with Dekker. He now moved in the circle of Jonson, the Beaumonts and the pastoral poets Drummond and Browne. His passion for England, history and geography further expressed in *Poems lyric and pastoral* (1605) which brought his earlier pastorals up to date and added a famous Agincourt ballad ('Fair stood the wind for France'), the counterpart of Tennyson's *Light Brigade;* also, in topical heroics, The Virginia ode, etc.; culminated in *Nymphidia* 1627. See B. H. Newdigate *Drayton and his circle* Oxford 1941; *Works* ed. J. W. Hebel 5 vols. Oxford 1931.

from The shepherd's Sirena

Near to the silver Trent
   Sirena dwelleth:
She to whom nature lent
   all that excelleth;
By which the Muses late   5
   and the neat Graces
Have for their greater state
   taken their places,
Twisting an anadem°
   wherewith to crown her   10
As it belonged to them
   most to renown her.
        On thy bank
        In a rank
        Let thy swans sing her   15
And with their music
   along let them bring her.
      •   •   •

Our mournful Philomel,
   that rarest tuner,
Henceforth in Aperil   20
   shall wake the sooner
And to her shall complain
   from the thick cover,
Redoubling every strain
   over and over: 25
For when my love too long
   her chamber keepeth,
As though it suffered wrong
   the morning weepeth.
        On thy bank *etc.*
      •   •   •

The verdant meads are seen   30
   when she doth view them
In fresh and gallant green
   straight to renew them;
And every little grass
   broad itself spreadeth   35
Proud that this bonny lass
   upon it treadeth;
Nor flower is so sweet
   in this large cincture

But it upon her feet   40
   leaveth some tincture. *etc.*

    •   •   •

When she looks out by night
   the stars stand gazing
Like comets to our sight
   fearfully blazing   45
As wondering at her eyes
   with their much brightness
Which so amaze the skies
   dimming their lightness;
The raging tempests are calm   50
   when she speaketh,
Such most delightsome balm
   from her lips breaketh.
        On thy bank
        In a rank
        Let thy swans sing her   55
And with their music
   along let them bring her. . . .

9 **anadem** garland.

from *To my noble friend Master William Browne:
of the evil time*°

Dear friend, be silent and with patience see
What this mad time's catastrophe will be;
The world's first wise men certainly mistook
Themselves and spoke things quite beside the book,
And that which they have said of God untrue,
Or else expect strange judgement to ensue.   5
   This isle is a mere bedlam and therein
We all lie raving, mad in every sin;
And him the wisest most men use to call
Who doth alone the maddest thing of all.

    •   •   •

   This world of ours thus runneth upon wheels,   10
Set on the head, bolt upright with her heels;
Which makes me think of what the ethnics told,
The opinion the Pythagorists° uphold
That the immortal soul doth transmigrate:
Then I suppose by the strong power of fate   15

That those which at confusèd Babel were,
And since that time now many a lingering year
Through fools and beasts and lunatics have passed,
Are here embodied in this age at last;
And though so long we from that time be gone,   20
Yet taste we still of that confusïon.
For certainly, there's scarce one found that now
Knows what to approve or what to disallow,
All arsey-varsey,° nothing is its own
But to our proverb all turned upside-down.   25

   Into the clouds the devil lately got
And, by the moisture doubting much the rot,
A medicine took to make him purge and cast;
Which in short time began to work so fast
That he fell to it and from his backside flew   30
A rout of rascals, a rude ribald crew
Of base plebeians, which no sooner light
Upon the earth but with a sudden flight
They spread this isle and, as Deucalion° once
Over his shoulder back by throwing stones,   35
They became men, even so these beasts became
Owners of titles° from an óbscure name.

   As men oft laugh at little babes when they
Hap to behold some strange thing in their play,
To see them on the sudden strucken sad   40
As in their fancy some strange forms they had
Which they by pointing with their fingers show,
Angry at our capacities so slow
That by their countenance we no sooner learn
To see the wonder which they so discern: 45
So the celestial powers do sit and smile
At innocent and virtuous men, the while
They stand amazèd at the world o'er-gone
So far beyond imaginatïon
With slavish baseness that they silent sit   50
Pointing like little children in describing it . . .

                                      1627

° **of the evil time** cf. Donne's *Anniversaries*, Jonson to Colby, in Vol. I.
13 **Pythagorists** the doctrine of the transmigration of souls through
various incarnations was attributed to Pythagoras (a Greek philosopher
of the 6th century B.C.) along with the proof about the square on the
hypotenuse, the theory of the music of the spheres, manly beauty and a
thigh of gold. See Yeats *Among school children*. 24 **arsey-varsey** dialect
for upside-down. 34 **Deucalion** Greek equivalent of Noah. When the

flood was over he and his wife threw stones behind them; his turned
into men, hers into women. 37 **titles** Elizabeth created less than a
dozen peers; James I doubled the number of peers by creating 60, plus
many baronets and knights. From about 1615 peerages were being sold
through his favourite Buckingham at £10,000 each.

from To Master George Sandys,° treasurer for the English colony in Virginia

As if to symptoms we may credit give,
This very time wherein we two now live
Shall in the compass wound the Muses more
Than all the old English ignorance before:
Base ballatry is so beloved and sought,   5
And those brave numbers are put by for naught
Which, rarely read, were able to awake
Bodies from graves and to the ground to shake
The wandering clouds, and to our men at arms
'Gainst pikes and muskets were most powerful charms: 10
That, but I know, ensuing ages shall
Raise her again who now is in her fall
And out of dust reduce our scattered rhymes,
The rejected jewels of these slothful times.
Who with the Muses would mis-spend an hour   15
But let blind Gothish° barbarism devour
These feverous dog-days, blessed by no recórd,
But to be everlastingly abhorred . . .

1621

° **Sandys**   the religious poet and traveller, sailed to Virginia in May 1621
and arrived in October, having translated two books of Ovid's *Metamorphoses*. Virginia had been taken possession of, and named after the
Queen, by Raleigh in 1584. The first colonists went out in 1606. 16
Gothish   see Davenant *Gondibert*.

JOHN FLETCHER

Younger son of the Bishop of London; cousin of Phineas and Giles Fletcher the younger. Probably Cambridge. Trained as dramatist under Shakespeare and succeeded him as chief writer for the King's Men at the Blackfriars theatre. Chief independent work *The faithful shepherdess*, a pastoral tragicomedy c.1608. Collaborated with Beaumont c.1609–13: they shared rooms near the South Bank theatres "and had one wench in the house between them" (Aubrey). Died of plague. See C. Leech *The J. Fletcher plays* 1962 and cf. *Comus*.

from The Faithful Shepherdess

Shepherds all, and maidens fair,
Fold your flocks up, for the air
'Gins to thicken and the sun
Already his great course hath run.
See the dew-drops, how they kiss   5
Every little flower that is,
Hanging on their velvet heads
Like a rope of crystal beads;
See the heavy clouds low falling
And bright Hesperus° down calling   10
The dead night from under ground,
At whose rising mists unsound
Damps and vapours fly apace,
Hovering o'er the wanton face
Of these pastures where they come   15
Striking dead both bud and bloom.
Therefore from such danger lock
Everyone his lovèd flock;
And let your dogs lie loose without
Lest the wolf come as a scout   20
From the mountain and ere day
Bear a lamb or kid away,

Or the crafty thievish fox
Break upon your simple flocks.
To secure yourselves from these,   25
Be not too secure in ease:
Let one eye his watches keep
Whilst the other eye doth sleep;
So you shall good shepherds prove
And for ever hold the love   30
Of our great god.° Sweetest slumbers
And soft silence fall in numbers
On your eyelids. So, farewell,
Thus I end my evening's knell.

10 **Hesperus** evening star. 31 **god** Pan.

BEAUMONT AND FLETCHER

Francis Beaumont (1584–1616) was the son of a lawyer and brother of Sir John; Drayton was a family friend. Oxford, law student. His chief play written mainly alone was *The knight of the burning pestle*. Chief plays of collaboration with Fletcher were *The maid's tragedy*, a melodrama, and *Philaster*, a grandiose tragicomedy. See E. H. Fellows ed. *Songs and lyrics from the plays of B. and F.* 1928.

from The Maid's Tragedy

Masque of heaven. Cynthia [the moon]; Night.

Cynthia   Great queen of shadows, you are pleased to
        speak
     Of more than may be done. We may not break
     The gods' decrees; but, when our time is come,
     Must drive away and give the day our room.
     Yet, while our reign lasts, let us stretch our
        power   5
     To give our servants one contented hour,
     With such unwonted solemn grace and state
     As may for ever after force them hate
     Our brother's glorious beams; and wish the night
     Crowned with a thousand stars, and our cold
        light: 10
     For almost all the world their service bend
     To Phoebus, and in vain my light I lend,
     Gazed on, unto my setting from my rise,
     Almost of none but of unquiet eyes.

[*Aspatia, betrothed to Amintor; Antíphila and Olympias, her ladies-in-waiting. Aspatia has had her fiancé stolen by the king's tyrannical mistress.*]

Asp.   Then, my good girls, be more than women—wise;
     At least be more than I was; and be sure

You credit anything the light gives light to
Before a man. Rather believe the sea
Weeps for the ruined merchant when he roars;   5
Rather, the wind courts but the pregnant sails
When the strong cordage cracks; rather, the sun
Comes but to kiss the fruit in wealthy autumn
When all falls blasted. If you needs must love
(Forced by ill fate), take to your maiden bosoms   10
Two dead cold aspics and of them make lovers:
They cannot flatter nor forswear; one kiss
Makes a long peace for all. But man!
O that beast man! Come, let's be sad, my girls.
That downcast of thine eye, Olympias,   15
Shows a fine sorrow. Mark, Antiphila:
Just such another was the nymph Oenónë°
When Paris brought home Helen. Now, a tear:
And then thou art a piece expressing fully
The Carthage queen° when, from a cold sea rock,   20
Full with her sorrow, she tied fast her eyes
To the fair Trojan ships; and, having lost them,
Just as thine eyes do, down stole a tear. Antiphila,
What would this wench do if she were Aspatia?
Here she would stand till some more pitying god   25
Turned her to marble. 'Tis enough, my wench!
Show me the piece of needlework you wrought.

Anti. Of Ariadne,° madam?
                        Yes, that piece.
Asp. This should be Theseus, he has a cozening face.
You meant him for a man?
Anti.   He was so, madam.   30
Asp. Why then, 'tis well enough. Never look back:
You have a full wind and a false heart, Theseus!
Does not the story say his keel was split
Or his masts spent or some kind rock or other
Met with his vessel?
Anti.   Not as I remember.   35
Asp. It should have been so. Could the gods know this
And not, of all their number, raise a storm?
But they are all as ill! This false smile
Was well expressed—just such another caught me.
You shall not go on so, Antiphila: 40
In this place work a quicksand
And over it a shallow smiling water
And his ship ploughing it. And then a Fear.
Do that Fear to the life, wench.
Anti.   'Twill wrong the story.

Asp. 'Twill make the story, wronged by poets,   45
        Live long and be believed. But where's the lady?

Anti. There, madam.

Asp. Fie, you have missed it here, Antiphila!
        You are much mistaken, wench:
        These colours are not dull and pale enough   50
        To show a soul so full of misery
        As this sad lady's was. Do it by me;
        Do it again, by me, the lost Aspatia,
        And you shall find all true but the wild island.
        Suppose I stand upon the sea beach now,   55
        Mine arms thus and mine hair blown with the wind,
        Wild as that desart; and let about me
        Be teachers of my story. Do my face
        (If thou hadst ever feeling of a sorrow)
        Thus, thus, Antiphila. Strive to make me look   60
        Like Sorrow's monument. And the trees about me,
        Let them be dry and leafless; let the rocks
        Groan with continual surges; and, behind me,
        Make all a desolation. Look, look, wenches!
        A miserable life of this poor picture.   65

Oly. Dear madam!

Asp.   I have done. Sit down; and let us
        Upon that point fix all our eyes—that point there.
        Make a dull silence, till you feel a sudden sadness
        Give us new souls.

17 **Oenone** wife of Paris, who deserted her for Helen and so started
the Trojan war. 20 **Carthage queen** Dido; she fell in love with Aeneas
who was sailing from Troy to Italy; he left her behind and she burnt
herself to death. 28 **Ariadne** was deserted on the isle of Naxos by her
lover Theseus.

WILLIAM BROWNE OF TAVISTOCK

Born at Tavistock on Dartmoor. Oxford, law student. Married the daughter of a Sussex squire, had two sons, who both died in infancy; he survived his wife. Literary life, mainly writing pastorals, some in conjunction with Wither: *Britannia's pastorals* 1613 ff; influenced Milton, Keats. In 1624 returned to Oxford as tutor to the future Earl of Caernarvon; and spent the end of his life with the Pembroke family at Wilton.

On the death of Mary, Countess of Pembroke°

Underneath this marble hearse
Lies the subject of all verse:
Sidney's sister, Pembroke's mother.
Death, ere thou hast killed another
Fair and learn'd and good as she,   5
Time shall throw a dart at thee.

Marble piles let no man raise
To her name for after days;
Some kind woman born as she,
Reading this, like Níöbë°   10
Shall turn marble and become
Both her mourner and her tomb.

° **Countess of Pembroke** Mary Herbert, 1555?–1621: sister of Sir Philip Sidney; 3rd wife of Henry Herbert, 2nd Earl of Pembroke; mother of William Herbert, 3rd Earl of Pembroke who was a great patron of poets—Browne himself, Daniel (his tutor), Massinger, Jonson, Chapman. The first folio of Shakespeare's plays was dedicated to him and his brother Philip the 4th earl as "the incomparable pair of brethren". Aubrey reported that 'In her time Wilton House [near Salisbury] was like a college, there were so many learned and ingenious persons. She was the greatest patroness of wit and learning of any lady in her time . . . This curious seat of Wilton and the adjacent country is an Arcadian place and a paradise.' Bemerton, where George Herbert (a relative) and John Norris had parishes, is nearby. It was thought that the countess's second son Philip was the product of a union between her and her brother Sidney; certainly her father-in-law the 1st earl (who could not read) realised that she would cuckold his son and therefore had her kept away from court, at Wilton; she was said to amuse herself there by watching the stallions leap the mares, before making love with Cecil, the Earl of Salisbury. When her husband died she married her lover, Sir Matthew Lister of the College of Physicians. See A. Holaday 'Browne's epitaph' *Philological Quarterly* 1949. 10 **Níöbë** when all her children died she turned to stone which ran with the water of her tears.

from Britannia's pastorals

from Book II Song i

Glide soft, ye silver floods
　　And every spring;
Within the shady woods
　　Let no bird sing,
Nor from the grove a turtle-dove   5
Be seen to couple with her love:
But silence on each dale and mountain dwell
Whilst Willy bids his friend and joy farewell.

But, of great Thetis'° train,
　　Ye mermaids fair   10
That on the shores do plain
　　Your sea-green hair,
As ye in trammels knit your locks,
Weep ye; and so enforce the rocks
In heavy murmurs through the broad shores tell   15
How Willy bade his friend and joy farewell.

Cease, cease, ye murdering winds,
　　To move a wave;
But if with troubled minds
　　You seek his grave,   20
Know 'tis as various as yourselves,
Now in the deep, then on the shelves,°
His coffin tossed by fish and surges fell,
Whilst Willy weeps and bids all joy farewell.

Had he Aríon-like°   25
　　Been judged to drown,
He on his lute could strike
　　So rare a sown
A thousand dolphins would have come
And jointly strive to bring him home;   30

But he on shipboard died, by sickness fell,
Since when his Willy bade all joy farewell.

> Great Neptune, hear a swain!
>   His coffin take
> And with a golden chain   35
>   For pity make
> It fast unto a rock near land,
> Where every calmy morn I'll stand
And ere one sheep out of my fold I tell,°
Sad Willy's pipe shall bid his friend farewell.   40

9 **Thetis** chief of the 50 sea-nymphs or Nereids, daughters of Nereus the sea-god. See Poussin, e.g. *Triumph of Neptune,* for the sense of sea deities. 22 **shelves** shoals. 25 **Arion** legendary Greek poet who was thrown overboard but borne ashore on a dolphin. Cf. *Lycidas.* 39 **tell** count.

from Book II Song i

Now great Hyperion° left his golden throne
That on the dancing waves in glory shone,
For whose declining on the western shore
The oriental hills black mantles wore,
And thence apace the gentle twilight fled,   5
That had from hideous caverns usherèd
All-drowsy Night, who in a car° of jet,
By steeds of iron-grey, which mainly sweat
Moist drops on all the world, drawn through the sky,
The helps of darkness waited orderly.   10
First thick clouds rose from all the liquid plains;
Then mists from marishes,° and grounds whose veins
Were conduit-pipes to many a crystal spring;
From standing pools and fens were following
Unhealthy fogs; each river, every rill   15
Sent up their vapours to attend her will,
These pitchy curtains drew 'twixt earth and heaven.
And as Night's chariot through the air was driven,
Clamour grew dumb, unheard was shepherd's song
And silence girt the woods; no warbling tongue   20
Talked to the echo; satyrs° broke their dance
And all the upper world lay in a trance.
Only the curlèd° streams soft chidings kept,
And little gales, that from the green leaf swept
Dry summer's dust, in fearful whisperings stirred,   25
As loth to waken any singing bird.
  Darkness no less than blind Cimmerian,°

Of Famine's° cave the full possession wan,°
Where lay the shepherdess enwrapped with night,
The wishèd garment of a mournful wight.　　　　　30
Here silken slumbers and refreshing sleep
Were seldom found; with quiet minds those keep,
Not with disturbèd thoughts; the beds of kings
Are never pressed by them; sweet rest enrings
The tired body of the swarty clown,°　　　　　35
And oftener lies on flocks° than softest down.
　　Twice had the cock crown, and in cities strong
The bellman's° doleful noise and careful song
Told men whose watchful eyes no slumber hent,°
What store of hours theft-guilty Night had spent.　　40
Yet had not Morpheus° with this maiden been,
As fearing Limos,° whose impetuous teen°
Kept gentle rest from all to whom his cave
Yielded enclosure deadly as the grave;
But to all sad laments left her forlorn,　　　　　45
In which three watches° she had nigh outworn . . .

1 **Hyperion** sun-god. 7 **car** chariot. 12 **marishes** marshes. 21 **satyrs**
minor forest gods, goat from the waist down and the ears up. 23 **curlèd**
rippled. 27 **Cimmerian** the Cimmerians were supposed to inhabit a
land of perpetual night beyond the ocean. 28 **Famine** deprivation as
well as shortage of food; the villain of this pastoral. **wan** dark. 35
swarty clown sunburnt peasant. 36 **flocks** cheap mattress materials.
38 **bellman** watchman who called the hours all night. 39 **hent** seized.
41 **Morpheus** god of dreams. 42 **Limos** famine. **teen** violence. 46
watches periods of 3 or 4 hours; or complete nights.

from Book II Song ii

　　The Muses' friend, grey-eyed Aurora,° yet
Held all the meadows in a cooling sweat:
The milk-white gossamers° not upwards snowed,
Nor was the sharp and useful-steering goad
Laid on the strong-necked ox; no gentle bud　　　5
The sun had dried; the cattle chewed the cud
Low levelled on the grass; no fly's quick sting
Enforced the stonehorse° in a furious ring
To tear the passive earth, nor lash his tail
About his buttocks broad; the slimy snail　　　10
Might on the wainscot, by his many mazes,
Winding meanders and self-knitting traces,
Be followed where he stuck, his flittering slime
Not yet wiped off. It was so early time,
The careful smith had in his sooty forge　　　15

Kindled no coal; nor did his hammers urge
His neighbours' patience: owls abroad did fly,
And day as then might plead his infancy.
Yet of fair Albion° all the western swains
Were long since up, attending on the plains   20
When Nereus' daughter° with her mirthful host
Should summon them on their declining coast.

1 **Aurora** dawn-goddess. 3 **gossamers** fields may be spread with spider-webs which are blown into the air later when dry. 8 **stonehorse** stallion. 19 **Albion** Celtic name for Britain. 21 **Nereus' daughter** see first excerpt.

JOHN ASHMORE

Nothing known of him but *Certain selected odes of Horace, Englished* 1621. His delicate diction would be worth comparison with e.g. Stanley's translations, Marvell's odes, and Milton's *What slender youth bedewed with liquid odours*. This piece is not from Horace but Marcantonio Flaminio of Serravalle (1498–1550), an Italian poet who, as was common until the time of Milton and Crashaw, wrote in Latin. He had a villa on Lake Garda.

Ex M. Antonio Flaminio, Ad agellum suum. Sic incipit, Umbrae frigidulae . . .°

Cool shades, air-fanning groves
  With your soft whisperings,
Where pleasure smiling roves
  Through dewy caves and springs
  And bathes her purple wings;   5

With flower-enamelled ground,
  Nature's fair tapestry,
Where chattering birds abound
  Flickering from tree to tree
  With change of melody;   10

Sweet liberty and leisures
  Where still the Muses keep:
O if to those true treasures
  That from your bosom peep
  I might securely creep!   15

If I might spend my days
  Remote from public brawls,
Now running lovely lays,
  Now lightfoot madrigals,
  Ne'er checked with sudden calls.   20

Now follow sleep that goes
 Rustling i'th' greenwood shade,
Now milk my goat that knows
 (With her young fearful cade) °
 The pail i'th' cooly glade,   25

And with bowls filled to the brims
 Of milky moisture new
To water my dried limbs
 And to all the wrangling crew
 Of cares to bid adieu.   30

What life then should I lead!
 How like then would it be
Unto the gods that tread
 I'th' starry gallery
 Of true felicity!   35

But you, O virgins° sweet
 In Helicon that dwell,
That oft the fountains greet
 When you the pleasures tell
 I'th' country that excel: 40

If I my life, though dear,
 For your far dearer sake
To yield would nothing fear,
 From cities' tumults take me
 And free i'th' country make me.   45

° **Title** from Marcus Antonio Flaminio, *To his little acre*; starting 'Cool
shades . . .' **24 cade** kid. **36 virgins** Muses, who lived on Mount
Helicon.

THE REVEREND RICHARD CORBET, BISHOP OF NORWICH

Son of a Surrey market-gardener. Westminster School, Pembroke and Christ Church Colleges, Oxford. Holy orders; travel in France 1618; 1619, father died, leaving him some land in London. Occupied various church livings, then 1620 Dean of Christ Church (i.e. master of the college as well as dean of Oxford cathedral); 1624 Bishop of Oxford, 1632 Bishop of Norwich. He is said to have obtained preferment in the church by currying favour with the Duke of Buckingham, but Fulke Greville helped him as a writer. *Certain elegant poems* 1627. Friend of Ben Jonson, and Strode was his chaplain at Christ Church. Married, one daughter, one son Vincent born 1627 who became a wastrel; wife died of smallpox 1628. Aubrey says his wife was rumoured to be his own daughter; 'A very handsome man but somewhat apt to abuse, and a coward.' See *Poems* ed. J. A. W. Bennett and H. R. Trevor-Roper, Oxford 1955.

from Iter boreale°

There we crossed Trent and on the other side
Prayed to St Andrew, and uphill we ride;
Where we observed the cunning men, like moles,   The houses
Dwell not in houses but were earthed in holes: in the rock
So did they not build upwards but dig thorough,   5
As hermits' caves, or conies° do their borough.
Great underminers sure as anywhere:
'Tis thought the powder-traitors° practised there.
Would you not think the men stood on their heads
When gardens cover houses there, like leads?°   10
And on the chimney's top the maid may know
Whether her potage boil or not below,
There cast in herbs and salt, or bread° their meat,
Contented rather with the smoke than heat?
This was the rocky parish; higher stood   15
Churches and houses, buildings stone and wood;

Crosses° not yet demolished; and Our Lady Crosses in
Nottingham
With her arms on, embracing her whole Baby.
(Where let us note, though those are northern parts,
The Cross finds in them more than southern hearts.)   20
     The castle's next; but what shall I report The castle
Of that which is a ruin, was a fort? ruined
The gates two statues keep, which giants° are, Guy and
To whom it seems committed was the care Colebrand
Of the whole downfall. If it be your fault, Where King
If you are guilty, may King David's vault David of Scots
Or Mortimer's° dark hole contain you both— was kept prisoner
A just reward for so profane a sloth; which is within
And if hereafter tidings shall be brought the castle
And the left lead or unbegged timber yet   30
Shall pass, by your consent to purchase it,
May your deformèd bulks endure the edge
Of axes, feel the beetle and the wedge,
May all the ballads be called in and die
Which sing the wars of Colebrand and Sir Guy.   35
O you that do Guildhall° and Holmby keep
So carefully, when both the founders sleep,
You are good giants and partake no shame
With those two worthless trunks of Nottinghame.
Look to your several charges; we must go,   40
Though grieved at heart to leave a castle so.

° **Title** northern journey. Here he describes Nottingham. **6 conies** rabbits. **8 powder-traitors** of the Gunpowder Plot 1605 (cf. P. Fletcher *Locusts*). Nottingham is a mining district—cf. D. H. Lawrence's descriptions of it, and Defoe in his *Tour through Great Britain* 1724–26. **10 leads** roofs. **13 bread** dress with breadcrumbs. **17 Crosses** public crosses and religious statues were supposed to have been demolished at the reformation. **21 castle** its ruin still dominates the main road and there is a picture of it on a cigarette packet. **23 giants** Guy of Warwick, a legendary knight who killed many giants including the Danish Colbrand. Many versions from 12th century including a popular 14th-century verse romance and a section in Drayton's *Polyolbion*. **27 Mortimer** c.1287–1330; lover of Queen Isabella, deposed and murdered Edward II, was effective dictator under Edward III; captured at Nottingham Castle, hanged in London. **36 Guildhall** see Taylor *Dick Swash*.

from A proper new ballad entitled The Fairies'
Farewell, or God-a-mercy Will; to be sung or
whistled to the tune of The Meadow Brow by the
learned; by the unlearned, to the tune of Fortune

Farewell, rewards° and fairies,
   Good housewives now may say:
For now foul sluts in dairies
   Do fare as well as they,
And though they sweep their hearths no less   5
   Than maids were wont to do,
Yet who of late for cleanliness
   Finds sixpence in her shoe?

Lament, lament old abbeys,°
   The fairies' lost command: 10
They did but change priests' babies°
   But some have changed your land;
And all your children stolen from thence
   Are now grown puritanes
Who live as changelings ever since   15
   For love of your domains.

At morning and at evening both,
   You merry were and glad,
So little care of sleep and sloth
   These pretty ladies had;   20
When Tom came home from labour,
   Or Ciss to milking rose,
Then merrily went their tabor°
   And nimbly went their toes.

Witness those rings and roundelays   25
   Of theirs which yet remain,
Were footed in Queen Mary's days
   On many a grassy plain;
But since of late Elizabeth
   And later James came in,   30
They never danced on any heath
   As when the time had been.

By which we note the fairies
   Were of the old profession,
Their songs were *Avë Maries*,   35
   Their dances were procession;

But now, alas! they all are dead
   Or gone beyond the seas,
Or further from religion fled,
   Or else they take their ease ...   40

1 **rewards** fairies left coins for good housework, and punished the lazy
with pinches; cf. Herrick *Oberon* in Vol. I, Milton *L'allegro, Midsummer
night's dream*. There are helpful books by Katharine M. Briggs, notably
Pale Hecate's team 1962. The point of this poem is that belief in fairies
is dying with Roman catholicism. 9 **abbeys** Henry VIII dissolved the
monasteries 1534–39; their lands were redistributed as rewards for
loyalty and service. 11 **babies** illegitimate babies, as well as malformed
ones, were said to have been changed or left by the fairies. 23 **tabor**
drum.

ANONYMOUS

A song bewailing the time of Christmas,° so much decayed in England

Christmas is my name, for have I gone, have I gone,
      have I gone,
Have I gone without regard;
  Whereas great men by flocks they be flown to London-
    ward
  Where they in pomp and pleasure do waste   5
That which Christmas had wont to feast,
     Welladay!
Houses where music was wonted to ring,
  Nothing but bats and owls now do sing.
Welladay, welladay, welladay, where should I stay?   10

Christmas bread and beef is turnèd into stones, into stones,
      into stones,
  Into stones and silken rags.
And Lady Money, it doth sleep, it doth sleep, it doth sleep,
  It doth sleep in misers' bags.
Where many gallants once abound,   15
  Nought but a dog and a shepherd is found,
     Welladay!
Places where Christmas revels did keep
  Are now become habitations for sheep.
Welladay, welladay, welladay, where should I stay?   20

Pan, the shepherds' god, doth deface, doth deface, doth
      deface,
  Doth deface Lady Ceres' crown;
And tillages doth decay, doth decay, doth decay,
  Doth decay in every town;
Landlords their rents so highly enhance   25
  That Piers the ploughman barefoot doth dance,
     Welladay!

Farmers that Christmas would entertain
   Hath scarcely withal themselves to maintain.
Welladay, welladay, welladay, where should I stay?   30

Go to the protestant, he'll protest, he'll protest, he'll protest,
   He will protest and boldly boast;
And to the puritan, he is so hot, he is so hot, he is so hot,
   He is so hot he will burn the roast.
The catholic good deeds will not scorn,   35
   Nor will he see poor Christmas forlorn,
      Welladay!
Since holiness no good deeds will do,
   Protestants had best turn papists too.
Welladay, welladay, welladay, where should I stay?   40

Pride and luxury doth devour, doth devour, doth devour,
   Doth devour housekeeping quite,
And beggary doth beget, doth beget, doth beget,
   Doth beget in many a knight.
Madam, forsooth, in coach she must reel   45
   Although she wear her hose out at heel,
      Welladay!
And on her back were that for her weed
   That would both me and many other feed.
Welladay, welladay, welladay, where should I stay?   50

Briefly for to end, here I find, here I find,
   Here I find such great vacation
That some great houses do seem to have, seem to have,
      seem to have,
   For to have some great purgation:
With purging pills such effects they have showed   55
   That out of doors their owners they have spewed.
      Welladay!
And when Christmas goes by and calls,
   Nothing but solitude and naked walls.
Welladay, welladay, welladay, where should I stay?   60

Philomel's cottages are turned into gold, into gold,
   Into gold for harbouring Joan;
And great men's houses up for to hold, up for to hold,
   Up for to hold, make great men moan;
But in the city they say they do live   65
   Where gold by handfuls away they do give,
      Welladay!

And, therefore, thither I purpose to pass,
   Hoping at London to find the Golden Ass.
I'll away, I'll away, I'll away, I'll no longer stay!   70
                              —British Museum MS. c. 1624

° **Christmas** festivities put down by the puritans as pagan and sensual.
Note echoes of Langland. See Tawney *Religion and the rise of capital-
ism*.

COMMENTARY 3

James I
1603–1625

Religion: Scriptures and Emblems

For most of the 17th century, religious poetry was of more various, serious interest than secular. All poets wrote both kinds. They distinguished them, by separate title-pages in their works such as sacred and profane, divine and idle, holy and amatory; but 'religious' has a much wider meaning for them than it does for us. Until about 1660 the concepts of Christianity embraced the cosmos; they were the ultimate terms towards which serious discussion moved. Everything was potentially religious; most things were in practice symbolic. (To investigate this, list the *objects* that are named or depicted or stand in any small church, in a gospel, and in one of the poems in this section. From there you could go to a Bible concordance, Herbert's poems, *Paradise lost*.)

Therefore, religious poetry of this period is essentially metaphysical (in a conceptual sense), whereas secular poetry does not by any means have to be. Christianity is based on a series of conceits: 'the Word was made flesh'. So Sylvester, writing about the fifth day of creation, anticipates Marvell's wit about Appleton House: both see tortoises as examples of God's art; Sylvester sees the cosmos as a garden, Marvell the estate as a microcosm.

At that time, too, poetry was used to transmit a lot of information which other media convey now. Most information was religious and therefore had meaning beyond its mere fact. For example, the factual statement 'Diamonds are transparent' implied the ethical proposal 'Clarity depends on hardness' and the imperative 'Be hard, be pure'. Sermons in stones; infinity in a grain of sand. Here is another ground of metaphysical imagery. Thus in Sylvester's second piece in this section he says men were created upright,

>   toward the azure skies'
> Bright golden lamps lifting his lovely eyes,

That through their nerves his better part might look
Still to that place from whence his birth he took.

Marvell tightened the image to a 'Soul hung up, as 'twere, in chains Of nerves and arteries and veins' (*Dialogue between soul and body*). These materials were not poetic; they were physiology. It was when physiology became incomprehensible, when it ceased to be taught in schools and discussed by gentlemen, when it ceased to have a religious derivation, that it ceased to be available, except as a gimmick, for poetry. Look at the pictures in an original copy of Quarles's *Emblems* and express some of them as conceits of your own.

It was also in religious poetry that the ambition of the 17th-century poets to produce a vernacular epic was most convincing. All the ingredients of epic, as established by Homer and Virgil for the pagan world, were held in suspension in Christianity—the mythology of Europe, its history, piety, world-view, even actual current heroism. The Fletchers attempted epics on the Gunpowder Plot (so did Milton, in Latin), on the life of Christ and so on. All failed. Perhaps the themes are too highly charged. The time-scales of the *Iliad* and other classical epics are long, the virtues and vices of this world and work themselves slowly out. Certainly the Fletchers struck the wrong note. They are deservedly unread for their Spenserianism. By their time it was old-fashioned, not yet remodelled into the baroque of Crashaw (that later baroque worked: why? because it was denser?). They followed the worst of Spenser anyway, the hectic antithetic rhetoric of his *Four hymns*. Giles's 'To him that died to live, and would not be, To be there where he would' achieves a sort of word but quite abandons the flesh. It is worth reading more of Giles, though, to discover his *métier*. Phineas' was for the language of fact, of history: his conspirators scattering in terror—'A third into an empty hogshead crawling Locks up his eyes, draws up his straggling heels'—share a racy realism with Quarles.

Quarles is usually anthologised for piety or a cosmetic beauty ('The still commandress of the silent night' quoted out of context). Actually he was one of the most widely-read poets of the century and what they read him for, under the piety, was a homely version of Dekker's documentary realism, tuned to decent virtues instead of harsh journalism. At this Quarles excels. If it were possible to be great on the hearthrug, he would be great. His Jesus is a toddler (cf. Holbrook's *Doubts about Messiah* and *Christ in the cupboard* in his *Imaginings* 1960). Quarles's bowling-green Devil walks every

golf links. His emblem of greed as a sucking at the work
teat is intimidatingly valid. His *Samson* would survive reading
aloud to the family (and Milton's?).

Little effective critical work has been done in this area. I
would recommend Quarles for major independent work on
almost any line. For Sylvester and the Fletchers I have made
some suggestions *en courant;* diction is the crucial topic—the
paradox at the heart of metaphysical writing in Sylvester's
'flimsy burghers'! Lathum and Townsend introduce the dialogue form. Its secular use could be pursued in this volume
in E. Herbert's *Ode,* Carew, Habington, Katherine Philips and
then out into the masque and drama (e.g. Durfey's *New dialogue sung by a boy and a girl,* Lawes's volume of *Airs and
dialogues*); all this would lead back to the 'dialogue of one'
in Donne's *Ectsasy.* The religious dialogue leads forward to
Marvell's pair between soul and body, soul and pleasure; it
is a meditative technique—see Norris *It must be done, my
soul;* and I believe that two voices can be heard in G. Herbert's *Collar* apart from God's at the end.

Lathum and Townsend are not otherwise very interesting;
Beedome would repay further reading though.

Drummond is an awkward case. Because Scottish he was
doing in the 1610s and '20s what English poets were doing
in the 1590s (e.g. Southwell, Constable; both will repay study
as manipulators of the religio-erotic convention). Drummond's
work has an Elizabethan gravity; but also a precious Jacobean
delicacy and smugness. These qualities only rarely combine
as in the 'eye of gold' in his bubble poem. He does not easily
yield to study; but he is useful for establishing Petrarch and
Plato as poetic forces.

JOSHUA SYLVESTER

Businessman. His translations started 1592, first collected 1605 as *Du Bartas his divine weeks and works*. Guillaume de Saluste, seigneur du Bartas, was a Huguenot who published in French verse *La semaine* (Paris 1574), an account of the week of creation in Genesis, and *La seconde semaine* (1584), an unfinished account of the subsequent history of the world. These poems were puritan encyclopaedias and bourgeois epics. They were translated into many European languages, Sidney and James I, as well as Sylvester, tried translations; Sylvester's was one of the most popular works of the 17th century and influenced William Browne of Tavistock, Milton, and Dryden, who confessed to a boyhood pleasure in it but later found it "abominable fustian." Sylvester also a miscellaneous writer; e.g. like James I he wrote against smoking: *Tobacco battered and the pipe shattered by a volley of holy shot* (verse, 1617). *Works* ed. A. B. Grosart 1880; *Du Bartas* ed. V. T. Holmes et al. 3 vols. Chapel Hill 1935–40.

from Du Bartas his divine weeks and works

1st Week 5th Day

As a rare painter draws, for pleasure, here
A sweet Adonis, a foul satyr there,
Here a huge Cyclops,° there a pygmy elf,
Sometimes no less busying his skilful self
Upon some ugly monster seldom seen   5
Than on the picture of fair beauty's queen:
Even so the Lord, that in his works' variety
We might the more admire his powerful deity,
And that we might discern by differing features
The various kinds of the vast ocean's creatures,   10
Forming this mighty frame he every kind
With divers and peculiar signet signed.
Some have their heads grovelling betwixt their feet,

As the inky cuttles and the many-feet;°
Some in their breast, as crabs; some headless are,   15
Footless and finless, as the baneful hare°
And heatful oyster, in a heap confused,
Their parts unparted, in themselves diffused.
　　The Tyrian° merchant or the Portugese
Can hardly build one ship of many trees;   20
But of one tortoise, when he lift to float,
The Arabian fisherman can make a boat;
And one such shell him in the stead doth stand
Of hulk° at sea and of a house on land.
　　Shall I omit the monstrous whirlabout   25
Which the sea another sea doth spout,
Wherewith huge vessels, if they happen by,
Are overwhelmed and sunken suddenly?

---

3 **Cyclops** one-eyed giant who captured Odysseus. 14 **cuttles . . . many-feet** cuttlefish, squids etc. 16 **hare** sea-hare, a kind of shellfish. 19 **Tyrian** Phoenician, Levantine. 24 **hulk** hull.

1st Week 6th Day

　　Almighty Father, as of watery matter
It pleased thee make the people of the water,
So of an earthly substance mad'st thou all
The flimsy burghers of this earthly ball,
To the end each creature might by consequent   5
Part-sympathise with his own element.
Therefore, to form thine earthly emperor
Thou tookest earth, and by thy sacred power
So temperedst it that of the very same
Dead shapeless lump didst Adam's body frame;   10
Yet, not his face down to the earthward bending
Like beasts that but regard their belly, ending
For ever all, but toward the azure skies'
Bright golden lamps lifting his lovely eyes,
That through their nerves his better part° might look   15
Still to that place from whence his birth he took.
　　Also thou plantedst the intellectual power°
In the highest stage of all this stately bower
That thence it might, as from a citadel,
Command the members° that too oft rebel   20
Against his rule; and that our reason there
Keeping continual garrison, as 'twere,
Might avarice,° envy and pride subdue,
Lust, gluttony, wrath, sloth and all their crew

Of factious commons that still strive to gain   25
The golden sceptre from this sovereign.

15 **better part** soul. 17 **intellectual power** reason; cf. Drummond
That learned Grecian etc. 20 **members** 'I see another law in my members, warring against the law of my mind': *Romans* viii. The doctrine
affected by political theory—see 25–26. 23 **avarice** 7 deadly sins start
here.

THE REVEREND PHINEAS FLETCHER

Elder brother of Giles. Eton; fellow of King's College, Cambridge; private chaplain; from 1621 rector of Hilgay in Norfolk. Married c.1622, at least 6 children; friend of Quarles, Benlowes. *The locusts or Apollyonists* 1627, an attack on the Jesuits, and *Purple island or Isle of man* 1633, a physiological allegory, stand halfway between Spenser and Bunyan; but really most interesting for diction. *Piscatory eclogues* 1633 = fish pastorals. *Poetical works* (with Giles') ed. F. S. Boas, 2 vols. Cambridge 1908–9. See A. B. Langdale *P.F. man of letters, science and divinity* 1937.

from The locusts° or Appolyonists

Now are they met: this armèd with a spade,
That with a mattock, void of shame and fear
The earth (their grandam earth) they fierce invade
And all her bowels search and rent and tear;
Then by her ruins fleshed, much bolder made,   5
They ply their work; and now near hell they hear
    Soft voices, murmurs, doubtful whisperings:
    The fearful conscience pricked with guilty stings
A thousand hellish forms into their fancy brings:

This like a statue stands—cold fright congeals   10
His marble limbs; to the earth another falling,
Creeping behind a barrel softly steals;
A third into an empty hogshead crawling,
Locks up his eyes, draws up his straggling heels;
A fourth, in vain for succour loudly calling,   15
    Flies through the air as swift as gliding star;
    Pale, ghastly, like infernal sprites afar
Each to his fellow seems; and so, or worse, they are.

So when in sleep's soft grave dead senses rest,
An earthly vapour clambering up the brain   20

Brings in a meagre ghost, whose lancèd breast
Showers down his naked corpse a bloody rain;
A dull-blue-burning torch about his crest
He ghastly waves; half-dead with frightful pain
    The leaden foot would, but can not fly;   25
    The gaping mouth fain would, but can not cry;
And now awake, still dreams, nor trusts his open eye;

At length those streams of life which, ebbing low,
Were all retired into the frighted heart,
Back to their wonted channels 'gan to flow: 30
So peeping out, yet trembling every part,
And listening now with better heed, they know
Those next adjoining rooms hollowed by art
    To lie for cellarage; which glad they hire
    And cram with powder and unkindled fire.   35
Slack agèd time with plaints and prayers they daily tire.

° **locusts** come out of hell in *Revelation* ix, led by Apollyon (the destroyer; he fights Christian in *Pilgrim's progress*); common metaphor for devils and Roman catholics. This excerpt, from Canto V, is about the Gunpowder Plot (cf. Corbet *Iter boreale*). The scene is the cellars of the Houses of Parliament.

To my soul in its blindness

How is't, my soul, that thou giv'st eyes their sight
    To view their objects, yet hast none
        To see thine own?
Earth's, air's, heaven's beauties they discern; their light
    Fair flowers admires, their several dresses,   5
        Their golden tresses;
The lily, rose, the various tulip, scorning
The pride of princes in their choice adorning.

They joy to view the air's painted nations:
    The peacock's train which the head outvies   10
        With fairer eyes
And emulates the heavenly constellations;
    The ostrich whose fair plume embraves
        Kings, captains, slaves;
The halcyons° whose Triton-bills appease   15
Curled waves and with their eggs lay stormy seas.

Pilots'° fixed eyes observe the arctic Bear°
    With all her unwashed starry trains
        In heavenly plains;

Night-travellers behold the moon to steer   20
    Her ship, sailing, while Eol° raves,
        Through cloudy waves;
Our less world's suns with pleasure view the light
Which gives all beauties beauty, them their sight.

Thou that giv'st sight to clay, to blackness light,   25
    How art so dull, so dim in duty
        To view his beauty
Who quickens every life, lights every light?
    His height, whose eagles' eyes surpasses?
        Thou wants thy glasses:°   30
Take up that pérspective° and view those streams
Of light, and fill thy waning orb° with beams.

Then see the flowers clad in his liveries
    And from his cheek and lovely face
        Steal all their grace;   35
See fowls from him borrow their braveries
    And all their feather-painted dresses
        From his fair tresses;
See stars, and moon, the sun and all perfectiön
Beg light and life from his bright eyes' reflectiön.   40

Look on his lips: heaven's gate there open lies,
    Thence that grace-breathing Spirit blows,
        Thence honey flows.
Look on his hands: the world's full treasuries.
    Fix all thy looks his heart upon: 45
        Love's highest throne.
And, when thy sight that radiant beauty blears
And dazzles thy weak eyes, see with thine ears.

15 **halcyons** birds of calm, supposed to rest on the sea at Christmas.
17 **Pilots** navigators. **Bear** constellation called Great Bear, Arcturus
or Plough, by which Nórth Star is found. Greek *arktos* = bear. Her
trains are 'unwashed' perhaps because never declining below horizon.
21 **Eol** Aeolus, wind god. 30 **Thou . . . glasses** you need your spectacles. 31 **perspective** telescope. 32 **orb** the moon was thought to
suck up supplies of light from the sun; so here the soul from God. Cf.
Nashe *Valentine*.

Drop, drop, slow tears

Drop, drop, slow tears
    And bathe those beauteous feet

Which brought from heaven
  The news and Prince of peace.
Cease not, wet eyes,   5
  His mercies to entreat;
To cry for vengeance
  Sin doth never cease;
In your deep floods
  Drown all my faults and fears;   10
Nor let his eye
  See sin but through my tears.

THE REVEREND GILES FLETCHER
THE YOUNGER

So-called because father also Giles and a poet. Younger
brother of Phineas. Westminster School; Trinity College,
Cambridge and taught there 1608–18; then various church
livings. Married. *Christ's victory and triumph in heaven and
earth, over and after death* 1610, an epic on the life of Christ
formally similar to Spenser's *Hymns*. *Poems* ed. D. C. Shel-
don, Madison 1938 and see Phineas.

from Christ's victory and triumph

Therefore° above the rest Ambition sat:
His court with glitterant pearl was all enwalled,
And round about the walls in chairs of state
And most majestic splendour were enstalled
A hundred kings, whose temples were impaled   5
   In golden diadems set here and there
    With diamonds and gemmèd everywhere,
And of their golden verges° none dis-sceptred were.

High over all, Panglory's blazing throne,
In her bright turret, all of crystal wrought,   10
Like Phoebus' lamp° in midst of heaven shone;
Whose starry top, with pride infernal fraught,
Self-arching columns to uphold were taught;
   In which her image still reflected was
    By the smooth crystal, that most like to glass   15
In beauty, and in frailty, did all others pass.

A silver wand the sorceress did sway
And, for a crown of gold, her hair she wore;
Only a garland of rosebuds did play
About her locks, and in her hand she bore   20
A hollow globe of glass that long before

She full of emptiness had bladderèd,
    And all the world therein depicturèd,
Whose colours, like the rainbow, ever vanishèd.

Such watery orbicles young boys do blow   25
Out from their soapy shells, and much admire
The swimming world, which tenderly they row
With easy breath till it be wavèd higher;
But if they chance but roughly once aspire,
    The painted bubble instantly doth fall.   30
    Here when she came she 'gan for music call
And sung this wooing song to welcome him withal:

Love is the blossom where there blows
Everything that lives or grows;
Love doth make the heavens to move   35
And the sun doth burn in love;
Love the strong and weak doth yoke
And makes the ivy climb the oak,
Under whose shadows lions wild,
Softened by love, grow tame and mild.   40
Love no medicine can appease—
He burns the fishes in the seas;
Not all the skill his wounds can staunch,
Not all the sea his fire can quench;
Love did make the bloody spear   45
Once a levy-coat° to wear,
While in his leaves there shrouded lay
Sweet birds, for love that sing and play;
And of all love's joyful flame
I the bud and blossom am.   50
    Only bend thy knee to me,
    Thy wooing shall thy winning be . . .

° **Therefore** in the court of Panglory, who now tempts Christ. 8
verges sceptres. 11 **lamp** sun. 46 **levy-coat** conscript's uniform.

WILLIAM DRUMMOND OF HAWTHORNDEN

Father laird of Hawthornden, an estate near Edinburgh. Edinburgh University, law schools of Bourges and Paris. Succeeded father 1610 and stayed at Hawthornden for the rest of his life. Read assiduously, especially modern poetry, in several languages. An inventor—e.g. a type of telescope and a wind-speed counter. *Poems* 1610. Engaged c.1614 but she died just before or after the wedding. Visited by Ben Jonson on his walk to Edinburgh 1618. Corresponded with Drayton. Fell ill in 1620; in 1623 fire and famine devastated Edinburgh. *Flowers of Zion*, religious poems, published that year (enlarged 1630); also *Cypress grove*, prose meditation on death. Married 1632, 9 children of whom 3 survived him. A royalist and sympathiser with Montrose, q.v. *Poetical works* ed. L. E. Kastner 2 vols. 1913.

Like the Idalian queen

Like the Idalian queen,°
Her hair about her eye,
With neck and breasts ripe apples to be seen
At first glance of the morn
In Cyprus gardens gathering those fair flowers°   5
Which of her blood were born,
I saw, but fainting saw, my paramour's.
The Graces° naked danced about the place,
The winds and trees amazed
With silence on her gazed,   10
The flowers did smile like those upon her face,
And as their aspen stalks those fingers band,
That she might read my case
A hyacinth° I wished me in her hand.

1 queen Aphrodite, goddess of love; from Idalium, a town in Cyprus sacred to her. As goddess also of fertility she was worshipped in gardens. **5 flowers** don't know. From the blood of her lover Adonis the anemone sprang up. **8 Graces** the three goddesses of beauty, youth and pleasure who attended Aphrodite. They are shown dancing hand in hand. Cf. Spenser *Faery Queen* VI.x; Milton, epilogue to *Comus*; see Wind, *Pagan mysteries in the renaissance*. **14 hyacinth** unknown Greek flower supposed to have had its petals marked with the cries of woe, *ai ai*.

This life which seems so fair

This life which seems so fair
Is like a bubble blown up in the air
By sporting children's breath,
Who chase it everywhere
And strive who can most motion it bequeath;   5
And though it sometime seem of its own might,
Like to an eye of gold, to be fixed there,
And firm to hover in that empty height,
That only is because it is so light;
But in that pomp it doth not long appear;   10
   For even when most admired, it in a thought
    As swelled from nothing doth dissolve in nought.

This world a hunting is

This world a hunting is,
The prey poor man, the Nimrod° fierce is Death;
His speedy greyhounds are
Lust, sickness, envy, care,
Strife that ne'er falls amiss,   5
With all those ills which haunt us while we breathe.
Now, if by chance we fly
Of these the eager chase,
Old age with stealing pace
Casts up his nets,° and there we panting die.   10

2 Nimrod a mighty hunter before the Lord: *Genesis* x.9. **10 nets** for snaring birds.

The nativity°

Run, shepherds, run where Bethlehem blest appears:
We bring the best of news, be not dismayed,
A Saviour there is born more old than years,
Amidst heaven's rolling heights this earth who stayed.°
In a poor cottage inned, a Virgin maid,   5
A weakling did him bear who all upbears.
This is he poorly swaddled, in manger laid,
To whom too narrow swaddlings are our spheres.°

Run, shepherds, run and solemnise his birth:
This is that night—no, day grown great with bliss   10
In which the power of Satan broken is.
In heaven be glory, peace unto the earth!

    Thus singing through the air the angels swam
    And cope of stars re-echoèd the same.

° **nativity**   cf. poems by Quarles, Herrick, Crashaw, Joseph Beaumont, Watkyns, Milton, Donne. 4 **stayed**   steadied. 8 **spheres**   of the planets, etc. See E. Herbert *Platonic love*.

FRANCIS QUARLES

Father a civil servant and Essex squire; Francis the 3rd son. Country school; Christ's College, Cambridge; Lincoln's Inn; studied music. Entered service of Princess Elizabeth and went with her court to Heidelberg (see Wotton *Queen of Bohemia*). In 1618 married 17-year-old Ursula: 18 children. Patronised by William Herbert, 3rd earl of Pembroke, and the Countess of Dorset. 1629 in Dublin as secretary to Archbishop Ussher; and was a royalist later on; but spent his 30s and 40s publishing devotional verse which gave him the reputation of 'an old puritannical poet . . . the sometime darling of our plebeian judgement' (Antony à Wood). In *Theatrum poetarum* (1675) Edward Phillips, Milton's nephew, said that Quarles' verses 'have been ever, and still are, in wonderful veneration among the vulgar.' By Pope's time he was despised. Work included versions of *Jonah, Esther, Job*; 1631; miscellaneous devotional verses called *Divine fancies* 1632; and *Emblems* 1635 et seq. This was his most famous work, though only some of his verses and some of the pictures were original. The great emblem vogue began with Alciati, a Milanese who published a book of emblems in 1531 which went through 90 editions before 1600 and was widely translated and imitated, especially in France, and in the Low Countries where it gave scope for the domestic realism of Dutch and Flemish engravers. The Jesuits produced emblems for missionary purposes, e.g. Hugo *Pia desideria* 1624. England lagged—the first was Whitney's *Choice of emblems* 1586, an anthology of continental work; and Quarles's emblems are mostly drawn from Hugo and from another work called *Typus mundi*; but Quarles's verses raised the literary level of emblems considerably. Wither also published a *Collection of emblems* 1634–35. Emblems may be regarded as the graphic parallel to the metaphysical conceit and the sermon. In 1638 Quarles gave a friend of his, John Josselyn, metrical versions of Psalms 16, 25, 51, 88, 113, and 137 to take to Winthrop and Cotton in America; they were printed in the *Whole book of Psalms* Boston 1640.

On the infancy of our Saviour

Hail! blessèd Virgin, full of heavenly grace,
Blest above all that sprang from human race,
Whose heaven-saluted womb brought forth in one
A blessèd Saviour and a blessèd Son.
O what a ravishment 't had been to see   5
Thy little Saviour perking on thy knee!
To see him nuzzle in thy virgin breast,
His milk-white body all unclad, undressed;
To see thy busy fingers clothe and wrap
His spraddling limbs in thy indulgent lap;   10
To see his desperate eyes with childish grace
Smiling upon his smiling mother's face;
And when his forward strength began to bloom
To see him diddle up and down the room.
O who would think so sweet a babe as this   15
Should ere be slain by a false-hearted kiss?
Had I a rag, if sure thy body wore it,
Pardon, sweet babe, I think I should adore° it;
Till then, O grant this boon, a boon far dearer:
The weed not being, I may adore the Wearer.   20

18 **adore**   worship of relics, as of the Virgin, now forbidden.

from The history of Samson°

When lusty diet and the frolic cup
Had roused and raised their quickened spirits up
And brave triumphing Bacchus° had displayed
His conquering colours in their cheeks, they said:
    Call Samson forth. He must not work today,   5
'Tis a boon feast, we'll give him leave to play.
Does he grind bravely? does our mill-horse sweat?
Let him lack nothing—what he wants in meat,
Supply in lashes. He is strong and stout
And with his breath can drive the mill about.   10
He works too hard, we fear: go down and free him.
Say that his mistress, Délila, would see him.
The sight of him will take our whores short!
Go fetch him, then, to make our honours sport.
Bid him provide some riddles; let him bring   15
Some songs of triumph: he that's blind may sing
With better boldness. Bid him never doubt

To please—what matter though his eyes be out?
'Tis no dishonour that he cannot see:
Tell him the god° of love's as blind as he!   20
  With that they brought poor Samson to the hall,
And as he passed he gropes to find the wall;
His pace was slow, his feet were lifted high—
Each tongue would taunt him, every scornful eye
Was filled with laughter. Some would cry aloud,   25
He walks in state! His lordship is grown proud!
Some bid his honour, Hail! while others cast
Reproachful terms upon him as he passed.
Some would salute him fairly and embrace
His wounded sides, then spit° upon his face.   30
Others would cry, For shame! forbear to abuse
The high and great redeemer of the Jews!
Some jibe and flout him with their taunts and quips
Whilst others flirt him on the starting lips.
  With that, poor Samson, whose abundant grief   35
Not finding hopes of comfort or relief,
Resolved for patience. Turning round, he made
Some shift to feel his keeper out, and said:
  Good sir, my painful labour in the mill
Hath made me bold (although against my will)   40
To crave some little rest; if you will please
To let the pillar but afford some ease
To my worn limbs, your mercy should relieve
A soul that has no more but thanks to give.
  The keeper yielded. Now the hall was filled   45
With princes and their people that beheld
Abusèd Samson, whilst the roof retained
A leash of thousands more whose eyes were chained
To this sad object with a full delight
To see this flesh-and-blood-relenting sight.   50
With that, the prisoner turned himself and prayed,
So soft that none but heaven could hear, and said:
  My God, my God, although my sins do cry
For greater vengeance, yet thy gracious eye
Is full of mercy. O remember now   55
The gentle promise and that sacred vow
Thou mad'st to faithful Abram and his seed.
O hear my wounded soul, that has less need
Of life than mercy! Let thy tender care
Make good thy plenteous promise now, and hear!   60
See how thy cursèd enemies prevail
Above my strength: behold how poor and frail
My native power is; and, wanting thee,

What is there, O what is there, Lord, in me?
Nor is it I that suffer: my desert   65
May challenge greater vengeance if thou wert
Extreme to punish; Lord, the wrong is thine;
The punishment is just, and only mine.
I am thy champion, Lord. It is not me
They strike at: through my sides they thrust at thee;   70
Against thy glory 'tis their malice lies;
They aimed at that when they put out these eyes.
Alas! their blood-bedabbled hands would fly
On thee wert thou but clothed in flesh as I.
Revenge thy wrongs, great God! O let thy hand   75
Redeem thy suffering honour, and this land!
Lend me thy power; renew my wasted strength
That I may fight thy battles; and at length
Rescue thy glory that my hands may do
That faithful service they were born unto.   80
Lend me thy power that I may restore
Thy loss, and I will never urge thee more.
  Thus having ended, both his arms he laid
Upon the pillars of the hall, and said:
  Thus with the Philistines I resign my breath   85
And let my God find glory in my death.
  And, having spoke, his yielding body strained
Upon those marble pillars that sustained
The ponderous roof; they cracked; and with their fall   90
Down fell the battlements and roof and all
And with their ruin slaughtered at a blow
The whole assembly: they that were below
Received their sudden deaths from those that fell
From off the top, whilst none was left to tell   95
The horrid shrieks that filled the spacious hall,
Whose ruins were impartial and slew all.
They fell; and, with an unexpected blow,
Gave everyone his death, and burial too.

° **Samson** *Judges* xvi. The first lines refer to the Philistines, who are
feasting. Samson had been captured some time before by the treachery
of his wife Delilah and is now 'Eyeless in Gaza, at the mill, with slaves'
(Milton *Samson Agonistes*). Samson was a favourite subject with painters
at this time; see Rembrandt especially. His giant size, violence and,
sensuality made him one of the few biblical rivals to classical heroes.
3 **Bacchus** god of wine. 20 **god** Cupid often has his eyes bandaged.
30 **sides . . . spit** cf. Christ of whom Samson was an important ante-
type, in the way that e.g. Moses was as shepherd and leader of his
people. See R. Tuve *Reading of G. Herbert* 1952.

Emblem V. 4°

One holding the case of an arctic needle, pointing to Christ

'I am my beloved's, and his desire is toward me.'
                                        Canticles vii.10.°

Like to° the arctic needle° that doth guide
  The wandering shade by his magnetic power
And leaves his silken gnomon to decide
  The question of the controverted hour,
First frantics up and down from side to side   5
    And restless beats his crystalled ivory case,
    With vain impatience jets from place to place
And seeks the bosom of his frozen bride;
    At length he slacks his motion and doth rest
His trembling point at his bright pole's belovèd breast: 10

Even so my soul, being hurried here and there
  By every object that presents delight,
Fain would be settled, but she knows not where:
  She likes at morning what she loathes at night;
She bows to honour; then she lends an ear   15
    To that sweet swan-like voice of dying pleasure;
    Then tumbles in the scattered heaps of treasure;
Now flattered with false hopes, now foiled with fear;
    Thus finding all the world's delight to be
But empty toys, good God, she points alone to thee.   20

But hath the virtued° steel a power to move?
  Or can the untouched needle point aright?
Or can my wandering thoughts forbear to rove,
  Unguided by the virtue of thy Sprite?
O, hath my leaden soul the art to improve   25
    Her wasted talent and, unraised, aspire
    In this sad moulting time of her desire?
Not first beloved, have I the power to love?
    I cannot stir but as thou please to move me,
Nor can my heart return thee love until thou love me.   30

The still commandress of the silent night
  Borrows her beams from her bright brother's eye;
His fair aspéct fills her sharp horns with light;
  If he withdraw, her flames are quenched and die:

Even so the beams of thy enlightening Sprite,   35
 Infused and shot into my dark desire,
 Inflame my thoughts and fill my soul with fire,
That I am ravished with a new delight;
 But if thou shroud thy face, my glory fades
And I remain a nothing, all composed of shades.   40

Eternal God! O thou that only art
 The sacred fountain of eternal light,
And blessèd lodestone of my better part!°
 O thou my heart's desire, my soul's delight:
Reflect upon my soul, and touch my heart,   45
  And then my heart shall prize no good above thee;
  And then my soul shall know thee; knowing, love
   thee;
And then my trembling thoughts shall never start
 From thy commands, or swerve the least degree,
Or once presume to move but as they move in thee.   50

If man can love man with so entire affection, that the
one can scarce brook the other's absence; if a bride can
be joined to her bridegroom with so great an ardency of
mind, that for the extremity of love she can enjoy no rest,
nor suffer his absence without great anxiety: with what
affection, with what fervency ought the soul, whom thou
hast espoused by faith and compassion, to love thee, her
true God, and glorious bridegroom?

        ST. AUGUSTINE *Meditations* X

Epigram

 My soul, thy love is dear: 'twas thought a good
 And easy pennorth° of thy Saviour's blood;
 But be not proud: all matters rightly scanned,
 'Twas over-bought: 'twas sold at secondhand.

° **Emblem** This is the full apparatus for the picture—legend, Biblical
text, sermon-poem, authority, epigram. 1 **Like to** frequent formula for
starting poems at this time. **arctic needle** compass needle, which points
to the magnetic north. **Shade** = shadow; **gnomon** = vertical element of
a sundial. The idea seems to be that the needle, suspended on a silken
thread, casts a moving shadow as it seeks the north, so that it is left to
the shadow of the thread to tell the time. Compasses can be used to tell
the time by. 21 **virtued** endowed with special power. 43 **better part**
soul. 63 **pennorth** pennyworth.

Emblem I.12

A child sucking out of paps on a globe, another holding
a sieve below

'Ye may suck, but not be satisfied with the breasts of her
consolations.'   *Isaiah* lxvi.11.

What, never filled? Be thy lips screwed so fast
  To the earth's full breast? For shame, for shame unseize
    thee!
Thou tak'st a surfeit where thou shouldst but taste,
  And mak'st too much not half enough to please thee.
    Ah fool, forbear! thou swallowest at one breath   5
Both food and poison down; thou draw'st both milk and
    death.

The uberous° breasts, when fairly drawn, repast
  The thriving infant with their milky flood;
But, being overstrained, return at last
  Unwholesome gulps composed of wind and blood.   10
    A moderate use does both repast and please;
Who strains beyond a mean, draws in and gulps disease.

But O that mean, whose good the least abuse
  Makes bad, is too too hard to be directed.
Can thorns bring grapes, or crabs° a pleasing juice?   15
  There's nothing wholesome where the whole's infected.
    Unseize thy lips! earth's milk's a ripened core?
That drops from her disease, that matters from her sore.

Thinkst thou that paunch that burlies out thy coat
  Is thriving fat? or flesh, that seems so brawny?   20
Thy paunch is dropsied and thy cheeks are bloat,
  Thy lips are white and thy complexion tawny,
    Thy skin's a bladder blown with watery tumours,
Thy flesh a trembling bog, a quagmire full of humours.°

And thou, whose thriveless hands are ever straining   25
  Earth's fluent breasts into an empty sieve,
That always hast, yet always art complaining,
  And whin'st for more than earth has power to give;
    Whose treasure flows and flees away as fast,
That ever hast, and hast, yet hast not what thou hast: 30

Go, choose a substance, fool! that will remain
  Within the limits of thy leaking measure;

Or else go seek an urn that will retain
  The liquid body of thy slippery treasure.
    Alas! how poorly are thy labours crowned: 35
Thy liquor's never sweet, nor yet thy vessel sound.

What less than fool is man to prog° and plot
  And lavish out the cream of all his care
To gain poor seeming goods which, being got,
  Make firm possession but a thoroughfare;   40
    Or, if they stay, they furrow thoughts the deeper;
And, being kept with care, they lose their careful keeper.

If we give more to the flesh than we ought, we nourish
an enemy; if we give not to her necessity what we ought,
we destroy a citizen: the flesh is to be satisfied so far as
suffices to our good; whosoever alloweth so much to her
as to make her proud, knoweth not how to be satisfied; to
be satisfied is a great art; lest, by the satiety of the flesh,
we break forth into the iniquity of her folly.
                ST. GREGORY *Homily* III Part ii *Ezekiel.*

The heart is a small thing, but desireth great matters.
It is not sufficient for a kite's dinner; yet the whole world
is not sufficient for it.
                HUGO *De anima*

Epigram

What makes thee, fool, so fat? Fool, thee so bare?
Ye suck the self-same milk, the self-same air;
No mean betwixt all paunch, and skin and bone?
The mean's a virtue, and the world has none.

7 uberous copious. **15 crabs** crab apples. **17 core** ulcer. **24 humours**
fluids. **37 prog** poke about searching.

Emblem I. 10

A bowling-green, the Devil handing the bowls°

'Ye are of your father the devil, and the lusts of your father
        ye will do.'   *John* viii.44

Here's your right ground. Wag gently o'er this black.
  'Tis a short cast: you're quickly at the jack.

Rub, rub an inch or two. Two crowns to one
  On this bowl's side. Blow, wind! 'Tis fairly thrown:
The next bowl's worse that comes. Come, bowl away!   5
  Mammon,° you know the ground, untutored play.
Your last was gone, a yard of strength well spared
  Had touched the block: your hand is still too hard.
Brave pastime, readers, to consume that day
  Which, without pastime, flies too swift away.   10
See how they labour, as if day and night
  Were both too short to serve their loose delight;
See how their curvèd bodies wreathe and screw
  Such antic shapes as Proteus° never knew.
One raps an oath, another deals a curse—   15
  He never better bowled, this never worse;
One rubs his itchless elbow, shrugs and laughs,
  The other bends his beetle brows, and chafes.
Sometimes they whoop, sometimes their Stygian° cries
  Send their black santos° to the blushing skies.   20
Thus mingling humours° in a mad confusion
  They make bad premises and worse conclusion.

° **bowls** the game of lawn bowls goes back to at least the 13th century.
Until c.1550 it was legislated against because it took people away from
archery practice; and in the 17th century puritans objected to it along
with other games; but James I and Charles I were keen on bowls and introduced wagering to it. Bad language was frequently heard on the green.
The object is to roll a large biassed black ball as close as possible to a
small white one called the jack. 6 **Mammon** devil of worldliness. 14
Proteus legendary Greek who could assume any shape. 19 **Stygian**
hellish. 20 **santos** hats? or oaths, from Spanish saint? 21 **humours**
moods, temperaments, determined by the mixture in the constitution of
phlegm, blood, choler, bile; hence phlegmatic, sanguine, choleric, melancholic.

[THE REVEREND GEORGE HERBERT]
WILLIAM LATHUM

Little known of him. *Phyala lachrymarum, or a few friendly tears* 1634, mourns a Cambridge scholar.

Prosopopoeia corporis animae valedicturi: adios: arrivederci°

My lovely friend, that long hast been content
To dwell with me in my poor tenement
Whose bulk, and all the stuff, both warp and woof,
Is all of clay, the floor and the roof,
Though yet thou ne'er found'st fault, ye didst upbraid   5
This homely hermitage so meanly made:
O mine own darling, my dear dainty one,
And wilt thou now indeed from me be gone?
Ah! for thou seest all running to decay:
The thatchy covering's now nigh fallen away;   10
The windows, which give light to every room,
Broken and dim and misty been become.
The mill-house and self miller's° out of frame;
My kitchen smokes, my larder is to blame
And from the studs° watch where the home doth shrink   15
And the breme° cold blows in at every chink;
The brasses° and supporters of my house
Tremble and waxen wondrous ruinous.
  So that albe it grieve me to the heart
To think that thou and I, old friends, must part;   20
Yet, sith my cabin's all out of repair,
Darling, farewell, go sojourn now elsewhere
In some clean place until that premier main°
That built me first rebuild me up again,
All of the selfsame stuff but with such art,   25
So polished and embellished every part,
That it shall ne'er be out of culture more.
Then shalt thou come again, as heretofore,

And dwell with me for ever and for aye:
So God us both bless until that happy day. 30

° **Title** = the body's farewell to the soul: goodbye [Spanish]: goodbye [Italian]. Prosopopoeia = dramatisation. 13 **self miller** miller himself. 15 **studs** upright timbers. 16 **breme** harsh. = Spenserian archaism. 17 **brasses** pillars? See *Ecclesiastes* xii.3 about 'the day when the keepers of the house shall tremble,' etc. 23 **main** power.

AURELIAN TOWNSEND

Served in households of Sir Robert Cecil (later 1st Earl of Salisbury) and Earl of Dorset. Accompanied Herbert of Cherbury (q.v.) to continent, visiting Henri IV of France and the Duc de Montmorenci, virtual ruler of Provence. Also a friend of Carew. Wrote masques for Charles I's court after Ben Jonson had been pushed out by Inigo James. Married, at least 5 children. Fell into poverty; fate unknown. *Poems and masques* ed. E. K. Chambers 1912.

A dialogue° between Time and a pilgrim

Pilgrim	Agèd man that mows these fields—
Time	Pilgrim, speak, what is thy will?
Pilgrim	Whose soil is this that such sweet pasture yields?
	Or who art thou whose foot stands never still?
	Or where am I? 5
Time	In love.
Pilgrim	His lordship° lies above.
Time	Yes, and below, and round about
	Wherein all sorts of flowers are growing
	Which, as the early spring puts out,
	Time falls as fast a-mowing. 10
Pilgrim	If thou art Time, these flowers have lives,
	And then I fear
	Under some lily she I love
	May now be growing there.
Time	And in some thistle or some spire of grass 15
	My scythe thy stalk before hers come may pass.
Pilgrim	Wilt thou provide it may?
Time	No.
Pilgrim	Allege the cause.
Time	Because Time cannot alter, but obey, Fate's laws.
Chorus	Then happy those whom Fate, that is the stronger,

Together twists their threads° and yet draws hers   20
                                      the longer.

° **dialogue**   it was set to music by Lawes and published in his *Airs and dialogues* 1653. 6 **His lordship**   presumably Love, meaning that love is heavenly. Possibly Adonis, lord of life. In Spenser's *Fairy queen* III.vi, Venus and Adonis live in a garden which is the nursery of souls before birth and after death; but the gardener of the souls is 'wicked Time, who with his scythe addressed Does now the flowering herbs and goodly things And all their glory to the ground down flings.' 20 **threads**   in Greek mythology the three Fates spun, and cut, the thread of life.

THOMAS BEEDOME

Nothing known. *Select poems* ed. F. Meynell 1928.

The inquisition°

Where art thou, God? or where is he
That can discover thee to me?
The world's without thee, sure. for here
        Doth domineer
Hell, flesh and sin: thou art not there.   5

Doth air thy blessèd Spirit hold
And from our eyes thy sight unfold?
Thou art not there, my God, for here
        Doth domineer
Satan, air's prince:° thou art not there.   10

Or doth thy sacred essence keep
Court in the chamber of the deep?
No, sure, my God, not so, for here
        Doth domineer
Leviathan:° thou art not there.   15

Doth flames, too subtle for our sense
To spy, empale thy excellence?
No, sure, my God, not so, for here
        Doth domineer
The fiery prince: thou art not there.   20

In none of these confined, yet thou dost scatter
Thy presence through both earth, air, fire and water.°

Each place contains thee, God, yet thou
Art nowhere, nowhere dost remain;
Though every place we thee allow,   25
No place we know can thee contain.
Then I have found thee now: though here
Nor here thou art not, yet thou art
Both there and here: be anywhere,

So thou be in my heart;   30
Where being, Lord, let that my closet be,
To keep thee safe in me, and me in thee.

Poems divine and human 1641

° **inquisition** inquiry, examination as a spiritual exercise. No reference here to the ecclesiastical court set up in the 13th century to counter heresy, which used torture to interrogate. 10 **air's prince** *Ephesians* ii.2, 'the prince of the power of the air' because the air thought to be the abode of spirits. 15 **Leviathan** whale, sea-serpent, crocodile or dragon in *Job* xli and elsewhere; also used to represent Satan. Job says 'he is a king over all the children of pride'. 22 **earth ... water** the 4 elements; also thought of as layers or regions of the earth and its emotions.

To the noble Sir Francis Drake°

Drake, pererrati novit quem terminus orbis,
   Et cujus faciem vidit uterque polus:
Si taceant homines facient te sidera notum,
   Sol nescit comitis non memor esse sui.

The translation

Drake, who the world hast conquered like a scroll,   5
Who saw'st the arctic and antarctic pole:
If men were silent, stars would make thee known;
Phoebus° forgets not his companion.

° **Drake** circumnavigated the world 1577–80, defended England against the Spanish armada, died in Nombre de Dios 1596. 8 **Phoebus** the sun too goes round the world from east to west.

COMMENTARY 4

Courtly Sex

The intellects of Donne and Jonson are needed to make this section autonomous. At the same time their range would draw other sections more clearly into view. Above all, they would bring in something that the dramatists and journalists of sections 1 and 2 have: a sense of action and the environment's reaction; an acknowledgement that beauty can be bought and there are people who can't afford it; that loving is done in the same world as making money; that though orgasm may call on death for metaphor, dying is not like sex.

Without them, these other poets lack that sense. These are courtiers in the flimsier sense that prevailed after the statesmen's court of Elizabeth ended and especially after the accession of Charles I in 1625 (though all started under James, Kynaston and Carew had most of their court careers under Charles). There had been scandals, and terrors, at Elizabeth's court; but it was a centre of government, conducted with state. James' court was more the centre of his own inclinations—confused, extravagant, full of foreigners, homosexuals, new peers, upstarts. They hunted and played games but did not visit the realm outside. His queen, Anne, liked entertainment, masques, dancing. That grave affront was absent which at Elizabeth's court met immorality.

Charles reorganised, insisted on form, spent his money with splendid taste on international works of art. But the artificiality continued. It was not his money and it was soon therefore not going to be his kingdom. Whitehall was not the seat of government so much as of fashion. Its arbiter was Queen Henrietta-Maria. She saw herself as a modern Eleanor of Aquitaine, queen of a court of love. The history of courtly love and Platonic love is complicated but we can say roughly this: like any other highly specific community, a court will tend to play with and gossip about its domestic relationships—love, jealousy, aspiration, rejection—just as about its political ones; but the effect of that, and the tone of the court, will

still depend on its leaders. Henrietta-Maria gave it abnormal
status. She encouraged masques even more than Anne had—
and they turn easily into exhibitionistic little charades of
flattery and intrigue (see Davenant and Shirley in section 6).
In the same way Platonic love can turn into something else:
the doctrine that you can move up a ladder of knowledge
from physical attraction to beatific vision is, for amateurs, an
elevated excuse for flirting:

> O Plato! Plato! you have paved the way
>   With your confounded fantasies to more
> Immoral conduct, by the fancied sway
>   Your system feigns o'er the controlless core
> Of human hearts, than all the long array
>   Of poets and romancers; you're a bore,
> A charlatan, a coxcomb, and have been,
> At best, no better than a go-between.
>   —BYRON *Don Juan* I.cxvi

The allied notions of courtly love, in their overblown
renaissance form, gave special authority to the court as a
place for loving in; and so, again, ignored ordinary life and
ordinary death. Court, in fact, was no longer a place of
judgement but a kind of theatre. The model for it was the
religiose, Platonising court of Urbino in the early 16th century, specifically queen-centred, which Castiglione described
in *Il cortegiano*, translated into *The courtier* by Sir Thomas
Hoby in 1561; and in 1651 the poet Stanley translated Pico
della Mirandola's *Platonic discourse upon love*. [See Broadbent
Poetic love, Cassirer *Platonic renaissance*, Richmond *School
of love* in booklist; pursue the less erotic kind of Platonism
with More, Vaughan, Duchess of Newcastle.]

Of course these influences operated in the 16th century;
one of the senses in which Sidney was a courtier was wooer;
Love's labours lost is about the subject; but I would suggest
that they were dealing with courtly *love*—a sentiment and a
manner, at the least; while about 1610 there was a shift to
sex. The philosophy of love, long available to the learned,
was now both popular and chic. The queen, centre of any
erotic court, was now not sovereign but consort. So we find
Donne using these materials seriously, on his own initiative,
with strain; an exploring effort still thickens the platonising
and courting of Herbert of Cherbury, even Carew; but, put
together with Kynaston, they are revealed as less intelligent
than Donne, and more courtly in the narrow wooing sense.

By calling their section court sex I mean that they are limited to the erotic—erogenous zones, sensations, sexual techniques, fetishes; rarely is anything not already erotic made so; rarely is there any reference to emotion, environment, action, or what we call relationship. Why should there be? There is always a temporary autonomy for sex. Within the history of culture, it is probably better to be able to write sexy poems than not to be able to write anything erotic at all, or—the Romantics' way—to have to say it in myths and mountains. Sexuality was acknowledged.

I start the section with a poem, *Gaze not on swans*, attributed rather dubiously to a poet who may have died before this anthology opens. This is to establish in time a technique which began in the 16th century but was important for our writers: abandoning or, in either sense, blowing up the conventional simile for beauty. It is familiar from Shakespeare—'My mistress' eyes are nothing like the sun' (*Sonnet* 130). It was practised with increasing economy. This poem says: Don't look at swans for beauty, or at snow as an emblem of virginity, for my mistress is more beautiful, more chaste. But it doesn't end with that negative comparison. The swan and snow, which would at an earlier date have been elaborated richly for their own sake, are here little more than named; yet their beauty all the same squeezes into the poem and over the girl by means of that K-ration of multiple reference that we call a conceit and which, interpreted, expands into a meal. A conceit operates, like K-rations, by concentration. When it is opened out it directs us to the essence of the subject, where Elizabethan poetry would have left us with the surface. In this case we are directed to the essence of both swan and girl: 'In whose soft breast A full-hatched beauty seems to nest' = consider the special beauty of swans, that their pouting breasts seem like beauties (cupids? girls?) nesting in the swan, as the swan itself nestles—beauty cradling beauty. That is a peculiarly swan-type beauty. Now apply it, though, to the girl's breasts—swan's eggs, or hatched eggs—and they become also not merely white and soft but *nestly*. They nestle in the body of the girl but are for nestling in; they are like hatched birds but are for hatching babies in; and so on. It sounds silly, a hall of mirrors; yet the mirrors allow repeated explorations of nature. They are a series of answers to the question, *What's it like?*

'Nor snow, which falling from the sky Hovers in its virginity': a pleasing evocation of snow's action, without the Elizabethan insistence on whiteness, coldness and so on; but it also says this: Before I deny that snow can compare with

her, notice that she is like snow in having descended (in
Platonic and Christian theory) from a celestial origin; but is
now uncertain of her virginity. So a psychological dimension
is opened up; or it may be a scientific one—the Milky Way
and Indian mine of this poem, 'kissing chemistry' and 'diamond's refracted light' in Herbert, Kynaston's lapidaries,
Carew's surgey.

The environment within which conceits work remains,
however, intellectual; and remains an environment for sex
rather than anything more permanent and elaborate. I don't
know whether that means that it 'mentalises' sexuality, as
Lawrence would claim; or whether that would be a bad thing.
But it was an important event in history when poetry acquired
this consciousness of sex. It was parallel to the publicising of
sexual techniques by 'love's great master' Aretino (see Carew
Rapture). And it cannot be dismissed as *merely* sexy, or
technical, or conscious, because in the poems it operates so
often through conceits which aim at essence. Sex is knowledge.
The neo-Platonist Plotinus had said 'Desire generates intelligence'; and vice versa?

Kynaston is the most representative poet here. He wrote a
Spenserian romance, *Leoline and Sydanis*, which is not printed
here: its stanzas softly sell the goods of Elizabethan romance—
'aromatic incense . . . dainty virgin beauties . . . precious
odoriferous breath'—sauced with old-fashioned Petrarchan
oxymorons like 'soft ivory and warm snow'; Venus appears as
an Elizabethan deity. The next stage is shown in *To Cynthia,
on concealment of her beauty* (Kynaston's most commonly
anthologised poem so I have not included it). Cynthia's beauties are catalogued in terms of their absolutes—blown up: her
breath is now not just odoriferous, it supplies the entire
orient with perfume. This hyperbole is the analogue of *Gaze
not on swans* and Carew's *Ask me no more* (and much of
Herrick, Habington *To roses*, Jordan's epitaph). Renaissance
glamour is artfully inflated till it loses value; then, attention
shifts to the art, the logic, to the curious nexus between beautiful thing and beautiful ikon (instead of either in itself).

This is, in spite of its failure to talk about love, the poetry
of nexus, of relationship. Consider all the poems in this
section which use the inter-reflection of eyes as image—series
of mirror-images—of mutual love on the analogy of Donne's
Ecstasy; then pursue the image through Nashe, Habington
Of true delight and *Reward of innocent love*, Suckling *To a
lady*, Cleveland *Mark Antony*, Davenant *Come melt thy soul*,
Cartwright *Come, my sweet*, Philipot *Epithalamium*. Is it
still in all cases artificial? Then take it through section 8,

where it is domesticated; then it fades, and we can ask if there is any reason why it should run from about the time of *Romeo and Juliet* to about the end of the Commonwealth?

The third development of erotic imagery exemplified by Kynaston runs on, however, into the Restoration. It is the fetish. It starts from his poems on sugar, mirror, diamond etc. The mistress is admired now not for her beauty, and not by comparison, nor by hyperbole: she is examined for sexual characteristics. The method is parallel to meditation in religious poetry. You select something with object-lesson potential and contemplate it in such a way as to teach yourself the lesson. The object may for our poets be itself erotic (Cynthia's saliva, the mole on Celia's bosom) or it may be a neutral object onto which the poet displaces erotic significance. It usually turns out to be loaded already. A mirror is not neutral (though Kynaston and Lovelace do not exploit it fully; see also Carew's, not printed here, and his hair-combing poem); Celia's blood is not neutral—indeed, the surgeon bleeding her is used by Donne as a metaphor for the lover. These things lead swiftly into the adored petticoats of Herrick and Waller, the smarter fans and coiffures of Lovelace. Occasionally Herrick and Lovelace reach the level of Baudelaire in say *Les bijoux*:

> *Ce monde rayonnait de métal et de pierre*
> *Me ravit en extase, et j'aime à la fureur*
> *Les choses où le son se mêle à la lumière.*

In *Her muff* Lovelace reaches the romantic-contemporary end of the line, where clothes *are* genitals, fetish becomes what it signals. Reflection on the nature of fetishes can be aided by reference to Freud's *Collected papers* and Brigid Brophy, *Black and white: a portrait of Aubrey Beardsley* 1968 (expanded from *Atlantic monthly*).

Further suggestions. For major independent work, Kynaston. But mostly it is a matter of constructing literary history bit by bit. What objects and classes of object dominate in these poems? Do they change in time?—see later sections. What objects were actually familiar? Trace the Platonic line from Herbert of Cherbury. Trace the dialogue line from Townsend. To judge the intellectual pressure of these poets relative to Donne, paraphrase his *Ecstasy* and Herbert's *Ode*. Check Kynaston for diction: does slang or poeticism predominate? Compare Kynaston's treatment of psychic impotence in *Leoline and Sydanis* with Nashe, Rochester, Aphra Behn. Investigate the history of mirrors and the theory of light as background to the eye images; but see also Petrarch's sonnet no. 94 *Quando giugne per gli occhi al cor profundo L'imagin donna*. Trace the treatment of angels in Herbert *Platonic love* and Kynaston *Learn'd lapidaries* back to Donne *Air and angels*, forward to Randolph *Platonic elegy*, Habington *Qui quasi*, Cleveland *State of love*, Lovelace *Love made in the first age*, Cartwright *No Platonic love*, Benlowes *Might souls converse*, Vaughan passim, Stanley *Killing kiss*, Philips *Friendship's mystery*, Cowley *Platonic love*, Traherne *Wonder*. Several of these poems deal with soul unions, and also deal in erotic primitivism—cf. Carew *Love's force* and his raptures, the pastorals of section 2, Herrick, Randolph, Cleveland, perhaps Crashaw *Music's duel*, Waller *Fall*, Rochester *Fall* and some of Aphra Behn. See also the anti-Platonism of Desportes and Ronsard—'*Bien que l'esprit humain s'enfle par le doctrine Du Platon*'. Is there a religious equivalent? Trace the symbolism of bees and honey from Kynaston and Carew through Herrick, Cleveland, Newcastle *Love's flowers*, Durfey *Bee-hive*, and consider its religious uses in Benlowes *Might souls converse*, Cary *Hymn*, Joseph Beaumont *For as the honey*. Are there other symbols of equal status? What might be said of the merits of the poets in this section relative to each other?

This would be the place to consider Scottish poetry. Apart from Drummond, Sir William Aytoun (1569–1638) is the equivalent of E. Herbert; *English and Latin poems* ed C. B. Gullans 1963.

[THE REVEREND DR. JOHN DONNE]
[BEN JONSON]

HENRY NOEL

Beauty's excellency°

Gaze not on swans, in whose soft breast
A full-hatched beauty seems to nest;
Nor snow, which falling from the sky
Hovers in its virginity.

Gaze not on roses, though new blown,   5
Graced with a fresh complexiön;
Nor lilies, which no subtle bee
Hath robbed by kissing chymistry.

Gaze not on that pure Milky Way
Where night vies splendour with the day;   10
Nor pearl, whose silver walls confine
The riches of an Indian mine.

For if my empress appears,
Swans moulting die, snow melts to tears,
Roses do blush and hang their heads,   15
Pale lilies shrink into their beds;

The Milky Way rides post° to shroud
Its baffled glory in a cloud;
And pearls do climb into her ear,
To hang themselves for envy there.   20

So have I seen stars big with light
Prove lanthorns to the moon-eyed night,
Which, when Sol's rays were once displayed,
Sunk in their sockets and decayed.

° **Title** printed in Lawes ed. *Airs and dialogues* 1653; and Anon. ed.
Wit's interpreter 1671. 17 **post** fast. The rider changed horses in relays
at staging-posts on the road.

LORD HERBERT OF CHERBURY

Edward Herbert, 1st Baron Herbert of Cherbury; brother of George Herbert; eldest son of the squire of Montgomery Castle and Magdalen Herbert: see Donne in Vol. I. Edward was educated privately on the Welsh border and entered University College, Oxford, in 1596. Shortly afterwards his father died; and a marriage was arranged between Edward, who was 16, and his 20-year-old kinswoman Mary Herbert (under her father's will she inherited his estate only if she married someone named Herbert). The couple were married and returned to Oxford together with Mrs. Magdalen Herbert. In 1600 he went to court in London and in 1603 was knighted on the accession of James I. He retired to Montgomery Castle to continue his studies, with a special interest in languages. When his mother remarried he went on a continental tour with Aurelian Townsend, and came to spend the next 10 years in foreign travel, love affairs and duelling—adventures of which he left a vainglorious account in his autobiography (one of the first in England); but it seems that on one of his visits home he was beaten up in Scotland Yard by Sir John Ayres for flirting with Lady Ayres. He was friendly with a wide circle of writers including Jonson, Carew, Selden and of course Donne and George Herbert. 1618 sent as ambassador to Paris and lived there until recalled, somewhat out of the King's favour and heavily in debt, 1624. However, created baron 1629 (Cherbury was an estate of his in Shropshire); and it was in Paris that his treatise *De veritate* was written and first published (1624): it was an attempt to reduce religion to a few propositions which all reasonable men could accept; it therefore stripped religion of mythology and God of personal attributes: deism. In 1639 accompanied Charles I against the Scots (wrote the Alnwick poem en route) but during the English civil war tried to stay neutral (though his sons were active royalists). A battle was fought over Montgomery Castle while he and his daughter were in it, and won by the parliamentary army. He went now to live in London. When dying sent to his old friend Archbishop Ussher for extreme unction, saying it could do no harm and might do

good; the archbishop refused. His wife had died in 1634;
3 children survived them. *Occasional verses* posthumously
1665. *Poems* ed. G. C. Moore Smith, Oxford 1923; chief
authority M. M. Rossi (Italian). Portraits at Powys Castle,
open to public.

Platonic° love

Madam, your beauty and your lovely parts
Would scarce admit poetic praise and arts,
As they are love's most sharp and piercing darts;
    Though, as again they only wound and kill
    The more depraved affections of our will,   5
    You claim a right to commendation still.

For as you can unto that height refine
All love's delights, as while they do incline
Unto no vice they so become divine,
    We may as well attain your excellence,   10
    As without help of any outward sense
    Would make us grow a pure intelligence.°

And as a soul, thus being quite abstráct,
Complies not properly with any act
Which from its better being may detract,   15
    So through the virtuous habits you infuse,
    It is enough that we may like and choose,
    Without presuming yet to take or use.

Thus angels° in their starry orbs proceed
Unto affection, without other need   20
Than that they still on contemplation feed;
    Though, as they may unto this orb descend,
    You can, when you would so much lower bend,
    Give joys beyond what man can comprehend.

Do not refuse then, madam, to appear,   25
Since every radiant beam comes° from your sphere
Can so much more than any else endear,
    As while through them we do discern each grace,
    The multiplièd lights from every place
    Will turn, and circle, with their rays, your face.   30

° **Platonic** as the last stanza hints, the Platonic love of the renaissance
was 'not so pure and abstract as they use To say which have no mistress
but their muse . . . Love sometimes would contémplate, sometimes do'
(Donne *Love's growth*). The theory, in Plato's *Phaedrus* and *Symposium*,

was popularized by the translations and commentaries of Ficino, a scholar in the Medici household in Florence, and other 15th-century Italian scholars and humanists, e.g. Pico della Mirandola. Your love moves up a ladder, from a person's body to their soul, from individual soul to abstract ideas, until at the top of the ladder you are knowing ultimate truth, goodness, beauty. By the 16th century the doctrine had become a part of courtly and poetic behaviour. Some, e.g. Spenser, emphasised the ascent to a more soulful kind of loving; others, including E. Herbert and Donne, used the drama of the theory—you cannot get to the top except by starting at the bottom. This realised its value as a medium for conflict between soul and body and so on, and as a target for violent feelings—the 'antiplatonic' became a little genre of its own in the 17th century (see Cleveland, Cartwright, Cowley). So Platonism helps 17th-century poems to define relationships, and explore polarities, within an intellectual and religious framework. 12 **grow a pure intelligence** turn into pure mind, quite abstracted from the body. 19 **angels** sometimes inhabited and guided the revolving spheres which carried the stars and planets round the earth (their revolution produced the music of the spheres). The spheres were made of the purest kind of matter; see Chapman *To Harriots*. It was thought by some that angels might in some way make love, although 'there be neither lust nor difference of sex amongst them, whence the kindest commotions of mind will never be anything else but an exercise of intellectual love whose object is virtue and beauty' (Henry More *Immortality of the soul* 1659). Cf. Milton,

> Easier than air with air, if spirits embrace,
> Total they mix, union of pure with pure
> Desiring. *Paradise lost* VIII.626.

26 **comes** that comes. What she gives will reflect to her glory again.

The idea.° Made of Alnwick, in his expedition to Scotland with the army, 1639

All beauties vulgar eyes on earth do see,
At best but some imperfect copies be
Of those the heavens did at first decree.

For though the ideas of each several kind,
Conceived above by the eternal Mind,   5
Are such as none can error in them find

(Since from his thoughts and presence he doth bear
And shut out all deformity so far
That the least beauty near him is a star):°

As Nature yet from far the ideas views,   10
And doth besides but vile materials choose,
We in her works observe no small abuse.

Some of her figures therefore, foiled and blurred,
Show as if heaven had no way concurred
In shapes so disproportioned and absurd;   15

Which, being again vexed with some hate and spite
That doth in them vengeance and rage excite,
Seem to be tortured and deformèd quite.

While so being fixed, they yet in them contain
Another sort of ugliness and stain,   20
Being with old wrinkles interlined again.

Lastly, as if Nature even did not know
What colour every several part should owe,
They look as if their galls did overflow.

Fair is the mark of good,° and foul of ill,   25
Although not so infallibly, but still
The proof depends most on the mind and will:

As good yet rarely in the foul is met,
So 'twould as little by its union get
As a rich jewel that were poorly set;   30

For since good first did at the fair begin,
Foul being but a punishment° for sin,
Fair's the true outside to the good within.

In these the súpreme Power then so doth guide
Nature's weak hand, as he doth add beside   35
All by which creatures can be dignified;

While you in them see so exact a line
That through each several part a glimpse doth shine
Of their original and form divine.

Therefore the characters of fair and good   40
Are so set forth and printed in their blood
As each in other may be understood;

That beauty so accompanied with grace,
And equally conspicuous in the face,
In a fair woman's outside takes the place;   45

Thus while in her all rare perfection meets,
Each as with joy its fellow beauty greets,
And varies so into a thousand sweets.

Or if some tempting thought do so assault,
As doubtful she 'twixt two opinions halt,   50
A gentle blush corrects and mends the fault,

That so she still fairer and better grows,
Without that thus she more to passion owes
Than what fresh colour on her cheeks bestows;

To which again her lips such helps can add   55
As both will chase all grievous thoughts and sad,
And give what else can make her good or glad.

As statuaries° yet, having framed in clay
An hollow image, afterwards convey
The molten metal through each several way,   60

But when it once unto its place hath passed
And the inward statua perfectly is cast,
Do throw away the outward clay at last:

So, when that form the heavens at first decreed
Is finished within, souls do not need   65
Their bodies more, but would from them be freed.

For who still covered with their earth would lie?
Who would not shake their fetters off and fly,
And be at least next to a deity?

However then you be most lovely here,   70
Yet when you from all elements are clear
You far more pure and glorious shall appear.

Thus from above I doubt not to behold
Your second self renewed in your own mould,
And rising thence fairer than can be told;   75

From whence ascending to the elect and blest,
In your true joys you will not find it least
That I in heaven shall know and love you best.

For while I do your coming there attend,
I shall much time on your idea° spend   80
And note how far all others you transcend.

And thus, though you more than an angel be,
Since being here to sin and mischief free
You will have raised yourself to their degree,

That, so victorious over death and fate   85
And happy in your everlasting state,
You shall triumphant enter heaven-gate:

Hasten not thither yet, for as you are
A beauty upon earth without compare,
You will show best still where you are most rare.   90

Live all our lives then: if the picture can
Here entertain a loving absent man,
Much more the idea where you first began.

° **idea** Plato said everything perceived by the senses is an imperfect
copy of an originating 'idea' or 'form' which exists at the ultimate true
level of reality; only the elevated and truth-desirous mind can begin to
apprehend the idea of anything. 9 **star** made of absolutely pure stuff.
25 **good** Platonic doctrine that the good soul showed itself in a
beautiful body, the bad in an ugly one—with exceptions. 32 **punishment**
Adam and Eve were created perfect and beautiful; after the fall they
began to ache and age. Herbert tries to equate Platonic ideas with pre-
lapsarian origins. 58 **statuaries** sculptors. 80 **your idea** the 'idea' of
you. A painting still at Alnwick Castle, called Platonic allegory, illus-
trates poem.

An ode° upon a question moved, Whether love should continue forever?

Having interred her infant-birth,
  The watery ground that late did mourn
  Was strewed with flowers for the return
Of the wished bridegroom of the earth.

The well-accorded birds did sing   5
  Their hymns unto the pleasant time
  And in a sweet consorted chime
Did welcome in the cheerful spring;

To which soft whistles of the wind
  And warbling murmurs of a brook   10
  And varied notes of leaves that shook,
An harmony of parts did bind,

While doubling joy unto each other
  All in so rare concent° was shown,
  No happiness that came alone   15
Nor pleasure that was not another;

When with a love none can express
  That mutually happy pair,
  Melander and Celinda fair,
The season with their love did bless.   20

Walking thus towards a pleasant grove
  Which did, it seemed, in new delight
  The pleasures of the time unite
To give a triumph to their love,

They stayed at last and on the grass   25
  Reposèd so as o'er his breast
  She bowed her gracious head to rest,
Such a weight as no burden was.

While over either's compassed waist
  Their folden arms were so composed   30
  As if in straitest bonds enclosed
They suffered for joys they did taste.

Long their fixed eyes to heaven bent
  Unchanged, they did never move,
  As if so great and pure a love   35
No glass° but it could represent.

When with a sweet though troubled look
  She first brake silence, saying,
    Dear friend,
  O that our love might take no end
Or never had beginning took!   40

I speak not this with a false heart
  (Wherewith his hand she gently strained)
  Or that would change a love maintained
With so much faith on either part.

Nay, I protest, though death with his   45
  Worst counsel should divide us here,
  His terrors could not make me fear
To come where your loved presençe is;

Only if love's fire with the breath
  Of life be kindlèd, I doubt   50
  With our last air 'twill be breathed out
And quenched with the cold of death;

That if affection be a line
  Which is closed up in our last hour,
  O, how 'twould grieve me any power   55
Could force so dear a love as mine!

She scarce had done when his shut eyes
  An inward joy did represent
  To hear Celinda thus intent
To a love he so much did prize.   60

Then with a look, it seemed, denied
  All earthly power but hers, yet so
  As if to her breath he did owe
This borrowed life, he thus replied:

O you,° wherein they say souls rest   65
   Till they descend pure heavenly fires,
   Shall lustful and corrupt desires
With your immortal seed be blest?

And shall our love, so far beyond
   That low and dying appetite,°   70
   And which so chaste desires unite,
Not hold in an eternal bond?

Is it because we should decline
   And wholly from our thoughts exclude
   Objects that may the sense delude,   75
And study only the divine?

No, sure, for if none can ascend
   Even to the visible degree°
   Of things created, how should we
The invisible comprehend?   80

Or rather, since that Power expressed
   His greatness in his works alone,
   Being here best in his creatures known,
Why is he not loved in them best?

But is't not true, which you pretend,°   85
   That since our love and knowledge here
   Only as parts of life appear,
So they with it should take their end?

O no, beloved, I am most sure
   Those virtuous habits we acquire,   90
   As being with the soul entire
Must with it evermore endure;

For if, where sins and vice reside,
   We find so foul a guilt remain
   As, never dying in his stain,   95
Still punished in the soul doth bide,

Much more that true and real joy
   Which in a virtuous love is found
   Must be more solid in its ground
Than fate or death can e'er destroy;   100

Else should our souls in vain elect,
   And vainer yet were heaven's laws
   When to an everlasting cause
They give a perishing effect.

Nor here on earth then, nor above,   105
  Our good affection can impair;
  For where God doth admit the fair,
Think you that he excludeth love?

These eyes° again, then, eyes shall see,
  And hands again these hands enfold,   110
  And all chaste pleasures can be told
Shall with us everlasting be.

For if no use of sense remain
  When bodies once this life forsake,
  Or they could no delight partake,   115
Why should they ever rise again?

And if every imperfect mind
  Make love the end of knowledge here,
  How perfect will our love be where
All imperfection is refined?   120

Let then no doubt, Celinda, touch,
  Much less your fairest mind invade;
  Were not our souls immortal made,
Our equal loves can make them such:

So when one wing can make no way,   125
  Two joinèd can themselves dilate,
  So can two persons propagate,
When singly either would decay.

So when from hence we shall be gone
  And be no more, nor you nor I,   130
  As one another's mystery°
Each shall be both, yet both but one.

This said, in her uplifted face
  Her eyes, which did that beauty crown,
  Were like two stars that having fallen down   135
Look up again to find their place;

While such a moveless silent peace
  Did seize on their becalmèd sense,
  One would have thought some influence°
Their ravished spirits did possess.   140

° **ode** one of a series of poems about this time in which lovers lie out
of doors communing silently, or talking about their souls, in an extended
contemplative foreplay. Cf. Sidney's *In a grove most rich of shade* and
Donne's *Ecstasy*. See G. Williamson in *17th-century contexts*, repr. in
Keast. 14 **concent** harmony. 36 **glass** mirror. 65 **you** God, heaven,

Abraham's bosom or a Platonic equivalent? Or Venus or Adonis—see Townsend *Dialogue*; Drayton *To Browne*. 70 **dying appetite** cf. Yeats' 'dying animal' in *Sailing to Byzantium*. 78 **degree** step on the ladder of creation, and of contemplation and love. 85 **pretend** claim. 109 **eyes** cf. T. S. Eliot *Hollow men, Eyes that last I saw in tears* and his essay on *The metaphysical poets*; also Sidney, 'While their eyes, by love directed, Interchangeably reflected.' It is the start of the tradition of eyes as emblems of reciprocity. 131 **mystery** sacrament; or religious secret, e.g. Trinity? or emblem. Cf. Donne in *Canonisation* and *Ecstasy*. 139 **influence** astrological, perhaps angelic. In a trance.

SIR FRANCIS KYNASTON

Eldest son of Shropshire squire. Oriel College, Oxford; Trinity College, Cambridge; Lincoln's Inn; concluded his studies and married 1613; one son. Court career, knighted by James I in 1618, M.P. for Shropshire 1621. Proctor of Cambridge University 1634. At Charles I's court became centre of literary coterie and founded a courtiers' academy called Musaeum Minervae in his house in Covent Garden. *Cynthiades* published with his romance *Leoline and Sydanis* posthumously 1642. Ed. Saintsbury.

To Cynthia: learn'd lapidaries

Learn'd lapidaries say the diamond,
Bred in the mines and mountains of the east,
Mixèd with heaps of gold ore is often found
In the half-bird's, half-beast's, the gryphon's° nest,
Is first pure water easy to be pressed,   5
   Then ice, then crystal, which great length of time
   Doth to the hardest of all stones sublime.

I think they say the truth, for it may be;
And what they of the diamond have said,
My brightest Cynthia, may be proved by thee,   10
Who, having lived so long so chaste a maid,
Thy heart with any diamond being weighed
   Is harder found, and colder than that stone,
   Thy first years' virgin-softness being gone.

For now it is become impenetrable   15
And he that will or° form or cut it must
(If he to purchase such a gem be able)
Use a proportion of thy precious dust;
Although the valuation be unjust,
   That pains which men to pierce it must bestow   20
   Will equal dear in price unto it grow.
But thou, it may be, wilt make this profession,

That diamonds are softened with goats' blood
And, mollified by it, will take impression;
This of slain lovers must be understood.   25
But trust me, dearest Cynthia, 'tis not good,
    Thy beauties so should lovers' minds perplex
    As make them think thee angel without sex.°

4 gryphon fabulous lion with eagle head and wings; it guarded gold in
Scythia (Russia). **16 or** either. **28 sex** gender, or genitals. See E.
Herbert *Platonic love.*

To Cynthia, on sugar and her sweetness°

Those, Cynthia, that do taste the honey-dew
Of thy moist rosy lips (who are but few),
Or sucketh vapour of thy breath more sweet
Than honeysuckle's juice, they all agree't
To be Madeira's sugar's quintessence—   5
Or some diviner syrup brought from thence.
And for the operation, they believe
It hath a quality provocative:
For Venus° in the sugar's propagation
Is said to have a sovereign domination.   10
But I must not think so, for I have read
Of an extracted sugar out of lead°
Of which I once did taste, which chemists call
Sugar of Saturn,° for they therewithal
Cure all venereal heats, for it doth hold   15
A winter in it like that planet's cold
And, though it be strangely sweet, yet doth it quench
All courage towards a mistress or a wench.
Such must I think thy sweetness for to be,
By that experience that is found in me: 20
For he that shall those sweets of thine but taste
Shall like thyself become, as cold, as chaste:
For, like the mildew° new-fallen from the sky,
Though dropped from heaven yet doth it mortify.

° **sugar . . . sweetness** slang for sex and saliva; (sugar-stick = penis;
cf. candy, honey, honeypot = vulva, etc. in current usage). Also poeti-
cisms for being sweet = lovable, nice. **9 Venus** goddess of love; here,
the planet influencing the production of Cynthia's sugar. **12 lead** sugar
of lead, lead acetate. **14 Saturn** leaden, gloomy and baleful planet. **23
mildew** honeydew, a sweet sticky stuff found on leaves, excreted by
aphids; it was thought to come with the dew.

To Cynthia, on her looking-glass

Give me leave, fairest Cynthia, to envý
Thy looking-glass, far happier than I,
To which thy naked beauties every morn
Thou showest so freely while thou dost adorn
Thy richer hair with gems and neatly deck   5
With oriental pearls thy whiter neck—
Which take the species° of thy naked breast,
So white, I doubt if it can be expressed
By the reflection of the purest glass;
Which swans, snows, ceruses° doth so surpass   10
As, in comparison of it, these may
Rather than white be termèd hoar or grey;
Besides, all whites but thine may take a spot;
Thine, the first matter of all whites, can not.
Maybe thou trusts thy glass's secrecy   15
With dainties yet unseen by any eye.
All these thy favours I will well allow
Unto my rival glass, but so, that thou
Wilt not permit it justly to reflect
Thy eye upon itself: I shall suspect,   20
And jealous grow, that such refléx may move
Thee, fair Narcissus-like,° to fall in love
With thine own beauty's shadow; love's sharp dart
Shot 'gainst a stone may bound,° and wound thy heart:
Which if it should, alas! how sure were I   25
To be past hope, and then past remedy.
This to prevent, may'st thou when thou dost rise
Vouchsafe to dress thy beauties in my eyes.
If these shall be too small, may, for thy sake,
Hypochondriac melancholy make   30
My body all of glass, all which shall be
So made and so constéllated° by thee
That, as in crystal mirrors many a spot
Is by infection of a look begot,
This glass of thine, if thou but frown, shall fly   35
In thousand shivers broken by thine eye.
Since then it hath this sympathy with thee,
Let me not languish in a jealousy
To think this wonder may be brought to pass,
Thy fair looks may inanimate thy glass   40

And make it my competitor: 'tis all one
To give life to a glass, as make me stone.

7 species shape (pearl = breast). **10 ceruses** white cosmetic. **22 Narcissus** fell in love with his own reflection in a pool, thinking it a nymph; he fell in and drowned. **24 bound** rebound. **32 constellated** fated, by being made under the influence of a particular constellation (her eyes).

THOMAS CAREW

Son of a judge. Oxford, Middle Temple, idling. Served the ambassador to Venice and the Hague but dismissed. Served Lord Herbert of Cherbury when he was ambassador in Paris 1619 . . . In 1628 gained a post in Charles I's court; became a friend of the King, and of Queen Henrietta-Maria (supposed to have stumbled and put out the light when, lighting the king to her chamber, he found Lord St. Alban's there). Associated also with Jonson, Townsend, Davenant, Feltham, Suckling. Painted with Thomas Killigrew by Van Dyck 1638 (at Windsor). Wrote a famous elegy on Donne (printed in the Donne volume in this series). *Poems* published posthumously 1640 (ed. with masque R. Dunlap, Oxford 1949, 1957). Some readers admired his 'sharpness' and 'elegancy', others thought his verse costive. E. I. Selig, *The flourishing wreath* 1958.

Love's force

In the first ruder age,° when love was wild,
Not yet by laws reclaimed, not reconciled
To order, nor by reason° manned, but flew
Full-summed by nature on the instant view
Upon the wings of appetite at all   5
The eye could fair or sense delightful call,
Election° was not yet: but as their cheap
Food from the oak or the next acorn-heap,
As water from the nearest spring or brook,
So men their undistinguished° females took   10
By chance, not choice. But soon the heavenly spark
That in man's bosom lurked broke through this dark
Confusion: then the noblest breast first felt
Itself for its own proper object° melt.

1 **ruder age** cf. Lovelace *Love made in the first age*. 3 **reason** cf. Cherbury *Idea*; see Montaigne's essay *Epistle to Raymond de Sebonde* and Lovejoy et al. *Primitivism*, for attitudes to nature. 7 **Election** choice, selection. 10 **undistinguished** undifferentiated. 14 **object** in

Plato's *Symposium* the origin of soulmates is explained thus: at first there were hermaphroditic beings; they split in half, one male, the other female, and ever afterwards seek to find their 'other halves'.

Upon a mole in Celia's bosom

That lovely spot which thou dost see
In Celia's bosom was a bee°
Who built her amorous spicy nest
In the Hyblas° of her either breast;
But from close ivory hives she flew   5
To suck the aromatic dew
Which from the neighbour vale distils,
Which parts those two twin-sister hills;
There feasting on ambrosial meat,
A rolling file° of balmy sweat   10
(As in soft murmurs before death
Swan-like° she hung) choked up her breath:
So she in water did expire
More precious than the phoenix' fire.°
    Yet still her shadow there remains   15
Confined to those Elysian° plains,
With this strict law, that who shall lay
His bold lips on that milky way
The sweet and smart from thence shall bring
Of the bee's honey and her sting.   20

2 bee an erotic insect in 17th-century poetry—sting, long tongue for sucking nectar from flowers, its hairy thighs; see Kynaston *Sugar and sweetness*. **4 Hyblas** Hybla is a mountain in Sicily which was famous for honey. **10 file** thread. **12 swan-like** the swan, normally mute, is supposed to sing as it dies; perhaps a reference also to death as orgasm, for the bee could represent either Celia or her lover. **14 fire** meaning that Celia's sweat is superior to the sacred fire that burns the phoenix. There is only one phoenix at a time; it does not reproduce itself but after living 500 years flies to the spicy forests of Arabia, sings itself a dirge, and burns itself up; from its ashes a new phoenix rises. It is an emblem of Christ, sacred love, unity, etc. See Shakespeare *Phoenix and turtle*; Donne *Canonisation*. **16 Elysian** paradisal.

Celia bleeding:° to the surgeon

Fond man, that canst believe her blood
    Will from those purple channels flow;

Or that the pure untainted flood
  Can any foul distemper know;
Or that thy weak steel can incise   5
The crystal case wherein it lies.

Know, her quick blood, proud of his seat,
  Runs dancing through her azure veins;
Whose harmony no cold nor heat
  Disturbs, whose hue no tincture° stains: 10
And the hard rock wherein it dwells
The keenest darts of love repels.

But thou repli'st, 'Behold, she bleeds!'
  Fool! thou'rt deceived, and dost not know
The mystic knot° whence this proceeds,   15
  How lovers in each other grow:
Thou struck'st her arm, but 'twas my heart
Shed all the blood, felt all the smart.

° **bleeding** being bled, having blood drawn off by leeching or lancing—
a common remedy for all sorts of ills. 10 **tincture** intrusive colouring.
15 **knot** the true-lovers'-knot was one of many continuous intertwined
patterns popular in 17th-century printing, embroidery etc.

Ask me no more°

Ask me no more where Jove bestows,
When June is past, the fading rose:
For in your beauties' orient deep
These flowers, as in their causes,° sleep.

Ask me no more whither do stray   5
The golden atoms of the day:
For in pure love heaven did prepare
Those powders to enrich your hair.

Ask me no more whither doth haste
The nightingale when May is past: 10
For in your sweet dividing° throat
She winters and keeps warm her note.

Ask me no more where those stars light°
That downwards fall in dead of night:
For in your eyes they sit and there   15
Fixèd become, as in their sphere.°

Ask me no more if east or west
The phoenix° builds her spicy nest:
For unto you at last she flies
And in your fragrant bosom dies.   20

° **Ask me no more** adapted by Tennyson in his *Princess.* 4 **causes**
origins (Aristotelian philosophy). 11 **dividing** descanting. 13 **light**
alight. 16 **sphere** see E. Herbert, *Platonic love.* 18 **phoenix** see *Upon
a mole.*

from A rapture°

I will enjoy thee now, my Celia—come
And fly with me to love's Elysium.°
The giant Honour, that keeps cowards out,
Is but a masquer,° and the servile rout
Of baser subjects only bend in vain   5
To the vast idol; whilst the nobler train
Of valiant lovers daily sail between
The huge Colossus'° legs and pass unseen
Unto the blissful shore. Be bold and wise,
And we shall enter. The grim Swiss° denies   10
Only to tame fools a passage, that not know
He is but form, and only frights in show
The duller eyes that look from far; draw near
And thou shalt scorn what we were wont to fear:
We shall see how the stalking pageant goes   15
With borrowed legs, a heavy load to those
That made and bear him; not, as we once thought,
The seed of gods but a weak model wrought
By greedy men that seek to enclose° the common,
And within private arms impale free woman.   20
   Come, then, and mounted on the wings of love
We'll cut the flitting air and soar above
The monster's head and in the noblest seats
Of those blest shades quench and renew our heats.
There shall the queens of love and innocence,   25
Beauty and nature, banish all offence
From our close ivy-twines; there I'll behold
Thy barèd snow and thy unbraided gold;
There my enfranchised hand on every side
Shall o'er thy naked polished ivory slide.   30
No curtain there, though of transparent lawn,°
Shall be before thy virgin-treasure drawn;
But the rich mine,° to the inquiring eye

Exposed, shall ready still for mintage lie,
And we will coin young Cupids.° There a bed   35
Of roses and fresh myrtles° shall be spread
Under the cooler shade of cypress groves;
Our pillows of the down of Venus' doves,
Whereon our panting limbs we'll gently lay
In the faint respites of our active play,   40
That so our slumbers may in dreams have leisure
To tell the nimble fancy our past pleasure,
And so our souls, that cannot be embraced,
Shall the embraces of our bodies taste.
Meanwhile the bubbling stream shall court the shore; 45
The enamoured chirping wood-choir shall adore
In varied tunes the deity of love;
The gentle blasts of western winds shall move
The trembling leaves and through their close boughs
    breathe
Still music, whilst we rest ourselves beneath   50
Their dancing shade till a soft murmur, sent
From souls entranced in amorous languishment,
Rouse us and shoot into our veins fresh fire
Till we in their sweet ecstasy expire.
    Then, as the empty bee that lately bore   55
Into the common treasure all her store
Flies 'bout the painted field with nimble wing
Deflowering the fresh virgins of the spring,
So will I rifle all the sweets that dwell
In my delicious paradise, and swell   60
My bag° with honey drawn forth by the power
Of fervent kisses from each spicy flower;
I'll seize the rose-buds in their perfumed bed,
The violet knots° like curious mazes spread
O'er all the garden; taste the ripened cherry,   65
The warm firm apple tipped with coral berry;
Then will I visit with a wandering kiss
The vale of lilies° and the bower of bliss;°
And where the beauteous region doth divide
Into two milky ways, my lips shall slide   70
Down those smooth alleys, wearing as I go
A tract for lovers on the printed snow;
Thence climbing o'er the swelling Apennine,
Retire into thy grove of eglantine°
Where I will all those ravished sweets distil   75
Through love's alembic,° and with chemic skill
From the mixed mass one sovereign balm° derive,
Then bring that great elíxir to thy hive.

   Now in more subtle wreaths I will entwine
My sinewy thighs, my legs and arms with thine;   80
Thou like a sea of milk shalt lie displayed,
Whilst I the smooth calm oceän invade
With such a tempest as when Jove of old
Fell down on Danaë° in a storm of gold;
Yet my tall pine shall in the Cyprian° strait   85
Ride safe at anchor and unlade her freight;
My rudder with thy bold hand, like a tried
And skilful pilot, thou shalt steer, and guide
My bark into love's channel, where it shall
Dance as the bounding waves do rise or fall.   90
Then shall thy circling arms embrace and clip
My willing body and thy balmy lip
Bathe me in juice of kisses, whose perfúme
Like a religious incense shall consume
And send up holy vapours to those powers   95
That bless our loves and crown our sportful hours,
That with such halcyon° calmness fix our souls
In steadfast peace as no affright controls.°
There no rude sounds shake us with sudden starts;
No jealous ears, when we unrip° our hearts,   100
Suck our discourse in; no observing spies
This blush, that glance traduce; no envious eyes
Watch our close meetings; nor are we betrayed
To rivals by the bribed chambermaid.°
No wedlock bonds unwreathe our twisted loves;   105
We seek no midnight arbour, no dark groves
To hide our kisses; there the hated name
Of husband, wife, lust, modest, chaste or shame
Are vain and empty words whose very sound
Was never heard in the Elysian° ground;   110
All things are lawful there that may delight
Nature or unrestrainèd appetite;
Like and enjoy, to will and act is one:
We only sin when love's rites are not done.
   The Roman Lúcrece° there reads the divine   115
Lectures of love's great master, Aretine,°
And knows as well as Laïs how to move
Her pliant body in the act of love:
To quench the burning ravisher she hurls
Her limbs into a thousand winding curls   120
And studies artful postures such as be
Carved on the bark of every neighbouring tree
By learnèd hands, that so adorned the rind
Of those fair plants which, as they lay entwined,

Have fanned their glowing fires. The Grecian° dame,   125
That in her endless web toiled for a name
As fruitless as her work, doth there display
Herself before the youth of Ithaca,
And the amorous sport of gamesome nights prefer
Before dull dreams of the lost traveller.°   130
Daphne° hath broke her bark, and that swift foot
Which the angry gods had fastened with a root
To the fixed earth doth now unfettered run
To meet the embraces of the youthful sun:
She hangs upon him like his Delphic lyre;   135
Her kisses blow the old, and breathe new fire;
Full of her god, she sings inspirèd lays,
Sweet odes of love such as deserve the bays,
Which she herself was. Next her, Laura° lies
In Petrarch's learnèd arms, drying those eyes   140
That did in such smooth-pacèd numbers flow
As made the world enamoured of his woe.
These, and ten thousand beauties more that died
Slave to the tyrant,° now enlarged deride
His cancelled laws and for their time misspent   145
Pay into love's exchequer double rent.
    Come then, my Celia, we'll no more forbear
To taste our joys, struck with a panic fear,
But will depose from his imperious sway
This proud usurper, and walk free as they,   150
With necks unyoked. Nor is it just that he
Should fetter your soft sex with chastity,
Which nature made unapt for abstinence,
When yet this false impostor can dispense
With human justice and with sacred right   155
And, maugre both their laws, command me fight
With rivals or with emulous loves that dare
Equal with thine their mistress' eyes or hair:
If thou complain of wrong, and call my sword
To carve out thy revenge, upon that word   160
He bids me fight and kill; or else he brands
With marks of infamy my coward hands.
And yet religion bids from bloodshed fly,
And damns me for that act. Then tell me why
    This goblin Honour, which the world adores,   165
    Should make men atheists and not women whores?

° **rapture** ecstasy in the sense of excitement, being carried away, rather
than in the sense of Donne's *Ecstasy*. Belongs to a tradition of loose or
'libertine' poetry; cf. Donne's elegies, Lovelace's *Aramantha*; Cowley in
his *Ecstasy* is rapt up to heaven. 2 **Elysium** heaven. 4 **masquer** pre-

tence. Carew produced a masque at court. 8 **Colossus** the colossus of Rhodes was a 105-foot-high statue of the sun god Helios; it came to be believed that it had bestrid the harbour so that ships sailed between its legs. 10 **Swiss** mercenary guard from Switzerland. 19 **enclose** enclosures of common land for private farming had occurred in the 16th century, and continued to the end of the 18th. 31 **lawn** see Lovelace *Strive not.* 33 **mine** could mean ore, bullion, or mine in the ground. Cf. Donne *Sun-rising.* **Mintage** often sexual in 17th century—stamping the impression of a head on softened metal. 35 **Cupids** the god of love as *putto.* 36 **myrtles** sacred to Venus, as are the doves. 61 **bag** see Carew *Upon a mole,* for the bee. The nectar it sucks from flowers goes into a kind of crop where it is mixed with saliva and turned into honey; but the bag may refer to the bulge of pollen carried on its thighs. Cf. Herrick's bee poems. 64 **knots** flower-beds in the complicated patterns fashionable in the Jacobean period. Allegorising veins. 68 **lilies** see *Solomon's song.* Usually refers to whiteness of the belly, hence navel here; though as a symbol = virginity. **bower of bliss** sensual garden in *Fairy Queen* II. xii; pudendum. 74 **eglantine** rose-bush. Must be one of the earliest references to cunnilinctus, and posterior coitus, in courtly or printed poetry. 76 **alembic** retort (Arabic *al ambiq.*). 77 **sovereign balm** supreme remedy, an aromatic ointment to cure all ills. The alchemists sought to 'derive' gold from base metals, the apothecaries a panacea from herbs. An important metaphor with poets of the 17th century, whether for semen or, as in Donne, some kind of redeeming virtue of the soul: see Vol I; cf. also 'summer's distillation' in Shakespeare's sonnets 5 and 6. 84 **Danaë** see Nashe *Dildo.* 85 **Cyprian** Cyprus was the birthplace of Aphrodite. 78 **hive** slang as well as poeticism for vulva. See D'Urfey *Beehive.* 97 **halcyon** bird of peace. 98 **controls** ends. 100 **unrip** open; with almost the connotation of modern unzip. 104 **chambermaid** cf. Donne *Window valediction* and *Elegies* I, IV, XVI. 110 **Elysian** heavenly. 115 **Lucrece** virtuous Roman wife raped by Tarquin (see Heywood, and Shakespeare's poem). With the other women in the list she is actually a type of chastity; but Laïs was a famous Greek courtesan. 116 **Aretine** Pietro Aretino (1492–1556), Italian writer. His sonnets on coital postures, in which the man tells the woman what to do at climax, were illustrated with engravings by Giulio Romano and constituted one of the first sophisticated texts of sexual instruction in the west. 125 **Grecian** Penelope. While her husband Odysseus was at the Trojan war and adventuring on the way back, she was pressed by the young men of Ithaca to marry one of them. She promised to when she had finished a tapestry, but every night undid what she had woven in the day. 130 **lost traveller** Odysseus; also a mysterious figure in epilogue to Blake's *For the sexes: the gates of paradise.* 131 **Daphne** lustfully pursued by Apollo, she changed into a laurel tree. Apollo was god of the sun, music, poetry; his chief temple was at Delphi. Bay, a kind of laurel, was used to crown poets. 139 **Laura** young wife of a burgher of Avignon in Provence. Francesco Petrarca (1304–1374), classical scholar, antiquary and poet, is supposed to have seen her once in church there. He wrote sonnets about his hopeless love for her for many years and long after her death in the plague in 1348, developing an introspective and quasi-religious form of erotic discussion which was influential throughout the renaissance. Laura = laurel, and Petrarch was crowned poet laureate in Rome in 1341. 144 **tyrant** honour.

A pastoral dialogue°

Shepherd. Nymph. Chorus.°

Shepherd	This mossy bank they pressed. *Nymph* That agèd oak
	Did canopy the happy pair
	All night from the damp air.
Chorus	Here let us sit and sing the words they spoke 5
	Till the day breaking their embraces broke.

Shepherd	See, love, the blushes of the morn appear
	And now she hangs her pearly store,
	Robbed from the eastern shore,
	In the cowslip's bell and roses rare. 10
	Sweet, I must stay no longer here.
Nymph	Those streaks of doubtful light usher not day
	But show my sun must set; no morn
	Shall shine till thou return:
	The yellow planets and the grey 15
	Dawn shall attend thee on thy way.
Shepherd	If thine eyes gild my paths they may forbear
	Their useless shine. *Nymph* My tears will quite
	Extinguish their faint light.
Shepherd	Those drops will make their beams more clear, 20
	Love's flames will shine in every tear.

Chorus	They kissed and wept and from their lips and eyes
	In a mixed dew of briny sweet
	Their joys and sorrows meet.
	But she cries out: *Nymph* Shepherd, arise! 25
	The sun betrays us else to spies.
Shepherd	The wingèd hours fly fast whilst we embrace
	But when we want their help to meet
	They move with leaden feet.
Nymph	Then let us pinion time, and chase 30
	The day for ever from this place.
Shepherd	Hark! *Nymph* Aye me, stay! *Shepherd* For ever! *Nymph* No, arise!
	We must be gone. *Shepherd* My nest of spice!
Nymph	My soul! *Shepherd* My paradise!

Chorus   Neither could say farewell, but through their   35
           eyes
        Grief interrupted speech with tears' supplies.

° **dialogue** See introduction to Section 3. This is also in the genre
of the aubade or dawn-poem; cf. Donne   *Goodmorrow* etc; *Romeo
and Juliet* III.v; Yeats *Parting*. In the first 3 lines the Shepherd and
Nymph sing as members of the chorus. With the last line cf. E. Herbert
Ode.

An Hymeneal° dialogue

Bride and Groom

Groom   Tell me, my love, since Hymen tied
        The holy knot hast thou not felt
    A new-infusèd spirit slide
        Into thy breast, whilst thine did melt?

Bride   First tell me, sweet, whose words were those?   5
        For though your voice the air did break
    Yet did my soul the sense compose
        And through your lips my heart did speak.

Groom   Then I perceive, when from the flame
        Of love my scorched soul did retire,   10
    Your frozen heart in her place came
        And sweetly melted in that fire.

Bride   'Tis true, for when that mutual change
        Of souls was made, with equal gain
    I straight might feel diffused a strange   15
        But gentle heat through every vein.

Chorus   O blest disunion! that doth so
        Our bodies from our souls divide
    As two do one, and one four grow,
        Each by contraction multiplied.   20

Bride   Thy bosom then I'll make my nest,
        Since there my willing soul doth perch.

Groom   And for my heart in thy chaste breast
        I'll make an everlasting search.

Chorus   O blest disunion! that doth so   25
        Our bodies from our souls divide

As two do one, and one four grow,
Each by contraction multiplied.

° **Hymeneal** wedding. See pastoral dialogue above, though this is
more in the line of such unity poems as *The phoenix and the turtle*
and E. Herbert *Ode*. Hymen is god of weddings.

Epitaph on the Lady Mary Villiers°

The Lady Mary Villiers lies
Under this stone; with weeping eyes
The parents that first gave her birth,
And their sad friends, laid her in earth.
If any of them, reader, were   5
Known unto thee, shed a tear;
Or if thyself possess a gem
As dear to thee, as this to them,
Though a stranger to this place,
Bewail in theirs thine own hard case: 10
For thou, perhaps, at thy return
Mayst find thy darling in an urn.

° **Villiers** identity doubtful.

Maria Wentworth°

And here the precious dust is laid,
Whose purely tempered clay was made
So fine that it the guest betrayed;

Else the soul grew so fast within,
It broke the outward shell of sin   5
And so was hatched a cherubin.

In height it soared to God above,
In depth it did to knowledge move,
And spread in breadth to general love.

Before, a pious duty shined   10
To parents; courtesy behind;
On either side an equal mind.

Good to the poor, to kindred dear,
To servants kind, to friendship clear,°
To nothing but herself severe.   15

So, though a virgin, yet a bride
To every grace, she justified
A chaste polygamy, and died.

Learn from hence, reader, what small trust
We owe this world, where virtue must,   20
Frail as our flesh, crumble to dust.

° **Wentworth**   daughter of Thomas earl of Cleveland. She died 1633
aged 18; the poem is on her magnificent tomb in St. George's church,
Toddington, Bedfordshire. Her effigy has a sewing-basket: she was said
to have died after pricking her finger while sewing on a Sunday. 14 **clear**
noble.

THE REVEREND HENRY KING,
BISHOP OF CHICHESTER

Eldest son of Bishop of London. Westminster School; Christ Church, Oxford, with brother who also became an eminent divine. M.A. 1614 followed by rapid preferment in the church, based on St. Paul's. Member of the literary and ecclesiastical circle which inluded Donne—also Jonson, Sandys, Izaak Walton. Married Anne Berkeley c.1617 and had 6 children of whom two survived; wife, to whom the *Exequy* is addressed, died 1624. He remarried 1630. Became Bishop of Chichester 1642, first year of the civil war, and was in his palace when the town surrendered to the parliamentary army 1643: deprived of bishopric and lived in country till restored in 1660. Wrote 'A deep groan, fetched at the funeral of that incomparable and glorious monarch Charles I . . . on whose sacred person was acted that execrable, horrid and prodigious murther . . .' and other amazing elegies. *Poems* published anonymously and piratically 1657, 1664. Ed. Margaret Crum, Oxford 1966. See R. Berman *H.K. and the 17th century* 1964.

The surrender

My once dear love—hapless that I no more
Must call thee so: the rich affection's store
That fed our hopes lies now exhaust and spent,
Like sums of treasure unto bankrupts lent.
  We that did nothing study but the way   5
To love each other, with which thoughts the day
Rose with delight to us, and with them set,
Must learn the hateful art, how to forget.
  We that did nothing wish that heaven could give
Beyond ourselves, nor did desire to live   10
Beyond that wish, all these now cancel must,
As if not writ in faith, but words and dust.
  Yet witness those clear vows which lovers make;

Witness the chaste desires that never brake
Into unruly heats; witness that breast   15
Which in thy bosom anchored his whole rest:
'Tis no default in us. I dare acquit
Thy maidenfaith, thy purpose fair and white
As thy pure self. Cross planets did envý
Us to each other, and heaven did untie   20
Faster than vows could bind. O that the stars,
When lovers meet, should stand opposed in wars!
  Since, then, some higher destinies command,
Let us not strive nor labor to withstand
What is past help. The longest date of grief   25
Can never yield a hope of our relief;
And though we waste ourselves in moist laments,
Tears may drown us but not our discontents.
  Fold back our arms, take home our fruitless loves
That must new fortunes try, like turtle-doves   30
Dislodgèd from their haunts. We must in tears
Unwind a love knit up in many years.
In this last kiss I here surrender thee
Back to thyself. Lo! thou again art free.
Thou in another, sad as that, re-send   35
The truest heart that lover e'er did lend.
  Now turn from each. So fare our severed hearts
As the divorced soul from her body parts.

An exequy: to his matchless never-to-be-forgotten friend

Accept, thou shrine of my dead saint,°
Instead of dirges this complaint;
And for sweet flowers to crown thy hearse
Receive a strew of weeping verse
From thy grieved friend, whom thou might'st see   5
Quite melted into tears for thee.
  Dear loss! since thy untimely fate
My task hath been to meditate
On thee, on thee: thou art the book,
The library whereon I look,   10
Though almost blind. For thee, loved clay,
I languish out, not live, the day,
Using no other exercise
But what I practise with mine eyes:
By which wet glasses° I find out   15

How lazily time creeps about
To one that mourns; this, only this
My exercise and business is:
So I compute the weary hours
With sights dissolvèd into showers.   20
Nor wonder if my time go thus
Backward and most preposterous:
Thou hast benighted me, thy set
This eve of blackness did beget,
Who wast my day (though overcast   25
Before thou hadst thy noontide passed)
And I remember must in tears,
Thou scarce hadst seen so many years
As day tells hours. By thy clear sun
My love and fortune first did run;   30
But thou wilt never more appear
Folded within my hemisphere,
Since both thy light and motiön,
Like a fled star, is fallen and gone,
And 'twixt me and my soul's dear wish   35
The earth now interposèd is,
Which such a strange eclipse doth make
As ne'er was read in almanake.
I could allow thee for a time
To darken me and my sad clime: 40
Were it a month, a year, or ten,
I would thy exile live till then;
And all that space my mirth adjourn,
So thou wouldst promise to return
And, putting off thy ashy shroud,   45
At length disperse this sorrow's cloud.

    But, woe is me! the longest date
Too narrow is to calculate
These empty hopes: never shall I
Be so much blessed as to descry   50
A glimpse of thee, till that day come
Which shall the earth to cinders doom,
And a fierce fever must calcine
The body of this world, like thine,
My little world!° That fit of fire   55
Once off, our bodies shall aspire
To our souls' bliss: then we shall rise
And view ourselves with clearer eyes
In that calm region where no night
Can hide us from each other's sight.   60

    Meantime, thou hast her, earth: much good
May my harm do thee. Since it stood
With heaven's will I might not call
Her longer mine, I give thee all
My short-lived right and interest   65
In her, whom living I loved best;
With a most free and bounteous grief
I give thee what I could not keep.
Be kind to her, and prithee look
Thou write into thy Doomsday Book   70
Each parcel° of this rarity
Which in thy casket shrined doth lie.
See that thou make thy reckoning straight,
And yield her back again by weight,
For thou must audit on thy trust   75
Each grain and atom of this dust,
As thou wilt answer him that lent,
Not gave thee, my dear monument.

    So close the ground, and 'bout her shade
Black curtains draw: my bride is laid.   80
Sleep on, my love, in thy cold bed
Never to be disquieted.
My last goodnight! Thou wilt not wake
Till I thy fate shall overtake:
Till age, or grief, or sickness must   85
Marry my body to that dust
It so much loves, and fill the room
My heart keeps empty in thy tomb.
Stay for me there: I will not fail
To meet thee in that hollow vale.   90
And think not much of my delay:
I am already on the way
And follow thee with all the speed
Desire can make, or sorrows breed.
Each minute is a short degree   95
And every hour a step towards thee.
At night when I betake to rest,
Next morn I rise nearer my west
Of life, almost by eight hours' sail,
Than when sleep breathed his drowsy gale.   100
Thus from the sun my bottom steers,
And my day's compass downward bears;
Nor labour I to stem the tide
Through which to thee I swiftly glide.

'Tis true, with shame and grief I yield, 105
Thou, like the van, first took'st the field,
And gotten hast the victory
In this adventuring to die
Before me, whose more years might crave
A just precédence in the grave; 110
But, hark! my pulse like a soft drum
Beats my approach, tells thee I come;
And slow howe'er my marches be,
I shall at last sit down by thee.

The thought of this bids me go on, 115
And wait my dissolutïon
With hope and comfort. Dear (forgive
The crime) I am content to live
Divided, with but half a heart,
Till we shall meet and never part. 120

1 **saint** endearment as well as religious title; cf. Milton *I thought I saw my late espoused saint.* 15 **wet glasses** crude magnifying glass. 55 **little world** the microcosm (man relative to world, world to universe, etc., mirrored the macrocosm. Cf. Donne *Goodmorrow, Sun-rising.* 71 **parcel** area of land.

COMMENTARY 5

King Charles I
1625–1649

Pre-War Poets

This is the most difficult phase of the century to pattern into literary history. It is usually done by calling these poets Caroline, or Cavalier, lyrists; or The School of Jonson. Indeed, Marmion, Randolph and Suckling were disciples of Jonson; so was Herrick; but Herrick was 20 years older than the others, and Jonson another 20 older than him. In any case, as I have tried to show in Vol. I, lyric is not the point for Jonson, but mordant satire and an arctic gloom. Many of the poems here were written for singing, and set by a friendly talent such as Lawes, and performed at home or in a masque or play. But the best writing does not lie there; it is in the curt epigram, whether tart or, like Herrick's to Julia, lascivious; and in the longer discursive poems such as the farewells of Suckling and Herrick. The sense of writing *words* predominates. The originality is mainly verbal. It is modern. Randolph, for example, has a candid rather awkward forcefulness with words; Suckling has it too:

> We are too dull and lumpish rather:
> Would they could find us both in bed together.

But it is not helpfully classed as cavalier, and so restricted to an area of society and a political allegiance. Strode has it—admittedly a royalist clergyman but as a poet it is his documentary ability that matters:

> the open back below
> And three long legs alone do make it show
> Like a huge trivet or a monstrous chair
> With the heels turned upward.

We are somewhere between Larkin's *Whitsun weddings* and Ferlinghetti's *Away above a harborful*. It is the uncertainty that's modern. Baron writes with it: 'these small clicking orbs' of the watch hold but fail to grasp the rich confusion of a universe which clockmaker Newton was soon to take over from 'the eternal Mind's poetic thought'.

It is presumably their uncertainty that makes them so difficult to categorise. They write insipid pop that enchants the entire century—Strode's *On Chloris walking in the snow,* Habington's *Roses in the bosom of Castara,* ditties in which all serious virtue drains out of the great symbols they use, snow, cloisters, phoenix, marble. Yet they can also write with profound original vision—Strode about nature, Habington about time and eternity. Uncertainly, they war within their own talents.

The one constant theme is awareness of war, and of royalty. Marmion, Suckling and Fane served in the civil war, Godolphin was killed in it. I have put this section together in such a way that by the end of the war nearly all its members were dead or had stopped writing. Military allusions beat quietly all through their work: Randolph uses civil war as an image in the first poem here, Suckling, Fane, Harding sound it more loudly at the end; in the next section it is taken up fully by Shirley, Cleveland, Lovelace.

The technical peculiarity of this section is the conceit. It shines in epitaphs, which are themselves a characteristic genre of the period. The new kind of conceit differs even from Carew's contemporary epitaphs on Maria Wentworth—the corpse as broken china, or an eggshell which the soul has hatched out of, the 'chaste polygamy' of being a bride to all the virtues. The epitaphs of Herrick, or Barksdale, are less intellectual than that; prettier. Looking further, to include Herrick's Julia poems, and popular set-pieces such as the anonymous *Complimental and amorous poems* here, Strode's Chloris, Habington's roses, we find the prettiness developed into an attention to the *thing*—the thing being talked about, or its image—rather than the idea. This is Elizabethan but smaller scale: rococo. These poems are filled like a toy snowstorm with tiny glamours—crystal, roses, lilies, cherries, birds, gems. These things stand as ikons for things potentially too big for them, things of vital importance on the other side of the snowstorm's glass—breasts, breath, babies, eyes. Should we draw the obvious moral conclusions? Certainly Strode handles his conceits in such a way as to depersonalise Chloris; she is aesthetic object, in classically allusive anonymity. Then the gold of Danaë turns into silver snow, the snow into birds, then tears and diamonds—the prettiness mutation. An inherently sensuous theme, snowflakes melting on a girl's breasts, is treated with so much aesthetic 'purity'—softly, silver, whiteness, tear, froze—that we suspect prurience, or at least frigidity, in the poet.

Another way of looking at this phase is to see it as a time when greatness could not yet be achieved. Milton was waiting. Marvell, who was really the only poet to find a way of incorporating the uncertainties and fears of the civil war creatively into poetry, was too young. These poets repeatedly anticipate him. Strode's 'legs of skin', for instance, and in Habington 'our loving coffins' which are 'thrust' like genitals of the grave. Stanzas 3 and 7 of Habington *To Castara: of true delight* fit Eliot's definition of Marvellian wit—'tough reasonableness beneath the slight lyric grace'—more exactly than Marvell does (for Marvell, more strenuously bizarre, is never reasonable). To pursue this line, work backwards from Marvell's geometrical images to Strode's in *Westwell Downs*, then Cleveland *Mark Antony* in section 6 and *Complimental and amorous poems* to see that both the intellectualist and the bizarre kinds of image work at a fairly popular level. What kinds work in our own popular songs? Can we draw conclusions from the prevalence of a particular kind? Beyond that, can we ask what it means for a culture to be so taken with *comparison*, as a way of admiring, as the Caroline was?

Further suggestions. Major independent work could still be done on Randolph, Strode, Jordan, Barksdale and, especially, the miscellanies. The miscellanies rise about 1640 and are of great importance for about 50 years. Start from the appendix to Ault's *17th-century lyrics*. Habington needs building into the structure of 17th-century poetry, secular and religious (but then the structure hardly exists yet; what we most need is a serious and catholic literary historian for the period). The following topics could be taken up on a smaller scale. Fairies; and see section 2. Fetishes: see section 4, and include Herrick (fixated on clothes and breasts and, to less effect, legs, tears, bees); follow up through a really detailed history of costume. For other fetish poems see, apart from section 4, Cleveland (bee); Davenant *Lark* and *This lady* (lawn); Lovelace; Cartwright *Circumcision* (can a fetish be religious? see Crashaw on the wardrobe of Christ crucified, and section 7 generally); Heath *Dancing;* Cowley *Light* (his *Clad all in white* is part of a sidetrack where clothing turns out to be skin; cf. Lovelace in *Aramantha* and *Bonaroba,* Newcastle *Love's commission,* Duchess of Newcastle *Soul's garment,* Traherne *Preparative*); Waller *Tree, Fall* (also his *Girdle* and others not printed here). Leigh, Ayres and Aphra Behn treat fetishes differently—the fixations are shifting.

The pastoral of this section may be compared with that of

2; start from Randolph and W. W. Greg *Pastoral poetry and pastoral drama* 1906, for classical and continental excursions. It is from Randolph that we can move forward in pastoral too, to Milton (*Paradise lost* IV, VII; *L'allegro, Il penseroso*), Marvell, Duchess of Newcastle *Hare,* Cotton *Evening* and so into 18th-century nature poetry. See P. V. Marinelli *Pastoral* 1971.

The epitaph should be studied. Why is it more important in some periods—mortality rates, or vehicle for a favoured style or content? Which dead are mourned? See Jonson, and others in section 1; W. Browne *Pembroke,* Beedome, Carew *Villiers, Wentworth;* Herrick, Barksdale, Fane, Shirley, James and Cleveland as a pair, Montrose, Lady Dyer. Compare some with another period, e.g. Collins *How sleep the brave;* consider the religious poems on death and resurrection, e.g. G. Herbert, Traherne, Wanley, Norris.

Epithalamions: start from Donne and others writing for the wedding of Elizabeth of Bohemia (see Wotton); *Solomon's song,* Spenser, Jonson, the endings of comedies, masques, *Paradise lost* IV, Hopkins, Carew *Hymeneal dialogue,* Herrick in Volume I, Randolph *Milkmaid's epithalamion* not printed here, Suckling *Ballad upon a wedding* not printed here, Lovelace's poem for Stanley's wedding anniversary (not here), Philipot.

Finally, idiom. In these poems alien and complicated vocabularies have been digested; but the language is still alive; it can be simple without being insipid, complicated without pomposity: 'Such delicate bodies sleep, and are laid by In their repositories. They do not die'. The syntactical ease which 18th-century critics thought was the invention of Waller and Denham (possibly learned from Fairfax as a translator of Tasso in 1600) is already here in the ranging capable syntax and casual idiom of a most various lot of writing. These qualities are worth documenting; then on to the *peculiarities* of language observable in Herrick (rustic diction) and in the micro-bizarre more generally. Language is the approach to Suckling: like Jonson and Shelley he is best when beastly: see his *Farewell* and cf. Jonson *Courtworm, Sir V. Beast* and the language of his masques, e.g. the witches in *Masque of queens;* cf. Shelley's angrier work, e.g. *Peter Bell, Oedipus.*

THOMAS RANDOLPH

Son of a nobleman's steward in Northamptonshire. Wrote a poem on the incarnation at the age of 9. Westminster School; Trinity College, Cambridge. Although a 'son of Ben', he stayed in Cambridge writing and producing plays till c.1632. Then devoted himself to dissipation in London, fell into debt and bad health, died of smallpox aged 29. *Poems* and 2 plays, 1638, ed. J. J. Parry 1917; *Poetical and dramatic works* ed. W. C. Hazlitt 2 vols. 1875; *Poems* ed. G. Thorn-Drury 1929.

An ode to Master Anthony Stafford, to hasten him into the country°

      Come, spur away!
I have no patience for a longer stay
        But must go down
And leave the chargeable° noise of this great town.
    I will the country see,   5
      Where old simplicity,
        Though hid in grey,°
      Doth look more gay
Than foppery in plush and scarlet clad.
    Farewell, you city wits that are   10
      Almost at civil war;
'Tis time that I grow wise when all the world grows mad.

      More of my days
I will not spend to gain an idiot's praise,
        Or to make sport   15
For some slight puisnë of the inns of court.°
    Then, worthy Stafford, say,
      How shall we spend the day,
        With what delights
        Shorten the nights,   20

When from this tumult we are got secure?—
   Where mirth with all her freedom goes,
     Yet shall no finger lose;°
Where every word is thought, and every thought is pure.

      There from the tree   25
We'll cherries pluck, and pick the strawberry,
     And every day
Go see the wholesome country girls make hay,
    Whose brown hath lovelier grace
    Than any painted face   30
        That I do know
        Hyde Park can show;
Where I had rather gain a kiss than meet
   (Though some of them in greater state
    Might court my love with plate)   35
The beauties of the Cheap° and wives of Lombard Street.

      But think upon
Some other pleasures—these to me are none.
     Why do I prate
Of women, that are things against my fate?   40
    I never mean to wed
    That torture to my bed:
        My Muse is she
        My love shall be.
Let clowns° get wealth, and heirs; when I am gone,   45
   And the great bugbear, grisly Death,
    Shall take this idle breath,
If I a poem leave, that poem is my son.

      Of this, no more!
We'll rather taste the bright Pomona's° store: 50
     No fruit shall 'scape
Our palates, from the damson to the grape;
    Then, full, we'll seek a shade
    And hear what music's made:
        How Philomel°   55
        Her tale doth tell
And how the other birds do fill the choir—
   The thrush and blackbird lend their throats,
    Warbling melodious notes.
We will all sports enjoy which others but desire: 60

      Ours is the sky,
Where at what fowl we please our hawk shall fly;
     Nor will we spare

To hunt the crafty fox or timorous hare,
 But let our hounds run loose   65
  In any ground they'll choose;
   The buck shall fall,
   The stag, and all.
Our pleasures must from their own warrants be,
 For to my Muse, if not to me,   70
  I'm sure all game is free:
Heaven, earth, are all but parts of her great royalty.°

  And when we mean
To taste of Bacchus'° blessings now and then,
  And drink by stealth   75
A cup or two to noble Barkley's health,
  I'll take my pipe and try
  The Phrygian° melody,
   Which he that hears
   Lets through his ears   80
A madness to distemper all the brain;
  Then I another pipe will take
  And Doric music make,
To civilise° with graver notes our wits again.

° **country** cf. other rural retreat poems, e.g. Strode *Westwell Downs*; Lovelace *Grasshopper*; Cotton *Evening*. 4 **chargeable** wearisome and expensive. 7 **grey** uncoloured cloth. 16 **puisne of the inns of court** junior student of the law schools. Origin of the word puny. The 4 inns of court—Inner Temple, Middle Temple, Lincoln's Inn, Gray's Inn— are colleges constituting the English bar. At this time they were used as postgraduate finishing-schools. 23 **no finger lost** mirth will not diminish by even a little? or, mirth will not degenerate from freedom into license of the kind indicated by rude gestures? 36 **Cheap** Cheapside, then a market area, and Lombard Street, where the bankers live, in the City of London. 45 **clowns** fools. 50 **Pomona** goddess of fruit. The circumlocution has an 18th-century ring. 55 **Philomel** see Brathwaite *I am not.* 72 **royalty** realm. 74 **Bacchus** wine god. 78 **Phrygian** the exciting one of the 'modes' of ancient Greek music; the Dorian was solemn and restraining, the Lydian relaxing and sensual. 84 **civilise** first recorded use 1601.

ANONYMOUS

from Complimental and amorous poems

On her paps

Her paps like two fair apples in their prime:
From those blessed sweets love sucks his summertime.

On her good thoughts

Her mindful breast perfumes with frankincense
And sweetest odours every fainting sense.

On her waist and ribs

Fitly so named since it doth waste   5
Men's lives until it be embraced;
Her ribs with white all arm̀d be,
Compact with curious symmetry.

On her skin and flesh

Her lovely skin is white, like curds new pressed,
And snowy flesh as soft as wool new dressed.   10

On her navel

Here love delights the wandering thought
Whilst that mine eyes astray are brought,
Since nature here would fain unite
In curious circles busy sight.

Academy of Compliments
1640, 1648, 1650, 1663
etc.

THE REVEREND WILLIAM STRODE

Came from a family of Devonshire squires. Westminster School; entered Christ Church, Oxford, in 1617 and stayed to become chaplain to Bishop Corbet, public orator and proctor; 'a most florid preacher'. In 1636 wrote a tragi-comedy, *The floating island*, with music by Lawes, which was acted by students before Charles I and Queen Henrietta-Maria on a visit to Oxford. Poems remained uncollected till 1907 when ed. B. Dobell.

On Chloris° walking in the snow

I saw fair Chloris walk alone,
Whilst feathered rain came softly down,
And Jove° descended from his tower
To court her in a silver shower.
The wanton snow flew on her breast   5
Like little birds unto their nest;
But overcome with whitness there,
For grief it thawed into a tear;
Thence falling on her garment's hem,
To deck her, froze into a gem.   10

—W. PORTER ed. *Madrigals and airs* 1632; etc.

° **Title** about the most frequently printed of all 17th-century poems in contemporary miscellanies. 3 **Jove** see Danaë in Nashe *Valentines*.

The commendation of music

When whispering strains, with creeping wind,
    Distil soft passion through the heart;
And when at every touch we find
    Our pulses beat, and bear a part;

When threads can make 5
A heart-string shake:
    Philosophy
    Can not deny
Our souls consist of harmony.

When unto heavenly joys we feign 10
    Whate'er the soul affecteth most,
Which only thus we can explain,
    By music of the heavenly host,
        Whose lays, methink,
        Make stars to shrink: 15
        Philosophy
        May judge thereby
Our souls consist of harmony.

O lull me! lull me! charming air,
    My senses rock with wonder sweet; 20
Like snow on wool thy fallings are;
    Soft as a spirit's are thy feet;
        Grief who need fear
        That hath an ear?
        Down let him lie 25
        And slumbering die
And change his soul for harmony.

On the Bible

Behold this little volume here enrolled:°
'Tis the Almighty's present to the world.
Harken, earth's earth! each senseless thing can hear
His Maker's thunder, though it want an ear.
God's word is senior to his works; nay rather, 5
If rightly weighed the world may call it father:
God spake, 'twas done; this great foundatïon
Is the Creator's exhalatïon
Breathed out in speaking. The best work of man
Is better than his word; but if we scan 10
God's word aright, his works far short do fall:
The word is God,° the works are creatures all.
The sundry pieces of this general frame
Are dimmer letters, all which spell the same
Eternal word; but these cannot express 15
His greatness with such easy readiness,

And therefore yield. The heavens shall pass away,
The sun and moon and stars shall all obey
To light one general bonfire; but his word,
His builder-up, his all-destroying sword,   20
That still survives; no jot of that can die;
Each tittle measures immortality.
    The word's own Mother, on whose breast did hang
The world's upholder drawn into a span,
She, she was not so blest because she bare him   25
As 'cause herself was new-born and did hear him:
Before she had brought forth she heard her Son
First speaking in the annunciatiön;
And then, even then, before she brought forth child,
By name of blessèd she herself enstyled.°   30
    Once more this mighty word his people greets,
Thus lapped and thus swathed up in paper sheets:
Read here God's image with a zealous eye,
The legible and written Deity.

1 **enrolled**   literally volume = scroll. 12 **The word is God**   see *John* i.
1–3. 30 **enstyled**   'for, behold, from henceforth all generations shall call
me blessed'—Mary in the Magnificat at the annunciation (*Luke* i), also
sung daily at evensong in the Church of England. Cf. nativity poems
here by Drummond, Quarles, Crashaw, Joseph Beaumont, Watkyns.

On Westwell Downs°

When Westwell Downs I 'gan to tread,
Where cleanly winds the green did sweep,
Methought a landscape there was spread,
Here a bush and there a sheep:
    The pleated wrinkles on the face   5
    Of wave-swollen earth did lend such grace
    As shadowings in imagery
    Which both deceive and please the eye.

The sheep sometimes did tread a maze
By often winding in and in,   10
And sometimes round about they trace,
Which milkmaids call a fairy ring:
    Such semi-circles have they run,
    Such lines across so trimly spun,
    That shepherds learn, whene'er they please,   15
    A new geometry with ease.

The slender food upon the down
Is always even, always bare,
Which neither spring, nor winter's frown
Can aught improve or aught impair: 20
    Such is the barren eunuch's chin
    Which thus doth evermore begin
    With tender down to be o'ercast
    Which never comes to hair at last.

Here and there two hilly crests   25
Amidst them hug a pleasant green,
And these are like two swelling breasts
That close a tender fall between:
    Here could I read, or sleep, or pray
    From early morn till flight of day.   30
    But hark! a sheep's bell calls me up,
    Like Oxford college bells, to sup.

° **Westwell Downs** in Oxfordshire. Cf. Arnold *Thyrsis, Scholar-gipsy*.

On a great hollow tree

Prithee stand awhile and view this tree
Renowned and honoured for antiquity
By all the neighbouring twigs—for such are all
The trees adjoining, be they ne'er so tall,
Compared to this. If here Jack Maypole° stood,   5
All men would swear 'twere but a fishing-rod.
Mark but the great trunk, which when you see,
You see how many woods and groves there be
Comprised within one elm. The hardy stock
Is knotted like a club, and who dares mock   10
His strength by shaking it? Each brawny limb
Could pose° the centaur° Monychus, or him
That waved a hundred hands,° ere he could wield
That sturdy weight, whose large extent might shield
A poor man's tenement. Great Ceres' oak   15
Which Erysíchthon° felled, could not provoke
Half so much hunger for his punishment
As hewing this would do by consequent.
    Nothing but age could tame it. Age came on,
And lo, a lingering consumptïon   20
Devoured the entrails, where an hollow cave,

Without the workman's help, began to have
The figure of a tent: a pretty cell,
Where grand Silenus° might not scorn to dwell,
And owls might fear to harbour though they brought   25
Minerva's° warrant for to bear them out
In this their bold attempt.
                           Look down into
The twisted curls, the wreathing to and fro
Contrived by nature, where you may descry
How hall° and parlour, how the chambers lie.   30
And were't not strange to see men stand alone
On legs of skin without or flesh or bone?
Or that the selfsame creature should survive
After the heart is dead? This tree can thrive
Thus maimed and thus impaired: no other prop   35
But only bark remains to keep it up.
Yet thus supported it doth firmly stand,
Scorning the sawpit, though so near at hand:
No yawning grave this grandsire elm can fright,
Whilst youngling trees are martyred in his sight.   40
   O learn the thrift of nature, that maintains
With needy mire stolen up in hidden veins
So great a bulk of wood. Three columns rest
Upon the rotten trunk, whereof the least
Were mast for Argos.° The open back below   45
And three long legs above do make it show
Like a huge trivet or a monstrous chair
With the heels turned upward. How proper, O how fair
A seat were this for old Diógenës°
To grumble in, and bark out oracles,   50
And answer to the raven's augury
That builds above. Why grew not this strange tree
Near Delphos? Had this wooden majesty
Stood in Dodona forest, then would Jove
Forgo his oak and only this approve.   55
Had those old Germans that did once admire
Deformèd groves, and worshipping with fire
Burnt men unto their gods, had they but seen
These horrid stumps, they canonised had been,
And highly too: this tree would calm more gods   60
Than they had men to sacrifice, by odds.
   You hámadryadës,° that wood-born be,
Tell me the causes how this portly tree
Grew to this haughty stature? Was it then
Because the mummies of so many men   65
Fattened the ground? or 'cause the neighbour spring

Conduits of water to the root did bring?
Was it with Whitsun° sweat, or ample snuff
Of my lord's beer, that such a bigness stuffs
And breaks the bark? O this it is, no doubt!   70
This tree, I warrant you, can number out
Your Westwell animals and distinctly tell
The progress of this hundred years, as well
By lords and ladies as ere Rome could do
By consulships.° These boughs can witness too   75
How goodman° Berry tripped it in his youth
And how his daughter Joan° of late forsooth
Became her place. It might as well have grown,
If Pan° had pleased, on top of Westwell Down
Instead of that proud ash, and easily   80
Have given aim to travellers passing by
With wider arms. But see, it more desired
Here to be loved at home than there admired;
And porter-like it here defends the gate
As if it once had been great Askapate.°   85
Had warlike Arthur's° days enjoyed this elm,
Sir Tristram's blade and good Sir Lancelot's helm
Had then bedecked his locks with fertile store
Of votive relics which those champions wore;
Until perhaps (as 'tis with great men found)   90
Those burdenous honours crushed it to the ground.
But in these merry times 'twere far more trim
If pipes and citterns° hung on every limb;
And since the fiddlers it hath heard so long,
I'm sure by this time it deserves my song.   95

5 **Maypole** centre of the May Day fertility rites and holiday-making. In the country it would be a birch trunk. Dancers held onto ribbons tied to the top. Parliament forbade maypoles as heathen in 1644; they returned at the Restoration but the last known was a 134-foot cedar pole erected in the Strand, London, 1661. It was taken down in 1717 and Newton moved it to Essex to take the weight of a telescope. Jack may be a confusion with Jack i' the Green, a man dressed up as a green tree, which was another feature of May Day. 12 **pose** puzzle, nonplus. **centaur** half horse, half man. I can't trace one with this name. 13 **hundred hands** Briareus, a titan with 100 hands. 16 **Erysichthon** the earth-ripper, cut down trees in a grove sacred to Demeter (Ceres, corn goddess) and was punished with such hunger that he ate his own arms and legs. 24 **Silenus** wood-dwelling friend of Bacchus, lustful and riotous. 26 **Minerva** goddess of wisdom; the owl was her emblem. 30 **hall . . . parlour . . . chambers** public room, private day room, bedrooms, in a great house. 45 **Argos** Greek for swift; name of Jason's galley when he and the other Argonauts sailed for the golden fleece. 49 **Diogenes** Greek philosopher c.412–323 B.C. Said to have lived in a barrel. For the Delphic oracle see Herrick *Unlacing*. The oldest oracle

in Greece was Zeus' at Dodona; the messages came from the tops of the oaks there. The oak was sacred to Zeus, as to other thunder gods, such as the Norse Thor and the Teutonic Donar referred to at 56. Comparative religion and anthropology advanced with the 17th-century theologians and antiquaries. 62 **hamadryades** dryads, tree-nymphs. 68 **Whitsun** used to be celebrated by midsummer feasting called W. ale. The lord's beer refers to a tenant's dinner, perhaps at the end of harvest. The tree = a fat old peasant. 75 **consulships** in republican Rome supreme authority was vested in two consuls. They were elected annually so years dated by their names. 76 **goodman** yeoman; farmer. 77 **Joan** standard name for country girl. 79 **Pan** nature god. 85 **Askapate** Ascapart or Asclopard, a giant in the 14th-century verse romance *Bevis of Hampton*, very popular in the 17th century. 86 **Arthur** several 14th-century romances told his story; Malory's prose version, *Le morte Darthur*, was published by Caxton in 1485; Arthur was the shadowy central figure of Spenser's *Fairy Queen*; Milton considered him as a hero for a tragedy. 93 **cittern** cithern, a kind of guitar.

ROBERT BARON

Little known of him and nothing after 1650. Law student? Friend of James Howell. Paris. Plagiarised large passages from Milton's 1645 *Poems* in his *Cyprian academy* [i.e. school of love] 1647. See K. C. Slagle, R. B. Cavalier poet, *Notes and queries* 12 Oct 1935.

To Eliza, with a tulip-fashioned watch

Lady,
This measure of time accept with serene eye
From him whose love to you shall time out-vie.
See what disguise this spy of day doth wear:
A tulip—as the forge its garden were! 5
Indeed, heat procreates even flowers; but this
A piece of an Egyptian° mystery is.
   Time by a flower denotes how suddenly
Earth's frailer crops bloom, flourish, fade and die;
In special, beauty (that sweet tulip) hastes 10
To wait on time. Then use it while it lasts.
When these small clicking orbs you busy hear
Panting in their round journey like the spheres,°
Think so my constant heart doth palpitate
Towards you, and the pulse of my affections beat, 15
Ne'er to stand till she that each happy thing
Envies, the peevish Sister,° cuts the string.

7 **Egyptian** perhaps alluding to the tale that the sun's heat bred snakes out of Nilus' slime. 13 **spheres** see Herbert *Platonic love*. 17 **Sister** Fate. See Townsend *Dialogue*.

WILLIAM HABINGTON

Son of wealthy R.C. antiquary of Worcestershire who had been involved in Gunpowder Plot. Jesuit education in France. Refused to join the order, returned to England and married Lucy, youngest daughter of William Herbert, 1st baron Powis, a distant relative of Herbert of Cherbury and George Herbert, and the Pembrokes. *Castara*, his poems to her, first published anonymously in 1634, soon after the marriage. He left one son. Knew Cromwell. *Poems* ed. K. Allott, Liverpool 1948.

To roses in the bosom of Castara

Ye blushing virgins happy are
  In the chaste nunnery° of her breasts
(For he'd profane so chaste a fair,
  Who'er should call them Cupid's nests).

Transplanted thus, how bright ye grow,   5
  How rich a perfume do ye yield!
In some close garden, cowslips so
  Are sweeter than in the open field.

In those white cloisters live secure
  From the rude blasts of wanton breath,°   10
Each hour more innocent and pure,
  Till you shall wither into death.

Then that which, living, gave you room,
  Your glorious sepulchre shall be:
There wants no marble for a tomb,   15
  Whose breast hath marble been to me.

2 **nunnery** cf. Herrick *Upon roses*. These are red. 10 **breath** instead of the wind outside.

[192]

To Castara: of true delight

Why doth the ear so tempt° the voice
  That cunningly divides° the air?
Why doth the palate buy the choice
  Delights of the sea to enrich her fare?

As soon as I my ear obey,   5
  The echo's lost even with the breath;
And when the sewer° takes away
  I'm left with no more taste than death.

Be curious in pursuit of eyes,°
  To procreate new loves with thine: 10
Satiety makes sense despise
  What superstition thought divine.

Quick fancy, how it mocks delight!
  As we conceive, things are not such:
The glow-worm is as warm as bright   15
  Till the deceitful flame we touch.

When I have sold my heart to lust
  And bought repentance with a kiss,
I find the malice of my dust,
  That told me hell contained a bliss.   20

The rose yields her sweet blandishment,
  Lost in the fold of lovers' wreaths;
The violet enchants the scent
  When early in the spring she breathes;

But winter comes and makes each flower   25
  Shrink from the pillow where it grows;
Or an intruding cold hath power
  To scorn the perfume of the rose.

Our senses like false glasses show
  Smooth beauty where brows wrinkled are,   30
And makes the cosened° fancy glow:
  Chaste virtue's only true and fair.

---

1 **tempt** be tempted by, perhaps? 2 **divides** sings, descants. 7 **sewer** head waiter. 9 **eyes** cf. Herbert *Ode*. The meaning seems to be: Make eyes assiduously so as to excite plenty of girls to fall in love with you (and, perhaps, so as to produce plenty of reflections of yourself to fall in love with); yet the more you do, the less you'll really admire. 31 **cosened** conned, swindled.

To Castara: of what we were before our creation

When Pelion° wondering saw that rain, which fell
But now from angry heaven, to heavenward swell;
When the Indian Ocean did the wanton play,
Mingling its billows with the Baltic Sea,
And the whole earth was water: O where then   5
Were we, Castara? In the fate of men
Lost underneath the waves? or, to beguile
Heaven's justice, lurked we in Noah's floating isle?
We had no being then. This fleshly frame,
Wed to a soul long after, hither came   10
A stranger to itself. Those months that were
But the last age, no news of us did hear.
What pomp is then in us, who the other day
Were nothing and, in triumph now, but clay?

1 **Pelion** mountain range in Greece, near Olympus, home of the gods.
The gods drowned the original inhabitants in a flood, except for
Deucalion and his wife who were saved in an ark he had built (cf.
Drayton *To Browne*).

To Castara

Why should we fear to melt away in death,
May we but die together? When beneath
In a cool vault we sleep, the world will prove
Religious° and call it the shrine of love.
There, when o'th' wedding-eve some beauteous maid,   5
Suspicious of the faith of man, hath paid
The tribute of her vows, o'th' sudden she
Two violets sprouting from the tomb will see
And cry out, Ye sweet emblems of their zeal
Who live below, sprang ye up to reveal   10
The story of our future joys, how we
The faithful patterns of their love shall be?
If not, hang down your heads, oppressed with dew,
And I will weep and wither hence with you!

4 **Religious** cf. Donne *Canonization*.

A dialogue between Araphil and Castara

Ara. Castara, you too fondly court
　　　The silken peace with which we covered are:
　Unquiet Time may, for his sport,
　　　Up from its iron den rouse sleepy war.

Cas. Then in the language of the drum　　　　　　5
　　　I will instruct my yet affrighted ear;
　All women shall in me be dumb
　　　If I but with my Araphil be there.

Ara. If fate—like an unfaithful gale
　　　Which, having vowed to the ship a fair event,　　10
　O' th' sudden rends her hopeful sail—
　　　Blow ruin, will Castara then repent?

Cas. Love shall in that tempestuous shower
　　　Her brightest blossom, like the blackthorn, show;
　Weak friendship prospers by the power　　　　　　15
　　　Of fortune's sun; I'll in her winter grow.

Ara. If on my skin the noisome scar
　　　I should o'th' leprosy or canker wear,
　Or if the sulphurous breath of war
　　　Should blast my youth: should I not be thy fear?　20

Cas. In flesh may sickness horror move
　　　But heavenly zeal will be by it refined:
　For then we'd like two angels love,
　　　Without a sense, embrace each other's mind.

Ara. Were it not impious to repine,　　　　　　25
　　　'Gainst rigid fate I should direct my breath
　That two must be, whom heaven did join
　　　In such a happy one, disjoined by death.

Cas. That's no divorce. Then shall we see
　　　The rites in life were types° of the marriage state;　30
　Our souls on earth contracted° be,
　　　But they in heaven their nuptials consummate.

30 **types** see Quarles *Samson*. 31 **contracted** engaged.

To Castara: the reward of innocent love

We saw and wooed each others' eyes,
  My soul contracted then with thine
And both burnt in one sacrifice
  By which our marriage grew divine.

Let wilder youth, whose soul is sense,   5
  Profane the temple of delight
And purchase endless penitence
  With the stolen pleasure of one night.

Time's ever ours while we despise
  The sensual idol of our clay,   10
For though the sun doth set and rise,
  We 'joy one everlasting day

Whose light no jealous clouds obscure
  While each of us shine innocent;
The troubled stream is still impure;   15
  With virtue flies away content.

And though opinions often err,
  We'll court the modest smile of fame;
For sin's black danger circles her
  Who hath infection in her name.   20

Thus when to one dark silent room
  Death shall our loving coffins thrust,
Fame will build columns on our tomb
  And add a perfume to our dust.

from Quoniam ego in flagella paratus sum. David°

Fix me on some bleak precipice
  Where I ten thousand years may stand,
Made now a statue of ice,
  Then by the summer scorched and tanned;

Place me alone in some frail boat   5
  'Mid the horrors of an angry sea
Where I, while time shall move, may float
  Despairing either land or day;

Or under earth my youth confine
  To the night and silence of a cell   10
Where scorpions may my limbs entwine,
  O God!—so thou forgive me hell! . . .

° **Title** Vulgate version of A. V. *Psalm* xxxviii. 17, on of the Penitential
Psalms: 'and my sorrow is continually before me.'

THE REVEREND CLEMENT
BARKSDALE

From west country to Oxford, holy orders, chaplain of Lincoln College. Master of Hereford cathedral school; when Hereford occupied by parliamentary army he withdrew into the service of the Chandos family in the Cotswold Hills. *Nympha Libethris or the Cotswold Muse, presenting some extempore verses to the invitation of young scholars* 1651. Translated the Dutch poet Grotius and some of Crashaw's Latin epigrams.

Upon the decease of my infant lady

E'en so the nipping wind in May doth come
And blast the choicest fruit in the first bloom.

Yet shall this blossom of nobility,
Preserved by angels' care, immortal be.

Such delicate bodies sleep, and are laid by   5
In their repositories. They do not die.

SIDNEY GODOLPHIN

Son of the squire of Godolphin in Cornwall. Exeter College, Oxford, law student, travel. M.P. for a Cornish town; an adherent of Strafford; one of the last royalist members to leave the Long Parliament in 1642 (the reforming session which went to war with Charles I). Raised troops in Cornwall for the King but was shot in a skirmish at Chagford, Devon, while leading them back. A friend of Falkland, Clarendon, Hobbes and Suckling, who called him Little Sid. Small, shy, melancholy, widely liked. Mainly a writer of songs but not published in his lifetime. Ed. Saintsbury; and W. Dighton, Oxford 1931.

'Tis affection but dissembled

'Tis affection but dissembled,
  Or dissembled liberty,
To pretend thy passion changèd
  With change of thy mistress' eye
  Following her inconstancy.   5

Hopes which from favour flourish
  May perhaps as soon expire
As the cause which did them nourish;
  And, disdained, they may retire;
  But love is another fire.   10

For if beauty cause thy passion,
  If a fair resistless eye
Melt thee with its soft impression,
  Then thy hopes will never die
  Nor be cured by cruelty.   15

'Tis not scorn that can remove thee,
  For thou either wilt not see
Such loved beauty not to love thee,
  Or wilt else consent that she
  Judges as she ought of thee.   20

Thus thou either canst not sever
    Hope from what appears so fair;
Or, unhappier, thou canst never
    Find contentment in despair
    Nor make love a trifling care.   25

There are soon but few retiring
    Steps in all the paths of love
Made by such who, in aspiring,
    Meeting scorn their hopes remove:
    Yet even those ne'er change their love.   30

SIR JOHN SUCKLING

Born at Twickenham, of a Norwich family. Father comptroller of James I's household. Mother died when Suckling 4; father then married a widow. Suckling to Trinity College, Cambridge and Gray's Inn. 1628 inherited his father's estates and went to continent. 1631 joined army to help Gustavus Adolphus and was at Leipzig and other sieges (see Fanshawe *Ode*). 1632 returned to an extravagant life at Charles I's court, notorious especially for his repartee, and for gambling on bowls at the Piccadilly green, and at Tunbridge Wells where he once won £2000 at skittles. Invented cribbage. Visited Bath with Davenant; particularly close with George Goring; other friends included Carew, Lovelace and the philosophically-minded Hales, Falkland, Boyle, Stanley. Beaten up in quarrel over a girl. His play *Aglaura* staged 1637. 1639 raised a troop of horse (known for its colourful uniform) to help the King against the rebel Scots (see Godolphin). Involved in plot to take over the army for the King, fled to France 1641, fell into poverty and took poison in Paris. Unmarried. Portrait by Van Dyck. Poems collected in *Fragmenta aurea* 1646. *Works* ed A. H. Thompson 1910; *Poems and letters from MSS.* ed H. Berry 1960.

To a lady that forbade to love before company

What! no more favours? Not a ribband more,
Not fan nor muff to hold as heretofore?
Must all the little blisses then be left,
And what was once love's gift become our theft?
May we not look ourselves into a trance,   5
Teach our souls' parley at our eyes?° not glance,
Not touch the hand, not by soft wringing there
Whisper a love that only yes can hear?
Not free a sigh, a sigh that's there for you?
Dear, must I love you and not love you too?   10

Be wise, nice° fair: for sooner shall they trace
The feathered choristers from place to place
By prints they make in the air, and sooner say
By what right line the last star made his way
That fled from heaven to earth, than guess to know   15
How our loves first did spring, or how they grow.
Love is all spirit: fairies sooner may
Be taken tardy, when they night-tricks play,
Than we. We are too dull and lumpish rather:
Would they could find us both in bed together.   20

6 eyes   cf. Herbert *Ode*. 11 **nice**   coy.

O for some honest lover's ghost

O for some honest lover's ghost,
          Some kind unbodied post°
          Sent from the shades below!
          I strangely long to know
Whether the nobler chaplets wear,   5
Those that their mistress' scorn did bear
          Or those that were used kindly?

For whatsoe'er they tell us here
          To make those sufferings dear,
          'Twill there, I fear, be found   10
          That to the being crowned
To have loved alone will not suffice
Unless we also have been wise
          And have our loves enjoyed.

What posture can we think him in   15
          That, here unloved, again°
          Departs and's thither gone
          Where each sits by his own?
Or how can that Elysium° be
Where I my mistress still must see   20
          Circled in others' arms?

For there the judges all are just,
          And Sophonisba° must
          Be his whom she held dear,
          Not his who loved her here;   25
The sweet Philoclea since she died

Lies by her Pirocles his side,
        Not by Amphialus.

Some bays, perchance, or myrtle bough
            For difference° crowns the brow   30
            Of those kind souls that were
            The noble martyrs here;
And if that be the only odds
(As who can tell?), ye kinder gods,
            Give me the woman here.   35

2 **post** messenger. 16 **again** away. 19 **Elysium** heaven. 23 **Sophonisba**
the names are conventional. 30 **difference** recognition, heraldry.

Farewell to love

Well-shadowed landscape, fare ye well!
How I have loved you none can tell—
        At least, so well
        As he that now hates more
        Than e'er he loved before.   5

But, my dear nothings, take your leave:
No longer must you me deceive
        Since I perceive
        All the deceit, and know
        Whence the mistake did grow.   10

As he whose quicker eye doth trace
A false star shot to a marked place,
        Does run apace
        And, thinking it to catch,
        A jelly up does snatch: 15

So our dull souls, tasting delight
Far off, by sense and appetite,
        Think that is right
        And real good; when yet
        'Tis but the counterfeit.   20

O how I glory now that I
Have made this new discovery!
        Each wanton eye
        Inflamed before: no more
        Will I increase that score.   25

If I gaze now, 'tis but to see
What manner of death's-head 'twill be
    When it is free
    From that fresh upper skin,
    The gazer's joy and sin.   30

The gum and glistening which with art
And studied method in each part
    Hangs down the hair, it
    Looks just as if that day
    Snails there had crawled the hay.   35

The locks that curled o'er each ear be,
Hang like two master-worms to me,
    That (as we see)
    Have tasted to the rest
    Two holes, where they like it best.   40

A quick° corse, methinks, I spy
In every woman; and mine eye
    At passing by
    Checks and is troubled, just
    As if it rose from dust.   45

They mortify, not heighten me:
These of my sins the glasses be;
    And here I see
    How I have loved before.
    And so I love no more.   50

41 **quick**   living.

MILDMAY FANE
2ND EARL OF WESTMORLAND

Mildmay was his mother's maiden name. Northamptonshire estate; Emmanuel College, Cambridge. M.P. for Peterborough. Knighted at coronation of Charles I, royalist soldier, arrested by parliamentary forces, released on parole but estates sequestered and fined £2000; 1644 took the covenant, estates returned. One son, 5 daughters by first wife, who died 1640; four daughters, one son by second wife. *Otia sacra* printed privately 1648. Friend of Herrick and Cleveland. *Poems* ed. A. B. Grosart, Manchester 1879; see A. Harbage, 'An unnoted Caroline dramatist,' *Studies in philology* XXXI 1934 and E. Withington, 'The "fugitive" poetry of M.F.' *Huntington Library Bulletin* IX 1955.

Virtus vera nobilitas°

What doth he get who ere prefers
The scutcheons of his ancestors?
This chimneypiece of gold or brass,
That coat of arms blazoned in glass:
When those with time and age have end,   5
Thy prowess must thyself commend;
The smooty° shadows of some one
Or other's trophies carved in stone,
Defaced, are things to whet, not try
Thine own heroicism by.   10
For cast how much thy merit's score
Falls short of those went thee before:
By so much art thou in arrear
And stain'st gentility,° I fear.
True nobleness doth those alone engage   15
Who can add virtues to their parentage.

° **Title** Virtue the true nobility. **7 smooty** smutty, grimy. **14 gentility** nobility.

SAMUEL HARDING

Nothing known.

from Sicily and Naples, or the Fatal Union:
a tragedy

Noblest bodies are but gilded clay:
                Put away
  But the precious shining rind,
The inmost rottenness remains behind.
Kings, on earth though gods they be,   5
Yet in death are vile as we;
He, a thousands' king before,
Now is vassal unto more:
Vermin now insulting lie
And dig for diamonds in each eye,   10
Whilst the sceptre-bearing hand
Cannot their inroads withstand.
Here doth one in odours wade
By the regal unction made,
  While another dares to gnaw   15
  On that tongue, his people's law.
Fools! ah, fools are we, who so contrive
                And do strive
  In each gaudy ornament
Who shall his corpse in the best dish present.   20

1640

COMMENTARY 6

Civil War and Commonwealth
1642–1660

Casualties and Survivors

This section is designed to show the sweet sympathies of sections 4 and 5 shot with war. Lovelace's wartime goodbyes are hackneyed; but war also supplies Fanshawe's ode (it is world war), Shirley's epitaph on Strafford, Montrose's on himself, the desperate anonymous lovers in *The secret;* and, presumably, a good deal of Davenant's *Gondibert,* for real war must have its effect on epic.

More than that, the imagery of these poets is military. Shirley mostly uses conventional Caroline materials but sharply, like pikes; then suddenly brings in drum, laurel, sword, armour, sceptre; and his sacrificial altar prophesies the special fate of Charles king and martyr. Cleveland is sharp too: his language corkscrews into its topics and comes out with a pop. It is stuck with warlike references—in the *Bee-errant,* of course, which is mock (an erotic *Hudibras!*) but most tellingly in the plain sensuousness of *The antiplatonic,* where featherbed and candy are laid waste with words like flint, assails, soldier, wire, cuirassier, turnpikes, artillery.

There is plenty of smiling peaceful Caroline verse; but Shirley in *The triumphs of peace,* Davenant in *The triumphs of the Prince d'amour* can hear the coming war. They warn of it by warding it off. The date is 1635:

> Unarm! unarm! no more your fights
> Must cause the virgins' tears.

(This is the origin of Marvell's flowery militia, incidentally.) Lovelace on the whole uses pre-war imagery based on the fetishes of Herrick and Habington; yet his fan poem is prickly, the fan itself a 'shield of down'; Mars and Vulcan constantly accompany Venus:

> Not all the *arms* the god of *fire* e'er made.
> Can the soft *bulwarks* of nak'd love *invade.*

Lovelace expresses a more general sense of barbaric violence, corruption, impending doom. The 'blustering wind or swallowing wave' in his *Going beyond the seas* recurs all through Davenant—in the sinister storms and wet misty nights filled with sinning statesmen of his pre-war masques; in the crowbars and prongs of *The unfortunate lovers* in the second year of the war; in the satire of *The siege of Rhodes,* 1656; and in the acknowledgement of Leviathan's tyranny in *The law against lovers.* That in its turn echoes Lovelace in *Sannazar;* and that leads us toward the satiric despair of the Restoration.

Lovelace is often Augustan. Lucasta's fan is beyond emblem, conceit, fetish, halfway, as 'so divine an edifice' and 'plumy curtain,' to the instruments of vanity that populate *The rape of the lock;* whether regarded as fan or fanny, it is treated in terms of the possessor's moral tone, rather than in terms of its beauty or its emblematic significance.

Davenant's *Gondibert* presents other 18th-century qualities. The dreary theory of epic has muffled them, but his sentences tread with a Johnsonian air:

> And on her peopled bank they might behold
> > The toils of conquest paid with works of pride,
> The palace of King Agilulf the old
> > (Or monument: for, ere 'twas built, he died).

Davenant encompasses the crammed antitheses of Pope—'There from sick mirth neglected feasters reel'—and the scope of Shelley: 'Winds which have made the trembling world look old.'

In Davenant's gloomy brilliance, and Lovelace's 'invention tough', there is of course a lot of Milton. It is his period. Cleveland's elegy to King is companion to *Lycidas;* the masques of Davenant and Shirley to *Comus;* Gondibert to *Paradise lost.* But Milton's closest rival is Cartwright. Cartwright would have outshone Milton had he lived, and had he had the stamina. He can be exquisitely sweet and sexy in the manner of Shirley, but with clearer phrases—'this thin love . . . some strict downlooked men pretend . . . shuffling so our souls'. Usually though he is ironic, and can be funny—'one gaping haddock's head which will At least affright the stomach, if not fill'. His gloomiest verse takes strenuous liberties:

> Creeping o'er dead bones
> And cold marble stones

That I may mourn
Over thy urn
And appease thy groans.

In religious poems he is as rich as Crashaw, and more delicate; the early Milton was neither. But the blank verse of his plays reaches, easily, the vast familiarity of a Webster or Tennyson—'Things tumbling the common night o' th' world'; and, sometimes, almost the grand complicatedness of mature Milton: 'Through labyrinths of waters whose perplexed And interwoven banks shall be environed . . .'

We can distinguish between that and a smaller-scale ingenuity. The latter is typical of Cleveland—'inoculate carnation . . . nice phlebotomy'. It is an old trick but the areas alluded to are shifting, from scholasticism, alchemy, astronomy, to things closer at hand and more actual—horticulture, medicine, history (Davenant is particularly historical—another Augustan trait, surely?). Consider, for ingenuity, the elegies of Cleveland and Captain James. Cleveland's is notorious for it; therefore, perhaps, insincere, like *Lycidas* in Dr. Johnson's view? James on the other hand, a bluff skipper mourning his crew, must have been sincere. But he is ingenious too:

The winter's cold, that lately froze our blood,
Now were it so extreme might do this good
As make these tears bright pearls . . .

Ingenuity then was common to the age. What was its social function?

The bigger Miltonic complication becomes more common in sections 7–9 but it begins here, in Cartwright and also in Lovelace. Perversely, Lovelace uses pedantic diction in the primitivist *Aramantha*—expiate, officious, proscribe, eliminate. When abstract words come into play like this, what are the factors?

These poets are not easy to differentiate but two final points help. Notice Cleveland's *intimacy*—a function of linguistic penetration, perhaps—'coy pulse . . . jelly gloved'. He gets very close. Secondly, of them all Lovelace is the most surprising, the richest in implication. *Her muff* is an extraordinary poem. Ostensibly it is a conceit on muff as slang for vulva, given away in the last line. When you re-read it with this in mind it becomes more complicated, obviously. But it moves beyond that extra bawdy level, and beyond compliments of beauty, beyond the phase of emblems, in fact, into the phase of metaphor. He makes metaphors which are valuable for what they adumbrate rather than for their own prettiness, *or* their own significance in the 17th-century scheme of things. Fingers as 'your ten white nuns' has implications that stretch into our own time. It is a post-Imagist metaphor. It makes you think. The equations in this poem are not as obvious as they seem at first. The muff is of fur, the fur from an animal; but 'That beasts to thee a sacrifice should bleed, And strip themselves to make you gay' is a very complicated corollary. 'Thou wouldst thy hand should deeper pierce' is motto for Lovelace.

Suggestions beyond those intimated so far. Define and differentiate some of these poets (anthologies and literary histories often confuse and lump them). Follow on from Commentaries 4 and 5, e.g. about fetishes, miscellanies, anticipations of Marvell (cf. his *Horatian ode* and Fanshawe's). Work through some of the historical allusions in Fanshawe's *Ode;* to what extent were the British civil wars part of a European event? and how related to the events indicated by such titles as Industrial Revolution, French Revolution, Napoleonic Wars? Compare *Hollo my fancy* with Milton's *Vacation exercise* as a start to other obvious Miltonic comparisons. Study the masque backwards from Shirley and Davenant and forwards into opera and Shakespearean adaptations; see A. S. Knowland *Six Caroline plays* 1962, and Commentary 4.

For major independent work nearly all these writers offer opportunities, especially if studied aside from the history of the theatre, and the theory of epic, which have rather obscured them so far. On epic, see Commentary 3 and assemble *Gondibert* with Cowley *Davideis*, Waller *Summer Islands*, Milton (especially, for style, *Paradise lost* XI–XII and *Paradise regained* III–IV, where he is writing most obviously after the renaissance and in the 17th century), Dryden *Annus mirabilis*, Pope *Rape of the lock;* also the translators—Chapman trans Homer *Iliad* and *Odyssey* (cf. Dryden, Pope); Edward Fairfax trans Tasso *Godfrey of Boulogne or Jerusalem delivered* 1600; Fanshaw trans Camoens *Lusiad*. See G. Highet *The classical tradition*. N. B. Fairfax is not represented here because his Tasso is so characteristically Elizabethan. Consider this stanza:

> The knights passed through the castle's largest gate
>   (Though round about an hundred ports there shine);
> The door-leaves, framed of carvèd silver plate,
>   Upon their golden hinges turn and twine;

They stayed to view this work of wit and state:
  The workmanship excelled the substance fine,
For all the shapes in that rich metal wrought,
Save speech, of living bodies wanted naught.

Book XVI

SIR RICHARD FANSHAWE

Son of a Hertfordshire squire. Thomas Farnaby's famous
private school in London; Jesus College, Cambridge; Inner
Temple. 1627 abroad to learn languages; diplomacy in Paris
and Madrid. When civil war broke out 1642, joined Charles I
at Oxford and there met Anne Harrison, 19, an accomplished
girl (needlework, French, singing, lute, virginals, dancing,
riding) with a reputation for independence and high spirits.
They married in May 1644; a baby born 9 months later died
within a few months. Fanshawe was made secretary to Prince
Charles (the future Charles II) and followed him to Bristol,
where Anne joined him after the baby's death. Plague sent the
court to Barnstaple in Devon and thence they retreated to
Truro, Penzance, Land's End, the Scilly Isles, Jersey and Caen
in Normandy. Second child born 1646; and then they lived
for some time privately in London. He now published his
translation of Guarini's *Pastor fido*, with poems of his own;
and trans. *Selected parts of Horace* and *4th book* of *the Aeneid
on the loves of Dido and Aeneas*, both 1652. 1648 Fanshawe sent to conduct diplomacy in Ireland and Spain. Baronet
1650. Sent from Spain to Paris (travelling across the Bay of
Biscay from San Sebastian to Nantes), and Scotland. Lady
Fanshawe returned to London. He was taken prisoner at
battle of Worcester; she visited him at 4 every morning to
talk under his window where he was imprisoned in Whitehall.
Released for ill health and transferred to house-arrest in
Yorkshire. Here in 1654 at the age of 8 their daughter Anne
(the second child) died. 1655 published his translation of
The Lusiad, Camoens' epic of Portugal. 1658 both suffered
from ague but cured by a visit to the medicinal waters at Bath.
When Cromwell died, returned to London with Philip, Earl
of Pembroke; the diarist Evelyn was another friend. At the
Restoration Fanshawe became M.P. for Cambridge University
and ambassador to Portugal, then Spain; spent his last years
there. On Fanshawe's death in Madrid, the Queen Mother
tried to bribe his widow with a pension of 30,000 ducats to
become a Roman catholic, but though in financial straits she
refused. Her father died 1670. In 1676 she wrote a memoir

of her husband for her only surviving son, Richard (altogether she had 14 children but only 5 of them survived her husband). She died 1680. Richard, who had been rendered deaf and dumb by infection, died unmarried in 1694. *Shorter poems and translations* ed. N. W. Bawcutt, Liverpool 1964. *Pastor* ed. Staton and Simeone, Oxford 1964; *Lusiad* J. D. M. Ford, Cambridge Mass. 1940.

An ode upon occasion of His Majesty's proclamation° in the year 1630, commanding the gentry to reside upon their estates in the country.

Now war is all the world about
And everywhere Erínyës° reigns;
Or else, the torch so late put out,
       The stench remains.

Holland° for many years hath been   5
Of Christian tragedies the stage,
Yet seldom hath she played a scene
       Of bloodier rage.

And France, that was not long composed,
With civil drums again resounds   10
And, ere the old are fully closed,
       Receives new wounds.

The great Gustavus in the west
Plucks the imperial eagle's wing,
Than whom the earth did ne'er invest   15
       A fiercer king:

Revenging lost Bohemia
And the proud wrongs which Tilly did,
And tempereth the German clay
       With Spanish blood.   20

What should I tell of Polish bands
And the bloods boiling in the North?
'Gainst whom the furied Russiàns
       Their troops bring forth,

Both confident—this in his purse   25
And needy valour set on work;
He in his axe; which oft did worse
       The invading Turk—

Who now sustains a Persian storm;
There hell, that made it, suffers schism: 30
This war, forsooth! was to reform
        Mahometism.

Only the island which we sow
(A world without the world) so far
From present wounds it cannot show   35
        An ancient scar.

White Peace° (the beautifull'st of things)
Seems here her everlasting rest
To fix, and spreads her downy wings
        Over the nest;   40

As when great Jove, usurping reign,
From the plagued world did her exile
And tied her with a golden chain
        To one blest isle

Which in a sea of plenty swam,   45
And turtles sang on every bough—
A safe retreat to all that came,
        As ours is now.

Yet we, as if some foe were here,
Leave the despisèd fields to clowns   50
And come to save ourselves, as 'twere,
        In wallèd towns.

Hither we bring wives, babes, rich clothes
And gems—till now my Sovereign
The growing evil doth oppose,   55
        Counting° in vain

His care preserves us from annoy
Of enemies his realms to invade,
Unless he force us to enjoy
        The peace he made.   60

To roll themselves in envied leisure
He therefore sends the landed heirs,
Whilst he proclaims not his own pleasure
        So much as theirs.

The sap and blood o' th' land, which fled   65
Into the root and choked the heart,
Are bid their quickning power to spread
        Through every part.

O! 'twas an Act not for my Muse
To celebrate, nor the dull age,   70
Until the country air infuse
    A purer rage.

And if the fields as thankful prove
For benefits received, as seed,
They will, to quit° so great a love,   75
    A Virgil° breed,

A Tityrus that shall not cease
The Augustus of our world to praise
In equal verse, author of peace
    And halcyon° days.   80

Nor let the gentry grudge to go
Into those places whence they grew,
But think them blest they may do so.
    Who would pursue

The smoky glory of the town,   85
That may go till his native earth
And by the shining fire sit down
    Of his own hearth,

Free from the griping scrivener's bands°
And the more biting mercer's books?°   90
Free from the bait of oilèd hands
    And painted looks?

The country too even chops for rain:°
You that exhale it by your power,
Let the fat drops fall down again   95
    In a full shower.

And you bright beauties of the time,
That waste yourselves here in a blaze,
Fix to your orb° and proper clime
    Your wandering rays: 100

Let no dark corner of the land
Be unembellished with one gem;
And those which here too thick do stand,
    Sprinkle on them.

Believe me, ladies, you will find   105
In that sweet life more solid joys,
More true contentment to the mind,
    Than all town toys.

Nor Cupid there less blood doth spill,
But heads his shafts with chaster love,   110
Not feathered with a sparrow's° quill
        But of a dove.

There shall you hear the nightingale°
(The harmless Siren° of the wood)
How prettily she tells a tale   115
        Of rape and blood.

The lyric lark, with all beside
Of nature's feathered choir, and all
The commonwealth of flowers in'ts pride,
        Behold you shall: 120

The lily (queen), the (royal) rose,
The gilly-flower° (prince of the blood),
The (courtier) tulip° (gay in clothes),
        The (regal) bud,

The violet (purple senator)—   125
How they do mock the pomp of state
And all that at the surly door
        Of great ones wait.

Plant trees you may, and see them shoot
Up with your children, to be served   130
To your clean boards; and the fairest fruit
        To be preserved;

And learn to use their several gums:
  'Tis innocence in the sweet blood
Of cherry, apricots and plums   135
        To be imbrued.

° **proclamation** on his accession in 1603 James I had sent gentlemen
with no special business at court back to their country homes; Charles I
issued similar proclamations; Fanshawe is referring to one dated 9
September 1630. In 1629 Charles had also dissolved parliament, which
had passed three resolutions exercising authority for itself in religion and
taxation. He did not recall parliament for 11 years and civil war then
shortly broke out. 2 **Erinyes** the Furies, goddesses of vengeance for
wrongdoing. 5 **Holland** the period c.1560–1660 was one of almost
continuous war in varying parts of Europe. Most of the strife was
catholic v. protestant as well as empire v. people. Holland: by dynastic
marriages and annexations, the protestant Netherlands had become
subject to catholic Spain; persecution, insurrection, war on and off
1568–1648, with flare-ups in 1621 and 1629, ending in independence.
France: war between the catholics and the armed, political protestants
(Huguenots) on and off 1562–98, ending in the Edict of Nantes which
gave the Huguenots political equality, and possession of some cities,

but little religious freedom. They rebelled again in 1625 but 1627–28 their city La Rochelle was besieged and, in spite of help from England, taken. On 11 November 1630 Marie de'Medici tried unsuccessfully to bring down Richelieu. **Gustavus and Bohemia**: this refers to the 30 Years' War 1618–48, the worst war of the period. The protestant Bohemians (Czechs) elected to their throne Frederick (who had married James I's daughter Elizabeth—see Donne's epithalamion to them in Vol. I, and Taylor the Water Poet); but traditionally that throne belonged to the Holy Roman Emperor. This was the Emperor Ferdinand, who was head of the catholic German states. In alliance with Spain, Ferdinand attacked Frederick and extirpated protestantism from Bohemia. 1625–29 his successor employed General Tilly to defeat other protestants, who had come to Bohemia's aid, in Germany and Hungary. On 4 July 1630 the protestant King Gustavus Adolphus of Sweden (which then included most of the Baltic coastlands) invaded Germany and made Tilly withdraw. Tilly besieged Magdeburg, sacked and burnt it with terrible massacre, and occupied Leipzig; Gustavus besieged him there in 1631 (see Suckling) and defeated him. Gustavus was himself killed in 1632 at Lutzen but the Swedes won the battle. Later the French (although catholic) joined the Swedes and they devastated Germany until the Peace of Westphalia 1648. **Poland**: chronically at war with Russia since the 15th century, partly by the escapades of undisciplined bands of cavaliers. In 1612 the Orthodox Church in Russia was threatened by the presence of both catholic Poles and protestant Swedes; a popular rising expelled them. **Turks**: the Ottoman Empire included all the Balkans; it pressed N.W. into Austria and Poland. 15 **invest** install. 37 **peace** represented as a dove (turtle); and as the goddess Irene. 50 **clowns** peasants. 56 **counting** reckoning it vain to protect the realm from invasion unless peace is enjoyed inside it. 75 **quit** requite. 76 **Virgil** 70–19 B.C., poet of the *Pax Romana*. Author of the agricultural *Georgics* and the pastoral *Eclogues* as well as the epic of Rome, the *Aeneid*. Called himself Tityrus in the *Eclogues*. The name of the emperor Augustus, his patron, often applied to kings in 17th- and 18th-century verse. 80 **halcyon** bird of peace and calm. 89 **scrivener's bands** moneylender's bonds. 90 **mercer's books** silk-merchant's bills. 93 **chops for rain** cracks with drought. Rain = money? 99 **orb** sphere. 111 **sparrow** emblem of lust. 113 **nightingale** see Brathwaite *I am not*. 114 **Sirens** bird-women who lured sailors to danger with their singing. 122 **gilly-flower** wallflower or relation. 123 **tulip** usually striped.

ANONYMOUS

Hollo, my fancy!

In a melancholy fancy,
 Out of myself,
Thorough the welkin° dance I,
 All the world surveying,
 Nowhere staying,   5
Like unto the fiery elf:°
Over the tops of highest mountains skipping,
Over the plains, the woods, the valleys, tripping,
Over the seas without oar of shipping.
 Hollo, my fancy! whither wilt thou go?   10

Amidst the cloudy vapours
 Fain would I see
What are those burning tapers
 Which benight us
 And affright us,   15
And what the meteors be;
Fain would I know what is the roaring thunder
And the bright lightning which cleaves the clouds in sunder,
And what the comets° are at which men gaze and wonder.
 Hollo, my fancy! whither wilt thou go?   20

Look but down below me
 Where you may behold,
Where none can see or know me,
 All the world of gadding,
 Running, of madding—   25
None can their stations hold:
One he sits drooping all in a dumpish passion,
Another he is for mirth and recreation,
The third he hangs his head because he's out of fashion.
 Hollo, my fancy! whither wilt thou go?   30

See, see, see what a bustling!
 Now I descry

>   One another justling,
>   How they are turmoiling,
>   One another foiling,   35
>   And how I passed them by!
> He that's above, him that's below despiseth;
> He that's below doth envy him that riseth;
> Every man his plot and counter-plot deviseth.
>   Hollo, my fancy! whither wilt thou go?   40
>
>   Ships, ships, ships I descry now,
>   Crossing on the main!
>   I'll go too and try now
>   What they are projecting
>   And protecting   45
>   And when they turn again:
> One he's to keep his country from invading;
> Another he is for merchandise and trading;
> The other lies at home like summer's cattle shading.
>   Hollo, my fancy! whither wilt thou go?   50
>
>   Hollo, my fancy, hollo!
>   I pray thee come unto me,
>   I can no longer follow;
>   I pray thee come and try me,
>   Do not fly me,   55
>   Sith it will no better be;
> Come, come away! leave off thy lofty soaring;
> Come, stay at home, and on this book be poring;
> For he that gads abroad he hath the less in storing.
>   Welcome, my fancy! welcome home to me!

> —British Museum MS., variant in Douce Ballads; written
>   c.1639?

3 **welkin** sky or air. 6 **elf** Will o' the wisp, Jack o' Lantern, *ignis fatuus* (and other names), i.e. the flame-like glimmer seen over marshy ground caused by the spontaneous combustion of decaying vegetation; thought to be a demon. 19 **comets** more important because more visible before electric lighting; and of astrological significance though explained by Tycho Brache in the 1570s. Halley's comet passed in 1607.

Recipe° for toothache

> Take a pound of butter made in May,
> Clap it to her arse in a summer's day

And ever as it melts then lick it clean away:
'Tis a medicine for the toothache, old wives say.

New academy of compliments 1671 (1713 ed.)

° **Recipe**   followed in the miscellany by *Bess black as charcoal* (a song about copulation) and then by Shirley *The glories of our blood and state.*

JAMES SHIRLEY

Born London; Merchant Taylors' school; St. John's College, Oxford and St. Catharine's, Cambridge. Soon after 1619 took holy orders but by 1623 had become Roman catholic. Schoolmaster for two years, married, but 1625 went to London to write plays of all kinds, and elaborate masques such as *The Triumph of Peace* 1633, highly popular with the court audience. Acquainted with Ford, Massinger, Izaak Walton, Habington, Randolph, Stanley, Sherburne. Visited Dublin to entertain Strafford. Stricken with poverty when theatres closed 1642. Duke of Newcastle asked him to join royalist army but he seems to have made a living by teaching again. *Poems* 1646. Did not return to the theatre at the Restoration. In the great fire of London 1666, he and his wife Frances fled into the fields and died there two months later, on the same day. They left three sons and a married daughter; another daughter had already died. *Dramatic works and poems* ed. W. Gifford and A. Dyce 6 vols. 1833; *Poems* ed. R. L. Armstrong 1941. See Swinburne in *Fortnightly Rev.* XLVII 1890 repr. in *Contemporaries of Shakespeare* 1919; G. F. Sensabagh, 'Platonic love in *The lady of pleasure*' [comedy 1637] in *A tribute to G. C. Taylor*, Chapel Hill 1952.

from The Contention of Ajax and Ulysses°

The glories of our blood and state°
    Are shadows, not substantial things.
There is no armour against fate;
    Death lays his icy hand on kings:
        Sceptre and crown   5
        Must tumble down
And in the dust be equal made
With the poor crooked scythe and spade.

Some men with swords may reap the field
    And plant fresh laurels° where they kill;   10

But their strong nerves° at last must yield—
   They tame but one another still;
      Early or late
      They stoop to fate
And must give up their murmuring breath   15
When they, pale captives, creep to death.

The garlands wither on your brow:
   Then boast no more your mighty deeds.
Upon Death's purple altar now,
   See where the victor-victim bleeds.   20
      Your heads must come
      To the cold tomb.
Only the actions of the just
Smell sweet, and blossom in their dust.

° **Title** a masque; but the poem anthologized separately—see Anon. *Recipe.* 1 **blood and state** breeding and rank. 10 **laurels** emblems of victory. 11 **nerves** sinews.

from The Imposture°

A battle having been won, a male chorus enters waving branches of laurel to celebrate the victor.

You virgins that did late despair
   To keep your wealth from cruel men,
Tie up in silk your careless hair—
   Soft peace is come again.

Now lovers' eyes may gently shoot   5
   A flame that will not kill;
The drum was angry, but the lute
   Shall whisper what you will.

Sing io! io!° for his sake
   Who hath restored your drooping heads;   10
With choice of sweetest flowers make
   A garden where he treads;

Whilst we whole groves of laurel bring,
   A petty triumph to his brow
Who is the master of our spring   15
   And all the bloom we owe.°

° **Imposture** tragi-comedy 1640. See Davenant *Night's song.* 9 **io** Greek and Latin hurrah! 16 **owe** own.

Cupid's call

Ho! Cupid calls, come, lovers, come,
Bring his wanton harvest home!
The west wind blows, the birds do sing,
The earth's enamelled, 'tis high spring:
    Let hinds° whose soul is corn and hay   5
    Expect their crop another day.

Into love's spring-garden walk—
Virgins dangle on their stalk
Full-blown and playing at fifteen:
Come, bring your amorous sickles, then!   10
    See, they are pointing to their beds
    And call to reap their maidenheads.

Hark! how in yonder shady grove
Sweet Philomel° is warbling love
And with her voice is courting kings—   15
For since she was a bird she sings:
    There is no pleasure but in men,
    O come and ravish me again!

Virgins that are young and fair
May kiss and grow into a pair;   20
Then, warm and active, use your blood,
No sad° thought congeal the flood:
    Nature no medicine can impart
    When age once snows upon our heart.

5 **hinds** peasants. 14 **Philomel** see Brathwaite *I am not*. 22 **sad** grave.

CAPTAIN THOMAS JAMES

Captain of his own ship. May have sailed to Hudson's Bay in 1612. In 1631 the merchants of Bristol commissioned him to discover a northwest passage to Japan. Sailed on 3 May in the 70-ton *Henrietta Maria* (the Queen's name) with a crew of 22; no companion ships. 4 June, Greenland; 5 June, ice; July, Hudson's Bay; wintered by running the ship onto the ice and sailed it home the next summer, arriving October 1632 with the loss of 4 men. His *Strange and dangerous voyage* 1633 read by Coleridge who used it in *The ancient mariner.*

Lines on his companions who died in the northern seas

I were unkind unless that I did shed,
Before I part, some tears upon our dead;
And when my eyes be dry, I will not cease
In heart to pray their bones may rest in peace:
Their better parts (good souls) I know were given   5
With an intent they should return to heaven.
Their lives they spent, to the last drop of blood,
Seeking God's glory and their country's good;
And as a valiant soldier rather dies
Than yields his courage to his enemies,   10
And stops their way with his hewed flesh when death
Hath quite deprived him of his strength and breath:
So have they spent themselves; and here they lie,
A famous mark of our discovery.
We that survive perchance may end our days   15
In some employment meriting no praise,
And in a dunghill rot; when no man names
The memory of us but to our shames.
They have outlived this fear, and their brave ends
Will ever be an honour to their friends.   20

Why drop ye so, mine eyes? Nay, rather pour
My sad departure in a solemn shower:
The winter's cold, that lately froze our blood,
Now were it so extreme might do this good
As make these tears bright pearls, which I would lay   25
Tombed safely with you till doom's fatal day;
That in this solitary place, where none
Will ever come to breathe a sigh or groan,
Some remnant might be extant of the true
And faithful love I ever tendered you.   30

　O rest in peace, dear friends, and (let it be
No pride to say) the sometime part of me:
What pain and anguish doth afflict the head,
The heart and stomach, when the limbs are dead!
So grieved, I kiss your graves, and vow to die   35
A foster-father to your memory.

JOHN CLEVELAND

Father a poor priest and teacher in Leicestershire, and a royalist; but Cleveland educated locally by a presbyterian; Christ's College, Cambridge, with Milton, then St. John's, where he was elected a fellow in 1634. Ejected by parliament in 1645; joined royalist army at Oxford. After the war, tutoring and journalism in London. Friend of Samuel Butler. Pleased with the anagram on his name, Heliconean dew. *Poems* published 1647, 1651 and often reprinted and anthologzed in 17th century; ed. B. Morris and E. Withington, Oxford 1967.

On the memory of Mr. Edward King, drowned in the Irish Seas

I like not tears in tune, nor will I prize
His artificial grief that scans° his eyes;
Mine weep down pious beads, but why should I
Confine them to the Muses' rosary?
I am no poet here: my pen's the spout   5
Where the rain-water of my eyes run out,
In pity of that name whose fate we see
Thus copied out in grief's hydrography.
The Muses are not mermaids, though upon
His death the ocean might turn Helicon.°   10
The sea's too rough for verse: who rhymes upon't
With Xerxes° strives to fetter th' Hellespont.
My tears will keep no channel, know no laws
To guide their streams; but like the waves, their cause,
Run with disturbance till they swallow me   15
As a description of his misery.
    But can his spacious virtue find a grave
Within th' imposthumed bubble of a wave?
Whose learning if we sound, we must confess
The sea but shallow, and him bottomless.   20
Could not the winds, to countermand thy death,

With their whole card° of lungs redeem thy breath?
Or some new island in thy rescue peep
To heave thy resurrection from the deep?
That so the world might see thy safety wrought   25
With no less miracle than thy self was thought.
The famous Stagyrite,° who in his life
Had nature as familiar as his wife,
Bequeathed his widow to survive with thee,
Queen dowager of all philosophy: 30
An ominous legacy that did portend
Thy fate, and predecessor's second end!
Some have affirmed that what on earth we find
The sea can parallel for shape and kind:
Books, arts and tongues were wanting, but in thee   35
Neptune° hath got an university.
   We'll dive no more for pearl. The hope to see
Thy sacred relics° of mortality
Shall welcome storms and make the seaman prize
His shipwreck now more than his merchandise;   40
He shall embrace the waves and to thy tomb
(As to a Royaller Exchange)° shall come.
   What can we now expect? Water and fire,
Both elements° our ruin do conspire,
And that dissolves us which doth us compound;   45
One Vatican° was burnt, another drowned.
We of the gown our libraries must toss
To understand the greatness of our loss;
Be pupils to our grief, and so much grow
In learning as our sorrows overflow.   50
When we have filled the rundlets of our eyes,
We'll issue't forth, and vent such elegies
As that our tears shall seem the Irish Seas,
We floating islands, living Hebrides.

° **King** a promising young fellow of Christ's. He was on a voyage to
Ireland to visit his family in 1637 when the ship struck a rock and
sank and he was drowned. This was one of 23 Greek and Latin poems,
and 13 English (including Milton's *Lycidas*) published in *Justa Edou-
ardo King* 1638; other contributors included his brother Henry King,
and Henry More, both of Christ's, and Joseph Beaumont. 2 **scans** as
in scansion; with a pun on the scanning done by eyes. 10 **Helicon**
spring of inspiration. 12 **Xerxes** King of Persia, the Ahasuerus of the
Bible. Invaded Greece 480 B.C. via pontoons across the Dardanelles
(Hellespont); when the first bridge was swept away ordered the sea
to be given 300 lashes and put in chains. 22 **card** of the compass.
Stagyrite Aristotle, born at Stagira, most famous as a natural philosopher. 36 **Neptune** god of the ocean. 38 **relics** bones, as a saint's
bones are kept as sacred objects. 42 **Exchange** financial and commodity

market. The building Cleveland refers to was started in 1566, dubbed Royal by Queen Elizabeth and burnt in 1666. 44 **elements** see Beedome *Inquisition*. 46. **Vatican** nobody knows what this alludes to.

Mark Antony

Whenas the nightingale chanted her vespers
And the wild forester couched on the ground,
Venus invited me in the evening whispers
Unto a fragrant field with roses crowned,
    Where she before had sent   5
    My wishes' complement,
    Unto my heart's content
    Played with me on the green.
        Never Mark Antony
        Dallied more wantonly   10
With the fair Egyptian queen.°

First on her cherry cheeks I mine eyes feasted,
Thence fear of surfeiting made me retire;
Next on her warmer lips which, when I tasted,
My duller spirits made active as fire.   15
    Then we began to dart
    Each at another's heart
    Arrows that knew no smart,
    Sweet lips and smiles between.
        Never Mark Anthony *etc.*   20

Wanting a glass to plait her amber tresses,
Which like a bracelet rich deckèd mine arm,
Gaudier than Juno wears whenas she graces
Jove with embraces more stately than warm,
    Then did she peep in mine   25
    Eyes' humour crystalline:°
    I in her eyes was seen
    As if we one had been. *etc.*

Mystical grammar of amorous glances;
Feeling of pulses, the physic of love;   30
Rhetorical courtings, and musical dances;
Numbering of kisses arithmetic prove;
    Eyes like astronomy;
    Straight-limbed geometry;
    In her art's ingeny°   35
    Our wits were sharp and keen.

> Never Mark Antony
> Dallied more wantonly
> With the fair Egyptian queen.

11 **queen** Cleopatra. 26 **humour crystalline** fluid lens of the eye (scientific). Cf. Herbert *Ode*. 35 **ingeny** ingenuity.

Fuscara; or, the bee-errant

Nature's confectioner, the bee
(Whose suckets° are moist alchemy,
The still° of his refining mould
Minting the garden into gold),
Having rifled all the fields 5
Of what dainties Flora° yields,
Ambitious now to take excise
Of a more fragrant paradise,
At my Fuscara's sleeve arrived,
Where all delicious sweets are hived. 10
The airy freebooter distrains
First on the violets of her veins,
Whose tincture, could it be more pure,
His ravenous kiss had made it bluer.
Here did he sit and essence quaff 15
Till her coy pulse had beat him off,
That pulse which he that feels may know
Whether the world's long-lived or no.
    The next he preys on is her palm
(That almoner of transpiring balm), 20
So soft, 'tis air but once removed,
Tender as 'twere a jelly gloved.
Here, while his canting dronepipe° scanned
The mystic figures of her hand,
He tipples palmistry and dines 25
On all her fortune-telling lines.
He bathes in bliss and finds no odds
Betwixt this nectar and the gods'.
    He perches now upon her wrist,
A proper hawk for such a fist,° 30
Making that flesh his bill of fare
Which hungry cannibals would spare;
Where lilies in a lovely brown
Inoculate carnatïon°
(Her *argent* skin with *or*° so streamed 35

As if the Milky Way were creamed).
From hence he to the woodbine bends
That quivers at her fingers' ends,
That runs division on the tree
Like a thick-branching pedigree: 40
So 'tis not her the bee devours,
It is a pretty maze of flowers;
It is the rose that bleeds when he
Nibbles his nice phlebotomy.°
About her finger he doth cling   45
In the fashion of a wedding ring,
And bids his comrades of the swarm
Crawl like a bracelet 'bout her arm.
      Thus when the hovering publican°
Had sucked the toll of all her span,°   50
Tuning his draughts with drowsy hums
As Danes carouse by kettle-drums,
It was decreed, that posy gleaned,
The small familiar° should be weaned.
At this the errant's courage quails,   55
Yet aided by his native sails
The bold Columbus still designs
To find her undiscovered mines.
To the Indies of her arm he flies,
Fraught both with east and western prize;°   60
Which when he had in vain essayed,
Armed like a dapper lancepresade°
With Spanish pike, he broached a pore
And so both made and healed the sore:
For as in gummy trees there's found   65
A salve to issue at the wound,
Of this her breach the like was true,
Hence trickled out a balsam,° too.
But O, what wasp was't that could prove
Ravaillac° to my queen of love?   70
The king of bees, now jealous grown
Lest her beams should melt his throne,
And finding that his tribute slacks,
His burgesses and state of wax
Turned to a hospital,° the combs   75
Built rank and file like beadsmen's° rooms,
And what they bleed but tart and sour
Matched with my Danaë's° golden shower,
Live honey all—the envious elf
Stung her 'cause sweeter than himself.   80

Sweetness and she are so allied
The bee committed parricide.

Clievelandi Vindiciae; or Cleveland's Genuine Poems 1677

2 **suckets** sugar-plums. See Herrick's bee poems. 3 **still** distillation plant. Mould in the sense of vessel, as in jelly-mould, as a metaphor for the honeycomb. For alchemy see Carew *Rapture*. 6 **Flora** flower goddess. 23 **canting dronepipe** monotonously whining bagpipe—a rural instrument. 34 **Inoculate carnation** propagate carnations, by grafting lilies into brown skin; and/or, white and brown unite with flesh-pink. Either way, exact gardening terms. 35 **Argent . . . or** heraldic silver and gold. 44 **phlebotomy** surgical bleeding, as in Carew *Celia bleeding*. 49 **publican** tax- or toll-gatherer as in 'publicans and sinners'. 50 **span** of her fingers. 54 **familiar** member of a household; or, familiar spirit, attendant demon. 60 **prize** cf. Donne, 'Both the Indias of spice and mine'—*Sun-rising*. 62 **lancepresade** Spanish cavalryman. 68 **balsam** cf. Carew *Rapture*. 70 **Ravaillac** assassinated Henri IV of France by stabbing 1610; was executed in public by the rack, external and internal burning, butchery and being torn apart by four horses. Henri IV was grandfather of Henrietta-Maria, Charles I's queen. 75 **hospital** almshouse for old pensioners (beadsmen). 78 **Danaë** see Nashe *Valentines*.

To the state of love, or the senses' festival

I saw a vision yesternight
Enough to sate a Seeker's° sight—
I wished myself a Shaker there
And her quick pants° my trembling sphere:
It was a she so glittering bright   5
You'd think her soul an Adamite;°
A person of so rare a flame
Her body might be lined° with same.
Beauty's chiefest maid of honour;
You may break Lent° with looking on her.   10
   Not the fair abbess° of the skies,
   With all her nunnery of eyes,
   Can show me such a glorious prize.

And yet, because 'tis more renown
To make a shadow shine, she's brown: 15
A brown for which heaven would disband
The galaxy, and stars be tanned;
Brown by reflection, as her eye
Deals out the summer's livery;°

Old dormant° windows must confess   20
Her beams: their glimmering spectacles,
Struck with the splendour of her face,
Do the office of a burning-glass.
   Now where such radiant lights have shown,
   No wonder if her cheeks be grown   25
   Sunburned with lustre of her own.

My sight took pay but (thank my charms!)
I now empale her in my arms
(Love's compasses° confining you,
Good angels, to a circle too).   30
Is not the universe strait-laced°
When I can clasp it in the waist?
My amorous folds about thee hurled,
With Drake° I girdle in the world;
I hoop the firmament° and make   35
This, my embrace, the zodiac.
   How would thy centre° take my sense,°
   When admiration doth commence
   At the extreme circumference?

Now to the melting kiss that sips   40
The jellied philtre° of her lips,
So sweet there is no tongue can praise't
Till transubstantiate° with a taste.
Inspired like Mahomet° from above
By the billing of my heavenly dove,   45
Love prints his signets in her smacks,°
Those ruddy drops of squeezing wax
Which, wheresoever she imparts,
They're privy° seals to take up hearts.
   Our mouths encountering at the sport,   50
   My slippery soul° had quit the fort
   But that she stopped the sally-port.

Next to these sweets, her lips dispense
(As twin conserves of eloquence)
The sweet perfume her breath affords,   55
Incorporating with her words
(No rosary this votaress needs,
Her very syllables are beads).
No sooner 'twixt those rubies born
But jewels are in ear-rings worn;   60
With what delight her speech doth enter—
It is a kiss of the second venter;°
   And I dissolve at what I hear

As if another Ros'mond° were
Couched in the labyrinth of my ear.   65

Yet that's but a preludious bliss,
Two souls pickeering° in a kiss;
Embraces do but draw the line,°
'Tis storming that must take her in.
When bodies join and victory hovers   70
'Twixt the equal fluttering lovers,
This is the game. Make stakes, my dear!
Hark, how the sprightly chanticleer
(That Baron Tellclock of the night)
Sounds boutesel° to Cupid's knight.   75
    Then have at all, the pass is got,
    For coming off, O name it not!
    Who would not die upon the spot?

2 **Seekers** religious sect. The Shakers another sect (or = Quakers),
who practised devotional convulsions. They may already have practised
the celibate marriages for which the 18th-century Shakers were known.
4 **pants** heaving breasts. 7 **Adamite** hippy. There had been sects of
this name on and off for 1500 years. They were naturists who tried to
recover Adam's innocence by going naked, loving freely and so on. Cf.
Donne on Elizabeth Drury in his *Anniversaries*. 8 **lined** perhaps referring to a fashion for scarlet linings. 10 **Lent** included abstinence
from sex as well as meat etc. 11 **abbess** moon (classical moon goddesses = chastity) with attendant stars. 19 **livery** presumably the
reddish brown of early autumn, as in *Fuscara*. 20 **dormant** dormer. 29
compasses alluding to Donne's metaphor in *Mourning valediction*.
The angels of virtue are shut in as if by a magic circle? 31 **strait-laced**
tightly corsetted, hence narrow (as well as the metaphorical meaning,
prudish). The embrace narrows the universe and turns it into a girl.
34 **Drake** see Beedome. 35 **firmament** sky, hooped like a barrel. The
zodiac (see J. Taylor *Dick Swash*) is seen as a belt following the
ecliptic—the sun's apparent annual swoop north and south of the
equator. 37 **centre** of the earth; and poetic slang for vulva. **take my
sense** excite my senses; or, knock me out. 41 **philtre** love-potion. 43
transubstantiate(d) changed from one substance into another, as in
alchemy and especially theology (bread and wine into Christ's flesh and
blood). Perhaps the meaning is: the aphrodisiac jelly of her lips is so
sweet that no tongue can do it justice until made equally sweet by
tasting it. See Kynaston *Sugar and sweetness*. 44 **Mahomet** put grains
of wheat in his ear so that his dove could sit on his shoulder and peck
them out; this made people think he was being inspired from heaven. 46
smacks kisses. 49 **privy** secret (legal terminology). 51 **slippery soul**
tongue. It was half thought that the soul could slip out through a kiss,
or in orgasm. 62 **second venter** anatomical term for throat (2nd of
the visceral cavities, abdomen, thorax, head). 64 **Ros'mond** the Fair
Rosamond, mistress of Henry II. He was said to have kept her in a
house called Labyrinthus, built like a maze; but Queen Eleanor found
and poisoned her 1170. She was buried in a nunnery with the epitaph
Hic jacet in tumba rosa mundi non rosa munda; Non redolet sed olet

que redolere solet (Here lies the rose that symbols sex, not purity; that is no perfumed petal but the smell of bed). 67 **pickeering** skirmishing. 68 **line** of battle or siege. 75 **boutesel** boot and saddle: stands ready like a squire to call the lover away.

The antiplatonic°

For shame, thou everlasting wooer,
Still saying grace and never falling to her!
Love that's in contemplation° placed
Is Venus drawn but to the waist.
Unless your flame confess its gender,   5
And your parley cause surrender,
You're salamanders of a cold desire
That live untouched amidst the hottest fire.

What though she be a dame of stone,
The widow of Pygmalion,°   10
As hard and unrelenting she
As the new-crusted Niobë,°
Or (what doth more of statue carry)
A nun of the Platonic quarry?
Love melts the rigour which the rocks have bred—   15
A flint will break upon a feather-bed.

For shame, you pretty female elves,
Cease for to candy° up your selves!
No more, you sectaries° of the game,
No more of your calcining flame!   20
Women commence by Cupid's dart
As a king hunting dubs a hart.°
Love's votaries enthral each other's soul
Till both of them live but upon parole.

Virtue's no more in womankind   25
But the green-sickness° of the mind;
Philosophy (their new delight)
A kind of charcoal° appetite.
There's no sophistry prevails,
Where all-convincing love assails,   30
But the disputing petticoat will warp,°
As skilful gamesters are to seek at sharp.°

The soldier, that man of iron,
Whom ribs of horror all environ,

That's strung with wire instead of veins,   35
In whose embraces you're in chains,
Let a magnetic° girl appear,
Straight he turns Cupid's cuirassier:
Love storms his lips and takes the fortress in
For all the bristled turnpikes of his chin.   40

Since love's artillery then checks
The breastworks of the firmest sex,
Come, let us in affections riot!
They're sickly pleasures keep a diet.
Give me a lover bold and free   45
Not eunuched with formality
Like an ambassador that beds a queen
With the nice caution of a sword between.

° **antiplatonic** see Herbert *Platonic love;* cf. Cartwright *No Platonic love;* Daniel *Pure Platonic;* Cowley *Platonic love.* 3 **contemplation** of the Platonic forms or, in Christianity, the beatific vision of God; also in religion one might have a vocation for either the contemplative or the active life. Cf. Donne 'Love sometimes would contémplate, sometimes do'—*Love's growth.* 10 **Pygmalion** fell in love with the statue of a goddess he had sculpted. 12 **Niobë** see W. Browne *Pembroke.* 18 **candy** to crystallise, preserve in sugar. Ironic because sugar = sex, as in *Fuscara.* 19 **sectaries** members of a religious sect, i.e. puritans. 22 **hart** a male red deer was called a hart royal when the crown of its antler had grown and it had been hunted by a king; so women take on full womanhood when struck by love. 26 **green-sickness** see Herrick *To music.* 28 **charcoal** eaten to purify the system. 31 **will warp** will pervert it. 32 **sharp** as skilful cardplayers like to practise sharping for fun? 37 **magnetic** cf. Jonson's *Magnetic Lady.*

Epitaph on the Earl of Strafford°

Here lies wise and valiant dust
Huddled up 'twixt fit and just:
Strafford, who was hurried hence
'Twixt treason and convenience.
He spent his time here in a mist,   5
A Papist, yet a Calvinist;
His prince's nearest joy and grief,
He had, yet wanted, all relief;
The prop and ruin of the state;
The people's violent love and hate;   10
One in extremes loved and abhorred.

Riddles lie here, or, in a word,
Here lies blood; and let it lie
Speechless still and never cry.

° **Strafford** Thomas Wentworth, Earl of Strafford, 'Black Tom tyrant',
beheaded 1641 before a crowd of 200,000 who had spent the night
yelling for his blood. A Yorkshire M.P., he had been opposed to
Charles I and his court advisers, not because he was either a puritan
or a parliamentarian but because he hated incompetence. In 1628 the
way began to open for him to exercise his own genius for government
so he joined the court and became, in 1639, the King's chief minister,
notorious for ruthless despotism in Ireland and feared lest he subjugate
England with an army: 'eloquent, sagacious, adventurous, intrepid, ready
of invention, immutable of purpose, in every talent which exalts or
destroys nations pre-eminent, the lost archangel, the Satan of the
apostasy' (Macaulay 1828). The revolutionary Long Parliament impeached him for treason as soon as it met in 1640; the trial lasted for
weeks without treason being proved so parliament passed a bill of
attainder (i.e. vote of guilt) and Charles signed it for fear of the mob.
'I am not afraid of death,' Strafford said on the scaffold, 'but do as
cheerfully put off my doublet this time as ever I did when I went to
bed'. One of Van Dyck's portraits of him is at Welbeck, where Newcastle lived.

SIR WILLIAM DAVENANT

Father died 1621 as mayor of Oxford and innkeeper of the Crown where Shakespeare stayed when travelling between Stratford and London. The innkeeper liked theatrical people but was a melancholic, whereas his wife was vivacious and attractive. Persistent legend that William was Shakespeare's illegitimate son. Educated privately in Oxford; aged 11 when Shakespeare died, wrote ode to him; Lincoln College, Oxford, for a brief time, then page to Duchess of Richmond. Service of Fulke Greville; when Greville murdered in 1628, hung about the royal court leading a rather debauched life. 'He got a terrible clap,' Aubrey reported, 'of a black handsome wench that lay in Axe Yard, Westminster, whom he thought on when he speaks of Dalga in *Gondibert*, which cost him his nose'. In the same year, 1638, published *Madagascar with other poems*. Turned to writing plays and masques for the court. Friendly with Endymion Porter, Edward Hyde (the future Earl of Clarendon), Carew, Habington, Suckling, Benlowes. In civil war fled to France but returned and was knighted for bravery on the king's side at siege of Gloucester. When the royalist army was defeated he served as a courier for the exiled court of Queen Henrietta-Maria in Paris. Became Roman catholic. Started *Gondibert* in his apartments in the Louvre. The Queen sent him on business to Virginia but off the French coast his ship was captured by the parliamentarian navy and Davenant imprisoned in Cowes Castle (now a yachting centre) and then for 2 years in the Tower of London. *Gondibert*, with preface on epic, published (1651) ed. D. F. Gladish 1971. Said to have been released by Milton's influence. Returned to private dramatic work; started opera in England with *Siege of Rhodes* 1656. At Restoration, to full public drama under the licenses which Charles II granted to him and to Killigrew. Davenant's theatre was under the patronage of the Duke of York (James II to be). His later work included operatic versions of some of Shakespeare's plays. Twice married (first wife died 1655), several children. *Dramatic works* ed. J. Maidment and W. H. Logan 5 vols. Edinburgh 1872–74 repr. New York 1964 (limited ed.). See A. Harbage *Sir W. Davenant* Philadelphia 1935.

The winter storms

Blow, blow! The winds are so hoarse they cannot blow.
Cold, cold! Our tears freeze to hail, our spittle to snow.
 The waves are all up, they swell as they run:
  Let them rise and rise
  As high as the skies   5
 And higher to wash the face of the sun.

Port, port! The pilot is blind! Port at the helm!
Yare, yare! For one foot of shore take a whole realm.
 A-lee, or we sink! Does no man know how to wind her?
  Less noise, and more room!   10
  We sail in a drum,
 Our sails are but rags, which lightning turns to tinder.

Aloof, aloof! Hey, how those carracks and ships
Fall foul and are tumbled and driven like chips!
 Our bosun, alas, a silly weak gristle,   15
  For fear to catch cold
  Lies down in the hold,
 We all hear his sighs but few hear his whistle.

from Luminalia or the festival of light personated in a masque at court by the Queen's Majesty and her ladies 1637

Night's song

In wet and cloudy mists I slowly rise,°
 As with mine own dull weight oppressed,
To close with sleep the jealous lovers' eyes
 And give forsaken virgins rest.

The adventurous merchant,° and the mariner   5
 Whom storms all day vex in the deep,
Begin to trust the winds when I appear,
 And lose their dangers in their sleep.

The studious, that consume their brains and sight
 In search where doubtful knowledge lies,   10
Grow weary of their fruitless use of light
 And wish my shades to ease their eyes.

The ambitious toiling statesman, that prepares
  Great mischiefs ere the day begins,
Not measures day by hours but by his cares: 15
  And night must intermit his sins.

Then why, when my slow chariot used to climb,
  Did old mistaking sages weep,
As if my empire did usurp their time
  And hours were lost when spent in sleep?   20

I come to ease their labours and prevent
  That weariness which would destroy:
The profit of their toils are still mis-spent
  Till rest enables to enjoy.

1 rise presumably on a piece of ascending machinery. The masque had reached a height of elaboration in Shirley's *Triumph of peace* 1633; see Jonson in Vol. I. **5 adventurous merchant** merchant venturer, i.e. one who conducts oversea trade.

---

from The Temple of Love: a masque presented by the Queen's Majesty and her ladies at Whitehall on Shrove Tuesday 1634. By Inigo Jones, surveyor of His Majesty's works, and William Davenant Her Majesty's servant.

Song

[Sunesis (= understanding); Thelema (= will)]

Sunesis	Come, melt thy soul in mine, that when unite We may become one virtuous appetite.°
Thelema	First breathe thine into me: thine is the part More heavenly and doth more adorn the heart.

Both	Thus mixed, our love will ever be discreet 5
	  And all our thoughts and actions pure;
	When perfect will and strengthened reason meet,
	  Then love's created to endure.

Chorus	Were heaven more distant from us, we would thrive. strive To reach't with prayers to make this union 10

Whilst this song continued, there came softly down from the
highest part of the heaven° a bright and transparent cloud,
which being come to the middle part of the air it opened, and
out of it came Amianteros,° or Chaste Love, flying down, clad
all in carnation and white, and two garlands of laurel in one
hand, and crowned with another of the same; whilst he descended, the cloud closeth again and returns upward and is
hidden in the heavens. Chaste Love being come down to the
earth, was accompanied by Sunesis and Thelema, Divine Poets,
Orpheus° and the rest of the poets, up to the state,° the great
Chorus following at a distance, where they sung this song:

Amianteros   Whilst by a mixture thus made one
          You're the emblem of my deity;
       And now you may in yonder throne
          The pattern of your union see:

       Softly as fruitful showers I fall
          And the undiscerned increase I bring
       Is of more precious worth than all
          A plenteous summer pays a spring.
       The benefit it doth impart
          Will not the barren earth improve
       But fructify each barren heart
          And give eternal growth to love.

Sunesis   To Charles, the mightiest and the best,
       And to the darling of his breast
          (Who rule by example as by power)
       May youthful blessings still increase
       And in their offspring never cease
          Till time's too old to last an hour.

Chorus   These wishes are so well deserved by thee
       And thought so modest too by destiny
       That heaven hath sealed the grant as a decree.

After which they all retire to the scene,° and Indamora and
her ladies begin the revels° with the King and the lords,
which continue the most part of the night. Thus ended this
mask, which for the newness of the invention, variety of
scenes, apparitions and richness of habits was generally approved to be one of the most magnificent that hath been done
in England.

2 **virtuous appetite** a contradiction in terms, the soul and appetite
normally being opposed. See Herbert *Platonic love*; and, for the sense of
unity, Carew *Hymeneal dialogue*. When the soul is harmonious, will is
ruled by understanding, not by appetite 12 **heaven** ceiling or canopy
over stage. 14 **Amianteros** . an invented name = loving return of love.

Milton used Anteros as the perfect mate for Eros in his *Divorce* pamphlet 1643. 20 **Orpheus** inventor of song. 20 **state** throne, where the King and Queen were sitting. 42 **scene** back of the stage. 43 **revels** dancing of cast with audience which ended a masque. Lady Ann Carr, daughter of the Somersets (see Anon *Masque of flowers*) played in this masque.

from The Triumphs of the Prince D'Amour: a masque presented by His Highness at his palace in the Middle Temple the 24th February 1635

The scene wholly changing again, there was observed in a grove of cypress intermingled with myrtle trees, the temple of Venus,° being an eight square° of the Corinthian order; within the temple her statue of silver standing in a niche, with Cupid by her, to whom she seems to deliver an arrow; the pilasters and ornaments were heightened with silver. From this temple the priests of Venus are discerned to come in loose white robes, their heads adorned with coronets of flowers, and playing on their instruments they descend and sing this:

Unarm! unarm! No more your fights
    Must cause the virgins' tears,
But such as in the silent nights
    Spring rather from their fears.

Such difference as when doves do bill   5
    Must now be all your strife:
For all the blood that you shall spill
    Shall usher in a life.

And when your ladies, falsely coy,
    Shall timorous appear,   10
Believe, they then would fain enjoy
    What they pretend to fear.

Breathe then each others' breath and kiss
    Your souls to union,
And whilst they shall enjoy this bliss   15
    Your bodies too are one.

Tomorrow will the hasty sun
    Be feared more of each lover
For hindering to repeat what's done
    Than what it may discover.   20

2 **temple of Venus** abode of love, as in Spenser's *Fairy Queen* IV.x. Cypress and myrtle are sacred to her. **eight square** octagon.

from Gondibert,° an heroic poem

The First Book
Canto the Fifth
The Argument

The battle in exact though little shape,
Where none by flight and few by fortune 'scape,
Where even the vanquished so themselves behave
The victors mourn for all they could not save,
And fear, so soon is fortune's fulness waned,   5
To lose in one all that by all they gained.

Now Hubert's page assists his wounded lord
   To mount that steed he scarce had force to guide
And wept to see his hand without that sword
   Which was so oft in dreadful battles tried.   10

Those who with Borgio saw his want of blood
   Cried out, If of thy strength enough remain,
Though not to charge, to make thy conduct good,°
   Lead us to add their living to our slain.

Hubert replied: Now you may justly boast,   15
   You sons of war, that Oswald was your sire,
Who got in you the honour I have lost
   And taught those deeds our ladies' songs admire.

But he (war's ancestor, who gave it birth,
   The father of those fights we Lombards fought)   20
Lies there embracing but his length of earth
   Who for your use the world's vast empire sought;

And cold as he lies noble Dargonet,
   And Paradine who wore the victor's crown,
Both swift to charge and slow in a retreat,   25
   Brothers in blood and rivals in renown.

This said, their trumpets sound revenge's praise;
   The hunters' horns (the terror of the wood)
Replied so meanly they could scarcely raise
   Echo so loud as might be understood.   30

The Duke, his fit of fury being spent,
   Which only wounds and opposition bred,
Does weep o'er the brave Oswald and lament
   That he, so great in life, is nothing dead.

But cried when he the speechless rivals spied,   35
   O worth above the ancient price of love!

Lost are the living, for with these love died,
   Or, if immortal, fled with them above;

In these we the intrinsic value know
   By which first lovers did love current deem;   40
But love's false coiners will allay° it now,
   Till men suspect what next they must contemn.

Not less young Hurgonil resents their chance,
   Though no fit time to practise his remorse,
For now he cries, finding the foe advance,   45
   Let death give way to life! to horse! to horse!

This sorrow is too soft for deeds behind
   Which I, a mortal lover, would sustain
So I could make your sister wisely kind
   And praise me living, not lament me slain.   50

Swift as Armenians in the panther's chase
   They fly to reach where now their hunters are,
Who sought out danger with too bold a pace,
   Till thus the Duke did them aloud prepare:

Impatient friends, stand, that your strength may last!   55
   Burn not in blaze, rage that should warm you long;
I wish to foes the weaknesses of haste,
   To you such slowness as may keep you strong.

Not their scorn's force should your fixed patience move
   (Though scorn does more than bonds free minds   60
      provoke);
Their flashy rage shall harmless lightning prove
   Which but fore-runs our thunder's fatal stroke.

For when their fury's spent, how weak they are
   With the dull weight of antic° Vandal arms!
Their work but short and little is in war   65
   Whom rage within, and armour outward, warms.

° **Gondibert** a fragment—Davenant got bored and never finished it.
In his preface, addressed to Hobbes and published separately with
Hobbes's sympathetic *Answer*, Davenant argued for epic which should
be Christian rather than classical, and, though fictional, not fantastic—
i.e. halfway between the romantic epic of the 16th century and the
classical realism of the 18th. This is a story of chivalry among the
Germanic tribes in the Lombardy in the dark ages. Prince Oswald is
Duke Gondibert's rival in love. 13 **make thy conduct good** make it
possible to go on leading us. 41 **allay** adulterate into an alloy. 64
antic clumsy, antiquated, barbarous. The Vandals were a tribe which
despoiled Gaul and sacked Rome in the 5th Century.

*The Second Book
Canto the First
The Argument*

Verona by the poet's pencil drawn,
Where Hurgonil did meet the early dawn:
Her wealth shown by each dweller's earlier care,
Which, sown by others' peace, she reaped by war;
The slain, whose life her safety was, and pride,   5
Are now in death their funeral rites denied.

Near to this evening region was the sun
    When Hurgonil with his lamented load,
And faithful Tybalt, their sad march begun
    To fair Verona where the court abode.   10

They slowly rode till night's dominion ceased,
    When infant morn, her scarce-waked beams displayed,
With a scant face peeped shyly through the east
    And seemed as yet of the black world afraid.

But by increase of swift expansive light   15
    The lost horizon was apparent grown
And many towers salute at once their sight:
    The distant glories of a royal town.

Verona, sprung from noble Vera's name,
    Whom careless time, still scattering old recórds   20
Where they are loosely gathered up by fame,
    Proclaims the chief of ancient Tuscan lords.

Verona borders on that fatal plain
    Whose barren thirst was quenched with valiant blood
When the rough Cimbrians by fierce Marius° slain   25
    Left hills of bodies where their engines stood.

So falsely proud this town did now appear
    As if it but immortal dwellers lacked,
As if Theodoric° had ne'er been there,
    Nor Attila° her wealth and beauty sacked.   30

Here Hurgonil might follow with his eye,
    As with deep stream it through the city passed,
The fruitful and the frightened Alicé
    Which thence from noise and nets to sea does haste;

And on her peopled bank they might behold   35
    The toils of conquest paid with works of pride,
The palace of King Agilulf the old
    (Or monument: for ere 'twas built, he died).

To it that temple joins whose lofty head
   The prospect of a swelling hill commands,   40
In whose cool womb the city springs are bred;
   On Doric pillars this tall temple stands.

This to soothe heaven the bloody Cephes built
   As if heaven's King so soft and easy were,
As meanly housed in heaven, and kind to guilt,   45
   That he would be a tyrant's tenant here.

And now they might arrest their wandering sight
   With that which makes all other objects lost,
Makes Lombard greatness flat to Roman height
   And modern builders blush that else would boast: 50

An amphitheatre which was controlled°
   Unheeded conquests of advancing age,
Winds which have made the trembling world look old
   And the fierce tempests of the Gothic rage;

This, great Flaminius° did in youth erect,   55
   Where cities sat to see whole armies play
Death's serious part; but this we may neglect
   To mark the business which begins with day.

As day new opening fills the hemisphere,
   And all at once, so quickly every street   60
Does by an instant opening full appear,
   When from their dwellings busy dwellers meet;

From wider gates oppressors sally there;
   Here creeps the afflicted through a narrow door,
Groans under wrongs he has not strength to bear   65
   Yet seeks for wealth to injure others more;

And here the early lawyer mends his pace;
   For whom the earlier client waited long;
Here greedy creditors their debtors chase
   Who 'scape by herding in the indebted throng.   70

The adventurous merchant whom a storm did wake
   (His ships on Adriatic billows tossed)
Does hope of eastern winds from steeples take
   And hastens there a courier to the coast.

Here through a secret postern issues out   75
   The scared adulterer who out-slept his time;
Day, and the husband's spy, alike does doubt
   And with a half-hid face would hide his crime.

There from sick mirth neglected feasters reel,
  Who cares of want in wine's false Lethes° steep;   80
There anxious empty gamblers homeward steal
  And fear to wake ere they begin to sleep.

Here stooping labourers slowly moving are,
  Beasts to the rich, whose strength grows rude with ease,
And would usurp, did not their ruler's care   85
  With toil and tax their furious strength appease.

There th'aged walk, whose needless carefulness
  Infects them past the mind's best medicine, sleep;
There some to temples early vows address
  And for the o'er-busy world most wisely weep.   90

To this vast inn, where tides of strangers flow,
  The morn and Hurgonil together came:
The morn, whose dewy wings appeared but slow
  When men the motion marked of swifter fame;

For fame, whose journeys are through ways unknown,   95
  Traceless and swift and changing as the wind,
The morn and Hurgonil had much outgone;
  Whilst truth moved patiently within behind . . .

25 **Marius** B.C. 157–86, Roman general who defeated the barbarian
tribes of Teutones and Cimbri. 29 **Theodoric** A.D. 455–526. King of the
Ostrogoths. Born Vienna, trained as a soldier in Constantinople, won
Italy from his barbarian predecessor, 493. One of his major victories
was near Verona. 30 **Attila** the Hun. Conquered Constantinople,
Germany, Lombardy, with fearful destruction. 51 **controlled** an amphitheatre it was which dominated time. 55 **Flaminius** a Roman general.
80 **Lethe** river of oblivion in hades.

from The Just Italian

A song between two boys

1   This lady, ripe and calm and fresh
      As eastern summers are,
    Must now forsake both time and flesh
      To add light to some small star.

2   Whilst yet alive, each star decayed   5
      She may relieve with light;
    But death leads beauty to a shade
      More cold, more dark than night.

1   The saucy faith of man doth blind   10
      His pride till it conduce
  To destiny all humankind
      For some eternal use.

2   But ask not bodies doomed to die
      To what abode they go:
  Since knowledge is but sorrow's spy,   15
      It is not safe to know.

                                      1630

*from The Siege of Rhodes° made a representation
by the art of prospective in scenes, and the story
sung in recitative music*

These are court-monsters, cormorants of the crown:
They feed on favour till they're overgrown;
Then saucily believe we monarchs' wives
    Were made but to be dressed
    For a continued feast,   5
To hear soft sounds and play away our lives;
They think our fulness is to wane so soon
As if our sex's governess, the moon,
Had placed us but for sport on fortune's lap.
They with bold pencils, by the changing shape   10
Of our frail beauty, have our fortune drawn;
And judge our breasts transparent as our lawn,°
    Our hearts as loose and soft and slight
    As are our summer vests of silk;
    Our brains like to our feathers light;   15
    Our blood as sweet as is our milk;
And think, when favourites rise, we are to fall
Meekly as doves, whose livers have no gall.
But they shall find I'm no Európean queen
Who in a throne does sit but to be seen   20
And lives in peace with such state-thieves as these
Who rob us of our business for our ease.

° **Title** the first English opera 1656, designed to evade the ban on
plays. Solyman the Magnificent, Sultan of the Ottomans, besieged
Rhodes 1522. This was one of a series of campaigns which marked the
greatest expansion of Turkish power—he took Baghdad, Belgrade and
Budapest but was repulsed from Vienna. Rhodes had been held for
over 200 years by the Knights of St. John of Jerusalem, descendants
of the Crusaders (hence the siege of Rhodes represents Christian v.
infidel: cf. Solyman's part in Tasso's *Gerusalemma liberata*). Rhodes
surrendered after 5 months. 12 **lawn** see *Lark*.

from The Law Against Lovers°

Wake all the dead! what ho! what ho!
How soundly they sleep whose pillows lie low!
They mind not poor lovers who walk above
On the decks of the world in storms of love.
   No whisper now nor glance can pass   5
   Through wickets or through panes of glass,
For our windows and doors are shut and barred.
Lie close in the church and in the churchyard:
   In every grave make room! make room!
The world's at an end and we come, we come!   10

   The State is now Love's foe, Love's foe,
Has seized on his arms, his quiver and bow,
Has pinioned his wings and fettered his feet
Because he made way for lovers to meet.
   But O sad chance! his judge was old: 15
   Hearts cruel grow when blood grows cold;
No man being young his process° would draw.
O heavens, that love should be subject to law!
   Lovers, go woo the dead, the dead!
Lie two in a grave and to bed, to bed!   20

° **Title** adaptation of *Measure for measure*. This is sung by Viola. 17
process prosecution, suit.

from The Unfortunate Lovers

You fiends and furies,° come along!
Each bring a crow° and massy prong;
Come, drag your shackles and draw near
   To stir up an old sea-coal cake
   Which in our hollow hell doth bake   5
Many a thousand thousand year.
Until your harvest-day at doom,
No grief like this will ever come
From whom you may that pleasure find
Which does your malice feed 'gainst humankind.   10

In sulphurous broth Tereus° hath boiled,
Basted with brimstone Tarquin° hath broiled
Long, long enough. Then make more room;

Like smoky flitches hang them by
  Upon our sooty walls to dry: 15
A greater ravisher will come.
No grief like this *etc.*

If you want fire, fetch a supply
From Etna and Puteoli;
Yet stay awhile, you need not stir   20
  Since if his glowing eyes shall chance
  To cast on Proserpine° a glance
He is so hot he'll ravish her.
No grief like this *etc.*

1643

1 **furies** see Fanshawe *Ode.* 2 **crow** crowbar. 11 **Tereus** see Brathwaite *I am not.* 12 **Tarquin** raped Lucrece. See Carew *Rapture.* 22 **Proserpine** see Campion *Hark.*

ANONYMOUS

The secret (written at the time of the Civil War)

Hark, Celia, hark! but lay thou close thine ear,
    There's for it a concerning reason:
For I've a secret now to tell, my dear,
    And 'tis no less than treason.

Let silly worldlings of their causes prate,   5
    From whence our civil rage begins;
Let wise men talk of errors in our state
    And churchmen of our sins;

Let others blame the stars' malignancy,
    Others the people's peevish call;   10
But, dearest, speak not of it, for, thou and I
    Are authors of it all.

We have all love engrossed; in us alone
    All kindness extant doth abide;
Nor have we left the land enough to atone   15
    One pair of hearts beside.

Then close, as men in famines viands do,
    Let us our loves in secret lay:
Such useful treasure, should the world but know,
    Alas! they'd take it away.   20

No, Celia, no: our love's transcendent worth
    No force, no injury can fear;
Then let it stream with all its glory forth
    And like itself appear;

That, when great Charles shall clear our troubled air   25
    And crown our orb with peaceful hours,
The nation all may unto us repair
    And light their loves at ours.

JAMES GRAHAM, 5TH EARL AND 1ST MARQUIS OF MONTROSE

Succeeded to his Scottish earldom at 12; at 15 to St. Andrew's University—hunting, hawking, archery and golf; at 17 married a peer's daughter; 21–24 continental travel. Sided with Charles I, as a Stuart, against the rebellious presbyterians and middle classes of his own country; imprisoned in Edinburgh Castle, released, defeated the Covenanters in 1643, and became notorious for his troops' habit of massacre and pillage; troops drifted away, he fled to Bergen, then Paris, became a mercenary. 1650 returned to Scotland to win it back for the throneless Charles II (Charles I having been executed 1649) but he lost 1000 of his 1200 men by shipwreck and was easily defeated by the presbyterians, and captured. Hanged, disembowelled, his intestines burnt, castrated and dismembered as a traitor on 21 May 1650 in the Grassmarket, Edinburgh, and his parts distributed through Scotland. He left one child. Later that year Charles II landed in Scotland and entered England but was defeated by Cromwell at Worcester and in exile for 10 years. *Poems* ed J. L. Weir 1938. See John Buchan *Life* 1913; C. V. Wedgwood, The poems of Montrose *Essays and studies* XIII 1960.

On himself, upon hearing what was his sentence

Let them bestow on every airth° a limb;
Open all my veins, that I may swim
To thee, my Saviour, in that crimson lake;
Scatter my ashes, throw them in the air:
Lord, since thou know'st where all these atoms are,   5
I'm hopeful once thou'lt re-collect my dust,
And confident thou'lt raise me with the just.

1 **airth** point of the compass.

RICHARD LOVELACE

Father a Kentish squire, died in Holland when Lovelace 10. Born at Woolwich, educated Charterhouse and Gloucester Hall, Oxford, where he was given the M.A. at the request of one of the Queen's ladies-in-waiting on account of his extreme good looks. To court, military expedition to Scotland 1639, imprisoned briefly by parliamentarians 1642 but released and lived extravagantly in London. Acquainted with Carew, Suckling, Marvell, Lawes, Cotton. Two of his younger brothers served Charles I in Wales and one was killed there in 1645; he also had three sisters. Joined Charles at Oxford but left England 1646 to fight for France against Spain; wounded at Dunkirk; news that he had been killed prompted his fiancée Lucy Sacheverell (Lucasta) to marry someone else. Returned 1648; prepared *Lucasta* (with illustrations by Lely) for publication during another term of imprisonment. Had spent his inheritance, so now sold his manor. Became, with poverty, depressed and unkempt; died in a cellar in Gunpowder Alley off Fleet St. His youngest brother, Dudley Posthumus Lovelace, edited his remaining poems in 1659 (there was a Dudley Lovelace in New York in 1673). *Poems* ed C. H. Wilkinson 2 vols. Oxford 1925, 1 vol. Oxford 1930. See C. H. Hartmann *The cavalier spirit* 1925; D. C. Allen on *Grasshopper* in *Image and meaning: metaphoric traditions in renaissance poetry* Baltimore 1960 repr. Keast.

Lucasta's fan,° with a looking-glass in it

Estrich, thou feathered fool and easy prey,
    That larger sails to thy broad vessel need'st;°
Snakes through thy gutter-neck hiss all the day,
    Then on thy iron mess at supper feed'st:

O what a glorious transmigration   5
    From this to so divine an edifice
Hast thou straight made! near from a wingèd stone
    Transformed into a bird of paradise!

Now do thy plumes for hue and lustre vie
    With the arch of heaven that triumphs o'er past wet,   10
And in a rich enamelled pinion lie
    With sapphires, amethysts and opals set.

Sometime they wing her side, then strive to drown
    The day's eye's piercing beams, whose amorous heat
Solicits still, till, with this shield of down,   15
    From her brave face his glowing fires are beat.

But whilst a plumy curtain she doth draw,
    A crystal mirror sparkles in thy breast,
In which her fresh aspéct whenas she saw,
    And then her foe retirèd to the west—   20

Dear engine, that o' th' sun got'st me the day,
    Spite of his hot assaults mad'st him retreat,
No wind (said she) dare with thee henceforth play
    But mine own breath to cool the tyrant's heat.

My lively shade thou ever shalt retain   25
    In thy enclosèd feather-framèd glass,
And, but unto ourselves, to all remain
    Invisible, thou feature of this face!

So said, her sad swain overheard and cried,
    Ye gods! for faith unstained this a reward!   30
Feathers and glass to outweigh my virtue tried!
    Ah, show their empty strength!
                        The gods accord:

Now fallen the brittle favourite lies, and burst.
    Amazed Lucasta weeps, repents, and flies
To her Alexis, vows herself accursed   35
    If hence she dress herself but in his eyes.

° **fan**   probably also pudendum as in modern English fanny; with complicated implications for the mirror, and its fate.

Lucasta taking the waters at Tunbridge:° ode

Ye happy floods! that now must pass
    The sacred conduits of her womb,
Smooth and transparent as your face
    When you are deaf and winds are dumb:

Be proud! and if your waters be   5
   Fouled with a counterfeited tear,
Or some false sigh hath stainèd ye,
   Haste, and be purifièd there.

And when her rosy gates ye've traced,
   Continue yet some orient wet,   10
Till, turned into a gem you're placed
   Like diamonds with rubies set.

Ye drops that dew the Arabian° bowers,
   Tell me, did you e'er smell or view
On any leaf of all your flowers   15
   So sweet a scent, so rich a hue?

But as through the organs of her breath
   You trickle wantonly, beware:
Ambitious seas in their just death
   As well as lovers must have share.   20

And see, you boil, as well as I!
   You that to cool her did aspire
Now troubled and neglected lie,
   Nor can yourselves quench your own fire.

Yet still be happy in the thought   25
   That, in so small a time as this,
Through all the heavens° you were brought
   Of virtue, honour, love and bliss.

° **Tunbridge** Tunbridge Wells, Kent, a fashionable spa. 13 **Arabian**
spicy. 17 **heavens** the head is the residence of virtue, etc.

Elinda's glove

Thou snowy farm with thy five tenements!
   Tell thy white mistress, here was one
   That called to pay his daily rents;
But she a-gathering flowers and hearts is gone
And thou left void to rude possessiön.   5

But grieve not, pretty ermine cabinet,
   Thy alabaster lady will come home;
   If not, what tenant can there fit
The slender turnings of thy narrow room,
But must ejected be by his own doom?   10

Then give me leave to leave my rent with thee:
   Five kisses, one unto a place;
   For though the lute's too high for me,
Yet servants, knowing minikin° nor bass,
Are still allowed to fiddle with the case.   15

14 **minikin**   treble string.

Her muff

'Twas not for some calm blessing to receive,
Thou didst thy polished hands in shagged furs weave;
   It were no blessing thus obtained:
   Thou rather wouldst a curse have gained
Than let thy warm driven snow be ever stained.   5

Not that you feared the discolouring cold
Might alchemise° their silver into gold;
   Nor could your ten white nuns so sin
   That you should thus penance them in,
Each in her coarse hair smock of discipline.   10

Nor hero-like, who on their chest still wore
A lion, panther, leopard or a boar
   To look their enemies in their hearse:
   Thou wouldst thy hand should deeper pierce
And, in its softness rough, appear more fierce.   15

No, no, Lucasta, destiny decreed
That beasts to thee a sacrifice should bleed,
   And strip themselves to make you gay;
   For ne'er yet herald did display°
A coat where sables upon ermine lay.   20

This for lay-lovers, that must stand at door,
Salute the threshold, and admire no more;
   But I, in my invention tough,
   Rate not this outward bliss enough,
But still contémplate° must the hidden muff.°   25

7 **alchemise**   see Carew *Rapture*. 19 **display**   describe or depict officially in heraldry. Technically *sable* = black, *ermine* = white spotted with black. 25 **contémplate** as in religion. See Cleveland *Antiplatonic*. **muff** slang for pudendum. The first images were of Jacob and Esau.

To Amarantha, that she would dishevel her hair

Amarantha sweet and fair,
Ah, braid no more that shining hair!
  As my curious hand or eye
  Hovering round thee let it fly!

Let it fly as unconfined   5
As its calm ravisher, the wind,
  Who hath left his darling, th'east,
  To wanton o'er that spicy nest.

Every tress must be confessed
But neatly tangled at the best,   10
  Like a clue of golden thread
  Most excellently ravellèd.

Do not then wind up that light
In ribands, and o'er-cloud in night,
  Like the sun in's early ray;   15
  But shake your head and scatter day.

See, 'tis broke! Within this grove,
The bower and the walks of love,
  Weary lie we down and rest
  And fan each other's panting breast.   20

Here we'll strip and cool our fire
In cream below, in milk-baths higher;
  And when all wells are drawèn dry,
  I'll drink a tear out of thine eye.

Which our very joys shall leave,   25
That sorrows thus we can deceive;
  Or our very sorrows weep
  That joys so ripe, so little keep.

Strive not, vain lover, to be fine

  Strive not, vain lover, to be fine:
  Thy silk's the silkworm's and not thine!
You lessen to a fly your mistress' thought
To think it may be in a cobweb caught.
  What though her thin transparent lawn°   5
  Thy heart in a strong net hath drawn?

Not all the arms the god of fire e'er made
Can the soft bulwarks of nak'd love invade.

    Be truly fine, then, and your self dress
    In her fair soul's immaculate glass: 10
Then by reflection you may have the bliss
Perhaps to see what a true fineness is,
    When all your gawderies will fit
    Those only that are poor in wit.
She that a clinquant° outside doth adore,   15
Dotes on a gilded statue, and no more.

5 **lawn** see-through cloth; this fashionable material is noticed in Cowley's *Light* as 'almost naked'. See commentary 5. 15 **clinquant** tinselled.

The snail

Wise emblem° of our politic world,
Sage snail, within thine own self curled,
Instruct me softly to make haste,
Whilst these my feet go slowly fast.
    Compendious snail! thou seem'st to me   5
Large Euclid's strict epitome;
And, in each diagram, dost fling
Thee from the point unto the ring;
A figure now triangular,
An oval now and now a square,   10
And then a serpentine dost crawl,
Now a straight line, now crook'd, now all.
    Preventing° rival of the day,
Th' art up and openest thy ray
And, ere the morn cradles the moon,   15
Th' art broke into a beauteous noon;
Then, when the sun sups in the deep,
Thy silver horns° ere Cynthia's peep,
And thou, from thine own liquid bed,
New Phoebus°, heav'st thy pleasant head.   20
    Who shall a name for thee create,
Deep riddle of mysterious state?
Bold nature, that gives common birth
To all products of seas and earth,
Of thee, as earthquakes, is afraid;   25
Nor will thy dire delivery aid.
Thou thine own daughter, then, and sire,
That son and mother art entire,

That big still with thyself dost go
And liv'st an aged embryo;   30
That, like the cubs of India,°
Thou from thyself a while dost play;
But frighted with a dog or gun
In thine own belly thou dost run;
And as thy house was thine own womb,   35
So thine own womb concludes thy tomb.

But now I must, análysed king,
Thy economic virtues sing:
Thou great staid husband° still within,
Thou thee, that's thine, dost discipline;   40
And when thou art to progress° bent,
Thou mov'st thyself and tenement:
As warlike Scythians° travelled, you
Remove your men and city too;
Then, after a sad dearth, and rain,   45
Thou scatterest thy silver train;
And when the trees grow naked and old
Thou clothest them with cloth of gold
Which from thy bowels thou dost spin
And draw from the rich mines within.   50

Now hast thou changed thee saint° and made
Thyself a fane that's cupola'd;
And in thy wreathèd cloister thou
Walkest thine own grey friar too;
Strict and locked up, th'art hood all o'er   55
And ne'er eliminat'st° thy door;
On salads thou dost feed severe,
And 'stead of beads thou dropp'st a tear;
And when to rest each calls the bell,
Thou sleep'st within thy marble cell,   60
Where, in dark contemplation° placed,
The sweets of nature thou dost taste;
Who now with time thy days resolve
And in a jelly thee dissolve
Like a shot star° which doth repair   65
Upward and rarefy the air.

1 **emblem** see Quarles; cf. Bunyan, and a poem on the snail by Thom
Gunn. 13 **preventing** first-comer. 18 **horns** tips of crescent moon. 20
Phoebus sun god. 31 **India** don't know unless it alludes to bear-cubs,
supposed to be amorphous until literally licked into shape by mother.
39 **husband** farmer. 41 **progress** royal tour. 43 **Scythians** oriental
nomads in Russia. 51 **saint** changed yourself into a saint. **eliminat'st**
crosseth; the literal Latin meaning of eliminate is cross the threshold;
jocosely pedantic. 61 **contemplation** cf. *Muff.* 65 **star** shooting stars
were thought to turn into jelly on landing.

from On Sannazar's° *being honoured with* 600
*ducats by the Clarissimi of Venice, for composing
an elegiac hexastich of the city: a satire*

. . . There is not in my mind one sullen fate
Of old, but is concentred in our state.
Vandal° o'errunners—Goths—in literature;
Ploughmen that would Parnassus° new manure;
Ringers of verse that all-in all-in chime   5
And toll the changes upon every rhyme;
A mercer° now by the yard does measure o'er
An ode which was but by the foot before;
Deals you an ell of epigram and swears
It is the strongest and the finest wears;   10
No wonder if a drawer° verses rack—
If 'tis not his't may be the spirit of sack;
Whilst the fair barmaid strokes the Muse's teat
For milk to make the posset° up complete.
  Arise, thou reverend shade, great Jonson,° rise!   15
Break through thy marble natural disguise!
Behold a mist of insects, whose mere breath
Will melt thy hallowed leaden house of death.
What was Crispinus that you should defy
The age for him? he durst not look so high   20
As your immortal rod, he still did stand
Honoured, and held his forehead to thy brand.
These scorpions with which we have to do
Are fiends, not only small but deadly too.
Well mightst thou rive° thy quill up to the back   25
And screw thy lyre's grave chords until they crack:
For though once hell° resented music, these
Devils will not, but are in worse disease.
How would thy masculine spirit, Father Ben,
Sweat to behold basely deposèd men   30
Justled from the prerogative of their bed,
Whilst wives° are periwigged with their husbands' head!
Each snatches the male quill from his faint hand
And must both nobler write and understand;
He to her fury the soft plume doth bow—   35
O pen! ne'er truly justly slit° till now!
Now as herself a poem she doth dress,
And curls a line as she would do a tress;
Powders a sonnet as she does her hair,
Then prostitutes them both to public air.   40

Nor is't enough that they their faces blind
With a false dye, but they must paint their mind;
In metre scold and in scanned order brawl:
Yet there's one Sappho° left may save them all . . .

° **Sannazar** Jacopo Sannazzaro 1458–1530. An Italian of Naples, which
was annexed by Spain in 1504. Famous for his *Arcadia* 1504, and
known as 'Christian Virgil' for his Latin epic on the nativity *De partu
virginis*. Also court poet for a succession of kings. 3 **Vandal** see Davenant *Gondibert*. 4 **Parnassus** mountain of the Muses. 7 **mercer** cloth-
merchant. 11 **drawer** barman. 14 **posset** wine and cream drink. 15
Jonson see Vol. I. Crispinus was Jonson's version of Marston in *The
poetaster*. 25 **rive** split. 27 **hell** Orpheus charmed it with his lyre.
32 **wives** Pope repeats the complaint that women are becoming literary.
Eleven poetesses figure in the latter part of this anthology. 36 **slit** in
the quill nib; and slang for vulva. 44 **Sappho** Greek poetess of the 7th
century B.C.

Love made in the first age:° to Chloris

In the nativity of time,
Chloris, it was not thought a crime
 In direct Hebrew° for to woo.
Now we make love as all on fire,
Ring retrograde our loud desire   5
 And court in English backward too.

Thrice happy was that golden age
When compliment was cónstrued rage,°
 And fine words in the centre hid;
When cursèd No stained no maid's bliss   10
And all discourse was summed in Yes,
 And naught forbade but to fore-bid.

Love then unstinted love did sip,
And cherries plucked fresh from the lip,
 On cheeks and roses free he fed;   15
Lasses like autumn plums did drop
And lads indifferently did crop
 A flower and a maidenhead.

Then unconfinèd each did tipple
Wine from the bunch, milk from the nipple;   20
 Paps tractable as udders were;
Then equally the wholesome jellies
Were squeezed from olive-trees and bellies,
 Nor suits of trespass did they fear.

A fragrant bank of strawberries   25
Díapered° with violets' eyes
    Was table, tablecloth and fare;
No palace to the clouds did swell,
Each humble princess then did dwell
    In the piazza of her hair.   30

Both broken faith and the cause of it,
All-damning gold, was damned to the pit;
    Their troth, sealed with a clasp and kiss,
Lasted until that éxtreme day
In which they smiled their souls away   35
    And in each other breathed new bliss.

Because no fault, there was no tear,
No groan did grate the granting ear;
    No false foul breath their delicate smell;
No serpent kiss poisoned the taste,   40
Each touch was naturally chaste
    And their mere sense a miracle.

Naked as their own innocence,
And unembroidered from offence,°
    They went, above poor riches, gay;   45
On softer than the cygnet's down
In beds they tumbled of their own,
    For each within the other lay.

Thus did they live; thus did they love,
Repeating only joys above,   50
    And angels were, but with clothes on,
Which they would put off cheerfully
To bathe them in the galaxy,
    Then gird them with the heavenly zone.°

Now, Chloris! miserably crave   55
The offered bliss you would not have;
    Which evermore I must deny
Whilst, ravished with these noble dreams,
And crownèd with mine own soft beams,
    Enjoying of myself I lie.   60

° **first age** see commentary 4 on erotic primitivism. 3 **Hebrew** gib-
berish; cf. double Dutch. But presumably Adam and Eve spoke Hebrew. 8 **rage** madness; or passion. Either the fine words were buried,
or went straight to the centre in the sense of vulva as in Cleveland's
State of love. 26 **Diapered** embroidered. 44 **offence** the fall of Adam
and Eve, after which they were ashamed and wore clothes. 54 **heavenly
zone** a region of the sky; but zone literally = belt.

The grasshopper: to my noble friend, Mr. Charles Cotton°

O thou that swing'st upon the waving hair
  Of some well-fillèd oaten beard,
Drunk every night with a delicious tear
  Dropped thee from heaven, where now thou'rt reared:

The joys of earth and air are thine entire,   5
  That with thy feet and wings dost hop and fly;
And when thy poppy° works, thou dost retire
  To thy carved acorn-bed to lie.

Up with the day, the sun thou welcom'st then,
  Sport'st in the gilt plaits of his beams;   10
And all these merry days mak'st merry men,
  Thyself, and melancholy streams.

But ah, the sickle! golden ears are cropped,
  Ceres and Bacchus° bid goodnight,
Sharp frosty fingers all your flowers have topped,   15
  And what scythes spared, winds shave off quite.

Poor verdant fool! and now, green ice! Thy joys,
  Large and as lasting as thy perch of grass,
Bid us lay in 'gainst winter rain, and poise
  Their floods with an o'erflowing glass.   20

Thou best of men and friends! we will create
  A genuine summer in each other's breast;
And spite of this cold time, and frozen fate,
  Thaw us a warm seat to our rest.

Our sacred hearths shall burn eternally   25
  As vestal° flames; the north wind, he
Shall strike his frost-stretched wings, dissolve and fly
  This Etna in epitome;°

Dropping December shall come weeping in,
  Bewail the usurping of his reign;   30
But when in showers of old Greek° we begin,
  Shall cry he hath his crown again!

Night as clear Hesper° shall our tapers whip
  From the light casements where we play,
And the dark hag from her black mantle strip   35
  And stick there everlasting day.

Thus richer than untempted kings are we
   That, asking nothing, nothing need:
Though lord of all what seas embrace, yet he
   That wants himself is poor indeed.   40

° **Cotton** see his poems below. **7 poppy** opiate. **14 Ceres . . . Bacchus** corn goddess, wine god. **26 vestal** in Rome the domestic hearth was sacred to the household gods. Vesta was goddess of the hearth in general and custodian of the sacred fire of the nation which Aeneas brought from Troy. The fire was kept in the forum and tended by 6 Vestal virgins of a particularly strict immaculacy. **28 epitome** model; flee this miniature volcano. **31 Greek** cards (cf. play below)? wine? talk (cf. Crashaw *Wishes* line 88). **33 Hesper** Hesperus, the evening star. Seems to mean that their candles shall be taken from the window and stuck in the sky as if they were evening stars, to perpetuate the day (Hesperus shines before dark).

La bella bona-roba°

I cannot tell who loves the skeleton
Of a poor marmoset, naught but bone, bone;
Give me a nakedness with her clothes° on:

Such whose white satin upper coat of skin,
Cut upon a velvet rich incarnadine,   5
Has yet a body (and of flesh) within.

Sure it is meant good husbandry in men,
Who do incorporate with airy lean,
To repair their sides and get their rib° again.

Hard hap° unto that huntsman that decrees   10
Fat joys for all his sweat, whenas he sees,
After his 'say,° naught but his keeper's fees.

Then Love, I beg, when next thou tak'st thy bow,
Thy angry shafts, and dost heart-chasing go,
Pass rascal° deer, strike me the largest doe.   15

° **bona-roba** girl, tart (Italian). Similarly marmoset (small monkey kept as a pet) and skeleton. **3 clothes** skin, as in *Aramantha*. **9 rib** Eve was made of Adam's rib. **10 hap** luck. **12 'say** essay, trying. **15 rascal** lean or immature deer.

THE REVEREND WILLIAM
CARTWRIGHT

His father squandered an inheritance and became an inn-keeper at Cirencester, Glos. Cartwright to school there, then Westminster, and Christ Church, Oxford, where he stayed to take holy orders and become 'the most florid and seraphical preacher in the university' (Anthony à Wood). Gained the friendship and admiration of Jonson, Izaak Walton, Vaughan. 'A miracle of industry and wit, sitting 16 hours a day at all manner of knowledge . . . and all this at 30 years of age!' Also wrote plays, songs and poems, mostly published 1651. Died of fever, widely mourned. *Plays and poems* ed. G. B. Evans, Madison 1951.

No Platonic love°

Tell me no more of minds embracing minds
 And hearts exchanged for hearts;
That spirits spirits meet, as winds do winds,
 And mix their subtlest parts;
That two unbodied essences may kiss   5
And then, like angels, twist and feel one bliss.

I was that silly thing that once was wrought
 To practise this thin love;
I climbed° from sex to soul, from soul to thought;
 But thinking there to move,   10
Headlong I rolled from thought to soul, and then
From soul I lighted at the sex again.

As some strict down-looked men pretend to fast,
 Who yet in closets eat,
So lovers who profess they spirits taste,   15
 Feed yet on grosser meat;
I know they boast they souls to souls convey:
Howe'er they meet, the body is the way.

Come, I will undeceive thee: they that tread
 Those vain aërial ways   20

Are like young heirs and alchemists,° misled
   To waste their wealth and days;
For, searching thus to be forever rich,
   They only find a medicine for the itch.

° **Platonic love** see Cleveland *Antiplatonic*. **9 climbed** see Herbert
Ode. **21 alchemists** see Carew *Rapture*.

*from The Royal Slave, a tragi-comedy presented
to the King and Queen by the students of
Christ Church, August 30, 1636*

Boy sings

Come, my sweet, whiles every strain
   Calls our souls into the ear,
Where they greedy listening fain
   Would turn into the sound they hear:
      Lest in desire   5
      To fill the choir
      Themselves they tie
      To harmony,
Let's kiss and call them back again.

Now let's orderly convey   10
   Our souls into each other's breast,
Where interchangèd let them stay,
   Slumbering in a melting rest;
      Then with new fire
      Let them retire   15
      And still present
      Sweet fresh content,
Youthful as the early day.

Then let us a tumult make,
   Shuffling so our souls that we,   20
Careless who did give or take,
   May not know in whom they be;
      Then let each smother
      And stifle the other
      Till we expire   25
      In gentle fire,
Scorning the forgetful lake.°

27 lake Lethe, river of oblivion in hades.

from The Siege, or Love's Convert

Leucasia	My most honoured father,
	Think not so ill of blest Misander, for
	I see him like a vigorous spark among
	Things tumbling the common night o' th' world,
	Sent to make what we call a pilgrimage 5
	Deserve the name of life. Without him, 'twere
	Only to stand without doors till it pleased
	The gods to call us in.
Misander	Fairest of things,
	And only like thyself, those pleasures which 10
	The laden bosom of this lower world
	Permits to careful mortals are too gross,
	Too earthy to be ours: let's mount the wings
	Of our desires and take a flight into
	Nature's sincerer kingdom, where she mints 15
	And shapes refined delights, delights like thee.
Leucasia	We'll to those places set apart for love
	Where trees kiss trees and branch entwineth branch.

   •   •   •

	And we,
	When we come there, what chaster pleasures shall we
	Indulge to our affections? 20
Misander	Thou shalt sit
	Queen of that kingdom in a chair of light
	And doves with 'nointed wings shall hover o'er thee
	Shedding perfúmes as if blest nature rained
	Delights and poured them on our tender loves 25
	To make 'em flourish. Fresh and well-tunèd winds
	Shall bring thee viands in, and at each change
	Of service° alter their respectful music;
	Fountains shall walk upon thy table, and
	Birds singing to the fall of their soft waters 30
	Shall by the marriage of their mingled sounds
	Create an harmony shall make the Sirens° sleep.
	Thence rising, thou shalt walk, and view young nymphs
	In currents gravelled with transparent amber
	Breaking their shapes at every step; thyself 35
	Outshining both the currents and them too.

Then shalt thou sail in one entire rich shell
Through labyrinths of waters whose perplexed
And interwoven banks shall be environed
With shady trees charged with delightful fruits,   40
Nature then making one continued season . . .

27 **service** course, dish. 31 **Sirens** angelic beings who rode on the
celestial spheres and made their music.

from A bill of fare

Expect no strange or puzzling meat, no pie
Built by confusion or adultery
Of forcèd nature; no mysterious dish
Requiring an interpreter, no fish
Found out by modern luxury. Our coarse board,   5
Pressed with no spoils of elements, doth afford
Meat, like our hunger, without art, each mess
Thus differing from it only, that 'tis less.
    Imprimis some rice porridge, sweet and hot—
Three knobs of sugar season the whole pot.   10
    Item, one pair of eggs in a great dish,
So ordered that they cover all the fish.
    Item, one gaping haddock's head which will
At least affright the stomach, if not fill.
    Item, one thing in circles which we take,   15
Some for an eel, but the wiser for a snake.
    We have not still the same—sometimes we may
Eat muddy plaice, or wheat; perhaps next day
Red, or white, herrings, or an apple-pie:
There's some variety in misery . . .   20

Sadness°

Whiles I this standing lake,
Swathed up with yew and cypress boughs,
    Do move by sighs and vows,
    Let sadness only wake;
That, whiles thick darkness blots the light,   5
My thoughts may cast another night;
    In which double shade,

By heaven and me made,
  O let me weep
    And fall asleep   10
And forgotten fade.

Hark! from yonder hollow tree
Sadly sing two anchorite° owls,
  Whiles the hermit wolf howls
And, all bewailing me,   15
The raven hovers o'er my bier;
The bittern on a reed I hear
  Pipes my elegy
  And warns me to die;
    Whiles from yond graves   20
    My wronged love craves
  My sad company.

Cease, Hylas,° cease thy call;
Such, O such was thy parting groan
  Breathed out to me alone   25
When thou disdained didst fall.
Lo, thus unto thy silent tomb
In my sad winding-sheet I come,
  Creeping o'er dead bones
  And cold marble stones   30
    That I may mourn
    Over thy urn
And appease thy groans.

° **Sadness** Coleridge copied a version of lines 7–11 into his common-place book; they were taken for his own. 13 **anchorite** hermit. 23 **Hylas** boy loved by Hercules. The water-nymphs also loved him and kept him at the bottom of a well. When Hercules shouted for him only a faint echo replied.

On the Circumcision: for the King's music°

1	Gently, O gently, father, do not bruise
	That tender vine° that hath no branch to lose.
2	Be not too cruel! See, the Child doth smile:
	His blood was but his Mother's milk erewhile.
1st Levite	Fear not the pruning of your vine, 5
	He'll turn your water into wine.°
2nd Levite	The Mother's milk that's now his blood
	Hereafter will become her food.

Chorus	'Tis done: so doth the balsam° tree endure
	The cruel wounds of those whom it must cure. 10
1st Levite	'Tis but the Passion's essay:° this young loss
	Only preludes unto his riper cross.
1	Avert, good heaven, avert that fate,
	To so much beauty so much hate!
2nd Levite	Where so great good is meant 15
	The blood's not lost but spent.
Chorus	Thus princes feel what people do amiss:
	The swelling's ours although the lancing° his.
1st Levite	When ye, fair heavens, white food° bled,
	The rose, say they, from thence grew red: 20
	O then, what more miraculous good
	Must spring from this diviner flood?
2nd Levite	When that the Rose° itself doth bleed,
	That blood will be the Church's seed.
Chorus	When that the Rose itself doth bleed, 25
	That blood will be the Church's seed.

° **music** set by Lawes. Milton attempted this subject. 2 **vine** 'I am the true vine' *John* xv; source of the communion wine; phallus, 'stem of Jesse'. 6 **wine** miracle of the marriage in Cana, *John* ii. 9 **balsam** see *Carew* Rapture. 11 **essay** trial. 18 **lancing** of a swollen infection, i.e. sin. 19 **white food** manna: *Exodus* xvi. 23 **Rose** Christ, on the basis of the rose of Sharon in Solomon's song, and e.g. Psalm cxxxii, 'There will I make the horn of David to bud'.

COMMENTARY 7

*Civil War and Commonwealth
1642–1660*

Baroque Religion

This section displays, not the mid-century's godliness, but its virtuosity with language. Perhaps the piety that Donne and Herbert wrote with was turning more aesthetic? That is a tendency of religious art, as it is a tendency of religion itself to turn into ecclesiastical polity. It would account for baroque extravagance as a desperation of devotion. Or was it the other way round? Perhaps during a quasi-religious war, and the rule of the saints, religion did more thoroughly imbue daily life, and in poetry too the frontiers between sacred and profane, worship and art, blurred? This would accord with puritan aims. Baroque would then be resistance to that normalising, an attempt to keep religion special by giving it special art.

These poets heard the battles while they wrote—'the ventriloquious drum' (Knevet) and 'sound of solid horses' hooves' (More). Their poems are packed with *things*; and they say simple things in absolute confidence against bathos: 'Christ had four beds' (Watkyns); 'Home, sweet home' (Beaumont). They pressgang rough thingy words—'the grizzled grey And cruddled clouds' in More's intellectualist devotions—just as Milton does; but, like him, they are more notable for domesticating learned vocabularies, or inventing neologisms—More's protopathy, Beaumont's ataxy and 'liberty Of unsolicitous delight', Vaughan's 'noiseless date and intercourse of times'. They have digested the mid-century wave of science, more practical, geocentric and biological than Donne's new philosophy—'man is a zoophyte' (Knevet), helix, intrinsic, 'flower-nibbling chemistry' (Benlowes). In metaphysics they operate at almost a professional level: 'Death is a noun' (Benlowes); 'Over to something's bank from nothing's side' (Beaumont).

I don't think we draw from the poets here, even Vaughan, so much convincing religious experience as we may find in Herbert and Hopkins, or Traherne and Norris in section 11, or in Eliot. They are at their most devout in the ethics of a

sombre commonsense. As they are always entirely serious,
their pontifications ring true: 'This base worm thou dost see
Has quite devoured thy parents; shall eat thee' (Cary); 'rotting men' (Hall). That comes not merely from the experience
of war: they have a vision of the whole world under eternity;
and they see visions. This was not true of the earlier poets.
It was of course a theocracy for them, but one apprehended
only very locally I think. Now it is global. This starts with
Davenant, goes on with Milton and Cowley, is characteristic
of the 1650s: 'Vast plains with lowly cottages forlorn' (More);
'my striving eye Dazzles at it, as at eternity' (Vaughan); and
Benlowes, that great boring genius, with his vision of the
earth as

> a dim spot . . . where mortals toil
> For shot-bruised mud walls (childish broil!),
> For pot-gun cracks 'gainst ant-hill works—O what a coil!

The baroque can be started here but English poets adopted
so much from Italian and Spanish models that we must go
first to Marino. Baroque is easier to appreciate in visual art
anyway (start from the iconography of saints; why are saints
baroque?) and in music (approach via Crashaw *Music's duel*
and its counterpart at *Paradise lost* XI.554). Cary's *Crucifixus*
ties back to the earlier baroque of Southwell, the Jesuit priest
who was martyred at Tyburn in 1595; Southwell in his turn
relates to Constable and to what may be regarded as a proto-
baroque in Spenser and the Fletchers—see Commentary 3.
But on the whole defining baroque is a boring game. It would
be more profitable to take a religious theme common to a
number of poems and survey its treatment (e.g. the nativity,
Easter, Mary Magdalene).

Hall is a good place to start looking at the interest in
science of later 17th-century poets—an interest more practical
and professional than Donne's. It culminates in Cowley's
membership of the Royal Society. See Hall's *Burning-glass*
(not here); Sir Thomas Browne's prose (and consider medical
poets as a group); Vaughan *Man*, Knevet *Progress*, Milton
Paradise lost V, VII, VIII, Duchess of Newcastle, Cowley
(*Ecstasy* and *Hymn to light* here) and Butler (sceptical about
science). In Beaumont, particularly, you will find a parallel
to scientific interest which we first noted in Davenant—an
interest in history replacing mythology.

Beaumont is the most obvious candidate for major independent work. He is meaty, concerned with meaning rather
than décor; he relates both to the dedicated learning of

Milton (compare them on chaos, and their use of abstractions) and to the more eccentric interests of the Duchess of Newcastle (Beaumont personifies Here and There!). His simplicity relates him to George Herbert (e.g. *The oath*) and the domestic poets of section 8.

Cary, Hall and Cudmore are also available; some of Benlowes; some of Vaughan's individual poems still need annotation and interpretation. Any work done in this area will also contribute to Miltonic studies, more than anything done on Milton himself.

I have referred here to Milton, Crashaw and Vaughan, who are included in Vol. I, because in this section on mid-century religion, as in the later section on Restoration satire, the greater poets write deeply inside the culture of the lesser ones; and the lesser repeatedly approach greatness because of that community of culture.

[JOHN MILTON]
[RICHARD CRASHAW]
[HENRY VAUGHAN]

THE REVEREND ROWLAND WATKYNS

A vicar in Becknockshire (cf. Vaughan), who probably practised medicine when dispossessed of his living by parliament.

Upon Christ's nativity, or Christmas

From three dark places Christ came forth this day:
First from his Father's bosom, where he lay
Concealed till now; then from the typic° law,
Where we his manhood but by figures saw;
And lastly from his mother's womb he came   5
To us, a perfect God and perfect man.
　　Now in a manger lies the eternal Word:
The Word° he is, yet can no speech afford;
He is the bread of life, yet hungry lies;
The living fountain, yet for drink he cries;   10
He cannot help or clothe himself at need
Who did the lilies° clothe and ravens feed;
He is the light of lights, yet now doth shroud
His glory with our nature as a cloud.
He came to us a little one, that we   15
Like little children° might in malice be;
Little he is, and wrapped in clouts, lest he
Might strike us dead if clothed with majesty.
　　Christ had four beds and those not soft nor brave:
The Virgin's womb, the manger, cross, and grave.   20
The angels sing this day, and so will I
That have more reason to be glad then they.

Flamma sine fumo 1662

3 typic typological: see Quarles *Samson*. The Old Testament law was 'a shadow of things to come; but the body is of Christ', *Colossians* ii. **8 Word** Logos, a Greek title of Christ; but Latin infans = unable to speak. **12 lilies** see Vaughan *Man* and, for ravens, *Religion*. **16 children** 'except ye become as little children . . .' *Matthew* xviii.

THE REVEREND HENRY MORE

Father a gentleman; both parents ardent Calvinists; More brought up by uncle who was an ardent flogger. Eton; Christ's College, Cambridge, where he took holy orders, was elected a fellow 1639 and spent the rest of his life except when staying with a private pupil, the Viscountess Conway at Ragley, Warwickshire. Went through several years of doubt and anxiety, then became one of group of liberal and idealist theologians known as Cambridge Platonists (it included Cudworth, the master of Christ's and Whichcote, the provost of King's). 'The language of Platonism at that time commanded assent with an authority second only to that of Scripture, and to use it in religious exhortation, therefore, was the happiest available method of implying, without aggressively proclaiming, that there were other ways of faith besides those laid down in the current formulae of the churches' (Willey, *17th-century background*). More produced his first doctrinal poetry in 1642 with *Psychodia platonica, or a Platonical song of the soul, consisting of four several poems*, expanded into *Philosophical poems* 1647. His prose includes *Conjectura cabbalistica, or a conjectural essay of interpreting the mind of Moses* 1653. *Philosophical poems* (a selection) ed. G. Bullough 1931.

from Psychozoia or the first part of the song of the soul, containing a Christiano-Platonical display of life

Canto i

There° you may see the eyelids of the morn
  With lofty silver arch displayed i'th' east,
And in the midst the burnished gold doth burn;
  A lucid purple mantle in the west
Doth close the day and hap the sun at rest;   5
  Nor doth these lamping shows the azure quell,

Or other colours: where't beseemeth best
   There they themselves dispose, so seemly well
Doth light and changing tinctures deck this goodly veil.

But 'mong these glaring glittering rows of light,   10
   And flaming circles, and the grizzle grey
And cruddled clouds with silver tippings dight,
   And many other deckings wondrous gay—
As Iris° and the halo—there doth play
   Still-paced Euphrona in her conic tire:°   15
By stealth her steeple-cap she doth essay
   To whelm on the earth—so schoolboys do aspire
With coppelled hat to quelm the bee all armed with ire.

1 **there** in the sky. 14 **Iris** rainbow goddess. The halo is one round
the sun or moon. 15 **tire** night was thought of as a cone shadowing
the globe.

Canto iii

I hear the clattering of an armèd troop,
   My ears do ring with the strong prancers' heels
(My soul, get up out of thy drowsy droop
   And look unto the everlasting hills!°);
The hollow ground, ah! how my sense it fills   5
   With sound of solid horses' hooves. A wonder
It is, to think how cold my spirit thrills
   With strange amaze. Who can this strength dissunder?
   Hark how the warlike steeds do neigh, their necks do
      thunder°

4 **hills** 'I will lift up mine eyes unto the hills, from whence cometh
my help.' Psalm cxxi. 9 **thunder** 'Hast thou given the horse strength?
Hast thou clothed his neck with thunder?' *Job* xxxix.

*from Psychathanasia or the second part of the song
of the soul, treating of the immortality of the soul*

Book III

The world's great soul° knows by protópathy°
   All what befalls this lower sprite; but we
Can only know't by deuteropathy,
   At least in sight and hearing. She doth see

In our own eyes, by the close unity   5
   Of ours and the world's life, our passion;°
Plainly perceives our idiópathy°
   As we do hers by the same union;
   But we can not see hers in that perfectiön.

Fresh-varnished groves, tall hills, and gilded clouds   10
   Arching an eyelid for the glorying morn,
Fair-clustered buildings which our sight so crowds
   At distance, with high spires to heaven yborne,
Vast plains with lowly cottages forlorn
   Rounded about with the low wavering sky,   15
Cragged vapours like to ragged rocks ytorn—
   She views those prospects in our distant eye:
   These and such like be the first centre's mystery.

1 **soul** *anima mundi*, world-soul, a familiar concept in ancient philosophy. In Plato it is what animates matter, the *élan vital* of all things.
More uses it like Wordsworth's 'impulse and a spirit' that rolls through
all things in *Tintern Abbey*. **protopathy** used by More to mean original
sympathy. *Deutero* means second. 6 **passion** experience. 7 **idiopathy**
experience peculiar to us as individuals.

EDWARD BENLOWES

Son of an Essex squire. St. John's College, Cambridge;
continental tour. Squandered inheritance. Friend of P.
Fletcher, Quarles, Davenant. *Theophila* 1652. Spent his last
8 years studying at Oxford. Changed from Roman catholic to
protestant. Died of privation. Ed. Saintsbury. See H. Jenkins
E. Benlowes . . . biography of a minor poet 1950; C. Hill,
'Benlowes and his times' *Essays in criticism* III 1953.

from Theophila, or love's sacrifice
The prelibation to the sacrifice

Canto I

Might souls converse with souls by angel-way,°
Enfranchised from their prisoning clay,
What strains, by intuition, would they then convey!

But spirits° sublimed too fast evaporate may
Without some interposed allay;   5
And notions subtilised too thin exhale away.

The gold (Sol's child) when in earth's womb it lay
As precious was, though not so gay
As, when refined, it doth itself abroad display.

Mount, fancy, then, through orbs to glory's sphere!   10
(Wild is the course that ends not there).
You who are virtue's friends lend to her tongue an ear.

Let not the wanton love-fights which may rise
From vocal fifes, flame-darting eyes
(Beauty's munition), hearts with wounds unseen sur-   15
  prise—

Whose basilisk-like° glances taint the air
Of virgin pureness and ensnare
Entangled thoughts i' th' trammels of their ambush-hair.

Love's captive view, whose days in warm frosts° spends;
On's idol dotes, to wit pretends;   20
Writes, blots, and rends, nor heeds where he begins or
    ends:

His stock of verse in comic fragments lies.
Higher than Teneriffe's° peak he flies—
Sol's but a spark—thou out-ray'st all diamonds of the
    skies:

Victorious° flames glow from thy brighter eye;   25
Cloud those twin-lightening orbs (they'll fry
An ice-veined monk), cloud them or, planet-struck, I die.

Indians, pierce rocks for gems; Negroes, the brine
For pearls! Tartars, to hunt combine
For sables: consecrate all offerings at her shrine.   30

Crouch low, O vermeil-tinctured cheek, for thence
The organs to my optic sense
Are dazzled at the blaze of so bright angelence.

Does Troy-bane Helen,° friend, with angels share?
All lawless passions idols are;   35
Frequent are fuco'd° cheeks, the virtuosa's rare,

A true authentic. Let not skin-deep white
And red perplex the nobler light
Of the intellect, nor mask the soul's clear-piercing sight.

Burn odes, lust's paper-blots; fly plays, its flame;   40
Shun guilty courtisms, forge for shame
No chains; lip-traffic and eye-dialogues disclaim.

    •   •   •

Shall larks with shrill-chirped matins rouse from bed
    Of curtained night Sol's orient head,
And shall quick souls lie numbed, as wrapped in sheets   45
    of lead?°

Awake from slumbering lethargy! the gay
    And circling charioteer of day
In's progress through the azure fields sees, checks our stay.

Arise! and rising, emulate the rare
    Industrious spinsters who with fair   50
Embroideries chequer-work the chambers of the air.

Ascend! Sol does on hills his gold display
    And, scattering sweets, does spice the day,
And shoots delight through nature with each arrowed ray.

The opal-coloured dawns raise fancy high;   55
  Hymns ravish those who pulpits fly:
Convert dull lead to active gold by love-chemy.°

As nature's prime confectioner, the bee,
  By her flower-nibbling chemistry
Turns vert to or:° so, verse gross prose does rarefy.   60

Stanzas 1–14 . . . 62–67

1 **angel-way** angels understood and communicated by intuition rather
than discourse. See *Paradise lost* V. 479–90. 4 **spirits** chemical sub-
stances (e.g. spirits of vitriol = sulphuric acid), here metaphors for
souls. Allay = alloy. 16 **basilisk** see Anon *Witch*. 19 **warm frosts**
typical oxymoron of the Petrarchan convention which Benlowes is
mocking. 23 **Teneriffe** peak in Canary Islands visible far in the Atlantic. 25 **victorious** start of 3 stanzas of parody. 34 **Helen** see Suckling *Dream*. 36 **fuco'd** fucus was a rouge. Virtuosa = female rectitude,
or truly honest woman. 45 **lead** used to wrap corpses. 57 **love-chemy**
for alchemy see Carew *Rapture*. 60 **vert to or** heraldic green to gold.

Canto II

Angels by one sin fell; so, man; how then
May sinners stand? Let's quit sin's den—
This moment's ours; life hastes away, delay's gangrene.

Conviction ushers grace; fall to prevent
Thy fall, Time's forelock take;° relent.   5
Shall is to come, and *was* is past; then, *now* repent.

Before the sun's long shadows span up° night,
Ere on thy shaking head snows light,
Ere round thy palsied heart ice be congealèd quite,

Ere in thy pocket thou thine eyes dost wear,   10
Ere thy bones serve for calendar,°
Ere in thy hand's thy leg, or silver in thy hair—

Preventing physic use. Think, now, ye hear
The dead-awaking trump! lo, there
The queasy-stomached graves disgorge worms-fattening   15
  cheer!

Sin's sergeants wait to attach° you! Then make haste
Lest you into despair be cast,
The judge unswayed. Take days at best, count each your
  last.

Time posts° on loose-reined steeds:
  The sun, ere it face   20

    To west, may see thee end thy race.
Death is a noun, yet not declined in any case.

The cradle's nigh the tomb. That soul has woe
    Whose drowsy march to heaven is slow
As drawling snails whose slime glues them to things below.   25

Anathema to lukewarm souls! Lo, here
    Theophila's° unhinged with fear,
Clammed with chill sweat whenas her rankling sins
    appear;

Perplexed in crime's meandering maze,
    God's law,   30
    And guilt, that does strict judgement draw,
And her too carnal, yet too stony heart, she saw.

                            Stanzas 46–55

---

5 **forelock take** snatch opportunity. **7 span up** wind up. **11 calendar** to register time. Might be calender, rollers for glazing cloth and paper. The series is based on *Ecclesiastes* xii, 'Remember now thy Creator in the days of thy youth'. 16 **attach** arrest. 19 **posts** hastens. 28 **Theophila** meaning lover of God.

Canto III

Muse! twang the powerful harp and brush each string
    O' the warbling lute, and canzons sing
May ravish earth and thence to heaven in triumph spring.

Noble Du Bartas,° in a high-flown trance
    Observed to start from his bed and dance,   5
Said, Thus by me shall caper all the realm of France!

As vicious meteors, framed of earthly slime,
    By motion fired,° like stars do climb
The woolly-curdled clouds and there blaze out their time

Streaming with burnished flames—yet those but ray   10
    To spend themselves and light our way;
And panting winds to cool ours, not their own lungs, play:

So when enlivened spirits ascend the skies,
    Wasting to make the simple wise,
Who bears the torch himself shades, lightens others' eyes.   15

As lust for hell, zeal sweats to build for heaven,
    When fervent aspirations, driven

By all the soul's quick powers, to that high search are
    given.

High is the sphere on which faith's poles are hinged;
    Pure knowledge, thou art not restringed,   20
Thy flames enfire the bushy heart, yet leave't unsinged.

Suburbs of paradise! thou saintly land
    Of visions wooed by wisdom's hand,
By dull mules in gold trappings how dost slighted stand!

—Whose world's a frantic sea more crosswinds fly   25
    Than sailor's compass knows: saints ply
Their sails through airy waves and anchor still on high.

'Tis holiness land'st here; where none distasted,°
    Rave with guilt's dread, nor with rage wasted,
Nor beauty-dazzled eyes with female wantons blasted;   30

No childish toys; no boiling youth's wild thirst;
    No ripe ambition; no accursed
Old gripping avarice; no doting sloth there's nursed;

No gluttony's maw-worm; nor the itch of lust;
    No tympany of pride; nor rust   35
Of envy; no wrath's spleen; nor obduration's crust;

No canker of self-love; nor cramp of cares;
    No schism-vertigo; nor nightmares
Of inward stings affright; here lurk no penal snares.

Hence, earth a dim spot shows, where mortals toil   40
    For shot-bruised mud walls (childish broil),
For pot-gun cracks 'gainst ant-hill works—O what a coil!

Where Gluttony is full-gorged; where Lust still spawns;
    Where Wrath takes blood, and Avarice pawns;
Where Envy frets, Pride struts and dull Remissness°   45
    yawns.

Where Mars° the ascendant is: how realms shattered lie
    With scattered courts beneath mine eye,
Which show like atoms chased by wind's inconstancy.

Here, the universe in nature's frame doth stand
    Upheld by truth and wisdom's hand;   50
Zanzummins° show from hence as dwarfs on pygmy-land.

How vile's the world! Fancy, keep up thy wings
    (Ruffled in bustle of low things,
Tossed in the common throng), then acquiesce° 'bove
    kings.

Thus, thou being rapt and struck with enthean° fire,   55
  In sky's star-chamber strike thy lyre.
Proud Rome, not all thy Caesars could thus high aspire!

Man's spiritual state, enlarged, still widening flows
  As the helix doth; a circle shows
Man's natural life, which death soon from its zenith   60
  throws.

Heaven's perspective° is over-reasoning faith
  Which soul-entrancing visions hath;
Truth's beacon, fired by love, joy's empire layeth.

This all-informing light i' th' pregnant mind
  The babe Theophila enshrined.   65
Grace dawns when nature sets—dawn for fair day de-
  signed.

Breathe in thy dainty bud, sweet rose: 'tis time
  Makes thee to ripened virtues climb
Whenas the Sun of grace shall spread thee to thy prime.

When her life's clock struck twelve (hope's noon), so   70
  bright
  She beamed that queens admired her sight,
Viewing, through beauty's lantern, her intrinsic light.

As when fair tapers burn in crystal frame
  The case seems fairer by the flame,
So does heaven's brighter love brighten this lovely dame.   75

Her soul the pearl, her shell out-whites the snow,
  Or streams that from stretched udders flow:
Her lips rock-rubies and her veins wrought sapphires
  show;

Attractive graces dance about her lips,
  Spice from these scarlet portals skips,   80
Thence Gilead's° mystic balm (grief's sovereign balsam)
  slips;

Such precious fume the incensèd altar vents:
  So, gums in air breathe compliments;
So, rose's damasked° robe, pranked with green ribbons,
  scents.

Her eyes amaze the viewers and inspire   85
  To hearts a warm yet chaste desire
(As Sol heats all); yet feel they in themselves no fire.

Those lights, the radiant windows of her mind,
  Who would portray as soon may find
A way to paint the viewless, poise the weightless wind.   90

But might we her sweet breast, love's Eden, see,
  On those snow-mountlets apples be
May cure those mischiefs wrought by the forbidden tree.

Her hands are soft as swanny down and much
  More white; whose temperate warmth is such   95
As when ripe gold and quickening sunbeams inly touch.

Ye sirens° of the groves who, perched on high,
  Tune guttural sweets—air-minstrels—why
From your bough-cradles rocked with wind to her d'ye
    fly?

See, lilies, gowned in tissue, simper by her,   100
  With marigolds in flaming tire;
Green-satinned bays, with primrose fringed, seem all on
    fire.

Thou art silver-voiced, teeth-pearled, thy head's gold-
    thatched;
  Nature's reviver, Flora,° 's patched,
Though tricked in May's new raiment, when with thee   105
    she's matched.

Thou, chaste as fair; Eve ere she blushed: from thee
  The liberal arts *in capite,*°
The virtues by knight-service, graces hold in fee.

                                    Stanza 1–37

4 **Du Bartas** see Sylvester. 8 **By motion fired** made incandescent by
friction. 28 **distasted** disgusted, disaffected. 45 **Remissness** Sloth,
completing the 7 Deadly Sins. 46 **Mars** planet of war, in astrological
dominance. 51 **Zanzummins** Zamzummins, giants of Canaan in *Deu-
teronomy* ii. Pygmies were known from the reports of Greek geogra-
phers, notably Pliny. 54 **acquiesce** keep still. 55 **enthean** divinely inspired. 61 **perspective** telescope. Heaven seen by mystical faith which
overbears reason. 81 **Gilead** famous for balm; cf. spices of Arabia.
See *Jeremiah* viii. 84 **damasked** embroidered. 97 **sirens** nightingales.
104 **Flora** flower goddess. 107 **in capite** land held directly from the
sovereign; knight-service and fee were ways of holding land on condition of service to the superior lord.

PATRICK CARY

Younger son of Henry Cary, 1st Viscount Falkland. Mother a learned woman, secret Roman catholic. Brother Lucius, the 2nd viscount, inherited house near Oxford called Great Tew, which he made famous as 'like a college, full of learned men' (Aubrey)——Jonson, Godolphin, Suckling, Waller, Cowley, Hobbes connected with it. Patrick sent to France to be educated as a catholic; spent 3 years there, then 12 in Italy where Pope Urban VIII gave him church emoluments (he did not become a priest). In 1650 he was returning to England in some distress and entered a Benedictine monastery for some months. *Trivial poems and triolets* known only from MS. dated 1651, edited in 1771 and again by Sir Walter Scott in 1820. Ed. Saintsbury. See K. Weber *Lucius Cary* 1940.

Hymn

Whilst I beheld the neck o' the dove,°
I spied and read these words:
This pretty dye
Which takes your eye
Is not at all the bird's;   5
The dusky raven might
Have with these colours pleased your sight,
Had God but chose so to ordain above.
This label wore the dove.

Whilst I admired the nightingale,   10
These notes she warbled o'er:
No melody
Indeed have I;
Admire me then no more:
God has it in his choice   15
To give the owl,° or me, this voice;
'Tis he, 'tis he that makes me tell my tale.
This sang the nightingale.

I smelt and praised the fragrant rose;
Blushing, thus answered she: 20
The praise you gave,
The scent I have,
Do not belong to me;
This harmless odour, none
But only God indeed does own;   25
To be his keepers, my poor leaves° he chose.
And thus replied the rose.

I took the honey from the bee,
On the bag° these words were seen:
More sweet than this   30
Perchance naught is,
Yet gall it might have been;
If God it should so please
He could still make it such with ease;
And as well gall to honey change can he.   35
This learnt I of the bee.

I touched and liked the down o' the swan
But felt these words there writ:
Bristles, thorns, here
I soon should bear   40
Did God ordain but it;
If my down to thy touch
Seem soft and smooth, God made it such;
Give more, or take all this away, he can.
This was I taught by the swan.   45

All creatures, then, confess to God
That they owe him all, but I.
My senses find
True, what my mind
Would still—oft does—deny.   50
Hence, pride! out of my soul!
O'er it thou shalt no more control:
I'll learn this lesson, and escape the rod.
I, too, have all from God.

1 **dove** all the creatures here are emblems of love. Cf. Noel *Gaze not on swans. The dove's neck-ring* is an early medieval Arabic treatise on courtly love. 16 **owl** traditional opposite to nightingale. 26 **leaves** there is a tradition which I cannot trace the source of that the rose, or its leaves, bears Christ in the world—perhaps because the Virgin is the mystic rose (cf. Vaughan *Night*); but then so is Christ (Cartwright *Circumcision*). 29 **bag** see Herrick *Bag of the bee*.

Nulla fides°

For God's sake mark that fly!
See what a poor, weak, little thing it is.
When thou hast marked, and scorned it, know that this,
This little poor weak fly
Has killed a pope; can make an emperor die.   5

Behold yon spark of fire:
How little hot! how near to nothing 'tis!
When thou hast done despising, know that this,
This contemned spark of fire,
Has burnt whole towns; can burn a world entire.   10

That crawling worm there see:
Ponder how ugly, filthy, vile it is.
When thou hast seen and loathed it, know that this,
This base worm thou dost see,
Has quite devoured thy parents; shall eat thee.   15

Honour, the world, and man—
What trifles are they! since most true it is
That this poor fly, this little spark, this
So much abhorrèd worm, can
Honour destroy; burn worlds; devour up man.   20

° **Title**   No faith.

Crucifixus pro nobis°

Christ in the cradle

Look how he shakes for cold!
How pale his lips are grown!
Wherein his limbs to fold
Yet mantle has he none:
His pretty feet and hands   5
(Of late more pure and white
Than is the snow
That pains them so)
Have lost their candour° quite;
His lips are blue   10
(Where roses grew),
He's frozen everywhere.
All the heat he has

Joseph, alas,
Gives in a groan; or Mary in a tear.   15

Christ in the garden

Look how he glows for heat!°
What flames come from his eyes!
'Tis blood that he does sweat,
Blood his bright forehead dyes.
See, see, it trickles down!   20
Look how it showers amain!
Through every pore
His blood runs o'er
And empty leaves each vein.
His very heart°   25
Burns in each part;
A fire his breast doth sear.
For all this flame,
To cool the same
He only breathes a sigh, and weeps a tear.   30

Christ in his passion

What bruises do I see!
What hideous stripes are those!
Could any cruel be
Enough to give such blows?
Look how they bind his arms   35
And vex his soul with scorns!
Upon his hair
They make him wear
A crown of piercing thorns;
Through hands and feet   40
Sharp nails they beat,
And now the cross they rear.
Many look on;
But only John
Stands by to sigh, Mary to shed a tear.   45

Why did he shake for cold?
Why did he glow for heat?
Dissolve that frost he could,
He could call back that sweat.
Those bruises, stripes, bonds, taunts,   50
Those thorns which thou didst see,
Those nails, that cross,

His own life's loss,
Why, O why suffered he?
'Twas for thy sake: 55
Thou, thou didst make
Him all those torments bear.
If then his love
Do thy soul move,
Sigh out a groan, weep down a melting tear.   60

° **title** Crucified for us. The phrase is in the Nicene creed, at eucharist.
9 candour whiteness. **16 heat** cf. *The Burning Babe* by Robert Southwell, a Roman catholic priest martyred 1595. The contrast is also Petrarchan: cf. Benlowes *Might souls converse*. The garden is Gethsemane.
25 heart Christ sometimes depicted with a flaming heart.

PROFESSOR JOSEPH BEAUMONT

Father a clothier in Hadleigh, a prosperous Suffolk wool-market. School there; Peterhouse, Cambridge; elected a fellow 1636 (cf. Crashaw). Expelled as royalist and high churchman 1644, but provided with various church emoluments. *Psyche* 1648. In 1650 chaplain to Bishop of Ely and married an heiress who was the bishop's ward. Lived at her manor in Suffolk, writing most of his minor poems, until 1662 when she died of fen fever, leaving 6 children (of whom one reached adulthood). At the same time, Beaumont elected master of Jesus College, Cambridge (restored the chapel at his own expense); a year later moved to be master of Peterhouse (where he painted the chapel altar with his own hand). Controversy with Henry More started 1665. In 1674, regius professor of divinity; still preaching robustly in his 80s. *Poetical works* ed. A.B. Grosart 2 vols. 1877–80.

Jesus inter ubera Mariae°
(to a bass and two trebles)

In the coolness of the day,
The old world's even,° God all undressed went
    down
  Without his robe, without his crown,
Into his private garden,° there to lay
    On spicy bed   5
    His sweeter head.

There he found two beds of spice,
A double mount of lilies in whose top
  Two milky fountains bubbled up.
He soon resolved: And well I like! he cries,   10
    My table spread
    Upon my bed.

Scarcely had he 'gun to feed
When troops of cherubs hovered round about,
   And on their golden wings they brought   15
All Eden's flowers. But we cried out: No need
      Of flowers here!
      Sweet spirits, forbear.

True, he needs no sweets, say they;
But sweets have need of him, to keep them so;   20
   Now paradise springs new with you,
Old Eden's beauty's all inclined this way;
      And we are come
      To bring them home.

Paradise spring new with you,   /   25
Where 'twixt those beds of lilies you may see
   Of life the everlasting tree.
Sweet is your reason, then said we: come strow
      Your pious showers
      Of eastern flowers.   30

Chorus   Winds awake! and with soft gale
Awake the odours of our garden too;
   By which yourselves perfumèd go
Through every quarter of your world, that all
      Your sound may hear   35
      And breathe your air.

° **title** Jesus between Mary's breasts. 2 **even** the end of the old dispensation of law; the beginning of the new, of grace. God walked in the garden of Eden in the cool of the day. 4 **garden** Mary, as in an allegorical reading of *Song of Solomon:* 'A garden enclosed is my sister, my spouse . . .' Mary is also the second Eden. Her breasts are two of the singers.

from Psyche° or love's mystery displaying the intercourse betwixt Christ and the soul

Canto II

For as the honey of heaven's lovely hives,
The summer's clouds, snugging in laps of flowers,
That correspondent dwelling quickly leaves
To churlish drops of less-deserving showers,
   Or rankling mildew which such venom sheds   5
   As soon deflowereth all those virgin beds:

So fared it now with Psyche's careless breasts,
On which more dainties dropped from Phylax'° tongue
Than e'er on Hybla° made their verdant nest.
Abroad she will, and please herself among   10
    The fields' wide sweets, forgetting that some wind
    Might steal upon and blast her honied mind.

Abroad she will because she understands
Not truly what it is to be abroad;
And knows as little what safe bliss commends   15
Her private home; that robbers haunt the road
    She never dreams; or that the broader way
    Gives danger room more ambushes to lay.

The sportful twins° of heaven now 'gan to reign
And brought a season fitting for their play: 20
Thick did they scatter upon every plain
A flowery verdure, and dishevel May
    Round Tellus'° springing face, who thus beguiles
    Her winter's sadness with this month of smiles.

And why, said Psyche, may not I comply   25
With heaven and earth, now both are of a mind?
Yet guilt's forerunner, doubtful jealousy,
Advisèd her this wild design to blind,°
    And by sly stealth to snatch those joys for which,
    Though earnest, yet still fearful was her itch.   30

She therefore plotted to slip out alone;
But sage Syneidesis, her trusty maid,
Hunted out every step where she had gone;
And Charis, an old friend of hers, afraid
    What might betide the wanderer, followed too,   35
    Yet in her company forbore to go.

Nor could her foolish craft escape the eye
Of wary Phylax: never-sleeping he
Discovered with what politic vanity
Her own betrayer she contrived to be;   40
    And all the way she went, with heavy sighs
    Pondered the dangers of her jollities.

As pleasure's paths she in the fields did trace,
It joyed her dreaming heart the lambs to see
Skipping in harmless sport from place to place;   45
And who would be so sad and dull, said she,
    To sneak at home, when thus abroad we may
    Behold how sweetly innocence doth play?

No smiling flower could meet her as she went
But, gathering it, she with a kiss would pay   50
The courteous price of that delicious scent
With which so kindly it perfumed her way;
    And still cries out, How poor a place is home,
     Which for such free full joys affords no room!

Stanzas 6–14

° **Psyche** soul. In the Greek myth she was a princess whom Cupid visited every night but would not let her see him. For Christ = Cupid see Crashaw *Weeper*. There are 24 cantos in the poem. The stanzas are those of Shakespeare's *Venus and Adonis*. 8 **Phylax** magical and holy guardian. As usual in romances, the heroine insists on an adventure. 9 **Hybla** see Carew *Mole*. 19 **twins** Castor and Pollux, constellation and sign of the zodiac for June. 23 **Tellus** earth. 28 **blind** conceal.

Canto V

A stately mirror's all-enamelled case
The second was. No crystal ever yet
Smiled with such pureness; never lady's glass
Its owner flattered with so smooth a cheat;
    Nor could Narcissus'° fount with such delight   5
     Into his fair destruction him invite.

For he in that, and self-love, being drowned,
Agenor from him plucked his doting eyes;
And shuffled in her fragments having found
Old Jezebel's,° he stole the dog's due prize;   10
    Goliah's staring basins too he got,
     Which he with Pharaoh's all together put;

But not content with these: from Phaëton,°
From Joab, Icarus, Nebuchadnezzar,°
From Philip° and his world-devouring son,   15
From Scylla,° Catiline, Tully, Pompey, Caesar,
    From Herod, Cleopatra and Sejanus,
     From Agrippina and Domitianus,

And many surly Stoics,° theirs he pulled;
Whose proudest humours° having drainèd out,   20
He blended in a large and polished mould;
Which up he filled with (what from heaven he brought)
    An extract of those looks of Lucifer
     In which against his God he breathèd war.

Then to the north, that glassy kingdom where   25
Established frost and ice for ever reign,
He sped his course, and meeting Boreas° there,
Prayed him this liquid mixture to restrain:
    When lo! as Boreas oped his mouth, and blew
    For his command, the slime all solid grew.   30

Thus was the mirror forgèd, and contained
The vigour of those self-admiring eyes
Agenor's witchcraft into it had strained—
A dangerous juncture of proud fallacies,
    Whose fair looks so enamoured him that he,   35
    Thrice having kissed it, named it Philauty.°

Enchanted Psyche ravished was to see
The glass herself upon herself reflect
With trebled majesty. The sun when he
Is by Aurora's° roseal fingers decked   40
    Views not his repercussèd self so fair
    Upon the eastern main, as she did here.

New flames were kindled in her spriteful eye,
New roses on her smiling lips were strowed,
New loves' and graces' dainty luxury   45
Down with her golden streaming tresses flowed,
    New lilies trimmed her hands' and fingers' feature,
    New goodliness aggrandisèd her stature.

Her cheated soul sprung through her eye, and dwelt
So long upon the glass that it grew new;   50
Such mighty thoughts till now she never felt,
As all about his high-swollen fancy flew;
    Which breaking from her mouth at length, she cries,
    How long have I been strange to mine own eyes!

Am I that worm, whom Phylax put in mind   55
So oft of dust and vileness? Could this face,
These eyes, these looks, these hands, this person find
No better parallels? I see the case
    Is plain how Aphrodisius came to be
    So hideous: Phylax made the like of me.   60

Fool that I was to dream it could be true
Which proud he daily preached to my disgrace!
Who could believe I ne'er till now should view
The wonders of mine own accomplished face?
    O most ingenious glass, which tells me more   65
    Than Phylax or than Charis did before!

I see what case there was to guard each port
Whose key doth hither any way unlock,
That such ingrateful envious guests' resort
No more may me and all my favours mock: 70
  'Tis just that they should hence exilèd be
  Whose spiteful fraud did banish me from me.

No marvel now if heaven's apparent heir
Disdains all beauties that he finds above,
And, doing right to what's supremely fair,   75
By stooping down to me exalts his love.
  I little thought I could so much have shown
  Why this my head should fit an heavenly crown.

O pardon me, bright eyes! that ignorant I
With briny tears so oft have sullied you;   80
Had not your flames by their divinity
Securèd been, they had been quenched e'er now;
  And pardon me, sweet cheeks! I will no more
  Blubber and scald your roses as before.

And you, all-lovely lips, no more shall kiss   85
The dust (which foolish I took for your mother);
The tribe of oriental rubies is
Your precious kindred; nor must any other
  Your soft and living nectar hope to sip
  But my dear spouse's correspondent lip.   90

Nor shall rude usage rob thee of thy due,
My glorious body: all hair-clothes, farewell!
My liberal tresses yield me hair enough;
And by this girdle, heaven did plainly tell
  What other furniture would suit me best   95
  When with this siege of gems it girt my waist.

And since thy casket's wardrobe challenges
My proudest choice, I wish thyself wert here,
Royal Agenor, to admire how these
Fair limbs of mine would quit themselves, and wear   100
  In worthy triumph thy best jewels, which
  Shall by my purer beams their own enrich.

This said, Love, who stood fawning by her side,
Her delicate quaintness sets on work to dress
Her high conceited queen in equal pride.   105
A purple mantle, fringed with stateliness,
  Embroidered with ambition, laced round
  With vanity, she in the casket found;

About her this she plants; then for her neck
And wrists, three gaudy strings of gems she chose;　　110
A sparkling coronet her head to deck;
To trim her feet a pair of silver shoes;
　　A crisping° pin to multiply her hair;
　　Spruce lawn° to make her breast, though clothèd, bare.

Stanzas 197–215

5 **Narcissus** see Kynaston *Looking-glass*. 10 **Jezebel** made herself up
to seduce Jehu but he ordered her to be thrown out of the window; he
trampled her body and it was eaten by dogs. The wife of King Ahab of
Israel, she was an ambitious enemy of God, like Goliath and Pharaoh,
and Joab, a general, whom Solomon had executed. 13 **Phaeton** crashed
his father's sun-chariot; see Chapman *Ovid's banquet*. Icarus similarly
with his father's artificial wings. 14 **Nebuchadnezzar** king of Assyria,
builder of Babylon, enemy of Daniel, who fell into a depression and
lived like an animal. 15 **Philip** of Macedon, conqueror of Greece,
assassinated 336 B.C. when his son, Alexander the Great, was 20. Alexander conquered the Middle East and northern India but died at Babylon
aged 32. Like the orientals above and the Romans in the next section,
he combined indulgence with energy. 16 **Scylla** Sulla, dictator of Rome,
d. 78 B.C. Catiline, leader of anarchist conspiracy in Rome, killed 62 B.C.
after being impeached by Cicero (Tully), who was himself killed in 43
B.C. (aged 63) on the orders of Mark Antony, lover of Cleopatra, queen
of Egypt who committed suicide in 30 B.C. aged 39. Pompey, a Roman
general, was defeated by Julius Caesar in Greece and stabbed in the
back by one of his own officers in Egypt, 48 B.C. Caesar, dictator of
Rome, was stabbed to death in 44 B.C. by Antony and others. Sejanus,
a conspirator against the emperor Tiberius, who had him put to death
in A.D. 31. Agrippina was mother of the emperor Nero and regent in his
minority until he had her put to death A.D. 59. The emperor Domitian,
satirised by Juvenal, was assassinated on the orders of his wife and
officers A.D. 96. 19 **Stoics** philosophers of Greece and Rome famous for
indifference to pain. 20 **humours** fluids. 27 **Boreas** north wind. 36
Philauty self-love. 40 **Aurora** dawn goddess. 113 **crisping** waving.
114 **lawn** see Lovelace *Strive not*.

Canto VI

All things at first was God, who dwelt alone
In his unbounded self; but bounteous he
Conceived the form of this creatiön°
That other things by him might happy be.
　　A way to ease his streams his goodness sought　　5
　　And at the last into a world burst out.

Which world at first was but one single step
From simple nothing; yet that step was wide;
No power but his or could or yet can leap

Over to something's bank from nothing's side: 10
  If you those distances compare with this,
    The east and west are one, the poles will kiss.

This something, son of nothing, in the gulf
Of its own monstrous darkness wallowing lay,
And, strangely lost in its confounded self,   15
Knew neither where to go nor where to stay,
  Being hideously besieged on every side
    With Tohu's and with Bohu's° boundless tide.

     •   /•   •

All qualities ran wildly up and down,
Ne'er thinking of symbolic amity;°   20
All motions were transverse; as yet unknown
Were rest and quiet; hideous ataxy°
  Was everything; and neither here nor there
    Keeped their own homes, but all were everywhere.

No shores the ocean in this tempest knew   25
But swallowed up the sands and, rushing out
Whilst all things else were plunged in quarrels, threw
His billowy arms the universe about,
  Which in this civil° deluge drowned had been,
    Had not the kind Creator's help come in.   30

Forth flew the eternal Dove,° and tenderly
Over the floods' blind tumult hovering,
The secret seeds of vital energy
Waked by the virtue of his fostering wing;
  Much like the loving hen, whose brooding care   35
    Doth hatch her eggs and life's warm way prepare.

Stanza 115–7 . . . 121–3

3 creation cf. Sylvester *Almighty Father*. **18 Tohu . . . Bohu** chaos.
In *Genesis* i.2, matter was at first 'without form and void'. The Hebrew
is *thohu wa-bhohu*, emptiness and desolation. Beaumont personifies
tohubohu like the classical Chaos sometimes was; Milton's Chaos in
Paradise lost II, X and elsewhere is sometimes the region or stuff, sometimes 'the anarch old.' **20 amity** universal order, in the dimensions of
space and time, and in the elements (see Beedome *Inquisition*), sym-
bolises human order, in the state and the soul. **22 ataxy** disorder.
From Latin, first recorded 1615. **29 civil** as in civil war, because the
elements etc. were (as in Milton) at war with each other instead of
cohering. **31 Dove** God's spirit 'hovered' or 'brooded' over chaos in
the original Hebrew of *Genesis* i.2; cf. also the dove which marks the
end of the Flood in *Genesis* viii; and the Holy Ghost at Christ's bap-
tism, *Luke* iii.

The oath

Yes, as I live, I'll do't. —Nay, stay
My friends! if that be all, I may
   Not rest on this security:
     Your swearing by
Your life doth but my faith deter,   5
For you but by a vapour swear.

Your life! what lease makes life your own?
May not your flitting breath be blown
   Away by every moment's blast?
     Future, and past,   10
Quite out of thy possession are,
And present's gone as soon as here.

What mean'st thou then by *as I live*?
Death can thy confidence deceive
   And make thee die a perjured man   15
     Precisely when
Thou'rt swearing by thy life. Take heed,
That oath thy essence doth exceed:

An oath which only doth become
The mighty mouth of God, from whom   20
   Life learned to live. Ah, mortal wight,
     I sooner might
Yield on thy credit to rely
If thou but swearest, *as I die*!

The gnat°

One night, all tirèd with the weary day
And with my tedious self, I went to lay
   My fruitless cares
   And needless fears
    Asleep.   5

The curtains of the bed and of mine eyes
Being drawn, I hoped no trouble would surprise
   That rest which now
   'Gan on my brow
    To creep.   10

When lo, a little fly, less than its name
(It was a gnat) with angry murmur came:
    About she flew
    And louder grew
      Whilst I   15

Fain would have scorned the silly thing, and slept
Out all its noise. I resolute silence kept,
    And laboured so
    To overthrow
      The fly.   20

But still with sharp alarms vexatious she
Or challengèd, or rather mockèd, me.
    Angry at last,
    About I cast
      My hand.   25

'Twas well night would not let me blush, nor see
With whom I fought; and yet, though feeble she,
    Nor her nor my
    Own wrath could I
      Command.   30

Away she flies, and her own triumph sings,
I being left to fight with idler things—
    A feeble pair,
    Myself, and air.
      How true   35

A worm is man, whom flies their sport can make.
Poor worm! true rest in no bed can he take,
    But one of earth
    Whence he came forth
      And grew.   40

For there none but his silent sisters be,
Worms of as true and genuine earth as he,
    Which from the same
    Corruption came;
      And there,   45

Though on his eyes they feed, though on his heart,
They neither vex nor wake him; every part
    Rests in sound sleep
    And out doth keep
      All fear.   50

° **gnat**   cf. Cary *Nulla fides.*

Home

Home's home, although it reachèd be
Through wet and dirt and night. Though heartily
  I welcomed was, yet something still,
  Methinks, was wanting to fulfil
  Content's odd appetite. No cheer,   5
Say I, so good as that which meets me here,

Here, here at home. Not that my board
I find with quainter, richer dainties stored;
  No, my high welcome all in this
  Cheap simple word presented is—   10
  My home: a word so dearly sweet
That all variety in it I meet.

When I'm abroad,° my joys are so,
And therefore they to me seem strangers too;
  I may salute° them lovingly   15
  But must not too familiar be;
  Some ceremonious points there are
Which me from pleasure's careless freedom bar.

There must my mirth's tunes taken be
Not by mine own but by my convives'° key;   20
  My words and smiles must temporise,
  And I myself a sacrifice
  Must on that humour's altar yield
Which there the company shall please to build.

If there on every dish I taste,   25
'Tis not myself but some disease I feast;
  My friend suspects, if I forbear,
  That I neglect him and his cheer;
  Nor is it easy to prevent
Or mine own mischief, or his discontent.   30

But home, sweet home, releaseth me
From anxious joys into the liberty
  Of unsolicitous delight;
  Which, howsoever mean and slight,
  By being absolutely free   35
Enthrones me in contentment's monarchy.

---

13 abroad away from home, out. **15 salute** kiss, shake hands, etc. **20
convives** companions.

Honour

   Ambitious sir, take heed!
    For thou on glass dost tread:
No glass more beautiful and clear
Than all the paths of honour are;
No glass more slippery can be,   5
Or brittle, than deceitful she.

   Ambitious sir, take heed!
    Thou trustest to a reed:
No reed more tossed and scornèd by
All winds, than honour's bravery;   10
No reed will wound more deeply thee
Who lean'st on it, than treacherous she.

   Ambitious sir, take heed!
    Thou rid'st a dangerous steed:
No steed his crest doth more advance,   15
Or proudlier than honour prance;
No steed did e'er so fatally
Stumble, as most uncertain she.

   Ambitious sir, take heed!
    Thou dost on poison feed: 20
No poison in a goodlier cup
Than that of honour servèd up;
No poison e'er made drinker be
More swollen than doth baneful she.

ANN COLLINS

Nothing known except from *Divine songs and meditations* 1653 (ed. S. N. Stewart, Los Angeles 1961) and its preface: 'I inform you, that by divine Providence I have been restrained from bodily employment, suiting with my disposition, which enforced me into a retired course of life; wherein it pleased God to give me such enlargedness of mind and activity of spirit, so that this seeming desolate condition, proved to me most delightful. I became affected to poetry, insomuch that I proceeded to practise the same: and though the helps I had therein were small, yet the thing itself appeared unto me so amiable, as that it influenced my faculties to put forth themselves in a practice so pleasing'.

Another song

The winter of my infancy being over-past,
I then° supposèd suddenly the spring would haste,
Which useth everything to cheer
With invitation to recreation
This time of year.   5

The sun sends forth his radiant beams to warm the
        ground,
The drops distil, between the gleams delights abound,
Ver° brings her mate, the flowery queen;
The graves she dresses, her art expresses
On every green.   10

But in my spring it was not so, but contrary,
For no delightful flowers grew to please the eye,
No hopeful bud nor fruitful bough,
No moderate showers which causeth flowers
To spring and grow.   15

My April was exceeding dry, therefore unkind;
Whence 'tis that small utility I look to find,

For when that April is so dry
(As hath been spoken) it doth betoken
Much scarcity.   20

Thus is my spring now almost past in heaviness,
The sky of pleasure's overcast with sad distress,
For, by a comfortless eclipse,
Disconsolation and sore vexation
My blossom nips.   25

Yet as a garden is my mind enclosèd fast,
Being to safety so confined from storm and blast,
Apt to produce a fruit most rare,
That is not common with every woman
That fruitful are.   30

A love of goodness is the chiefest plant therein;
The second is (for to be brief) dislike of sin;
These grow in spite of misery,
Which grace doth nourish and cause to flourish
Continually.   35

But evil motions, corrupt seeds, fall here also,
Whence spring profaneness, as do weeds where flowers
        grow,
Which must supplanted be with speed—
These weeds of error, distrust and terror—
Lest woe succeed,   40

So that they not molest the plants before expressed,
Which countervails these outward wants, and purchase
        rest,
Which more commodious is for me
Than outward pleasures or earthly treasures
Enjoyed would be.   45

My little hopes of worldly gain I fret not at,
As yet I do this hope retain: though spring be late,
Perhaps my summer-age may be
Not prejudicial but beneficial
Enough for me.   50

Admit the worst, if be not so, but stormy too,
I'll learn myself to undergo more than I do;
And still content myself with this
Sweet meditation and contemplation
Of heavenly bliss,   55

Which for the saints reservèd is who persevere
In piety and holiness and godly fear,

The pleasures of which bliss divine
Neither logician nor rhetorician
Can define.°   60

Divine songs and meditations 1653

2 **I then** conjectural : gap in text. 8 **Ver** Primavera, post-classical
goddess of spring; with Flora. 60 **Can define** conjectural : gap in text.

JOHN HALL

Precocious, fat, intemperate journalist, friend of Shirley, Henry More, Hobbes, Hartlib the educationist, and protégé of Stanley. Son of gentleman, born and educated in Durham. St. John's College, Cambridge; published his *Poems* and a volume of essays aged 19, and complained at university 'for denying those honorary advancements which are as it were the indulgence of the university when there is an excess of merit' (published sensible tract on university reform 1649). Gray's Inn. *Emblems* 1648. Government pamphleteer; translator.

A dithyramb°

Still creeping, still degenerous soul,
On earth so wallowing still in mire?
Still to the centre dost thou roll,
When up to heaven thou shouldst aspire?
Did not thy jailer, flesh, deny   5
The freedom for to feed thine own insatiate eye,
   How might thou let it surfeit here
   On choicest glories! how it might
   Thick-flowing globes of splendour bear,
   And triumph in its native light!   10
   How't would hereafter sleep disdain!
The glorious Sun of righteousness uprise again!
   O who so stupid that would not
   Resolve to atoms° for to play
   'Mong the golden streamers he shall shut   15
   While he prolongs one endless day!
   How small three° evenings' darkness be
Comparèd once with measureless eternity!
   See how the joyous clouds make way
   And put a ruddy brightness on,   20
   How they their silken fleeces lay

For him to mount to heaven upon,
Where he may in full glory shine,
Whose presence made, before, a heaven of Palestine.
    That lovely brow, that was before   25
    Drowned in a flood of crimson sweat,
    Is now with brightness gilded o'er
    And all with burnished flames beset.
    Him, whom his drowsy sons° did leave
Sleepless, aërial legions triumph to receive.   30
    This innocent colúmbine,° he
    That was the mark of rage before,
    O cannot now admirèd be
    But, still admirèd, still needs more.
    Who would not stand amazed to see   35
Frail flesh become the garment of divinity?
    Appear no more, proud Olivet,°
    In tawny olives: from this time
    Be all with purple vines beset;
    The sprig of Jesse° from thee did climb   40
    Up to the skies, and spread those boughs
Whereon life's grapes, those paradisian clusters, grows.
    Why stare you, curious gazers, so?
    No eye can reach his journey's end:
    He'll pierce the rolling concave through   45
    And that expanded fabric rend;
    Then he's at home. He was before
A pilgrim, while he footed this round nothing o'er;
    If then his nimble feet could make
    A pavement° of the quivering stream,   50
    And cause those powerful spirits quake
    That fear not anything but him:
    Now can and will he turn to joys
Your fears, and or disarm or turn your enemies.
    He is not lost, though wafted hence,   55
    He's with you (darlings of his love);
    He's the supreme intelligence,°
    That all little orbs will move;
    He is the head (it cannot be
Members can perish where there's such a head as he):   60
    A head composed of majesty,
    Were't not by mercy all possessed,
    From which such charming glances fly
    As striking vengeance can arrest,
    From which such powerful frowns arise   65
As can strike palsies in the earth and headache in the
    skies.

What did you think he could remain
Disguised in such an inch° of land,
That convex° cannot him contain,
Though spun out by his own right hand?   70
'What did you think, that though he lay
Interred a while, the earth might swallow such a prey?
  That very dying did restore
  Banished life to rotting men,
  And fetched back breath that fled before   75
  Into their nostrils once again;
  That very death gave life to all
And to all mankind recovery of their father's fall.
  Suppose ye that the fatal tree,
  That happiest worst of punishments,   80
  Did punish such a sinless he,
  Or shame him that was excellence?
  No! no! the crime doth ever state
The punishment, and he sin could not act, but hate.
  Thought ye that stream did flow in vain   85
  That issued from his opened side?
  Your souls were foul, yet every stain
  By these pure drops were purified;
  He was, he, freely prodigal
To spend all's blood for some, when some might have   90
    saved all.
  Hark! hark! what melody, what choice
  Of sweetest airs, of charming sounds!
  Heaven seems all turned into a voice!
  Hear what loud shrieking joy rebounds!
  The very winds now whistle joy,   95
And make Hosannas! of the former Crucify!

° **dithyramb** wild poem (originally bacchanalian). This is about Easter.
14 **atoms** dissolve into atoms so as to play in the sunbeams of the
resurrection (Easter a solar festival). 17 **three** nights that Christ the
sun of righteousness was in the grave. 29 **sons** apostles who went to
sleep in Gethsemane. 31 **columbine** dove; see Joseph Beaumont *All
things*. 37 **Olivet** hill of the ascension: *Luke* xxiv. 40 **Jesse** father of
David, ancestor of Christ: 'there shall come forth a rod out of the
stem of Jesse'—*Isaiah* xi. 50 **pavement** walking on the water, *Matthew*
xiv. 57 **intelligence** angelic being that operates each of the celestrial
spheres. 68 **inch** his sepulchre. 69 **convex** outer sphere of the universe.
See Herbert *Platonic love*.

On an hour-glass

My life is measured by this glass, this glass
By all those little sands that thorough pass.
See how they press, see how they strive which shall
With greatest speed and greatest quickness fall;
See how they raise a little mount, and then   5
With their own weight do level it again;
But when they have all got thorough they give o'er
Their nimble sliding down and move no more.
    Just such is man, whose hours still forward run,
Being almost finished ere they are begun;   10
So perfect nothings, such light blasts° are we,
That ere we're aught at all we cease to be.
Do what we will, our hasty minutes fly,
And while we sleep what do we else but die?
How transient are our joys, how short their day!   15
They creep on towards us, but fly away.
How stinging are our sorrows! where they gain
But the least footing, there they will remain.
How groundless are our hopes, how they deceive
Our childish thoughts, and only sorrow leave!   20
How real are our fears! they blast us still,
Still rend us, still with gnawing passions fill.
How senseless are our wishes, yet how great!
With what toil we pursue them, with what sweat
(Yet most times for our hurts): so small we see,   25
Like children crying for some mercury.°
This gapes for marriage, yet his fickle head
Knows not what cares wait on a marriage bed;
This vows virginity, yet knows not what
Loneness, grief, discontent, attends that state.   30
Desires of wealth another's wishes hold,
And yet how many have been choked with gold?
This only hunts for honour, yet who shall
Ascend the higher shall more wretched fall.
This thirsts for knowledge, yet how is it bought?   35
With many a sleepless night, and racking thought.
This needs will travel, yet how dangers lay
Most secret ambuscados in the way!
These triumph in their beauty, though it shall
Like a plucked rose or fading lily fall.   40
Another boasts strong arms: 'las! giants have
By silly dwarfs been dragged unto their grave.
These ruffle in rich silk: though ne'er so gay,

A well-plumed peacock is more gay than they.
  Poor man! what art? A tennis-ball of error,   45
A ship of glass tossed in a sea of terror;
Issuing in blood and sorrow from the womb,
Crawling in tears and mourning to the tomb.
How slippery are thy paths! how sure thy fall!
How art thou nothing, when thou art most of all!   50

11 **blasts** gusts. 26 **mercury** keeps breaking into blobs (?).

THE REVEREND DANIEL CUDMORE

Graduate of Oxford, rector of Holsworthy, Devon. *Euchodia, or a prayer-song* 1655.

If could some Delius with divided hands

For from within, out of the heart of men, proceed evil thoughts, adulteries, fornications, murders, thefts, covetousness, wickedness, deceit, lasciviousness, an evil eye, blasphemy, pride, foolishness.

Mark vii. 21–22

If could some Delius° with divided hands
　　Sound the seas' depth and on his soul's recorder
Imprint the wracks, huge rocks and heaps of sands
　　Which there lie scattered in confused disorder—
　　　　This could he do by nature's strength or art: 　　5
　　　　Yet none could sound the bottom of the heart.

Should some shipmaster make 's foresplit the probe
　　Of nature's secrets and so bring to view
Land to make up a perfect earthly globe
　　Which Drake or Kit Columbus never knew: 　　10
　　　　Yet, as in the great world, so in his own,
　　　　He must confess there's yet much land unknown.°

The heart's a sea for depth; like Sodom lake°
　　Dead, thick and gross: in it will sink no good.
The heart's land's unknown, wherein what monsters make 　　15
　　Their hides and dens, few yet have understood.
　　　　The centre° may be purest earth; yet the heart,
　　　　The body's centre, 's the corrupter part.

Our heartstrings are the cords of vanity;
　　Their caverns are the devil's lurking-holes; 　　20
(No fit triangle° for the Trinity,
　　An habitatïon more fit for moles);

Their cauls° the veils of damned hypocrisy:
Thus is summed up man's wretched majesty.

If thus the sun within our firmament   25
  Into a meteor degenerate;
If thus the king within our continent
  Lets sin and lust usurp his royal state;
    If thus corrupted be the body's leaven,°
    How much shall we manchets be prepared for   30
    heaven?

Whether hell be in the earth's centre, I suspend;°
  But in man's centre's couched an hell of sin;
Nor do so many lines to the centre tend
  As in a wicked heart fiends make their inn:
    Which yet most know no more than can be found   35
    Where Arethusa° winds beneath the ground.

Lord, show me in the mirror of thy law
  The horror of my heart by bright reflectiön;
In that, thy glass, there falsehood is nor flaw,
  Though wickedly some scorn its true direction   40
    And whip the tutor for his discipline:
    Yet, Lord, direct mine by that glass of thine.

O deign my heart with graces to perfúme
  And throughly purge it from each noisome vapour
Whose rank infection chokes each neighbouring room   45
  And strives to damp my soul's aspiring taper.
    O make my heartstrings, Lord, thy cords of love:
    So mine according to thy heart shall prove.

---

1 **Delius** Apollo, god of knowledge, with outstretched arms. 12 **un-known** at this time: Australia, interior Africa, much of the east, Antarctica. 13 **Sodom lake** Dead Sea. 17 **centre** of the earth. 21 **triangle** heart-shaped. 23 **cauls** cardiac membranes, especially pericardium. (Anatomical term; usually refers to membrane round foetus.) 29 **leaven** fermented dough, which makes the bread rise (manchet is a small loaf); improving ingredient; kingdom of heaven (*Luke* xiii). Here (as in the correspondences in Vaughan's *Tempest*), sun : meteor :: king : usurping sin :: heart : body etc. 31 **suspend** leave the question open. The location of hell was a matter for controversy. 36 **Arethusa** river said to flow under the sea from Greece to Sicily.

THE REVEREND RALPH KNEVET

Chaplain to the great Paston family in Norfolk, in whose papers his 'Gallery to the Temple', a sequel to Herbert's poems, was left. Published *Statisticon, a discourse of military discipline* in verse 1628, and *Rhodon and Iris, as it was presented at the Florist's Feast in Norwich, May 3, 1631*. Rector of Ling 1652–71. There is plenty of writing about the Pastons but best to start with Nicholas Stone's tombs at Paston and Oxnead, 1629, 1635, 1636. *A gallery* ed. G. Pellegrini, Pisa 1954; *Shorter poems* ed. A. M. Charles, Columbus, Ohio 1966. See W. M. Merchant, 'R. Knevet of Norfolk, poet of civil war' *Essays and studies* xiii 1960.

The progress

Man in the womb is but a zoophyte,°
    There nourished like a plant;
But when he is produced to the daylight,
    Disclosed from that warm haunt
  He at the honour doth arrive   5
  To be a creature sensitive.

And memory with fancy in him reign
    Till time makes him mature;
Then reason sets her throne up in his brain
    And takes the sovereign° cure   10
  Of the frail microcosm, an empire
  Which oft commotions do distemper.

For will, seduced by carnal appetite,
    Her dictates doth despise;
Thus her prerogative she loseth quite,   15
    And her high dignities.
  But divine grace can her alone
  Restore unto the regal throne;

By whose assistance man acquireth power
   Unto an higher pitch to climb   20
And to become a glorious conqueror
   Over both death and time:
 Thus he who was a zoophyte
  At first, becomes an angel bright.

1 **zoophyte** creature intermediate between animal and plant, e.g. sea
anemone. First recorded use 1621. 10 **sovereign** complete; and (with a
pun) royal.

The deliverance

One blindfold went upon the narrow ridge
   Of a steep bridge
Which with an archèd bit did curl and chap
   A foaming flood.
He, having passed along free from mishap,   5
   Threw off his hood
And, looking on the danger he had 'scaped,
With infinite amazement he was rapt.

Then conscious of that providence sublime
   Which at that time   10
Had him preservèd from the jaws of hell,
   Immediately
In humble sort upon his knees he fell
   And zealously
No dry devotions did to him pour forth   15
Who from those waters deep did him secure.

The vote°

The helmet now an hive for bees becomes
And hilts of swords may serve for spiders' looms;
   Sharp pikes may make
   Teeth for a rake
And the keen blade, the arch-enemy of life,   5
Shall be degraded to a pruning-knife;°
   The rustic spade,
   Which first was made
For honest agriculture, shall retake

Its primitive employment and forsake   10
    The rampires° steep
    And trenches deep.
Tame conies in our brazen guns shall breed
Or gentle doves their young ones there shall feed;
    In musket barrels   15
    Mice shall raise quarrels
For their quarters. The ventrilóquious drum,
Like lawyers in vacation, shall be dumb.
    Now all recruits
    But those of fruits   20
Shall be forgot; and the unarmed soldier
Shall only boast of what he did whilere,
    In chimney's ends
    Among his friends.

If good effects shall happy signs ensue,   25
I shall rejoice, and my prediction's true.

° **vote** prayer, wish. The poem is based on an ancient emblem, of
bees in a helmet, used by Alciati and by Whitney. 6 **pruning-knife**
'they shall beat their swords into ploughshares, and their spears into
pruning-hooks.' *Isaiah* ii. 4. 11 **rampires** military earthworks.

COMMENTARY 8

Civil War and Commonwealth
1642–1660

Friendship and Marriage

The poems in this section show that about the time of the
Commonwealth there was a development out of Platonic love
into something more familiar. The poets call it sympathy, or
friendship. There was also a development out of the Stuart
version of courtly love into the poetry explicitly of marriage—
'love's matrimony' Newcastle calls it.

Was the Commonwealth a cause, or merely the temporal
context, of these developments? Were they developments of
behaviour or only of intellectual constructs for love poetry?
Certainly both are important for social as well as literary
history. Neither has been attended to. I think Donne initiated
them. Stanley and Feltham are obvious imitators of him,
Newcastle names him in a poem about 'the new love'; yet
none of the poets in this section appears in Kenner's anthology *17th-century poetry: the schools of Donne and Jonson*
(or, in case they should be too late for that, in Harold Love's
Penguin book of Restoration verse). Stanley is quoted once,
Feltham named twice, the others not at all, in Alvarez'
School of Donne. That is precisely the emphasis (to stay
with books that influence students) of both the *Pelican guide
. . . Donne to Marvell* and Helen Gardner's anthology *The
metaphysical poets*.

A lot of the error is due to the concepts 'metaphysical
poetry' and 'Restoration verse'. The first is a statement about
a certain kind of imagery content; but it has been expanded
into the name for a school of poetry supposed to exist in
time, and then expanded again (in the Gardner anthology
for instance) to cover 'everything I like in the 17th century,
starting about 1590'. The second concept is the name for a
period; but it has been contracted into the name for a style—
a style which does not exist. Together, they are stools for
impertinently individuated poets to fall between. It has been
getting worse. Grierson's originating anthology *Metaphysical*

lyrics and poems of the 17th century: Donne to Butler (1921) included Davenant, Milton and Katherine Philips. Their presence blunted the title's precision but at least it admitted that you might write a 'metaphysical' poem and still have an independent existence. But Eliot did not discuss those three in his review, which was reprinted to become authority for error as an essay on 'The metaphysical poets'. Helen Gardner excludes Katherine Philips but stirs in Traherne, Rochester and Richard Leigh. Neither she nor Grierson admits the Newcastles; yet what could be more metaphysical than the Duke's 'real-ly we lie Contracted in each other's eye', and the Duchess's 'cows of probability'? The first uses the eye imagery popularised by Donne, together with his habitual Platonic and Scholastic philosophy. The second is part of a new mode, in which not the images but the statements are metaphysical in the professional sense (we saw it starting in the last section with Benlowes; but Benlowes too is absent from all these anthologies).

We have to start again. The directions are plain. First, to clear the mind of cant, study the allocation of space in anthologies to a few more poets. What determines canonisation? Examinability? How do gaps get left? How do literary myths start? What myth of the 17th century would suit us better now than Eliot's of the dissociation of sensibility? (It seems clear from the poets of this section that some sensibilities or parts of them got closer together in the 1640s, not further apart.) Why do we not study the Commonwealth as a period (cf. Jacobean, Restoration, Augustan)? is it that we need a king's name to authorise us? if so, how do Americans label their periods? Perhaps, disliking puritanism, we can't believe it capable of art (cf. our attitude to communism). Maybe we are right: perhaps these were developments from defeat and exile, or simply from post-war relief, proto-Restoration euphoria, rather than from conditions special to the Commonwealth? To answer these questions we should have to look at the French and Russian revolutions. On the other hand, perhaps it is left-wing prejudice that has diminished this section: we cannot think a royalist general and bloodstock breeder like Newcastle could be genuinely tender, or that an eccentric stagestruck duchess could be as intelligent as his wife.

Consult the reading list under history and domestic arts to see if the historians propose any grounds for a change in the status of women at this time, or in the practice of marriage (note the frequency of divorce as a contradicted image; cf.

Donne in *Batter my heart*). Sympathy between lovers, as understood here, implies that man and woman are equal. This was, in poetry anyway, Donne's discovery: 'So to one neutral thing both sexes fit' (*Canonisation*); but it had by now become more widely experienced and might therefore be genuine even when almost quoted. In much the same way in the late 1960s in England and the States, young people dropped sex differences in hair and clothes—or rather adopted as neutral norm what had been the feminine one of long hair, loose torso coverings and tightness at the groin. This started as a mass imitation of what had always been the habit of 'intellectuals', Bloomsbury, Bohemia and so on; as an act it was merely imitative, fashionable and literary; yet it had the effect, eventually, of popularising some of the underlying experience of the initiators. That is to say, young men and women began to feel more *au fait* with each others' bodies, and sensibilities, than in the previous more differentiated period; therefore more open to 'co-animation'. The equality of status between men and women is now far more marked than any change in their economic positions, or the law of marriage, has been likely to produce.

Equality of this sort can merge into sentimental collusion, or a kind of conspiracy of depravity. Perhaps this is how Restoration comedy, so virulently antagonistic to marriage, can follow so soon on Newcastle and Anne Bradstreet—though the chief causes would still be social and commercial. In poetry, the gap between this section and the Restoration sections 9-10 may seem slight. I have put Cowley and Waller into 9 though they were middle-aged when Charles II was restored, and Cowley writes about Platonic love. But Cowley (a bachelor) and Waller both seem to me to treat women with an aggressive objectivity which is characteristic of the Restoration period; it is obvious in Rochester, and in Mrs. Behn.

The entry of women into poetry needs separate study, from A. Dyce *Specimens of British poetesses selected and chronologically arranged* 1825. The entry of married love coincides with the arrival of women poets but it is not restricted to them; and it is strongly present in pre-war domestic drama. The puritan dislike of virginity and respect for marriage may have had something to do with it; and no doubt it was one of the reactions against Petrarch and Plato. These motives join in Milton's celebration of 'wedded love' as source of 'Relations dear, and all the charities Of father, son, and brother' (*Paradise lost* IV.750). He goes on to reject the Caroline and Restoration alternatives—

> the bought smile
> Of harlots, loveless, joyless, unendeared,
> Casual fruition, nor in court amours—
> Mixed dance, or wanton masque, or midnight ball,
> Or serenade, which the starved lover sings
> To his proud fair, best quitted with disdain.

His divorce pamphlets need to be brought into the case too; and for a proper study of marriage poetry this section needs suport from epithalamions (see Commentary 5) and Habington.

On a smaller scale, or as a starting-point, we could simply look at unity as a topic inside this anthology. Stanley, though a frigid writer, sums up the doctrines in *The killing kiss*. So does Sir Kenelm Digby in his private memoirs (called 'Loose fantasies and castrations' in the MS.): 'all other language was stopped between them both, whilst their souls, ascending to the very extremities of their tongues, began a mystical discourse'. For Restoration versions see Cotton's 'conversation of the mind' in *Join once more*; Jane Barker's *Parting* (similar to Newcastle) and Ephelia's *Philocles*; for earlier versions see Commentaries 1 and 4 on Platonism and angels, and consider in what ways the topic has been altered.

Stanley employs spirits and cherubim; Newcastle equates coitus with eucharist; but it is Katherine Philips who uses the whole panoply of religio-erotic imagery in *Friendship's mystery* and *Dialogue of absence*: 'Let's prove there's a religion in our love'. For this convention's history see Donne (especially *Canonisation* and some Holy Sonnets), G. Fletcher *Thus spend we tears*, G. Herbert *Easter*, Herrick *Star song*, Habington, Cartwright *Circumcision*, Section 7 passim, and Norris in 11.

We would regard Mrs. Philips as a trite manipulator of stupendous themes, one of the women who come and go talking of Michelangelo; but *Orinda to Lucasia parting* is such sincere blackmailing bitchery that we are bound to think of her work as lesbian. You may not think special categories raise the interest of the writing they contain—children's writing, lesbian poetry and so on. Even if not, pursue the 'friendship' of the matchless Orinda and her circle. In his *Discourse of friendship* (1657) Jeremy Taylor, one of that circle, insisted on the practicality of friendship:

> I do not think that friendships are metaphysical things, created for contemplation, or that men and women should stare upon each others' faces, and make dialogues

of news and prettinesses, and look babies in one anothers' eyes . . . for there is a Platonic friendship as well as a Platonic love; but they being but the images of more noble bodies are but like tinsel dressings, which will show bravely by candlelight, and do excellently in a masque, but are not fit for conversation and the material intercourses of our life.

Two final notes on the Newcastles as individuals. He is as frankly sensual as Carew (his contemporary): *Love's flowers* introduces cunnilinctus, *Love's preparation* equates his erection with Christ's resurrection; but the most notable thing is that this is real folk poetry—simple, viable, crude—even though he was a duke. The Duchess has echoes of folk in her own simplicity, but it is the terrifying simplicity of arrogance and schizophrenic vision. She will use verse as she wants: 'I mean by atoms small as small can be'. Yet, if arrogant, she is not remote: the poems about food are fantastic but she has handled the stuff; the poems about war and hunting are more acridly true to death than any other writing in the language before, I suppose, Joyce:

> Their knees pulled up lest the bowels out should come,
> But all too little, through their blood they swom:
> Guts did, like sausages, their bodies twine.

Suppose she had met Marvell?

THOMAS STANLEY

Father an Essex squire, mother (the 2nd wife) a cousin of
Lovelace. Tutored at home by William Fairfax, son of the
poet Edward. Pembroke College, Cambridge, at 13; fine
classical and modern scholar but made an early marriage to
an heiress (one son 1650). Continental travel. *Poems and
translations* 1647. Took lodgings in Middle Temple and
started literary life in London. Friends included Shirley,
Sherburne, Hall (all of whom he helped with money), Jordan, Milton's nephew Edward Phillips. Royalist. Biographies
of Greek philosophers 1655–62 remained standard history of
philosophy for some time. Edited Aeschyulus and left volumes
of MS. notes on Greek poets, especially Callimachus, in University Library, Cambridge. Much of his verse translated or
paraphrased from continental poets of the 17th century: see
Sherburne. Buried in St. Martin-in-the-Fields. Poems etc. ed.
Saintsbury, and G. M. Crump, Oxford 1962. See L. I. Guiney
T. Stanley Hull 1907.

The killing kiss

When on thy lip my soul° I breathe,
    Which there meets thine,
  Freed from their fetters by this death
    Our subtle forms combine;
  Thus without bonds of sense they move   5
And like two cherubins converse° by love.

  Spirits to chains of earth confined
    Discourse by sense;
  But ours, that are by flames refined,
    With those weak ties dispense;   10
  Let such in words their minds display—
We in a kiss our mutual thoughts convey.

  But since my soul from me doth fly,
    To thee retired,

Thou canst not both retain, for I   15
   Must be with one inspired:
Then, dearest, either justly mine
Restore, or in exchange let me have thine.

Yet, if thou dost return mine own,
   O, take't again!   20
For 'tis this pleasing death alone
   Gives ease unto my pain:
Kill me once more, or I shall find
Thy pity than thy cruelty less kind.

---

1 **soul** its emission in a kiss meant literally; but also = semen; kiss
can be raised to a higher power; killing = orgasmic. See Carew
Hymeneal dialogue; Herbert *Platonic love*; Cleveland *State of love*. 6
converse cf. Benlowes *Might souls converse*; Davenant *Come melt*.
Stanley's poem summarises the doctrine of spiritual unity via bodily
fusion.

La belle confidante°

You earthly souls that court a wanton flame
   Whose pale weak influence
Can rise no higher than the humble name
   And narrow laws of sense:
   Learn by our friendship to create   5
      An immaterial fire,
   Whose brightness angels may admire
      But cannot emulate.

Sickness may fright the roses from her cheek
   Or make the lilies fade,   10
But all the subtle ways death doth seek
   Cannot my love invade.
   Flames that are kindled by the eye
      Through time and age expire;
   But ours, that boast a reach far higher,   15
      Can nor decay nor die.

For when we must resign our vital breath,
   Our loves by fate benighted,
We by this friendship shall survive in death,
   Even in divorce united.
   Weak love, through fortune or distrust,   20
      In time forgets to burn;

But this pursues us to the urn
　　And marries either's dust.

° **confidant(e)** Most commonly, friend of hero or heroine in French
drama of this period, who would be confided in particularly about love.
The word anglicised c.1700. Could be translated 'intimate'; Stanley uses
it with the sexual connotations of that word. Similarly the friendship
of line 5: its Platonic original was between men; now the confiding
intellectuality of that love is transferred to a heterosexual relationship.

OWEN FELTHAM

Son of a Suffolk squire and married the daughter of another, in the rich wool country round Melford. In his 20s and 30s published successive versions of *Resolves divine, moral, political* (essays praised by Randolph, q.v.). His poems were appended to the 1661 ed. with their own title *Lusoria*. Royalist. Spent most of his life in Northamptonshire in the service of the Earl of Thomond, and died there. Ed. O. Smeaton 1904.

The sympathy°

Soul of my soul! it cannot be
That you should weep, and I from tears be free.
  All the vast room between both poles
  Can never dull the sense of souls
    Knit in so fast a knot.   5
O! can you grieve, and think that I
Can feel no smart because not nigh?
    Or that I know it not?

They're heretic thoughts. Two lutes are strung
And on a table tuned alike, for song;   10
  Strike one, and that which none did touch
  Shall, sympathising, sound as much
    As that which touched you see.
Think then, this world, which heaven enrolls,
Is but a table round, and souls   15
    More apprehensive° be.

Know, they° that, in their grossest parts,
Mix by their hallowed loves entwinèd hearts,
  This privilege boast, that no remove
  Can e'er infringe their sense of love.   20
    Judge hence then our estate:
Since when we loved there was not put

Two earthen hearts in one breast, but
    Two souls co-animate.

° **sympathy** cf. next poem. The word came into use not much before
1600; but as a name for the community of feeling in these poems it
seems to date from the mid-century. Cf. Eve describing her reflection in
Paradise lost IV (1667): 'I started back, It started back, but pleased I
soon returned, Pleased it returned as soon with answering looks Of sympathy and love.' For the sentiment cf. Stanley *Killing kiss*. 16 **appre-
hensive** sensitive, intuitive. 17 **they** people whose grossest contact is
of the heart (rather than sexual). The poet and his soul are even more
refined—not hearts but souls.

ANONYMOUS

'Tis not the world nor what can please

'Tis not the world nor what can please
 With vain delights (the soul's disease)
 I care to lose;
For if the fates first call me
To that bliss whither we   5
Both shall go, I cannot choose;
 Nor do I grieve
 Those joys to leave
 Which we in females do conceive—

I 'joyed them never;   10
 Nor do I fear to pass the shade
 Of cruel death, for who is made
 To live here ever?
But O I die before I die
 To think that we   15
 'Twixt whom there is such sympathy°
 Should parted be.
     Bodleian Library MS. 1600–40?

16 **sympathy** see Feltham.

WILLIAM CAVENDISH, 1ST DUKE OF NEWCASTLE-UPON-TYNE

Son of a knight. St. John's College, Cambridge. Knighted 1610 in honour of Prince Henry (see Wither) becoming Prince of Wales. Continent with Wotton (q.v.). Married and gave James I two entertainments at Welbeck, Nottinghamshire) and in Derbyshire for which Jonson wrote the minor masques called *Love's welcome*; the receptions cost £20,000. In 1639 raised a troop for Charles I against Scotland. In civil war held Northumbria for the king; in 1643 defeated Fairfax in Yorkshire and was created marquis; in that year his wife died. To Scottish border next but forces weakened and Fairfax closed on him at York. Rescued by Prince Rupert but next day the prince rejected Newcastle's tactical advice and lost the battle of Marston Moor. Newcastle fought in it as a private individual, then sailed with some of his family from Scarborough to Hamburg; 1645 to Paris for 3 years. There met and married his second wife, Margaret Lucas. His poems were written to her at that time; she replied in prose letters but was herself a superior poet. Property sequestrated so borrowed money in exiled court, pawned wife's jewellery and profited from good marriages of his two sons and eldest daughter, so able to stage a grand entertainment for the exiled Charles II in 1658. In 1660 returned to his estates, was created duke and knight of the Garter and lived with the duchess at Welbeck, where he collected some fine paintings, built a racecourse, and bred Barbary horses; textbooks of horsemanship 1657 (French) and 1667. Also took an interest in the stage—encouraged Shirley and Shadwell and tried his hand at writing plays. Sir Philip Warwick, last secretary to Charles I, wrote of Newcastle: 'He was a gentleman of grandeur, generosity, loyalty, and steady and forward courage; but his edge had too much of the razor in it; for he had a tincture of a romantic spirit, and had the misfortune to have somewhat of the poet in him; so as he chose Sir William Davenant, an eminent good poet, and loyal gentleman, to be lieutenant-general of his ordinance. This inclination of his own and such kind of witty society (to be modest in the expressions of it) diverted many counsels and lost many opportunities.' *The phanseys [poems] of William Cavendish marquis of Newcastle addressed to Margaret Lucas and her letters in reply* collected by her, ed. Douglas Grant 1956. See her *Life* of the duke 1667 etc. ed. C. H. Firth 1886, 1906; and H. T. E. Perry *The first duchess of Newcastle and her husband as figures in literary history* Cambridge Mass. 1921.

Love's vision

Dear, let us two each other spy:
How curious in each other's eye
We're drawn to life;° and thus we see
Ourselves at once, both thee and me,
Distinctly two yet not alone,   5
Incorporated that's but one.

My picture in your eyes you bear,
I yours as much as mine you wear;
'Tis not our species° cannot pass,
Or shining makes a looking-glass,   10
Nor picture: really we lie
Contracted in each other's eye.

When that our milk-white purer lawn,°
Our eyelid-curtains, when they're drawn,
Soft sleep, made with sweet vapours' rain,   15
To cool us shrinks into each brain,
Rejoicing with love's running streams
Which grosser lovers calls but dreams:

Because we two must never part,
We move down to each other's heart;   20
And there, all passions turned to joy,
Our loving hearts feels no annoy,
Delated.° Lest our souls outskips
With joy, kiss quickly, stop our lips!

---

3 **to life** to the life, exactly. Cf. Herbert *Ode*. The last two lines of this stanza echo Shakespeare's *Phoenix and turtle*. 9 **species** image or form. It isn't that our images can't get through each others' pupils. 13 **lawn** gauze. 23 **delated** carried down.

Love's matrimony

There is no happy life
But in a wife;
The comforts are so sweet
When they do meet:
'Tis plenty, peace, a calm   5
Like dropping balm;
Love's weather is so fair,
Perfumèd air;
Each word such pleasure brings,
Like soft-touched strings;   10
Love's passion moves the heart
On either part;
Such harmony together,
So pleased in either,
No discords, concords still,   15
Sealed with one will.
By love, God man made one,
Yet not alone:
Like stamps of king and queen
It may be seen,   20
Two figures but one coin,
So they do join;
Only, they not embrace:
We, face to face.

Love's flowers

From your lips I will pluck
Fresh roses, kisses suck,
And blow those budding leaves,
Rob you and so disseaves°
Those odoriferous   5
Fragrant love's flowers, thus.

It is no theft, for when
I kiss, you take't again
And doth your lips renew
With your own honied dew°   10
And natural showers got
From your tongue's water-pot.

When my lips, heated, seeks
Love's cooler walks, your cheeks;
Or wandering loves to rove   15
In thickets, your hair's grove;
Or on love's mounts that's fair,
Your panting breasts, gives air;

Or bathe me in love's pool°
My heated love to cool;   20
Or in love's grotto shun
Your eyes, each a hot sun:
Fresh fountains there will please me,
With sweet fanned air to ease me.

4 **disseaves** dis-sheave, scatter; perhaps via dishevel. He often gets
final -s wrong in verbs. 10 **dew** see Carew *Rapture*. 19 **pool** and **grotto**
navel and vulva.

The unexpressible love

My love to you is so much—nay, 'tis more
Than ever lovers yet did know before:
Theirs no proportion, theirs is so much less;
Mine more than any language can express.
If a new alphabet was made, too small°   5
To express least part of our love, how then all?
Nay, algebraics, arithmetic all o'er
Will still fall short: our love will still be more.
Not the world's hieroglyphics° for ours stand—
Our love's small parts more numerous than the sand.   10
Poor lady Venus and her son, that youth—°
All fictions, far too little for our truth.
We must find out some new way how to move
The greatest wits to guess but at our love.
Love (that word's too little, like motes to the sun),   15
Love, forty years ago, served Dr Donne,°
But we're beyond it far; our wise delight
Is what we know, not know that's infinite:°
Then 'tis a God to all love else; then thus
All lovers as our creatures worship us.   20

5 **too small** it would be too small. 9 **hieroglyphics** alphabets, sacred
writings, especially pictorial alphabets such as the ancient Egyptian.
These were matters of recent knowledge; but secret signs had long been
used in religion. 11 **youth** Cupid. 16 **Donne** his love poetry written

when Newcastle was a small boy; 5 editions 1633 . . . 50. **18 infinite**
our delight is in our love, not in the knowledge of its infiniteness. A
joke against metaphysical poetry. Cf. Donne *Lovers' infiniteness.*

Love's commission°

'Tis love's commission—justly it may call:
For Hymen's° only use you have me all.
Your words such harmony, your ear doth feel
All music else scraped trenchers, ungreased wheel.
Your plump flesh with your nature-robe° so thin,   5
All others rough like a bear's or a seal's skin.
Ambrosia, nectar, nautiously should cast°
When hope but on your tempting lips to taste.
The fresher flowers, Spanish scents, they stink
To your balm's dew like privy or our sink.°   10
The handsomest of your sex to me appears,
Compared to you, like men of fourscore years,
Not women. Since I've left them all for you,
And they for that left me, your love is due
In justice for to love me, and love so   15
As love no other; else I'm lost, you know.

° **commission** charge to act in specific duty. 2 **Hymen** god of marriage. 5 **nature-robe** cf. Lovelace *Aramantha*. 7 **cast** nauseously should
cause to retch or vomit. The whole set of nausea words was of recent
coinage and Newcastle is using his own version. 10 **sink** cesspool or
drain.

Love's preparation

Just like a penitent that doth prepare
For to receive,° washing his soul with prayer
And sadder tears, repentance rubbing sin,
All spots thereof, so clean, though it be thin:
A better immortality 'twill be   5
To enjoy my heaven, which is only thee;
Which makes me now, in hopes for to be thine,
To purge me clean, fit for your holy shrine;
Thus be your living ark° and to me draw
Your virgin rod, blest manna, and your law,   10
And keep them sacred; and, with nothing fed

But pure marriage, your shew holy bread.
In me your consecrated ark shall lie,
So crystal-pure I'll be, for you I'll boast,
Fit to preserve you, my love's Holy Ghost.°   15
When joyfully receive you, I dare say
That may be justly called my Easter Day,
My resurrection; and you too shall see
My blest ascension° when I am with thee.
But a long Lent I've had, and do believe   20
Before our Easter had too long an eve,
Which crucified me to my only loss,
My dark Good Friday and my shameful cross.°
Old and New° Testament (some thinks us neither),
Sure we're love's Bible when we're bound together.   25

2 receive the sacraments. **9 ark** 'And after the second veil [see
Vaughan *Night*], the tabernacle which is called the holiest of all; which
had the golden censer, and the ark of the covenant overlaid round about
with gold, wherein was the golden pot that had manna [Cartwright
Circumcision], and Aaron's rod that budded [Crashaw *Easter*], and the
tables of the covenant' (*Hebrews* ix). The shew-bread was kept in the
outer shrine. The erotic application of religious imagery in this poem is
unusually extreme; the rod and law can hardly refer to specific parts
of her genitals but manna was associated with honey and dew (see
Kynaston *Sugar and sweetness*). **15 Holy Ghost** an unprecedented
claim, whether he means it for himself or her; but the Holy Ghost is
often in the Bible said to 'fill' men who receive it; and *I Corinthians* vi,
'your body is the temple of the H.G. which is in you.' **19 ascension**
erection. **23 cross** first marriage? loss of war? exile? **24 Old and New**
referring to their ages.

My lord
Your verses are more like you then your peckter though it
resembelles you very much but heer art has not bene so good
a courtier as it eues to be. My lord, the only blesing I wish
for heer is I may desarve your afeetshion which is onvalabell.
I have sent this hear in obedance to your commands which
I shall allways be redy to exsequit with that obsarvances as
becomes my lord your most
                umbell sarvant
                MARGARET LUCAS

MARGARET CAVENDISH, DUCHESS OF NEWCASTLE-UPON-TYNE

Born near Colchester where her father Sir Thomas Lucas was a landowner; he died in her infancy leaving 8 children of whom she was the youngest; but their mother ensured a decent education for them. When civil war broke out her 3 brothers joined the King's forces; two were killed; her mother and eldest sister died. She became maid-of-honour to Queen Henrietta-Maria and went with her in exile to Paris; there in 1645 she met the Duke (q.v.) and married him. She wrote most of her verse while abroad: *Poems and fancies* 1653, 1664; *Nature's pictures drawn by fancy's pencil* (stories in prose and verse, including *A true relation of my birth, breeding, and life*) 1656. On return to England published a large number of plays, mostly unacted (1662, 1668). Added to her reputation for stern virtue and intellect one for being eccentric: 'The whole story of this lady is a romance and all she does is romantic. Her footmen in velvet coats and herself in antique dress . . . a mad, conceited, ridiculous woman' (Pepys 12 April 1667 , , , 18 March 1668). In 1666 published *Observations upon experimental philosophy* (i.e. physics) together with a fantasy; and in 1667 her adoring *Life of the thrice noble, high and puissant prince William Cavendish, duke, marquis and earl of Newcastle*. See introduction to the Duke; her own works; Douglas Grant *Margaret the first: a biography* 1957. Her autobiography and some other writing ed. E. Jenkins as *The cavalier and his lady* 1872.

Epigraph to The theme of love

O love, how thou art tired out with rhyme!
Thou art a tree whereon all poets climb
And from thy tender branches every one
Doth take some fruit, which fancy feeds upon;
But now thy tree is left so bare and poor   5
That they can hardly gather one plum more.

What makes echo

That motion which doth from the mouth proceed
Runs through the air and doth an echo breed;
As several letters in one word do join,
So several figures through the air combine.
The air is wax, words seal and give the print,   10
And so an echo in the air do mint.
And while those figures last they life maintain;
When motion wears them out is echo slain:
As sugar in the mouth doth melt with taste,
So echo in the air itself doth waste.   15

part of *Nature calls a council . . . to advise about
making the world*

The bigness of atoms°

I mean by atoms small as small can be.
They do in quantity, weight, quality agree,
Not in their outward figure, for some may
Show bigger and some others less than they.
Take water fluid, and ice, and you will see   5
They do in weight but not in bulk agree.
So atoms, some are soft, others more knit,
According as each atom's figure fit:
Atoms whose form is hollow, long and round,
Bend more than flat, or sharp, which close are bound;   10
And being hollow they are spread more thin
Than other atoms, which are close within;
And atoms which are thin are softer much,
When atoms close are of a harder touch.

ibid.

Of loose atoms

In every brain there do loose atoms lie:
Those which are sharp, from them do fancies fly;
Long airy atoms nimble are and free,
But round and square ones dull and sleepy be.

ibid.

° **atoms** atomic theories of matter were propounded by the Greek
philosophers Democritus in 5th century B.C. and Epicurus in the 3rd,
and the Roman philosopher-poet Lucretius who d. 55 B.C. It was taken
up again in various ways in the 17th century, notably by Hobbes.

Nature's prospect°

Once at imagination's windows I
Standing, a prospect in the mind did spy;
The eye of ignorance I shut up close,
Lest the eye of knowledge should this prospect lose;
Drawing a circle round of fine conceit,°   5
Extravagant speeches contracting strait,
The more I viewed, my eye the farther went,
Till understanding's sight was almost spent.
An isle of thoughts within a church I viewed—
Filled full of fancy's light to me it showed: 10
Pillars of judgement thick stood on a row;
And in this isle motion walked to and fro;
Fear, love, humility kneeled down to pray,
Desires did beg of all that passed that way,
Poor doubts did shake as if they had some harm,   15
Yet mantles of good hope did keep them warm;
But generous faith seemed bountiful and free,
She gave to all that asked her charity.
All sorts of sects in pulpits seemed to preach—
Fables for truth, no doubt, did many teach,   20
But I heard not what their opinions were:
For prospect's in the eye, none in the ear.

° **prospect** view. 5 **conceit** imagination.

from Nature's landskip

I standing on a hill of fancies high
And viewing round with curiosity's eye,
Under my thoughts saw several landskips lie.

In champains of delight, I saw, did feed
Pleasures, as wethers fat and ewes to breed;   5
And cows of probability, which went
In hope's green pastures, gave milk of content . . .

From Nature's dessert

Sweet marmalade of kisses newly gathered,
Preservèd children which were never fathered;
Sugar of beauty which away melts soon,
Marchpane° of youth, and childish macaroon;
Sugarplum words which fall sweet from the lips,   5
And water promises mouldering like chips;°
Biscuits of love which crumble all away,
Jelly of fear which shaked and quivering lay.
Then was a fresh green-sickness° cheese brought in,
And tempting fruit like that which Eve made sin,   10
With cream of honour, which was thick and good;
Firm nuts of sincere friendship by it stood;
Grapes of delight, dull spirits to revive,
Whose juice, 'tis said, doth Nature keep alive.
All this dessert did Nature mightily please: 15
She ate and drank, then went to rest in ease.

4 **Marchpane** marzipan. 6 **chips** ice? 9 **green-sickness** see Herrick *To music.*

from Nature's cook

Death is the cook of nature, and we find
Creatures dressed several ways to please her mind.
Some, Death doth roast with fevers burning hot,
And some he boils with dropsies in a pot;
Some are consumed for jelly, by degrees,   5
And some with ulcers, gravy out to squeeze;
Some, as with herbs, he stuffs with gouts and pains;
Others for tender meat he hangs in chains;
Some in the sea he pickles up to keep,
Others he, as soused brawn, in wine doth steep;   10
Some flesh and bones he with the pox° chops small
And doth a French fricassée make withal;
Some on gridirons of calentures° are broiled;
And some are trodden down and so quite spoiled.
But some are baked, when smothered they do die;   15
Some meat he doth by hectic fevers fry;
In sweat sometimes he stews with savoury smell,
An hodge-podge of diseases he likes well.
Some brains he dresseth with apoplexy

Or sauce of megrims° swimming plenteously;   20
And tongues he dries with smoke from stomachs
Which as the second course he sends up still;
Throats he doth cut, blood-puddings for to make,
And puts them in the guts which colics rack;
Some hunted are by him for deer, that's red,   25
And some as stall-fed oxen knocked o' th' head;
Some singed and scalled for bacon seem most rare
When with salt rheum and phlegm they powdered are.

11 **pox** it is smallpox (endemic till mid-19th century) that is notorious
for the pockmarks it leaves, so the skin can look like mincemeat; but
French suggests syphilis, called French or Spanish pox in the 16th century. Actually brought from Haiti by Columbus' sailors to Portugal in
1494. The Tudors and Stuarts were infected but references to it (or
gonorrhea—also pox, or clap) intensify in the Restoration period. It
came under some control in the 18th century as sheaths of fine leather,
silk etc. came to be worn. 13 **calentures** delirious fevers. 20 **megrims**
migraine.

from The Convent of Pleasure *Act IV Scene i*

*The scene is opened, and there is presented a rock as in
the sea, whereupon sits the Princess and the Lady Happy;
the Princess as the sea-god Neptune, the Lady Happy
as a sea-goddess; the rest of the ladies sit somewhat lower,
dressed like water-nymphs; the Princess begins to speak a
speech in verse, and after her the Lady Happy makes her
speech.*

Lady Happy . . . My cabinets are oyster-shells
               In which I keep my orient pearls;
               To open them I use the tide,
               As keys to locks, which opens wide
               The oyster shells; then out I take   5
               Those orient pearls and crowns do make.
               And modest coral I do wear,
               Which blushes when it touches air.
               On silver waves I sit and sing
               And then the fish lie listening;   10
               Then sitting on a rocky stone
               I comb my hair with fishes' bone,
               The whilst Apollo with his beams
               Doth dry my hair from watery streams.
               His light doth glaze the water's face,   15

Makes the large sea my looking-glass:
So when I swim on waters high
I see myself as I glide by;
But when the sun begins to burn
I back into my waters turn   20
And dive unto the bottom low:
Then on my head the waters flow
In curlèd waves and circles round,
And thus with waters am I crowned.

Plays never before printed 1668

On a melting beauty

Going into a church my prayers to say,
Close by a tomb a mourning beauty lay:
Her knees on marble cold were bowed down low
And fixed so firm as if she there did grow;
Her elbow on the tomb did steady stand,   5
Her head hung back, the hind part in her hand;
Turning her eyes up to the heavens high
Left nothing but the white of each her eye;
Upon the lower shut did hang a tear
Like to a diamond pendant in an ear;   10
Her breast was panting sore, as if life meant
To seek after her heart, which way it went.
    I, standing there, observèd what she did:
At last she from her hand did raise her head
And casting down her eyes ne'er looked about;   15
Tears pulled her eyelids down as they gushed out;
Then with a gentle groan at last did speak,
Her words were soft, her voice sound low and weak:
O heavens! said she, O! what do you mean?
I dare not think you gods can have a spleen,°   20
And yet I find great torments you do give,
And creatures make in misery to live;
You show us joys, but we possess not one;
You give us life, for death to feed upon.
O cruel death! thy dart hath made me poor,   25
Thou struck'st that heart my life did most adore.
You gods, delight not thus me to torment
But strike me dead by this dear monument
And let our ashes mix both in this urn,
That both into one phoenix° we may turn.   30

Hearing her mourn, I went to give relief,
But O, alas! her ears were stopped with grief;
When I came near, her blood congealed to ice
And all her body changèd in a trice;
That ice straight melted, into tears did turn, 35
And through the earth's pores got into the urn.

20 **spleen**   seat of malice, ill-humour; later especially of melancholia.
30 **phoenix**   see Carew *Mole*.

from The Fort or Castle of Hope

A description of the fight

Some with sharp swords, to tell O most accursed!
Were above half into their bodies thrust,
From whence fresh streams of blood along did run
Unto the hilts and there lay clodded on;
Some, their legs dangling by the nervous strings 5
And shoulders cut hung loose like flying wings;
Heads here were cleft in pieces, brains lay mashed
And all their faces into slices hashed;
Brains only in the *pia-mater* thin
Did quivering lie within that little skin; 10
Their skulls, all broke and into pieces burst,
By horses' hoofs and chariot wheels were crushed.
Others, their heads did lie on their own laps,
And some again, half cut, lay on their paps;
Some thrust their tongues out of their mouths at length— 15
For why? the strings were cut that gave them strength.
Their eyes did stare, their lids were open wide,
For the small nerves were shrunk on every side.
In some again those glassy balls hung by
Small slender strings, as chains, to tie the eye, 20
Which strings when broke, the eyes fell trundling round,
And then the film was broke upon the ground.
In death their teeth strong set, their lips were bare,
Which grinning seemed as if they angry were;
Their hair upon their eyes in clodded gore 25
So wildly spread as ne'er it did before;
With frowns their foreheads did in furrows lie
As graves, their foes to bury, when they die.
Their spongy lungs, heaved up through pangs of death,
With pain and difficulty fetched short breath; 30

Some grasping hard their hands through pain provoked
Because the rattling phlegm their throats had choked.
Their bodies now bowed up, then down did fall
For want of strength to make them stand withal;
Some staggering on their legs did feebly stand,   35
Or leaning on their sword with either hand
Where on the pummel did their breast rely,
More grieved they could not fight than for to die.
Their hollow eyes sunk deep into their brain
And hard-fetched groans did from each heart-string strain;   40
Their knees pulled up lest the bowels out should come,
But all too little, through their blood they swom:
Guts did, like sausages, their bodies twine,
Or like the spreading plant or wreathing vine;
Their restless heads not knowing how to lie,   45
Through grievous pains did quickly wish to die,
Rolling from off their back upon their belly,
Did tumble in their blood as thick as jelly
And gasping lay with short breaths, and constraint,
With cold sweat-drops upon their faces faint;   50
Heaving their dull pale eyeballs up did look
As if through pain, not hate, the world forsook . . .

9 **pia-mater**   membrane enclosing brain.

from The hunting of the hare

  Betwixt two ridges of ploughed land sat Wat,°
Whose body pressed to the earth lay close and squat;
His nose upon his two forefeet did lie,
With his grey eyes he glarèd obliquely;
His head he always set against the wind,   5
His tail when turned his hair blew up behind
And made him to get cold; but he being wise
Doth keep his coat still down, so warm he lies.
Thus rests he all the day, till the sun doth set,
Then up he riseth his relief to get   10
And walks about, until the sun doth rise,
Then coming in's former posture lies.
  At last poor Wat was found as there he lay
By huntsmen which came with their dogs that way;
Whom seeing, he got up, and fast did run,   15
Hoping some ways the cruel dogs to shun;

But they by nature had so quick a scent
That by their nose they traced what way he went
And with their deep wide mouths set forth a cry
Which answered was by echo in the sky.   20
Then Wat was struck with terror and with fear,
Seeing each shadow thought the dogs were there,
And running out some distance from their cry
To hide himself, his thoughts he did employ.
Under a clod of earth in sand-pit wide   25
Poor Wat sat close, hoping himself to hide;
There long he had not been but straight in's ears
The winding horns and crying dogs he hears;
Then starting up with fear he leaped and such
Swift speed he made, the ground he scarce did touch;   30
Into a great thick wood straightways he got
And underneath a broken bough he sat
Where every leaf that with the wind did shake
Brought him such terror that his heart did ache.
That place he left, to champain° plains he went,   35
Winding about for to deceive their scent,
And while they snuffling were to find his track,
Poor Wat, being weary, his swift pace did slack;
On his two hinder legs for ease he sat,
His forefeet rubbed his face from dust and sweat,   40
Licking his feet, he wiped his ears so clean
That none could tell that Wat had hunted been;
But casting round about his fair grey eyes,
The hounds in full career he near him spies.
To Wat it was so terrible a sight,   45
Fear gave him wings and made his body light;
Though he was tired before by running long,
Yet now his breath he never felt more strong;
Like those that dying are think health returns,
When 'tis but a faint blast which life outburns,   50
For spirits seek to guard the heart about,
Striving with death, but death doth quench them out.
The hounds so fast came on and with such cry
That he no hopes had left, nor help could spy.
With that the winds did pity poor Wat's case   55
And with their breath the scent blew from that place;
Then every nose was busily employed
And every nostril was set open wide
And every head did seek a several way
To find the grass or track where the scent lay;   60
For witty industry is never slack,
'Tis like to witchcraft and brings lost things back.

But though the wind had tied the scent up close,
A busy dog thrust in his snuffing nose
And drew it out, with that did foremost run,   65
Then horns blew loud, the rest to follow on,
The great slow hounds their throats did set a bass,
The fleet swift hounds as tenors next in place,
The little beagles did a treble sing
And through the air their voices round did ring,   70
Which made such consort as they ran along
That, had they spoken words, 't had been a song.
The horns kept time, the men did shout for joy
And seemed most valiant, poor Wat to destroy:
Spurring their horses to a full career,   75
Swom rivers deep, leaped ditches without fear,
Endangered life and limbs, so fast they'd ride
Only to see how patiently Wat died.
    At last the dogs so near his heels did get
That their sharp teeth they in his breech did set;   80
Then tumbling down he fell, with weeping eyes
Gave up his ghost; and thus poor Wat he died . . .

1 **Wat**   conventional name for hare. 35 **champain**   open common.

[ANDREW MARVELL]

LADY (KATHERINE) DYER(?)

These poems are engraved on tablets at the Dyer tomb in the village church of Colmworth in Bedfordshire. Below them are effigies of husband and wife lying on their sides, holding their heads in their hands, one above the other. An inscription says they 'multiplied themselves into seven children' and below them are statuettes of their 4 sons and 3 daughters. Above the tablets is the inscription, 'Sir William Dyer, Knight . . . who put on immortality April 29th A.D. 1621 aet. 39 who married Katherine . . . of the ancient family of the Doyleys who in her life at her own charge out of her loyal respect to her husband did erect this monument A.D. 1641.' The first poem is here published for the first time probably; 13 lines of the second appeared in *English love poems* ed. Betjeman and Taylor 1957. Lady Dyer is not conclusively the author— she might have commissioned them. Donne visited in the neighbourhood.

Sir William Dyer, knight

If a large heart joined with a noble mind,
Showing true worth, unto all good inclined,
In faith, in friendship, justice unto all,
Leave such a memory as we may call
Happy, thine is. Then, pious marble, keep   5
His just fame waking though his loved dust sleep;
And though death can devour all that hath breath,
And monuments themselves have had a death,
Nature shan't suffer this to ruinate,
Nor time demolish it, nor an envious fate: 10
Raised by a just hand, not vainglorious pride,
Who'd be concealed were't modesty to hide

Such an affection did so long survive
The object of it; yet loved it as alive;
And this great blessing to his name doth give,   15
To make it by his tomb, and issue, live.

My dearest dust, could not thy hasty day
Afford thy drowsy patience leave to stay
One hour longer, so that we might either
Sat up, or gone to bed together?
But since thy finished labour hath possessed   5
Thy weary limbs with early rest,
Enjoy it sweetly; and thy widow bride
Shall soon repose her by thy slumbering side;
Whose business now is only to prepare
My nightly dress, and call to prayer.   10
Mine eyes wax heavy and the day grows old;
The dew falls thick, my blood grows cold.
Draw, draw the closèd curtains and make room:
My dear, my dearest dust, I come, I come!

MRS. ANNE BRADSTREET

Her father (Dudley) was steward to the Earl of Lincoln. At the age of 16 Anne had smallpox, and married Simon Bradstreet who had worked under her father and was now steward to the Countess of Warwick. In 1630 the Dudleys and Bradstreets joined an expedition sailing for New England and after a voyage of 6½ weeks landed at Salem. In 1634 they settled at Ipswich, Mass.; in 1638 Simon Bradstreet formed a plantation at Merrimac. Dudley became governor of Massachusetts. In 1640 Anne had her first baby; 1642 made a MS. collection of her poems: they were published in London in 1650 as *The tenth muse lately sprung up in America* (also 1678). She suffered a serious illness in 1661 when her husband was on state business in England. He remarried after her death and lived till 1697, aged 94. See John Berryman's volume of poems *Homage to Mistress Bradstreet* 1959.

A letter to her husband, absent upon public employment

As loving hind that, hartless, wants her deer
Scuds through the woods and fern with hearkening ear
Perplexed, in every bush and nook doth pry,
Her dearest deer might answer ear or eye:
So doth my anxious soul, which now doth miss   5
A dearer dear, far dearer heart, than this,
Still wait with doubts and hopes and failing eye
His voice to hear or person to descry.
Or as the pensive dove doth all alone
On withered bough most úncouthly bemoan   10
The absence of her love and loving mate
Whose loss hath made her so unfortunate,
Even thus do I with many a deep sad groan
Bewail my turtle true who now is gone,
His presence and his safe return still woo   15

With thousand doleful sighs and mournful coo.
Or as the loving mullet, that true fish,
Her fellow lost, nor joy nor life doth wish
But launches on that shore there for to die
Where she her captive husband doth espy—   20
Mine being gone, I lead a joyless life;
I have a loving fere° yet seem no wife,
But, worst of all, to him can't steer my course—
I here, he there, alas! both kept by force.
   Return, my dear, my joy, my only love   25
Unto thy hind, thy mullet and thy dove,
Who neither joys in pasture, house nor streams—
The substance gone, O me these are but dreams!
Together at one tree O let us browse
And like two turtles roost within one house   30
And like the mullets in one river glide;
Let's still remain but one till death divide.
   Thy loving love and dearest dear
   At home, abroad and everywhere,

                                            A.B.

22 **fere**   mate.

MRS. KATHERINE PHILIPS

Father, John Fowler, a merchant of Bucklersbury in the City of London; mother (also Katherine; a daughter of Dr. John Oxenbridge). To Mrs. Salmon's fashionable boarding-school at Hackney. When her father died, mother married a Hector Philips of Wales; and at 16 Katherine married James Philips, her stepfather Hector's eldest son by a former marriage; James had also been married before.

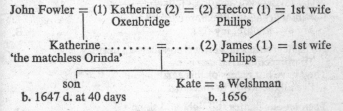

John Fowler = (1) Katherine (2) = (2) Hector (1) = 1st wife
               Oxenbridge   Philips

        Katherine .... = ... (2) James (1) = 1st wife
     'the matchless Orinda'   Philips

        son   Kate = a Welshman
   b. 1647 d. at 40 days   b. 1656

After her marriage she divided her time between Wales and London, where she gathered a literary circle c.1650, special-ising in friendship and 'sympathy'. The members had pastoral nicknames, e.g. Antenor = her husband, Sylvander = Sir Edward Dering, Palemon = Francis Fitch, Lucasia = Mrs. Anne Owen, Rosania = Mrs. Montagu. She was 'the matchless Orinda'. Jeremy Taylor was an important theorist: see his *Discourse of friendship* 1657. Other friends included Cowley, Flatman and Anne Killigrew (see next section). First pub-lished verses were lines prefaced to volumes by Vaughan and Cartwright in 1651. Trans. Corneille's *Pompey* 1663. Next year died of smallpox aged 33. *Poems by the incomparable Mrs. K.P.* pirated 1664. Ed. Saintsbury. See Edmund Gosse in his *17th-century studies* 1883; W. Souers *The matchless Orinda* Cambridge, Mass. 1931; W. G. Hiscock, Friendship: Francis Fitch's discourse and the circle of the matchless Orinda *Rev. Eng. Studs.* XV 1939.

To my excellent Lucasia, on our friendship°

I did not live until this time
   Crowned my felicity,
When I could say without a crime,
   I am not thine, but thee.

This carcase breathed and walked and slept   5
   So that the world believed
There was a soul the motions kept;
   But they were all deceived.

For as a watch by art is wound
   To motion, such was mine: 10
But never had Orinda found
   A soul till she found thine;

Which now inspires, cures and supplies,
   And guides my darkened breast:
For thou art all that I can prize,   15
   My joy, my life, my rest.

No bridegroom's nor crown-conqueror's mirth
   To mine compared can be:
They have but pieces of this earth,
   I've all the world in thee.   20

Then let our flames still light and shine
   And no false fear control,
As innocent as our design,
   Immortal as our soul.

° **friendship** see Stanley *Confidante.*

Friendship's mystery, to my dearest Lucasia

Come, my Lucasia, since we see
   That miracles men's faith do move
By wonder and by prodigy,
   To the dull angry world let's prove
   There's a religion° in our love.   5

For though we were designed to agree
   That fate no liberty destroys,
But our election° is as free

As angels', who with greedy choice
Are yet determined to their joys. 10

Our hearts are doubled by the loss:
Here mixture is addition grown;
We both diffuse, and both engross:
And we whose minds are so much one
Never yet ever are alone. 15

We court our own captivity,
Than thrones more great and innocent:
'Twere banishment to be set free
Since we wear fetters whose intent
Not bondage is but ornament. 20

Divided joys are tedious found,
And griefs united easier grow;
We are ourselves but by rebound,
And all our titles shuffled so—
Both princes and both subjects too. 25

Our hearts are mutual victims laid,
While they (such power in friendship lies)
Are altars, priests and offerings made:
And each heart which thus kindly° dies
Grows deathless by the sacrifice. 30

5 religion cf. Habington *Why should we fear*. **8 election** choice of
each other. The analogy is the doctrine of election, whereby a Christian
is not predestined to grace, for that would deny free will; but he is
'Elect according to the foreknowledge of God the Father' (*I Peter* i;
cf. *Romans* viii). Others disagree; and K.P. is using the contradictions
inherent in the doctrine as an analogy for the similar phenomena of
love—that in love we feel fated or made for each other, yet specially
free. She may also have in mind such texts as *Isaiah* xlii, 'mine elect,
in whom my soul delighteth,' and the 2nd epistle of *John* which is 'unto
the elect lady . . . whom I love in the truth'. The point about angels is
that they cannot stop being angels; see Herbert *Platonic love*; Benlowes
Might souls converse. **29 kindly** naturally; generously; perhaps, gently;
possibly, genitally.

A dialogue° of absence 'twixt Lucasia and Orinda.
Set by Mr. Henry Lawes

Luc.   Say, my Orinda, why so sad?
Orin.   Absence from thee doth tear my heart,
        Which, since with thine it union had,
            Each parting splits. *Luc.* And can we part?

Orin.	Our bodies must. *Luc.* But never we:	5
	Our souls, without the help of sense,	
	By ways more noble and more free	
	Can meet and hold intelligence.	
Orin.	And yet those souls, when first they met,	
	Looked out at windows through the eyes.°	10
Luc.	But soon did such acquaintance get,	
	Nor fate nor time can them surprise.	
Orin.	Absence will rob us of that bliss	
	To which this friendship title brings;	
	Love's fruits and joys are made by this	15
	Useless as crowns to captived kings.	
Luc.	Friendship's a science, and we know	
	There contemplation's° most employed.	
Orin.	Religion's so, but practic too,	
	And both by niceties destroyed.	20
Luc.	But who ne'er parts can never meet	
	And so that happiness were lost.	
Orin.	Thus pain and death are sadly sweet,	
	Since health and heaven such price must cost.	
Chorus	But we shall come where no rude hand shall sever	25
	And there we'll meet and part no more for ever.	

° **dialogue**   cf. Carew *Hymeneal dialogue.* 10 **eyes**   see Herbert *Ode.*
18 **contemplation**   see Cleveland *Antiplatonic.*

Orinda to Lucasia parting, October 1661, at London

Adieu, dear object of my love's excess,
And with thee all my hopes of happiness.
With the same fervent and unchangèd heart
Which did its whole self once to thee impart
(And which, though fortune has so sorely bruised,   5
Would suffer more to be from this excused)
I to resign thy dear convérse submit,
Since I can neither keep nor merit it.
   That hast too long to me confinèd been
Who ruin am without, passion within: 10
My mind is sunk below thy tenderness
And my condition does deserve it less;
I'm so entangled and so lost a thing,
By all the shocks my daily sorrows bring,

That wouldst thou for thy old Orinda call   15
Thou hardly couldst unravel her at all.
And should I thy clear fortunes interline
With the incessant miseries of mine?
No, no, I never loved at such a rate,
To tie thee to the rigours of my fate.   20
   As from my obligations thou art free,
Sure thou shalt be so from my injury:
Though every other worthiness I miss,
Yet I'll at least be generous in this;
I'd rather perish without sigh or groan   25
Than thou shouldst be condemned to give me one;
Nay, in my soul I rather could allow
Friendship should be a sufferer than thou.
   Go then, since my sad heart has set thee free,
Let all the loads and chains remain on me.   30
Though I be left the prey of sea and wind,
Thou, being happy, wilt in that be kind;
Nor shall I my undoing much deplore,
Since thou art safe whom I must value more.
O mayst thou ever be so! and as free   35
From all ills else as from my company;
And may the torments that thou had from it
Be all that heaven will to thy life permit;
And that they may thy virtue service do,
Mayst thou be able to forgive them too.   40
   But though I must this sharp submission learn,
I cannot yet unwish thy dear concern.
Not one new comfort I expect to see:
I quit my joy, hope, life and all, but thee;
Nor seek I thence aught that may discompose   45
That mind where so serene a goodness grows;
I ask no inconvenient kindness now
To move thy passion or to cloud thy brow;
And thou wilt satisfy my boldest plea
By some few soft remembrances of me,   50
Which may present thee with this candid thought—
I meant not all the troubles that I brought.
Own not what passion rules, and fate does crush,
But wish thou couldst have done't without a blush;
And that I had been, ere it was too late,   55
Either more worthy or more fortunate.
Ah! who can love the thing they cannot prize?
But thou mayst pity though thou dost despise;
Yet I should think that pity bought too dear
If it should cost those precious eyes a tear.   60

   O, may no minute's trouble thee possess
But to endear the next hour's happiness;
And mayst thou, when thou art from me removed,
Be better pleased, but never worse beloved.
O! pardon me for pouring out my woes   65
In rhymes, now that I dare not do it in prose;
For I must lose whatever is called dear,
Any thy assistance all that loss to bear,
And have more cause than e'er I had before
To fear that I shall never see thee more.   70

COMMENTARY 9

Commonwealth and Restoration
1649–1685

Satire and Panegyric

I have put Cowley here for his worship of science and light. That is more significant to us than his perplexing the fair sex with metaphysics, which placed him earlier for Johnson. His science is a Restoration characteristic, the obverse—the target—of Butler's and Rochester's scepticism. But Cowley does not easily fit anywhere. He is too representative, of too long a time, too many modes, and always at a mediocre level. This is why the chief question about him is why was he ever popular—'Who now reads Cowley?' The best use for Cowley is as excuse for reading the chapter of Alex Comfort's *Darwin and the naked lady* in which he is the centre of a discussion of evolutionary criteria for art. *Davideis* struggles for a harmonious cosmos but cannot construct it; the familiar *Ode of wit* (not printed here) is similar. Perhaps that is what the 17th century's epic ambition was about? From one point of view Cowley's *Ecstasy* is like his epic, a sentimental collocation of junk. The poem is in the line of the gloomy visions of section 6 and Milton's aspiring *Vacation exercise;* it was to be succeeded by a thousand febrile odes much like inner tubes blowing themselves up. But once again Cowley is not built for the job—he cannot manage astronautics: 'Where am I now? Angels and God is here'. The bathos of the 18th century enters with its pomp. Yet the *Ecstasy* is worth study as pop art. We have felt the pressure of folk idiom all through the century—at first mainly in bawdy and madness; then (with Quarles and Joseph Beaumont for instance) in the plainness of middle-class Sunday-go-to-meeting speech; finally in the Newcastles, Anne Bradstreet, Lady Dyer—'so that we might either Sat up, or gone to bed together': they handle poetry as a familiar tool. Perhaps Cowley's mediocrity is an advanced form of that familiarity? or a version of it that has been emasculated? At any rate I think we can see in the *Ecstasy* what the pop art, the decadent baroque, of a past age might be:

'Twas gawdy all, and rich in every part,
Of essences and gems and spirit of gold
    Was its substantial mould,
    Drawn forth by chymic angels' art;
Here with moonbeams 'twas silvered bright,
There double gilt with the sun's light,
    And mystic shapes cut round in it,
Figures that did transcend a vulgar angel's wit.

The chariot of wrath is a treacherous topic (see *Paradise lost*
VI–VII). But it is not just the glitter here that is pop; it is
the degradation of those potent and reverend ingredients into
cliché. Although at any given moment we must disapprove
of this, historically there seem to be times when it is good
from the point of view of social biology. It gives very extensive currency, in pre-digested form, to concepts which
without that processing might remain the prerogative of an
oligarchy, so that society as a whole would get stuck. Historical
pop can be followed up in the next section with Heyrick,
Anne Killigrew and Aphra Behn; to distinguish it from folk,
see Durfey and go back to Sylvester and Quarles in section 3.

I have put Butler next because he mocks Cowley's enlighten-
ment. He too writes with a special freedom that hints at pop,
though he is too clever and contemptuous to actually be
popular. He produced versions of *The elephant in the moon*
(the very title hinting at Houyhnhnms) in 'short verse' (i.e.
octosyllabic) and long. I think this was to mock poetry with
the measurements of science. Inside the poem he degrades
rhyme—'honour : upon her; cities there : civiller'; and he
forces into the verse words not only indecorous but unman-
ageably arhythmic—water-engines, jiggumbobs. He parodies
love poetry ('as if he meant to gaze her through') and epic; he
undermines the philosophers—'Surprised with wonder beforehand At what they did not understand'. All this makes him
tiresome, and little read (he would be read more if we shifted
attention off *Hudibras,* the dreariest of his works). Yet he is
not nihilistic. He draws into his poems a wonderful multitude
of things. They are there not as emblems but as themselves, as
those mere things—pumps, cooks, tiles, corns in the toe,
salmon. This is another form of familiarity. (For all the
panegyrics to Charles II, poetry is no longer of the court.
What was its social centre, then?) In his uncourtly language,
and his disgust with conventional science and with war, Butler
is the companion of the Duchess of Newcastle; but with the
Poetical thesaurus he reaches beyond her, to Blake and the
Proverbs of hell. What links sceptic with mystic?

For years Denham and Waller were purely nominal for me, counters to be used in answering exam questions on the 18th century, quoting Pope's 'praise the easy vigour of a line Where Denham's strength and Waller's sweetness join' (*Essay on criticism*). Dryden said it too; Johnson repeated them in his life of Denham. Denham remains not worth reading at any length; but the historical points to make about him turn out to differ from those expected by the examiners. He is indeed Augustan in precise ways—crammed with historical references (cf. Davenant, Joseph Beaumont); using mythology as form of periphrasis instead of a set of dramatic tales (Arachne's line = cobweb in a strictly synonym relationship); anti-zealous, antithetical, sceptical; using a wit of syntax rather than of trope:

> Uncharitable zeal our reason whets
> And double edges on our passion sets.

But isn't he Augustan because those are the forms into which satire naturally falls, at least when it is restrained by that fear of commitment that prevailed after the civil war until deep into the 18th century? Certainly parts of Rochester's *Satire against mankind* are indistinguishable from the *Dunciad*, written half a century later:

> Whilst the misguided follower climbs with pain
> Mountains of whimsies heaped in his own brain.

The distinction lies, actually, in the superior intellect of Restoration satire. The Augustans followed Dryden instead of his betters.

The point I am trying to propose is that Denham is like an Augustan not because he influenced them but because they went on doing things—notably, writing a particular kind of satire—which were effectively the invention of the Restoration.

Denham is interesting in his own right as a sceptic. He distrusts religion, *and* science:

> Through seas of ignorance we our course advance,
> Discovering still new worlds of ignorance;
> And these discoveries make us all confess
> That sublunary science is but guess.

His distrust leads him to McLuhanlike statements about printing.

The sceptical materialism of Hobbes lies behind Rochester's satire. It is only with Dryden that satire loses a metaphysic and gains a party; and even in that dwindled genre, Shadwell, it seems to me, is livelier and funnier than Dryden and Pope, who pilloried him over and over again.

Shadwell is also a better dramatist than Dryden. Otway, the Tourneur of the Restoration, is in every way more interesting than Dryden and than any of the established Restoration dramatists. This was acknowledged by his European popularity (he was translated into many languages including Russian); but somewhere in the mid-18th century his rank in literary history got distorted (see Warton's *History of English poetry*). As with so many others, we have continued to accept the canons of Pope and of Johnson, in spite of our entirely different literary needs. It is worth questioning the values Johnson rests on in his account of Otway:

> *The orphan* . . . is a domestic tragedy drawn from middle life. Its whole power is upon the affections; for it is not written with much comprehension of thought, or elegance of expression . . . *Venice preserved* . . . still continues to be one of the favourites of the public, notwithstanding the want of morality in the original design, and the despicable scenes of vile comedy . . . his images were by time become stronger, and his language more energetic. The striking passages are in every mouth; and the public seems to judge rightly of the faults and excellences of this play, that it is the work of a man not attentive to decency, nor zealous for virtue; but of one who conceived forcibly, and drew originally, by consulting nature in his own breast . . . Of the poems . . . the longest is *The poet's complaint of his muse,* part of which I do not understand; and in that which is less obscure I find little to commend. The language is often gross, and the numbers are harsh. Otway had not much cultivated versification, nor much replenished his mind with general knowledge.

Waller, on the other hand, had. His antitheses snap as safely as children's plastic scissors—'All that can, living, feed the greedy eye Or, dead, the palate, here you may descry' (the possibility of eye and palate changing places, which would have leapt from line with Marvell or Cleveland, doesn't occur to Waller). His poems are rich, smooth, commercial; he writes about comfort—animals are food, or ambergris; vegetables are harvests; the earth a park. Johnson said he improved our numbers; but surely he is only one part of that general 'improvement' which embraced London, St. James's Park, the commons, the manners of squires and eventually their agriculture? In the town it produced civil splendour; in the country, gradually, tameness. See Pope's moral essays on *The use of riches* and note that his *Windsor Forest* seems contemporaneous with Waller's (also royal) park; what happened in between? If you then compare Waller's panegyrics with Marvell's, Marvell comes out as belonging to an older, tarter world. Waller, however insincere about his rulers, is genuinely patriotic about his nation. It is a new kind of patriotism; or is it servility? It leads into Dryden's *Annus mirabilis,* Marlborough's wars (see Durfey in the next section), the mercantilist patriotism of James Thomson; it founders in Blake.

Further suggestions. For major independent work, Butler remains available, especially for linguistic study and outside *Hudibras;* Waller; Shadwell. Otway has in some ways been overworked but I don't think the psychological appeal of his plays (and it is mainly that) has been dealt with. Rochester has been spoilt by the air of naughtiness and censorship surrounding him. Now that we are allowed to read him unbowdlerised, and are less disturbed by his language, we might start asking questions about it. Etymologically, fuck and cunt are very old words but they seem to have been kept out of *printed* literature, at any rate in their full spelled-out magical form, except for the brief Restoration period and again since the *Lady Chatterley's lover* trial in England in the 1950s. Was that a form of folk censorship? or was it that alternative words were preferred anyway? For some cultures a euphemism may be more potent than the real thing. Why did these words enter printed books at the Restoration? Was there a change in the extra-literary habits of language, and if so which classes did it happen in? Why are Restoration poets so preoccupied with impotence and venereal disease and why do they so closely associate genital with urinary functions? Is there a relationship between sex and satire, parallel perhaps to that between love and hate? Rochester has a Swiftian horror (rather, Swift had a Rochesterian one) at the squalor of 'the reasoning engine'; yet Rochester also has a sense of tenderness and unity, expressed in strongly physical terms in *Imperfect enjoyment.* What had been said in terms of angels or Plato, Rochester now says as 'Her hand, her foot, her very look's a cunt'. What sort of change is that? How do these events in literary history affect one's reading of Lawrence's essays on love?

Finally, why did Johnson write lives of those and only those poets?

ABRAHAM COWLEY

Posthumous 7th son of London stationer who left £1000 amongst his children. Westminster School; infant prodigy— read the *Fairy Queen* as a child, wrote his own romance at 10, published *Poetical blossoms* at 15. Trinity College, Cambridge, where he was elected to a fellowship and wrote his unfinished epic *Davideis* (cf. Davenant, Waller), Latin poems and *The cutter of Coleman Street* 1641, a satirical comedy on the Puritans. Ejected by parliament 1643; to the King's court at Oxford, where he met Crashaw again and became friend of Lord Falkland (see Cary) and other royalists. Followed the Queen's court into French exile 1646; delicate diplomacy, cypher correspondence with Charles I. *The mistress* 1647. In 1655 came to England, arrested as a spy, released but suspected of being a double agent. Published *Davideis* and odes 1656. Studied medicine at Oxford and after the Restoration retired to Kent to study pharmacology and botany and write his essays and *A proposition for the advancement of experimental philosophy*. 15 editions of *Works* between the year of his death and 1721 but in the 1730s Pope asked "Who now reads Cowley?" (*Epistle to Augustus*). Friend of Denham, Hobbes, and Sprat, secretary of the Royal Society. Unmarried. Complete works ed. A. B. Grosart 2 vols. Edinburgh 1881; *English writings* ed. A. R. Waller 2 vols. Cambridge 1905–06. See Johnson *Lives of the poets* 1781; A. H. Nethercot *A. C. The muses' Hannibal* 1931; R. B. Hinman *A. C.'s world of order* Cambridge Mass. 1960; A. Comfort in his *Darwin and the naked lady*. 1961.

from Davideis Book I

Music

Such was God's poem, this world's new essáy;
So wild and rude in its first draft it lay—
The ungoverned parts no correspondence° knew,

An artless war from thwarting motions grew;
Till they to number and fixed rules were brought   5
By the Eternal Mind's poetic thought.
Water and air he for the tenor chose,
Earth made the bass, the treble flame arose;
To the active moon a quick brisk stroke he gave,
To Saturn's° string a touch more soft and grave;   10
The motions straight and round and swift and slow
And short and long were mixed and woven so,
Did in such artful figures smoothly fall,
As made this decent measured dance of all.
And this is music: sounds that charm our ears   15
Are but one dressing that rich science wears.
Though no man hear it, though no man it rehearse,
Yet will there still be music in my verse.
In this great world° so much of it we see;
The lesser, man, is all o'er harmony.   20
Storehouse of all proportions! single choir
Which first God's breath did tunefully inspire!
From hence blest music's heavenly charms arise,
From sympathy which them and man allies.
Thus they our souls, thus they our bodies win,   25
Not by their force, but party that's within;
Thus the strange cure on our spilt blood applied,
Sympathy to the distant wound does guide;
Thus when two brethren strings are set alike,
To move them both, but one of them we strike;   30
Thus David's lyre° did Saul's wild rage control
And tuned the harsh disorders of his soul.

3 **correspondence** cf. Joseph Beaumont *All things at first* and Vaughan
Tempest in Vol. I. 10 **Saturn** leaden planet. 19 **great world** macrocosm as opposed to the little world of man; see King *Exequy*. 31 **lyre**
see Rembrandt's picture of this event.

from Davideis Book I

Hell°

Beneath the silent chambers of the earth,
Where the sun's fruitful beams give metals birth,
Where he the growth of fatal gold does see,
Gold which, above, more influence has than he;
Beneath the dens where unfletched° tempests lie   5
And infant winds their tender voices try;

Beneath the mighty oceans' wealthy caves,
Beneath the eternal fountain of all waves,
Where their vast court the mother-waters keep
And, undisturbed by moons, in silence sleep: 10
There is a place, deep, wondrous deep, below
Which genuine night and horror does o'erflow;
No bound controls the unwearied space, but hell,
Endless as those dire pains that in it dwell.
Here no dear glimpse of the sun's lovely face   15
Strikes through the solid darkness of the place;
No dawning morn does her kind reds display;
One slight weak beam would here be thought the day.
No gentle stars with their fair gems of light
Offend the tyrannous and unquestioned night.   20
Here Lucifer, the mighty captive, reigns,
Proud midst his woes and tyrant in his chains.
Once general of a gilded host of sprites,
Like Hesper° leading forth the spangled nights;
But down like lightning, which him struck, he came,   25
And roared at his first plunge into the flame.
Myriads of spirits fell wounded round him there;
With dropping lights thick shone the singèd air . . .

° **Hell** cf. *Paradise lost* I and *Dunciad*. 5 **unfletched** unfledged. 24
Hesper 'How art thou fallen from heaven, O Lucifer, son of the
morning' [i.e. morning star] *Isaiah* xiv.

The ecstasy°

I leave mortality, and things below.
I have no time in compliments to waste,
    Farewell t'ye all in haste!
    For I am called to go.
  A whirlwind bears up my dull feet,   5
  The officious° clouds beneath them meet
    And lo! I mount, and lo!
How small the biggest parts of earth's proud title show.

Where shall I find the noble British land?
Lo! I at last a nothern speck espy   10
    Which in the sea does lie
    And seems a grain o' th' sand.
  For this will any sin, or bleed?
  Of civil wars in this the meed?

And is it this, alas, which we   15
(O irony of words!) do call Great Britainy?

I pass by the archèd magazines° which hold
The eternal stores of frost, and rain, and snow;
      Dry and secure I go,
       Nor shake with fear or cold;   20
    Without affright or wonder
    I meet clouds charged with thunder,
       And lightnings in my way
Like harmless lambent fires about my temples play.

Now into a gentle sea of rolling flame   25
I'm plunged, and still mount higher there
      As flames mount up through air;
      So perfect, yet so tame,
    So great, so pure, so bright a fire
    Was that unfortunate desire   30
      My faithful breast did cover
Then, when I was of late a wretched mortal lover.

Through several orbs which one fair planet bear,
Where I behold distinctly as I pass
      The hints of Galileo's° glass,   35
      I touch at last the spangled sphere:
    Here all the extended sky
    Is but one galaxy,
      'Tis all so bright and gay,
And the joint eyes of night make up a perfect day.   40

Where am I now? Angels and God is here.
An unexhausted ocean of delight
      Swallows my senses quite
      And drowns all what, or how, or where.
    Not Paul,° who first did thither pass,   45
    And this great world's Columbus was,
      The tyrannous pleasure could express:
O 'tis too much for man! but let it ne'er be less.

The mighty Elijah° mounted so on high—
That second man who leapt the ditch where all   50
      The rest of mankind fall,
      And went not downwards to the sky;
    With much of pomp and show,
    As conquering kings in triumph go,
      Did he to heaven approach,   55
And wondrous was his way, and wondrous was his coach:

'Twas gawdy all, and rich in every part,
Of essences of gems and spirit of gold
    Was its substantial mould,
      Drawn forth by chymic° angels' art;   60
Here with moonbeams 'twas silvered bright,
  There double-gilt with the sun's light,
    And mystic shapes cut round in it,
Figures that did transcend a vulgar angel's wit;

The horses were of tempered lightning made,   65
Of all that in heaven's beauteous pastures feed
    The noblest, sprightfullest breed,
    And flaming manes their necks arrayed;
They all were shod with diamond,
  Not such as here are found   70
    But such light solid ones as shine
On the transparent rocks o'th' heaven crystalline.°

Thus mounted the great prophet to the skies.
Astonished men who oft had seen stars fall,
    Or that which so they call,   75
    Wondered from hence to see one rise!
  The soft clouds melted him away,
  The snow and frosts which in it lay
    A while the sacred footsteps bore,
The wheels and horses' hoofs hissed as they past them o'er;   80

He passed by the moon and planets, and did fright
All the worlds there which at this meteor gazed,
    And their astrologers amazed
    With the unexampled sight.
  But where he stopped will ne'er be known   85
  Till phoenix'° nature, aged grown,
    To a better being do aspire
And mount herself, like him, to eternity in fire.

° **ecstasy** in sense of sublime vision, not as in Donne and Herbert's *Ode.* 6 **officious** .dutiful. 17 **magazines** he moves up from the earth through the layers or 'regions' of water, air and fire to the spheres of the moon, planets and stars. Cf. Milton's *Vacation exercise*; see Herbert *Platonic love.* 35 **Galileo** in 1543 Copernicus (Polish) asserted that the sun, not the earth, was central. Tycho Brahe (Danish) collected observations and in 1577 showed that a comet had passed through the 'crystalline sphere' of the old system. Kepler (German) took over from Brahe, who died in 1600, and worked out orbits (Wotton visited him to invite him to England but Kepler's mother was in custody during a 6-year trial for witchcraft and he stayed at home to save her from torture). The first telescope was probably made by Leonard Digges (Oxford, d. 1571), whose son Thomas argued that the universe was infinite; telescopes were also used early on by Harriot (see Chapman's poem to him above); but public development of the instrument rests with Lippersley, a Dutch optician, who took out a patent in 1608. Galileo Galilei heard of it in 1609 and it was he who put it to greatest use. Galileo was born in Pisa in 1564 on the day that Michelangelo died. His investigations proved the Copernician case in detail (e.g. unevenness of the moon's surface, Jupiter's satellites, Saturn's ring, sunspots, starry composition of the Milky Way). The Inquisition declared his doctrines absurd in 1616; in 1632 he was tried and abjured his findings. His daughter died in 1634 and he went blind in 1636. There is a story that Milton visited him in 1639. He died in 1642, the year Newton was born. **45 Paul** 'I will come to visions and revelations of the Lord . . . caught up to the third heaven. And I knew such a man . . . caught up into paradise, and heard unspeakable words.' *II Corinthians* xii. **49 Elijah** went to heaven in a fiery chariot, *II Kings* ii. The first was Enoch, 'translated that he should not see death,' *Hebrews* xi, *Genesis* v. Cf. Vaughan *Religion*. **60 chymic** alchemical; see Benlowes *Might souls converse*. **72 crystalline** transparent sphere outside the sphere of the stars. **86 phoenix** see Carew *Mole*.

SAMUEL BUTLER

Son of a farmer. King's School, Worcester. Service of Countess of Kent where he met Selden, who educated him. Studied painting. Magistrates' clerk in Worcestershire; his paintings at Earl's Coombe used to stop up broken windows in the 18th century. While clerk to a series of country gentlemen, including one of Cromwell's generals, wrote *Hudibras,* satire on a Presbyterian colonel. Friend of Cleveland. Travelled in France and Holland. In 1660 became steward of Ludlow Castle, where *Comus* had been performed 1634. Soon after, married and lived on wife's money until they lost it in bad investments. Published *Hudibras* 1663 (Parts II and III, 1664, 1678); suddenly famous; introduced at court by Earl of Dorset but his poverty not relieved—perhaps because of his own prickliness. *General remains* 1668 contains *Elephant in the moon* and satirical prose character-sketches. The rest of his life poor and obscure. *Collected works* ed. A. R. Waller and R. Lamar 3 vols. Cambridge 1905, 1908, 1928. See Aubrey *Brief lives*; Pepys *Diary*; R. Quintana, S. B.: a Restoration figure in a modern light *English literary history* XVIII 1951.

from The elephant in the moon: a satire: in short verse°

A learn'd society° of late,
The glory of a foreign state,
Agreed upon a summer's night
To search the moon by her own light:
To take an inventory of all   5
Her real estate and personal;
And make an accurate survey
Of all her lands and how they lay,
As true as that of Ireland, where
The sly surveyors stole a shire;   10

To observe her country, how 'twas planted,
With what she abounded most, or wanted;
And make the properest observations
For settling of new plantations°
(If the society should incline   15
To attempt so glorious a design).
This was the purpose of their meeting,
For which they chose a time as fitting:
When, at the full, her radiant light
And influence° too were at their height.   20
    And now the lofty tube, the scale°
With which they heaven itself assail,
Was mounted full against the moon;
And all stood ready to fall on,
Impatient who should have the honour   25
To plant an ensign first upon her.
When one, who for his deep belief
Was virtuoso- then in-chief,
Approved the most profound and wise
To solve impossibilities,   30
Advancing gravely to apply
To the optic glass his judging eye,
Cried, Strange! Then reinforced his sight
Against the moon with all his might
And bent his penetrating brow   35
As if he meant to gaze her through;
When all the rest began to admire
And, like a train,° from him took fire,
Surprised with wonder beforehand
At what they did not understand,   40
Cried out, impatient to know what
The matter was they wondered at.
    Quoth he: The inhabitants of the moon
Who, when the sun shines hot at noon,
Do live in cellars underground   45
Of 8 miles deep and 80 round,
In which at once they fortify
Against the sun and the enemy,
Which they count towns and cities there
Because their people's civiller   50
Than those rude peasants that are found
To live upon the upper ground,
Called Privolvans, with whom they are
Perpetually in open war;
And now both armies, highly enraged,   55
Are in a bloody fight engaged;

And many fall on both sides slain,
As by the glass 'tis clear and plain:
Look quickly then that everyone
May see the fight before 'tis done ...   60

° **short verse** he wrote a decasyllabic version as well. **1 society** satire
on the Royal Society, premier scientific academy of England. Developed
from disciples of Francis Bacon who met in 1645; interrupted by war,
chartered 1662, first transactions published 1665. Early membership was
widely 'philosophical' and included Cowley, Dryden, Waller, Aubrey
the biographer, the diarists Evelyn and Pepys, and Christopher Wren, as
well as Boyle the chemist and Bishop Sprat, who wrote a history and
defined the aims of the society. These included stripping concepts of
metaphor, and practising 'a close, naked, natural way of speaking; posi-
tive expressions; clear senses; a native easiness'. Committees handled
various projects, e.g. collecting reports of natural phenomena, experiments with gravity, vacuums, microscopy, the dissection of executed
persons (the society had a right to their bodies) and vivisection, and the
study of folklore topics such as natural 'sympathy' between objects, and
fabulous creatures such as unicorn and salamander. Similar societies
were founded in Paris and Berlin. The nearest project to Butler's parody
was a meteorological expedition to Teneriffe (see Benlowes *Might souls
converse*). **14 plantations** colonies. **20 influence** astrological, hence
anti-scientific; and causing lunacy. **21 scale** siege ladder. International
competition to land on the moon in the 1960s was quasi-military; Butler
is being mock-heroic and mock-antique here, but also mocking the
civil war. **38 train** fuse.

Arts and sciences

Rules

Were made for novices and fools.
    The old Egyptians steered their boats
And sailed down cataracts of spoats,°
Made spectacles to improve the sight   5
And see in the dark as well as light.
    'Tis strange how stubbornly industrious
Some men are found to appear preposterous,
That spare no drudgery and pains
To waste their little stock of brains: 10
All arts and sciences perplex
And with a thousand idle freaks
The government of nature vex
And, like fanatics, in their hearts
Have visions, and new lights in arts;   15
From old designs of water-engines
Steal gifts and lights of new inventions,

Make pumps for water (and their wit)
To raise 'em both so many feet,
And forge their gimcracks at the rate   20
Fanatics use in church and state,
And out of antique theorems
New jiggumbobs of light and dreams.
   Smatterers are more brisk and pert
Than those who understand an art,   25
As little sparkles shine more bright
Than glowing coals that give 'em light,
Whose sudden vanities and flashes
Are clouded by themselves with ashes.
   'Tis not the art of schools to understand   30
But make things hard instead of being explained;
And therefore those are commonly the learnedst
That only study between jest and earnest:
For when the end of learning's to pursue
And trace the subtle steps of false and true,   35
They ne'er consider how they are to apply
But only listen to the noise and cry
And are so much delighted with the chase,
They never mind the taking of their preys.
For books are but a kind of útensils   40
Of turning children upon potters' wheels
That, when they are o'erclogged with heavy men,
Reduce 'em naturally to boys again.
For books—were made for men, not men for books,
No more than meat was made for dressing cooks;   45
Are commonly the by-blows of an author
(Not one in forty has an honest mother).

from *The poetical thesaurus*

2 **spoats** spouts?

Nature

leaks like a tub and not a boat,
For the one runs in and the other out.
   The sphere of vapours rules the air
And makes the weather foul or fair.

     •   •   •

   Fishes with scales are tiled about   5
Like houses, to keep water out.
   An army, and a populous town
Infected with the plague, 's all one.

Men's corns are wont before a shower of rain
(But never when they're in it) to be in pain.   10
  So woodcocks that are coloured like dead leaves
The crafty fowler easily deceives.
  So in the western sea of Spain, the sun
Is like a taper put out, and goes down,
That in a moment shines and then goes out,   15
As the ancients, in his seabed chamber, thought.
  A single feather breaks the horse's back
And drops of water greatest vessels wrack.
  Sleep that wearied life redeems
Is fed with vain and idle dreams.   20
  The most divine of all the works of nature
Was not to make model but the matter;
As men may build without designs and rules
But not without materials and tools.
  A salmon is both bow and arrows   25
That is both shot himself and carries.
  The lady, like a fish's roe, had room
For such a shoal of infants in her womb.

                •   •

When no one person's able to understand
The vast stupendous uses of the hand,   30
The only engine helps the wit of man
To bring the world in compass of a span,
From raising mighty fabrics on the seas
To filing chains to fit the necks of fleas.

                •   •

For though the moon's commandress of the seas   35
And all her various, different nations sways,
She never yet has, at the full, been said
To make her natural subjects, fishes, mad,
Like those that, out of her supreme command,
Are born and bred and live upon the land.   40

                •   •

In all the year, the day and night
Have less of darkness than of light,
In twilights and the dawns of suns,
Besides six months of shining moons.
The light below, and upper darkness, dye   45
The natural blue tincture of the sky,
For all the heat and light we find appear
Extends no further than the atmosphere:
The rest all darkness, only where the moon
And other planets entertain the sun,   50
That holds no more proportion to the whole

Than glow-worms' tails or sparkles of a coal.
  Some guess the earth is but a shell
And all the inner concave hell—
The infernal dungeons and dark holes   55
Of reprobate departed souls,
Which poets call the Stygian lake,
From whence no traveller comes back.
     •   •   •

                      All phenomenas
May be expounded several ways.   60
     •   •   •

And if the sun does but draw near to us,
As great philosophers believe he does,
The date of this world's charter will expire
And all its movables consume in fire.

                    from *The poetical thesaurus*

from Hudibras:° *the first and second parts, written in the time of the late wars*

The argument of the first canto

> Sir Hudibras his passing worth,
> The manner how he sallied forth,
> His arms and équipage are shown,
> His horse's virtues and his own;
> The adventure of the bear and fiddle   5
> Is sung but breaks off in the middle.

When civil fury first grew high
And men fell out, they knew not why,
When hard words, jealousies and fears
Set folks together by the ears   10
And made them fight like mad or drunk
For Dame Religion as for punk°
(Whose honesty they all durst swear for,
Though not a man of them knew wherefore);
When gospel-trumpeter, surrounded   15
With long-eared rout, to battle sounded,
And pulpit—drum ecclesiastic—
Was beat with fist instead of a stick:
Then did Sir Knight abandon dwelling
And out he rode a-colonelling.   20
     •   •   •

He was in logic a great critic,
Profoundly skilled in analytic;
He could distinguish and divide
A hair 'twixt south and south-west side—
On either which he would dispute,   25
Confute, change hands and still confute.
He'd undertake to prove by force
Of argument a man's no horse;
He'd prove a buzzard is no fowl
And that a lord may be an owl,   30
A calf an alderman, a goose a justice
And rooks committee-men and trustees;
He'd run in debt by disputation
And pay with ratiocination;
All this by syllogism, true   35
In mood and figure, he would do.
  For rhetoric, he could not ope
His mouth but out there flew a trope;
And when he happened to break off
In the middle of his speech, or cough,   40
He'd hard words ready to show why
And tell what rules he did it by.

   •   •

He could reduce all things to acts
And knew their natures by abstracts,
Where entity and quiddity,°   45
The ghosts of defunct bodies fly;
Where truth in person does appear
Like words congealed in northern air.
He knew what's what, and that's as high
As metaphysic wit can fly;   50
In school divinity as able
As he that hight irrefragable;°
Profound in all the nominal°
And real ways beyond them all,
And with as delicate a hand   55
Could twist as tough a rope of sand,°
And weave fine cobwebs fit for skull
That's empty when the moon is full—
Such as take lodgings in a head
That's to be let unfurnishèd.   60

   •   •

  For his religion, it was fit
To match his learning and his wit:
'Twas Presbyterian true blue,°
For he was of that stubborn crew

Of errant saints whom all men grant 65
To be the true church militant,
Such as do build their faith upon
The holy text of pike and gun,
Decide all controversies by
Infallible artillery 70
And prove their doctrine orthodox
By apostolic blows and knocks,
Call fire and sword and desolation
A Godly-thorough-reformation
Which always must be carried on 75
And still be doing, never done—
As if religion were intended
For nothing else but to be mended . . .

° **Hudibras** a mock-epic modelled on Cervantes' *Don Quixote* (1610, trans. 1612). The hero is named after a minor hothead in Spenser's *Fairy Queen*. He is a presbyterian colonel of the crudest puritan pedantry who sets out with his squire Ralpho (an Independent in religion) and tries to put down bear-baiting in a Worcester-like town. 12 **punk** whore. 45 **quiddity** the whatness of a thing, its essence. 52 **irrefragable** Alexander of Hales, an English monk of the 13th century, was called (hight) the Irrefragable Doctor. 53 **nominal** nominalists attend to individual things and deny the existence of abstracts—horse is a name given to a class of quadrupeds; realists believe in the existence of ideal Horse. 56 **sand** see Herbert *Collar.* 63 **true blue** now means conservative but was colour of the Scottish Covenanters, and of presbyterian preachers, perhaps versus royal scarlet, perhaps because blue was a permanent, washable, stainless dye (so used in butchers' aprons).

SIR JOHN DENHAM

Born in Dublin, son of an Irish judge. Trinity College,
Oxford—slow and dreamy student; Lincoln's Inn. Married at
19, one son, two daughters. Quarrelled with father over
gambling, squandered inheritance when father died 1638.
Cooper's Hill belongs to this period. At civil war appointed
governor of Farnham Castle for the king but easily beaten
out of it by parliamentary army; captured but released. Wither
petitioned for some of his property but when he was himself
captured by the royalists Denham asked that Wither be kept
alive so that he, Denham, 'should not be the worst poet in
England'. Helped Cowley with correspondence for exiled
court but returned penniless. Fortunes somewhat restored in
1660; appointed chief government architect (Wren became
his deputy in 1668). A widower by now, remarried 1665;
his wife, who was 18, openly the mistress of the Duke of
York, who visited her at the Denham house in Scotland Yard;
she died the next year and Denham was suspected of poisoning her drinking chocolate; the post mortem found no trace
but rumours were widespread (Marvell refers to them); her
ghost was said to haunt the duchess. Denham had had a fit
of madness and claimed, before the King, to be the Holy
Ghost. *Cooper's Hill* became a model for topographical verse
in the 18th century but the first to praise it was Herrick.
Poems and translations 1668. *Poetical works* ed. T. H. Banks,
New Haven 1928. See Aubrey and Dr. Johnson.

from The progress of learning

Then darkness Europe's face did overspread,
From lazy cells° where superstition bred
Which, linked with blind obedience, so increased
That the whole world some ages they oppressed;
Till through those clouds the sun of knowledge brake   5
And Europe from her lethargy did wake;
Then first our monarchs° were acknowledged here

That they their churches' nursing fathers were.
When Lucifer no longer could advance
His works on the false grounds of ignorance,   10
New arts he tries and new designs he lays;
Then his well-studied masterpiece he plays:
Loyola, Luther,° Calvin he inspires
And kindles with infernal flames their fires,
Sends their forerunner (conscious of the event)   15
Printing,° his most pernicious instrument!
Wild controversy then, which long had slept,
Into the press from ruined cloisters leapt:
No longer by implicit faith we err
Whilst every man's his own interpreter;   20
No more conducted now by Aaron's° rod,
Lay-elders from their ends create their God.
But seven° wise men the ancient world did know;
We scarce know seven who think themselves not so.
When man learned undefiled religion,   25
We were commanded to be all as one;
Fiery disputes that union have calcined—
Almost as many minds as men we find;
And when that flame finds cómbustible earth,
Then *fatuus*° fires and meteors take their birth.   30
Legions of sects, and insects, come in throngs—
To name them all would tire a hundred tongues:
So were the centaurs° of Ixion's race
(Who a bright cloud for Juno did embrace);
And such the monsters of Chimera's° kind,   35
Lions before and dragons were behind.
    Then from the clashes between popes and kings
Debate, like sparks from flints' collision, springs;
As Jove's loud thunderbolts were forged by heat,
The like our Cyclops° on their anvils beat: 40
All the rich mines of learning ransacked are
To furnish ammunition for this war;
Uncharitable zeal our reason whets
And double edges on our passion sets.
'Tis the most certain sign the world's accursed   45
That the best things, corrupted, are the worst:
'Twas the corrupted light of knowledge hurled
Sin, death and ignorance o'er all the world;
That sun, like this from which our sight we have,
Gazed on too long, resumes the light he gave;   50
And when thick mists of doubts obscure his beams
Our guide is error and our visions, dreams.
'Twas no false heraldry when madness drew

Her pedigree from those who too much knew:
Who in deep mines for hidden knowledge toils,   55
Like guns o'ercharged, breaks, misses, or recoils;
When subtle wits have spun their thread too fine,
'Tis weak and fragile, like Arachne's° line.
True piety, without cessation tossed
By theories, the practic part is lost   60
And like a ball bandied 'twixt pride and wit,
Rather than yield, both sides the prize will quit;
Then, whilst his foe each gladiator foils,
The atheist, looking on, enjoys the spoils.

   Through seas of knowledge we our course advance,   65
Discovering still new worlds of ignorance;
And these discoveries make us all confess
That súblunary science is but guess;
Matters of fact to man are only known,
And what seems more is mere opinion.   70
The standers-by see clearly this event:
All parties say they're sure, yet all dissent.
With their new light our bold inspectors press,
Like Cham,° to show their fathers' nakedness,
By whose example after-ages may   75
Discover we more naked are than they.

   All human wisdom to divine is folly;
This truth the wisest° man made melancholy.
Hope, or belief, or guess gives some relief;
But to be sure we are deceived brings grief.   80
Who thinks his wife is virtuous, though not so,
Is pleased and patient, till the truth he know.

   Our God, when heaven and earth he did create,
Formed man, who should of both participate;
If our lives' motions theirs must imitate,   85
Our knowledge, like our blood, must circulate.°
When, like a bridegroom,° from the east the sun
Sets forth, he thither whence he came doth run;
Into earth's spongy veins the ocean sinks,
Those rivers to replenish which he drinks: 90
So learning, which from reason's fountain springs,
Back to the source some secret channel brings.
'Tis happy when our streams to knowledge flow
To fill their banks, but not to overthrow.

   Ut metit Autumnus fruges quas parturit Aestas,   95
   Sic ortum Natura, dedit Deus his quoque finem.°

---

2 **cells** of monks. Denham is attacking the middle ages as dark. 7
monarchs Henry VIII claimed headship of the church in England

independently of the Pope by the Act of Supremacy 1535. Then he suppressed monasteries. Such enactments as the Treaty of Augsburg (1555) had similar effect in parts of the Continent. 13 **Luther** Martin Luther 1483-1546, son of a German miner, monk, priest and professor of theology, exposed abuses in the church in 1517 and enforced reformation in the German states; was excommunicated, married a former nun. Preferred faith, conscience and Bible to works, reason and the church; regarded as fanatic. The Lutheran church dominant in the Baltic basin. John Calvin 1509-1564, son of a French lawyer, codified protestant theology in his *Institutes of the Christian religion* 1536. Appointed head of the reformed church in Geneva and governed it with intimate severity. Believed that men are predestined to salvation or damnation (see Philips *Friendship's mystery*). The Genevan church became notorious for intolerance but Calvinism dominated Scotland and parts of France and eastern Europe. St. Ignatius Loyola c.1491-1556, came of a noble Basque family; royal page, army officer, experienced conversion while convalescing from a wound; became for a time a hermit of extreme ascetic practices; had vision of the Trinity; wrote *Spiritual exercises* (published 1548). Pilgrimage to Holy Land. Founded Society of Jesus in Paris 1534. Papal approval of the Jesuits in 1540 marks the counter-reformation. The order was characterised by obedience, rigorous educational activities (they are said to have invented exam marks), and international missionary and confessional work. 16 **Printing** by moveable type said to have been invented in China in 9th century A.D. Various claims for the invention in the Rhine basin in the 15th century. Gutenberg was printing at Mainz c.1450; the Latin Bible ascribed to him was published 1456. Caxton, an English merchant, learned printing in Cologne c.1473 and published his first book (of Troy stories) at Bruges c.1474. Luther and Calvin insisted on individual reading and interpretation of the Bible. 21 **Aaron** was high priest, hence his rod stands for authority of the church. 23 **seven** the seven sages of ancient Greece were Solon, Chilo, Thales, Bias, Cleobulus, Pittacus, Periander. 30 **fatuus** see Anon *Hollo my fancy*. 33 **centaurs** half horse, half man, children of King Ixion. Ixion tried to seduce Hera (Juno), the wife of Zeus, so Zeus sent down a cloud which looked like her; Ixion lay with the cloudy image and it gave birth to a centaur. The centaurs multiplied rapidly. 35 **Chimera** so fabulous a monster that it stands for nightmarish illusion or fond fancy. 40 **Cyclops** one-eyed blacksmith giants. 58 **Arachne** spider goddess. 74 **Cham** Khan of Tartary. The story of the emperor's clothes is that the Khan and all his people were duped into admiring his non-existent new robes for fear of being thought impercipient if they said he was naked; but his little son said so. 78 **wisest** probably Socrates. 86 **circulate** circulation of the blood proposed by Servetus in 1553, experimentally confirmed by Harvey 1628. 87 **bridegroom** see *Psalm* xix. 96 **epigraph** As autumn reaps the fruits that summer brings forth, so nature gave rise to these but God completed them. Neo-Latin source unknown.

EDMUND WALLER

Father a squire in Buckinghamshire, d. 1616. Eton; King's College, Cambridge 1620; 1622 Lincoln's Inn and M.P., at 16. 1630 married daughter of a rich London mercer; employed Hobbes as tutor for their son. Wife died in childbirth 1634, and Waller brought George Morley, later bishop of Winchester, to live with him; Morley introduced him to the Falkland circle (see Cowley). Most poems first published 1645. Royalist at heart probably but cousin of the rebellious Bucks squire Hampden, and related by marriage to Cromwell. Went to Oxford to negotiate with the King and arrested by parliament for alleged conspiracy with him; gave information against other accused, of whom three released at once and two hanged at their own front doors. Waller debarred from parliament for ever, fined and banished. Before leaving the country remarried. To France, where he published his *Discourse on Gondibert* (see Davenant), but banishment revoked 1651 and at Restoration re-elected M.P. Favourite courtier of Charles II and James II; friend of Evelyn. See Anne Wharton. Second wife died 1677. *Divine poems* 1685. *Poems* ed. G. Thorn-Drury 1893, 2 vols. 1905. See Johnson *Lives*.

from A panegyric to my Lord Protector:° of the present greatness, and joint interest, of His Highness and this nation

While with a strong and yet a gentle hand
You bridle faction and our hearts command,
Protect us from ourselves and from the foe,
Make us unite and make us conquer too:

Let partial spirits still aloud complain,   5
Think themselves injured that they cannot reign

And own no liberty but where they may
Without control upon their fellows prey.

Above the waves, as Neptune shows his face
To chide the winds and save the Trojan race,   10
So has your Highness, raised above the rest,
Storms of ambition, tossing us, repressed.

Your drooping country, torn with civil hate,
Restored by you is made a glorious state,
The seat of empire, where the Irish come,   15
And the unwilling Scotch, to fetch their doom.

The sea's our own; and now all nations greet
With bending sails° each vessel of our fleet;
Your power extends as far as winds can blow
Or swelling sails upon the globe may go.   20

Heaven, that has placed this island to give law,
To balance Europe, and her states to awe,
In this conjunction does on Britain smile:
The greatest leader and the greatest isle!

Whether this portion of the world were rent   25
By the rude ocean from the continent,
Or thus created, it was sure designed
To be the sacred refuge of mankind.

Hither the oppressèd shall henceforth resort,
Justice to crave, and succour, at your court;   30
And then your Highness not for ours alone
But for the world's Protector shall be known. . . .

c.1655

° **Protector** Cromwell's title. Cf. Marvell's ode *Upon Cromwell's return
from Ireland* 1650. Cromwell 1599–1658, was an M.P. of the squirearchy
who made his name as a cavalry tactician in the civil war. In 1651, at
the end of all the fighting and after the execution of Charles I, the
army began to prod what remained of parliament to more radical and
quick reforms; Cromwell rose naturally to the top of the army and it
was he who forcibly ejected the Speaker and dissolved parliament in
1653, and ruled Britain for 5 years, first through an assembly of notables
selected by the army, with the provost of Eton as Speaker; then, in
1654, as protector (cf. American executive president) with dictatorial
powers over parliament; just before his death he was offered kingship.
Cromwell violently suppressed Ireland in 1649 and Scotland in 1650 for
their royalist sympathies; defeated Charles II's counter-revolution at
Worcester 1651; and defeated the Dutch (important commercial and
naval rivals, though protestant) in 1654. 18 **sails** the Dutch were
forced to agree to salute English warships in the Channel.

from To the King, upon His Majesty's happy return°

The rising sun° complies with our weak sight—
First gilds the clouds, then shows his globe of light
At such a distance from our eyes as though
He knew what harm his hasty beams would do.
But your full Majesty at once breaks forth   5
In the meridian of your reign.° Your worth,
Your youth, and all the splendour of your state
(Wrapped up till now in clouds of adverse fate)
With such a flood of light invade our eyes,
And our spread hearts with so great joy surprise,   10
That if your Grace° incline that we should live
You must not, sir, too hastily forgive!
Our guilt preserves us from excess of joy
Which scatters spirits and would life destroy.
All are obnoxious°; and this faulty land,   15
Like fainting Esther°, does before you stand,
Watching your sceptre . . .

                                          1660

° **return** Charles II, son of Charles I, was restored to the throne from
exile in 1660 by vote of a newly-elected parliament which came into
being as the result of Cromwell's death, his son's resignation, a left-
wing army coup, and a right-wing counter-coup by the professional
soldier General Monck. It was mainly the army's bullying priggishness
which altered sentiment enough to secure the restoration of the monarchy; more generally it might be said that the Commonwealth's consti-
tutional experiments and legal reforms, its religious tolerance and its
imperialism, were too modern for the age. 1 **sun** ancient emblem of
royalty; the sovereign star. 6 **reign** officially Charles II succeeded at
his father's execution in 1649. 11 **grace** by now a slightly old-fashioned
mode of address to a sovereign. The next line's Sir always normal. 15
obnoxious blameworthy. 16 **Esther** fasted for 3 days before begging
the King of Persia to save the lives of the captive Jews. When the King
held out his sceptre to her it meant she had permission to speak. *Esther*
v–vii.

from On St. James's Park° as lately improved by His Majesty

Of the first paradise there's nothing found:
Plants sent by heaven are vanished, and the ground;
Yet the description lasts. Who knows the fate

Of lines that shall this paradise relate?
　Instead of rivers rolling by the side　　　　　5
Of Eden's garden, here flows in the tide:
The sea, which always served his empire, now
Pays tribute to our Prince's pleasure too.
Of famous cities we the founders know,
But rivers, old as seas to which they go,　　　10
Are nature's bounty: 'tis of more renown
To make a river than to build a town.
　For future shade, young trees upon the banks
Of the new stream appear in even ranks;
The voice of Orpheus° for Amphíon's hand　　15
In better order could not make them stand:
May they increase as fast and spread their boughs
As the high fame of their great owner grows!
May he live long enough to see them all
Dark shadows cast, and as his palace tall!　　20
Methinks I see the love that shall be made,
The lovers walking in that amorous shade,
The gallants dancing by the river's side—
They bathe in summer, and in winter slide.
Methinks I hear the music in the boats　　　25
And the loud echo which returns the notes,
While overhead a flock of new-sprung fowl
Hangs in the air and does the sun control,
Darkening the sky; they hover o'er and shroud
The wanton sailors with a feathered cloud.　　30
Beneath, a shoal of silver fishes glides
And plays about the gilded barges' sides;
The ladies, angling in the crystal lake,
Feast on the waters with the prey they take:
At once victorious with their lines, and eyes,　35
They make the fishes and the men their prize.
A thousand Cupids on the billows ride
And sea-nymphs enter with the swelling tide,
From Thetis° sent as spies to make report
And tell the wonders of her sovereign's court.　40
All that can, living, feed the greedy eye
Or, dead, the palate, here you may descry:
The choicest things that furnished Noah's ark,
Or Peter's sheet,° inhabiting this park;
All with a border of rich fruit-trees crowned,　45
Whose loaded branches hide the lofty mound.
Such various ways the spacious alleys lead,
My doubtful muse knows not what path to tread:
Yonder, the harvest of cold months laid up,

Gives a fresh coolness to the royal cup;   50
There ice, like crystal firm, and never lost,
Tempers hot Júly with December's frost;
Winter's dark prison, whence he cannot fly,
Though the warm spring, his enemy, draws nigh.
Strange, that extremes should thus preserve the snow   55
High on the Alps, or in deep caves below . . .

                                        1661

° **Park**   westwards from Whitehall (then royal residence; burnt 1697)
and Westminster, a fashionable district. Henry VIII had reclaimed the
land from the marshes and built St. James's Palace at the N.W. corner;
Charles II improved it in 1668 with lime trees, a canal, ponds, the Mall
(a processional avenue), an ice-house, etc. 15 **Orpheus**   charmed nature
into harmony. Amphion made stones dance and form themselves into
houses and cities at the sound of his lute. 39 **Thetis**   chief sea nymph.
44 **sheet**   in a hungry trance the apostle Peter 'saw heaven opened, and
a certain vessel descending unto him, as it had been a great sheet knit
at the four corners, and let down to the earth: wherein were all manner
of four-footed beasts of the earth, and wild beasts, and creeping things,
and fowls of the air.' *Acts* x.

The fall

See how the willing earth gave way
To take the impression where she lay!
See how the mould, as loath to leave
So sweet a burden, still doth cleave
Close to the nymph's stained garment! Here   5
The coming spring would first appear
And all this place with roses strow,
If busy feet would let them grow;
Here Venus° smiled to see blind chance
Itself before her son advance   10
And a fair image to present
Of what the Boy so long had meant.
'Twas such a chance as this made all
The world into this order fall:
Thus the first lovers° on the clay   15
Of which they were composèd lay;
So in their prime, with equal grace,
Met the first patterns of our race.
Then blush not, fair! or on him frown,
Or wonder how you both came down;   20
But touch him and he'll tremble straight—
How could he then support your weight?

How could the youth, alas! but bend
When his whole heaven upon him leaned?
If aught by him amiss were done,   25
'Twas that he let you rise so soon.

9 **Venus** mother of the blind cupid. 15 **first lovers** the fall itself refers
to Adam and Eve too.

Of the last verses in the book

When we for age could neither read nor write,
The subject made us able to indite.
The soul with nobler resolutions decked,
The body, stooping, does herself erect:
No mortal parts are requisite to raise   5
Her that unbodied can her Maker praise.

The seas are quiet when the winds give o'er;
So calm are we when passions are no more:
For then we know how vain it was to boast
Of fleeting things, so certain to be lost.   10
Clouds of affection from our younger eyes
Conceal that emptiness which age descries.

The soul's dark cottage, battered and decayed,
Lets in new light through chinks that time has made.
Stronger by weakness, wiser men become   15
As they draw near to their eternal home:
Leaving the old, both worlds at once they view
That stand upon the threshold of the new.

                              Poems 1686

JOHN WILMOT
2ND EARL OF ROCHESTER

Father a royalist general, mother from a great puritan family. Born Ditchley House, Oxfordshire (an Allied HQ in 1944). Wadham College, Oxford, where at 13 he was introduced to the debauches that celebrated the Restoration. Continental tour. To court in 1665, a favourite of Charles II (who supported him financially) in spite of frequent disorders and banishments. Friends included Sedley, Etherege, Killigrew, Oldham and Otway (with whom he quarrelled); opposed to Sheffield and Dryden. Abducted an heiress, Elizabeth Malet, released her, fought in the navy as retribution, married her 1667. She lived in the west country where he visited (they had 4 children) in the intervals of a wild life at court. Apparently an alcoholic, with outbursts of destructive disorder; venereal disease worsening; numerous liaisons and illegitimate children (cf. the King); deathbed conversion on being read the 'suffering servant' passage in *Isaiah* liii. Much piratical editing; first reliable volume *Poems on several occasions* 1691. *Poems* ed. V. de S. Pinto 1953; *Complete poems* ed. D. M. Vieth 1968; see Pinto *Enthusiast in wit* rev. 1962.

from *A satire*° *against mankind*

Were I (who to my cost already am
One of those strange prodigious creatures, man)
A spirit free to choose for my own share
What case of flesh and blood I pleased to wear,
I'd be a dog, a monkey or a bear,   5
Or anything but that vain animal
Who is so proud of being rational.
The senses are too gross—and he'll contrive
A sixth to contradict the other five;
And before certain instinct will prefer   10
Reason, which fifty times for one does err—
Reason, an *ignis fatuus*° of the mind

Which, leaving light of nature, sense,° behind,
Pathless and dangerous wandering ways it takes
Through errors, fenny bogs and thorny brakes; 15
Whilst the misguided follower climbs with pain
Mountains of whimsies heaped in his own brain;
Tumbling from thought to thought falls headlong down
Into doubt's boundless sea, where like to drown;
Books bear him up awhile and makes him try 20
To swim with bladders of philosophy
In hopes still to o'ertake the escaping light.
The vapour dances in his dazzled sight,
Till, spent, it leaves him to eternal night;
Then old age and experience, hand in hand, 25
Lead him to death and make him understand,
After a search so painful and so long,
That all his life he has been in the wrong.
Huddled in dirt the reasoning engine lies
Who was so proud, so witty and so wise. 30

c.1675

° **satire** strongly influenced by Boileau. 12 **ignis fatuus** see Anon
Hollo my fancy. 13 **sense** Rochester followed Hobbes as an empiricist
and materialist.

The imperfect enjoyment°

Naked she lay, clasped in my longing arms,
I filled with love and she all over charms,
Both equally inspired with eager fire,
Melting through kindness,° flaming in desire;
With arms, legs, lips, close clinging to embrace 5
She clips me to her breast and sucks me to her face.
The nimble tongue (love's lesser lightning) played
Within my mouth and to my thoughts conveyed
Swift orders, that I should prepare to throw
The all-dissolving thunderbolt below. 10
My fluttering soul, sprung° with the pointed kiss,
Hangs hovering o'er her balmy limbs of bliss.
But whilst her busy hand would guide that part
Which should convey my soul up to her heart,
In liquid raptures I dissolve all o'er, 15
Melt into sperm and spend° at every pore.
A touch from any part of her had done't—
Her hand, her foot, her very look's a cunt,

Smiling, she chides in a kind murmuring noise
And from her body wipes the clammy joys;   20
When with a thousand kisses wandering o'er
My panting breast, And is there then no more?
She cries. All this to love and rapture's due;
Must we not pay a debt to pleasure too?

But I, the most forlorn lost man alive,   25
To show my wished obedience vainly strive.
I sigh, alas! and kiss, but cannot swive.°
Eager desires confound my first intent,
Succeeding shame does more success prevent,
And rage at last confirms me impotent.   30
Even her fair hand, which might bid heat return
To frozen age and make cold hermits burn,
Applied to my dead cinder warms no more
Than fire to ashes could past flames restore.
Trembling, confused, despairing, limber, dry,   35
A wishing, weak, unmoving lump I lie.

This dart of love, whose piercing point, oft tried
With virgin blood, ten thousand maids has dyed;
Which nature still directed with such art
That it through every cunt reached every heart;   40
Stiffly resolved, 'twould carelessly invade
Woman or boy, nor aught its fury stayed
Where'er it pierced—a cunt it found or made—
Now languid lies, in this unhappy hour,
Shrunk up, and sapless, like a withered flower.   45

Thou treacherous base deserter of my flame,
False to my passion, fatal to my fame!
By what mistaken magic dost thou prove
So true to lewdness, so untrue to love?
What oyster, cinder, beggar, common whore   50
Didst ere thou fail in all thy life before?
When vice, disease and scandal lead the way,
With what officious haste dost thou obey?
Like a rude roaring Hector° in the streets
That scuffles, cuffs and ruffles all he meets;   55
But if his king or country claim his aid,
The rascal villain shrinks and hides his head:
Even so thy brutal valour is displayed—
Breaks every stews,° does each small whore invade;
But if great Love the onset does command,   60
Base recreant to thy prince, thou dar'st not stand!
Worst part of me, and henceforth hated most,
Through all the town the common fucking-post
On whom each whore relieves her tingling cunt

As hogs on goats do rub themselves and grunt,　　　65
May'st thou to ravenous shankers° be a prey
Or in consuming weepings waste away;
May stranguries and stone thy days attend,
May'st thou ne'er piss who didst refuse to spend
When all my joys did on false thee depend;　　　70
And may ten thousand abler pricks agree
To do the wronged Corinna right for thee.

Poems on several occasions Antwerp 1680

° **enjoyment** fashionable word for coitus; cf. fruition; see Behn *Disappointment*. Psychological impotence often referred to in love poetry and comedy in this period; but cf. Nashe *Valentines*. 4 **kindness** natural sexuality. 11 **sprung** like a trap; or like a bird sprung from cover. At this period soul often means penis, or semen (cf. Cleveland *State of love*); heart can mean vagina. 16 **spend** then standard slang for orgasm. 18 **cunt** sometimes spelt out, sometimes not; cf. Durfey *Beehive*. An international and ancient word, reasonably polite until the spread of printing and literacy in 16th century, when it began to be censored; out of polite use by 1700; excluded from Oxford dictionaries. Fuck similarly but not such wide European usage. Both returned to literary use by Joyce and Lawrence in 1920s and returning to reasonably polite conversational use in late 60s with the return from literary to oral and visual culture. See Nashe *Valentines*. 27 **swive** fuck (17th-century slang). 54 **Hector** prince of Troy. At the Restoration, member of one of the groups of bullies who roamed the streets beating people up. London was less safe at night than it had been anyway for 50 years. 59 **stews** brothel. 66 **shankers** along with weepings, stranguries and stone: symptoms of venereal diseases and diseases of the urinary tract.

The fall:° *a song*

How blest was the created state
　Of man and woman ere they fell,
Compared to our unhappy fate:
　We need not fear another hell.

Naked beneath cool shades they lay,　　　5
　Enjoyment waited on desire;
Each member did their wills obey,
　Nor could a wish set pleasure higher.

But we, poor slaves to hope and fear,
　Are never of our joys secure:　　　10
They lessen still as they draw near,
　And none but dull delights endure.

Then, Chloris, while I duly pay
  The nobler tribute of my heart,
Be not you so severe to say   **15**
  You love me for a frailer part.

° **fall** cf. Waller *Fall*; Lovelace *Love made in first age.*

Upon nothing°

Nothing! thou elder brother even to Shade,
Thou hadst a being ere the world was made,
And (well fixed) art alone, of ending not afraid.

Ere Time and Place were, time and place were not,
When primitive Nothing Something straight begot;   **5**
Then all proceeded from the great united What.

Something, the general attribute of all,
Severed from thee, its sole original,
Into thy boundless self undistinguished fall.

Yet something did thy mighty power command   **10**
And from thy fruitful emptiness's hand
Snatched men, beasts, birds, fire, air and land.

Matter, the wickedest offspring of thy race,
By Form assisted, flew from thy embrace;
And rebel Light obscured thy reverend dusky face.   **15**

With Form and Matter, Time and Place did join;
Body, thy foe, with thee did leagues combine
To spoil thy peaceful realm and ruin all thy line.

But turncoat Time assists the foe in vain
And, bribed by thee, assists thy short-lived reign   **20**
And to thy hungry womb drives back thy slaves again.

Though mysteries are barred from laic eyes
And the divine alone with warrant pries
Into thy bosom (where the truth in private lies),

Yet this of thee the wise may freely say,   **25**
Thou from the virtuous nothing tak'st away;
And to be part with thee the wicked wisely pray.

Great Negative, how vainly would the wise
Inquire, define, distinguish, teach, devise,
Didst thou not stand to point their dull philosophies? **30**

Is, or Is Not, the two great ends of fate,
And True or False, the subject of debate,
That perfect, or destroy, the vast designs of fate,

When they have racked the politician's breast,
Within thy bosom must securely rest   35
And, when reduced to thee, are least unsafe and best.

But, Nothing, why does Something still permit
That sacred monarchs should at council sit
With persons highly thought, at best, for nothing fit?

Whilst weighty Something modestly abstains   40
From princes' coffers, and from statemen's brains,
And nothing there, like stately Nothing, reigns.

Nothing, who dwell'st with fools in grave disguise,
For whom they reverend shapes and forms devise
(Lawn sleeves,° and furs, and gowns) when they, like   45
   thee, look wise,

French truth, Dutch prowess, British policy,
Hibernian learning, Scotch civility,
Spaniards' dispatch, Danes' wit, are mainly seen in thee;

The great man's gratitude to his best friend,
Kings' promises, whores' vows—towards thee they bend,   50
Flow swiftly into thee, and in thee ever end.

° **nothing**   cf. chaos in Cowley *Light* etc. 45 **sleeves**   worn by bishops;
fur by scholars; gowns by lawyers.

[JOHN DRYDEN]

THOMAS SHADWELL

One of 11 children of a royalist lawyer who became a judge
and attorney-general at Tangier. Norfolk birth, school in
Bury St. Edmunds; Caius College, Cambridge; Middle Temple;
foreign travel. From 1668, a playwright in London, sometimes under the patronage of Duke of Newcastle, specialising
in comic documentary, e.g. *Epsom Wells* 1673 and *Lancashire
witches* 1681. See Duffett. Died probably of an overdose of
opium. *Complete works* ed. M. Summers 5 vols. 1927. See
A. S. Borgman *T.S.: his life and comedies* 1928.

from Timon of Athens, the Man-hater°

[Apemantus, a rigid philosopher; Aelius and Cleon, senators.]

Aelius	Well, babbling philosophical rascal,
	We shall make you tremble one day.
Apemantus	Never!
	Sordid great man! It is not in your power.
	I fear not man, no more than I can love 5
	him.
	'Twere better for us that wild beasts pos-
	sessed
	The empire of the earth, they'd use men
	better
	Than they do one another: they'd ne'er
	prey
	On man but for necessity of nature.
	Man undoes man in wantonness and sport; 10
	Brutes are much honester than he. My dog,
	When he fawns on me, is no courtier—
	He is in earnest. But a man shall smile,
	And with my throat cut.
Cleon	Money of me, saist thou? 15

° **Title**   adapted from Shakespeare 1678. III.ii.

[Demetrius, Timon's steward; Poet]

Dem.	But let me see your piece.°
Poet	I'll read it. 'Tis a good-morrow to the lord Timon.
Dem.	Do you make good-morrow sound loftily?
Poet	O, very lofty:

    The fringèd valance° of your eyes advance,   5
    Shake off your canopied and downy trance,
    Phoebus already quaffs the morning dew,
    Each does his daily lease of life renew.

Now you shall hear the description—'tis the very
life of poetry: 10

    He darts his beams on the lark's mossy house
    And from his quiet tenement doth rouse
    The little, charming and harmonious fowl
    Which sings its lump of body to a soul:
    Swiftly it clambers up in the steep air   15
    With warbling throat and makes each note a
       stair.

There's rapture for you, ha?

Dem.	Very fine!
Poet	This the solicitous lover straight alarms,

    Who too long slumbered in his Celia's arms;   20
    And now the swelling sponges of the night
    With aching heads stagger from their delight;
    Slovenly tailors to their needles haste;
    Already now the moving shops are placed
    By those who crop the treasures of the fields   25
    And all those gems the ripening summer yields.

Who d'ye think they are, now? Why, nothing but
herb-women: there are fine lofty expressions for
herb-women!

    Already now—

Dem.	But what's all this to my lord?	30
Poet	No, that's true. 'Tis description, though.	
Dem.	Yes, in twenty lines to describe to him that 'tis	

about the fourth hour in the morning. I'll in, and
let him know in three words 'tis the seventh.

                          [*Exit*]
                            I. i

---

1 piece of verse; and slang for penis. **5 valance** see Marston *What you
will*. These lines are usually quoted as straight Shadwell instead of
parody.

from *The medal of John Bays:*° a satire against folly and knavery

How long shall I endure without reply
To bear this Bays, this hackney° railer, lie?
The fool, uncudgelled° for one libel, swells
Where not his wit but sauciness excels;
Whilst with foul words and names which he lets fly   5
He quite defiles the satire's dignity:
For libel and true satire different be—
This must have truth, and salt, with modesty;
Sparing the persons, this doth tax the crimes,
Calls not great men but vices of the times   10
With witty and sharp, not blunt and bitter rhymes.
Methinks the ghost of Horace° there I see
Lashing this cherry-cheekèd dunce of fifty-three
Who, at that age, so boldly dost profane
With base hired libel the free satire's vein.   15
Thou styl'st it satire to call names—rogue, whore,
Traitor and rebel and a thousand more;
An oyster-wench is sure thy muse of late
And all thy Helicon's at Billingsgate.°
A libeller's vile name then may'st thou gain   20
And moderately the writing part maintain—
None can so well the beating part sustain:
Though with thy sword thou art the last of men,
Thou art a damned Boroski° with thy pen!
    As far from satire does thy talent lie   25
As from being cheerful or good company,
For thou art saturnine, thou dost confess—
A civil word thy dulness to express.
An old gelt mastiff hath more mirth than thou
When thou a kind of paltry mirth wouldst show;   30
Good humour then so awkwardly put'st on,
It sits like modish clothes upon a clown—
While that of gentlemen is brisk and high
When wine and wit about the room does fly;
Thou never mak'st, but art, a standing jest;   35
Thy mirth by foolish bawdry is expressed
And so debauched, so fulsome and so odd
As: Let's bugger one another now, by God—
When asked how they should spend the afternoon
This was the smart reply of the heroic clown.   40
    He boasts of vice which he did ne'er commit,
Calls himself whoremaster and sodomite,

Commends Reeves'° arse and says she buggers well
And silly lies of vicious pranks does tell.
This is a sample of his mirth and wit   45
Which he for the best company thinks fit.
  In a rich soil the sprightly horse you've seen
Run, leap and wanton o'er the flowery green,
Prance and curvet with pleasure to the sight—
But it could never any eyes delight   50
To see the frisking frolics of a cow;
And such another merry thing art thou . . .

° **Bays** John Dryden (see Vol. I), crowned with bay as poet laureate.
Dryden was a Roman catholic and tory, Shadwell a protestant and
whig. Patronage depended increasingly on party politics so their feud
was basically an economic struggle. Shots in the feud were: 1681 Dryden
Absalom and Achitophel, a satirical allegory against the whigs and
their attempts to exclude Roman catholics from the throne; 1681 Part
H, mainly by Nahum Tate but with 200 lines by Dryden including
Shadwell and Elkanah Settle (another rival dramatist) as Og and Doeg:
'With all this bulk there's nothing lost in Og, For every inch that is not
fool is rogue: A monstrous mass of foul corrupted matter, As all the
devils had spewed to make the batter'. 1682 Dryden *The medal*, a satire
on whigs as demagogues (they had struck a medal to celebrate a political
victory); Samuel Pordage *The medal reversed*; Shadwell *The medal of
John Bays*; Dryden *Mac Flecknoe*, pillorying Shadwell as king of
dulness (Flecknoe was an innocent Irish poet; the poem was the
precursor of Pope's *Dunciad*); Shadwell (?) *The tory poets*. 1687 Shadwell *10th Satire of Juvenal*. 1688 Shadwell displaces Dryden as poet
laureate when James II deposed in favour of the protestant William and
Mary. 2 **hackney** hack, hireling, jade. 3 **uncudgelled** Dryden had been
beaten up for an offensive passage in Sheffield's *Essay on satire* which
he was thought to have written. 12 **Horace** B.C. 65–8, Roman satirist
and lyric poet. 19 **Billingsgate** fish-market in London. Helicon is the
spring of inspiration. 24 **Boroski** Bur or Buri, the first man in Norse
creation myth. He was produced by the cow Andhumla licking rock-salt.
43 **Reeves** presumably a notorious woman.

from The Tory poets: a satire

Shadwell and Settle are both fools to Bays—°
They have no bawdy prologues to their plays;
These silly villains under a pretence
Of wit deceive us, and like men write sense.
Alas! says Bays, what are your wits to me?   5
Chapman's a sad dull rogue at comedy,
Shirley's an ass to write at such a rate,
But I excel the whole triumvirate.
In all my worthy plays show if you can

Such a rough character as Solyman;°   10
But though I have no plot, and verse be rough,
I say 'tis wit and that sure is enough.
The laurel makes a wit; a brave, the sword;
And all are wise men at a council board;
Settle's a coward 'cause fool Otway° fought him   15
And Mulgrave is a wit because I taught him.
   So hectors Bays, till one would think 'twas fit
That none but fools should write or judge of wit;
His pygmy wit and little infant sense
Rightly defined is naught but impudence.   20
His lines are weak, though of lewd catches° full,
And naught is strong about him but his skull,
The brave defensive headpiece of a fool.
   Of all mean hackney° jades, I'd never use
This mercenary parti-coloured muse;   25
Whoe'er beholds he straight must needs confess
She's clad at once in home and foreign dress.
Read Dryden's plays and read Corneille's° too,
You'll swear the Frenchman speaks good English now:
'Mongst borrowed sense some airy flashes drop   30
To please the feeble females and the fop;
So soft and gentle flourishes do move
The weak admiring maid, and fire love;
Quickens the dizzy soul with love beset
And tamely draws it to the golden net;   35
Stupid it lies and senseless of its pain
And kindly kisses the bewitching chain.
Cupid's the god and love is all the song,
The blest Elysium of the sportful young.
But eased of this so kind, so grateful pain   40
And brought unto its former sense again,
The glimmering lamp, its lustre once so bright,
Looks like the torches of eternal night;
The amorous paths with sweets enchanted strown
Looks like Acyna° when her paint was gone.   45
That wit upon the stage cried up today,
Tomorrow in the closet's thrown away;
Wit though with glory it may chance to rise
And mounting seems to kiss the very skies,
Yet if above the mounds of sense it get,   50
It is all wind and is no longer wit.
But Bays in all his wit is staunch and sound
Though in it all there's no proportion found;
But what he speaks, or writes, or does amiss,
It is all wit. But why? Because 'tis his.   55

'Tis wit in him if he all sense oppose,
'Twas wit in Davenant too to lose his nose;
If so, then Bays is Davenant's wisest son,
After so many claps° to keep his on.

1 **Bays** see preceding poem. This was published anonymously and is
not certainly by Shadwell. 10 **Solyman** perhaps referring to Davenant's
Siege of Rhodes, q.v. 15 **Otway** see him below. Sheffield was leader of
the tories and Dryden's patron. 21 **catches** songs. 24 **hackney** see
Medal. 28 **Corneille** 1606–84. French exponent of heroic tragedy. 45
Acyna don't know. 59 **claps** venereal infections. See Davenant.

from The Humourists°

[Theodosia, a rich heroine; Lady Loveyouth, a vain amorous
lady]

Theo.	They husbands! Why, a nunnery were more toler-
able, to be mewed up with nine but musty old
women, or your melancholy young eaters of
chalk. I had rather be kept waking at a conven-
ticle than hear the name of them!
L.L.	You are a foolish girl! I protest they are pretty
gallants and wits of the town.
Theo.	Gallants and wits! Buffoons and jack-puddings!
Rather condemn me to a little city shopkeeper,
with whom I may never have new gown and
handkercher, but half a year behind the fashion,
where I may be bred to rail against the ladies of
the court, among my public she-neighbours, and
to mince and simper at an up-sitting or a chris-
tening—
L.L.	Ay, ay! go on, go on!
Theo.	—to live all the week in a melancholy back room,
and on Sunday to go to church with my husband
in a broad hat, strutting before me, and the fore-
man of the shop having me in one hand, and a
huge-bossed Bible, as big as I am, in the other . . .

° **Humourists** comedy dedicated to Duchess of Newcastle 1670. Title
refers to indulgent whimsy.

THOMAS OTWAY

Son of a poor clergyman in Sussex. Winchester; Christ Church, Oxford—no degree. To London, introduced himself to Aphra Behn and wrote successful vehicles for Betterton, the great actor of heroic tragedy. Friend of Shadwell and Rochester; said to have been infatuated with Elizabeth Barry who acted the heroine in most of his plays; but she went with Rochester who had discovered her and had a daughter by him. Said to have been involved with Nell Gwynne, an actress who became mistress of Charles II. Reputation for drink and profligacy. Joined the army 1678. Returned to the theatre with *The orphan* 1680; *Venice preserved* 1681 was a tory-slanted play dedicated to the Duchess of Portsmouth (Charles II's Roman catholic mistress). Seems to have died in dubious circumstances in a public house on Tower Hill. Mermaid selections ed. R. Noel 1888; *Works* ed. J. C. Ghosh 2 vols. Oxford 1932. See Aline Mackenzie Taylor *Next to Shakespeare* 1950 (stage history); and note Brecht's interest.

from Venice Preserved, or a plot discovered III.ii.

[Antonio, a senator; Aquolina, a courtesan]

Antonio	Then look you now, suppose me a bull, a Basan° bull, the bull of bulls, or any bull. Thus up I get and with my brows thus bent— I broo, I say, I broo, I broo, I broo. You won't sit down, will you? I broo—[*Bellows like a bull and drives her about*]	5
Aquoline	Well sir, I must endure this. [*She sits down*] Now your honour has been a bull, pray what beast will your worship please to be next?	
Antonio	Now I'll be a senator again, and thy lover, little Nicky Nacky! [*Sits by her*] Ah, toad,	10

	toad, toad, toad! Spit in my face a little, Nacky—spit in my face, prithee spit in my face, ever so little; spit but a little bit—spit, spit, spit, spit when you are bid, I say! Do, prithee, spit! Now, now, now, spit! What, you won't spit will you? Then I'll be a dog.	15
Aquolina	A dog, my lord?	
Antonio	Yes, a dog—and I'll give thee this t'other purse to let me be a dog—and to use me like a dog a little. Hurry durry—I will—here 'tis. [*Gives the purse*]	20
Aquolina	Well, with all my heart. But let me beseech your dogship to play your tricks over as fast as you can, that you may come to stinking° the sooner, and be turned out of doors as you deserve.	25
Antonio	Ay, ay, no matter for that. [*Gets under the table*] That shan't move me—now, bough waugh waugh, bough waugh! [*Barks like a dog*]	30
Aquolina	Hold, hold, hold sir, I beseech you! What is't you do? If curs bite, they must be kicked, sir. Do you see? Kicked thus!	
Antonio	Ay, with all my heart: do, kick, kick on! Now I am under the table, kick again—kick harder —harder yet. Bough waugh waugh, waugh, bough—odd, I'll have a snap at thy shins— bough waugh waugh, waugh, bough—odd! she kicks bravely.	35
Aquolina	Nay then, I'll go another way to work with you: and I think here's an instrument for the purpose. [*Fetches a whip and a bell*] What, bite your mistress, sirrah! Out, out of doors, you dog, to kennel and be hanged! Bite your mistress by the legs, you rogue! [*She whips him*]	40 45

2 **Basan** valley famous for its cattle: 'Many bulls have compassed me: strong bulls of Bashan have beset me round', *Psalm* xxii. Cf. Genet *The maids* etc. Antonio is a burlesque on Anthony Ashley Cooper, 1st Earl of Shaftesbury 1621–83. He had been a royalist, and opposed to Cromwell during the interregnum; but under Charles II he was founder of the whig party, bent on securing protestant succession to the throne. Dryden satirised him as Achitophel in *Absalom and Achitophel* and *The medal* (see Shadwell). 25 **stinking** orgasm.

from The Orphan, or the unhappy marriage IV.ii.

[Polydore to his sister Monimia; they are lovers]

              Then thus let's go together
Full of our guilt, distracted where to roam,
Like the first wretched pair expelled their paradise.
Let's find some place where adders nest in winter,
Loathsome and venomous; where poisons hang   5
Like gums against the walls; where witches meet
By night and feed upon some pampered imp,
Fat with the blood of babes: there we'll inhabit
And live up to the height of desperation.
Desire shall languish like a withering flower   10
And no distinction of the sex be thought of:
    Horrors shall fright me from those pleasing harms
    And I'll no more be caught with beauty's charms.
    But, when I'm dying, take me in thy arms.

                           [*Exeunt*]
                           1680

from The Orphan V.ii.

[Castalio to Monimia; he loves her, she has left him]

Where am I? Sure I wander 'midst enchantment
And never more shall find the way to rest.
But O Monimia! art thou indeed resolved
To punish me with everlasting absence?
Why turn'st thou from me? I'm alone already.   5
Methinks I stand upon a naked beach
Sighing to winds and to the seas complaining,
Whilst afar off the vessel sails away
Where all the treasure of my soul's embarked.
Wilt thou not turn? O could those eyes but speak,   10
I should know all, for love is pregnant in them:
They swell, they press their beams° upon me still.
Wilt thou not speak? If we must part for ever,
Give me but one kind word to think upon
And please myself withal whilst my heart's breaking!   15

12 **beams** one theory of light was that objects emitted it as a series
of films from their surfaces.

from *The poet's complaint°* of his muse

To a high hill where never yet stood tree,
Where only heath, coarse fern and furzes grow,
    Where, nipped by piercing air,
The flocks in tattered fleeces hardly graze,
    Led by uncouth thoughts, and care   5
  Which did too much his pensive mind amaze,
  A wandering bard, whose Muse was crazy grown,
Cloyed with the nauseous follies of the buzzing town,
  Came, looked about him, sighed and laid him down.
'Twas far from any path, but where the earth   10
Was bare and naked all as at her birth
    When by the Word it first was made,
      Ere God had said
  Let grass and herbs and every green thing grow,
With fruitful trees after their kind; and it was so.   15
  The whistling winds blew fiercely round his head;
    Cold was his lodging; hard his bed.
  Aloft his eyes on the wide heavens he cast
  Where we are told peace only's found at last,
  And as he did its hopeless distance see,   20
Sighed deep and cried, How far is peace from me! . . .

° **complaint** cf. Petrarch's sonnets about wandering in the hills.

COMMENTARY 10

Restoration and Revolution
1660–1688

Sentiment and Burlesque

We think of the Augustan style as antithetical. The whole period of Restoration and Revolution, in which that style was being formed, is marked by antitheses: the panegyric and opposing satire of the previous section, the sensuality and hatred of Rochester, and so on. Here, panegyric and burlesque are represented together by Flatman. The imagery of his New Year's Day panegyric suggests that England used Charles II for something more than king: see Waller, and Cruttwell's Shakespearean moment. In his *Appeal to cats in the business of love* Flatman introduces the new burlesque note. It is a pert slapstick which denies tenderness and dignity. It sees men as pantomime animals or clowns, and life a farce (as Durfey, jolliest poet of all, pathetically calls it). Perhaps this was a way of stabilising themselves in a period of civil war, regicide, restoration, revolution, fire and plague, triumph, colonisation, wealth. Perhaps it was a way of dealing with an actuality too depressing to be borne seriously—the round of drunken lust and debt in Radcliffe's *Ramble* (cf. Rochester's *Ramble in St. James's Park* and his mock epic *How Tallboy, Killprick, Suckprick did contend*, not printed here; and see Commentary 2 on folk bawdy).

Yet there was also a new kind of tenderness. Cotton slapsticks with urine frozen into legs, and words into bullets (he has a good deal of military imagery; cf. Commentary 6, Aphra Behn *Ode to love* and especially—not printed here—her *Love armed*, and the flagellatory note in Ayres *Cynthia on horseback*). But he also has the hypnotic gentleness of *See how like twilight slumber falls* (and other poems not printed here, notably *Join once again, my Celia, join*). Something of that amorous susceptibility will be found in most of this section when it is not being coarse. There is a more popular parallel in the amorous pieces of Durfey. Even there it is feminine, in the sense of being empathetic of the female; or perhaps voyeuristic of her; but anyway much less ruggedly songs for men in a

man's world than in any earlier phase of popular verse: 'At
last impetuously her pulses move . . . and thus in soft convulsions dies'; 'My breasts do so heave, so heave, so heave'.
There must be a connection between this quality and the fact
of female authorship (see Commentary 8). None of the
women here is of the stature of the Duchess of Newcastle or
even Katherine Philips. Their work (if we have it all, which
is unlikely) is limited; they were shortlived. But consider the
simplicity of feeling in Jane Barker's *Coming from———in a
dark night:* the dropping of courtliness is behavioral as well as
linguistic—in this world the woman is active, it is she who
visits and returns from her lover. Anne Killigrew was a
genius, destroyed by smallpox at 25: in the verses printed
here (though not, unfortunately, in much else that is extant)
you can see her free, wild, totally original yet just linked to her
time by the gentle sentiment, and by the Gothick of 'Sea-
monsters there abide The coming of the tide'. We would say
it was Coleridgean but in fact it is a fantastic branch of the
burlesque, perhaps even of the pop. It is found also in Heyrick,
and Marvell.

Aphra Behn, a romantic figure but a repetitive and really
rather dull poet, displays an extreme softness. Is it female
exhibitionism, or merely the habit of a procuress? Her verses
are full of boudoir monosyllables—love, sweet, warm, fair,
press, all, and soft itself over and over again. She is the poet
of tender vulvas, limp penises, eyeballs, 'The little struggling of
the fair . . . The soft enchantments of the tongue'. It is a
tenderness of the body; but in the soul the antagonism of
Rochester, and of her own plays, sticks hard—see the military
imagery (verging to sadism), the elaborate Cupid vogue (arrows, broken hearts, resistance and yielding). These are the
terms of a sex war, the 'amorous cruel strife' of *The disappointment*. It was to be the model of literary sexual relations
for 100 years. Richardson starts here. Was all the Restoration
tenderness perhaps ointment on Adonis' gored thigh?

For further material on the Cupid vogue see the anonymous
pieces, and of course rococo art. The miscellanies reach their
peak now; refer to Commentaries 5 and 6. Note the loss in this
section of both traditional public forms (e.g. no epithalamions)
and intellectual frames (no Platonism, though Aphra Behn
quotes Herbert's *Ode* in *Disappointment* line 58). What replaced these scaffolds? politics?

For major independent work, most of these writers except
Cotton, Behn, and Sedley remain available, but would be
best treated in groups. Notice how the anticipations of Romantic poetry, always obvious in Milton, are multiplying now:

Butler and Blake in the previous section, here Cotton, Heyrick, Anne Killigrew with Wordsworth and Coleridge; T. S. Eliot had also clearly read Anne Killigrew (see Herrick similarly; but why was Pope not romantic?). The relaxed genius of Cotton is worth more brief study. For example, his *Evening* and other pastorals could be taken with Denham *Cooper's Hill,* Gray's *Elegy* and Wordsworth's *Evening walk* and *Descriptive sketches* to study changing uses of pastoral and topography (see Commentaries 2, 4, 5).

All these writers need inserting into the canon, as in the last section Shadwell and Otway did.

I have included Duffett as another example of Shakespearean adaptation, and of burlesque (both are fields for larger operations); and because his vulgar prose is so much richer than the polite verse contemporary with it. That richness was already being exported to America and this might be the place to take up that topic again: see Commentary 2.

THE REVEREND THOMAS HEYRICK

His grandfather was elder brother of Herrick. Born in Market Harborough, Leicestershire; Peterhouse, Cambridge; holy orders and became curate in birthplace. *Miscellany poems* 1691.

On an Indian° Tomineios, the least of birds

I'm made in sport by Nature when
  She's tired with the stupendous weight
Of forming elephants and beasts of state;
  Rhinocerots that love the fen;
  The elks that scale the hills of snow,   5
And lions couching in their awful den:
  These do work Nature hard and then
  Her wearied hand in me doth show
What she can for her own diversion do.

  Man is a little world, 'tis said,   10
  And I in miniature am drawn,
A perfect creature but in shorthand shown.
  The roc° in Madagascar bred
  (If new discoveries truth do speak),
Whom greatest beasts and armèd horsemen dread,   15
  Both him and me one artist made:
  Nature in this delight doth take,
That can so great and little monsters make.

  The Indians me a sunbeam name
  And I can be the child of one.   20
So small am I, my kind is hardly known:
  To some a sportive bird I seem
  And some believe me but a fly;
Though me a feathered fowl the best esteem.
  Whate'er I am, I'm Nature's gem   25
  And like a sunbeam from the sky
I can't be followed by the quickest eye.

I'm the true bird of paradise
    And heavenly dew's my only meat—
My mouth so small 'twill nothing else admit.   30
    No scales know how my weight to poise,
    So light I seem condensèd air;
And did at the end of the creation rise
    When Nature wanted° more supplies,
    When she could little matter spare   35
But in return did make the work more rare.

° **Indian**   South American or West Indian. 13 **roc**   fabulous white bird
which carried off Sinbad the Sailor. 34 **wanted**   lacked.

On a mandrake°

The play of Nature underground,
    The draft that from her hands doth fall
In regions where no light is found
    But sullen darkness covers all—
Like man—as like as drafts could be   5
Where Nature had no eyes to see.

Each limb and part exactly drawn
    Doth much our admiration raise:
Nature her mimic art hath shown
    And wantonly with mankind plays;   10
And, though it may seem useless, yet
The very sex she don't omit

(In this the picture doth excel
    And doth above the substance rise).
The mandrake doth in regions dwell   15
    Unseen, unknown to mortal eyes
And where our final rest we have
Doth live and flourish—in the grave.

° **mandrake**   see Anon. *Witch.*

from *The submarine voyage: a Pindaric° poem in four parts*

    . . . There two that struggling into the deep
    With deadly hate grasping each other fast,

    Even dead their hostile postures keep,
    The enmity seems yet to last:
    The senseless bones each other hold   5
Nor death the unkind embraces could unfold.
    But when the raging tempests blow
    And tides move all the deep below,
    The clashing bones yet seem to jar
    And keep up a perpetual war.   10
      Another lies hard by
That o'erboard fell with a far-stretched-out blow
    Aimed at his eager foe
And in the same posture fell, in the same doth lie:
His threatening arm his deadly sword doth wield,   15
    Menacing death in the watery field;
And to express his rancoured hate within,
    Dead he retains a ghastly grin.

                                      (i.16)

      •   •   •

    Neptune° sat in his chariot high
    Drawn by six hippopotami;°   20
Streamers of the English arms in the wanton air did fly,
A sea-green robe was o'er his shoulders spread
Enriched with all the unvaluable° store
    That seas do breed or storms devour;
      And on his head   25
    A crown of rays from Phoebus° sent
    Or as acknowledgement, or rent
    For revelling each night in the deep,
    For's hours of pastime or of sleep.
    On tuneful shells the Tritons° played,   30
    The winds and storms to sleep were laid
And a profound peace o'er the deep was spread;
Mermaids in melting strains their voices tried
    And sea-nymphs in soft airs replied
That even rude rocks and surly seas took in the music   35
      pride.

                                      (i.28)

      •   •   •

    Hence curiosity me led
      To view the neighbour sea
    Where 'tis with green Sargossa° spread
    And imitates a flowery mead;
Doth the unwearied eye to rove invite   40
And everywhere gives prospect of delight;
    Under whose shade the harmless fry,
      No fear nor danger nigh,

Their innocent revels keep
And deck with sparkling pearly scales the deep;   45
   Where tortoises from far resort
Journey again unto their well-known port,
   Do with unwearied feet repair
   Unto the place where they were bred
   Or where before their eggs they laid   50
And without guide, but nature being their friend,
Through devious ways are without Pole Star led
    And upon barren desolate isles
    They stupidly unto the care
Of hatching sands their shelly brood commend,   55
   Or to the sun's auspicious smiles . . .

                             (iii.1)

° **Pindaric**   irregular ode, named after Pindar of Thebes (c.522–442 B.C.) who wrote triumphal poems for athletes. In vogue from Cowley's 15 odes in *The mistress* 1647, for about 100 years till Gray and Collins. A vehicle for irregularity and excitement which came to be excluded from other forms. 19 **Neptune**   sea god. 20 **hippopotami**   hippopotamus is Greek for river-horse. 23 **unvaluable**   invaluable. 26 **Phoebus**   sun god. 30 **Triton**   fish god, who blows through a conch-shell. 38 **Sargossa** cf. Coleridge *Ancient mariner.*

CHARLES COTTON

Father owned estates in Staffordshire and Derbyshire and was friend of Jonson, Donne, Wotton, Selden, Herrick, Lovelace. Only child. Brasenose College, Oxford; ejected by parliament 1648, travelled on continent. Became a skilled angler, gardener and countryman, especially at his house at Beresford. In 1656 married his cousin Isabella (sister of Colonel Hutchinson, a parliamentary leader famous for his wife's memoir of him). She died about 14 years later, having borne 8 children. In 1675 Cotton married the widowed Countess of Ardglass. Creditors pestered his later years. Friend of Walton, Flatman, Lovelace (see *Grasshopper*). *Scarronides or Virgil travestie* 1664; trans. Corneille's *Horace* 1671; *Wonders of the Peak* (poems) 1681; trans. Montaigne's *Essays* 1685 (for long a standard version). *Poems* 1689. Wordsworth and Lamb admired his *Ode to winter. Poems* ed. J. Buxton 1958.

Evening

The day's grown old, the fainting sun
Has but a little way to run;
And yet his steeds,° with all his skill,
Scarce lug the chariot down the hill.

With labour spent, and thirst oppressed,   5
Whilst they strain hard to gain the west,
From fetlocks hot drops melted light,
Which turn to meteors in the night.

The shadows now so long do grow,
That brambles like tall cedars show;   10
Mole-hills seem mountains, and the ant
Appears a monstrous elephant.

A very little little flock
Shades thrice the ground that it would stock;
Whilst the small stripling, following them,   15
Appears a mighty Polypheme.°

These being brought into the fold
And by the thrifty master told,°
He thinks his wages are well paid
Since none are either lost or strayed.   20

Now lowing herds are each-where heard,
Chains rattle in the villeins'° yard,
The cart's on tail set down to rest,
Bearing on high the cuckold's crest;°

The hedge is stripped, the clothes brought in,   25
Naught's left without should be within;
The bees are hived and hum their charm,
Whilst every house does seem a swarm;

The cock now to the roost is pressed,
For he must call up all the rest;   30
The sow's fast pegged within the sty
To still her squeaking progeny.

Each one has had his supping mess;°
The cheese is put into the press,
The pans and bowls, clean scalded all,   35
Reared up against the milk-house wall;

And now on benches all are sat
In the cool air to sit and chat,
Till Phoebus, dipping in the west,
Shall lead the world the way to rest.   40

---

3 **steeds**   see Anon. *Tom of Bedlam*. 16 **Polypheme**   one-eyed giant, one
of the Cyclops. 18 **told**   counted. 22 **villeins**   peasants (feudal term).
24 **crest**   the cuckold's horns (sign that another man is sleeping with
your wife) imitated by the upended shafts of the cart. The allusion
seems pointless. 33 **mess**   meal.

from *Burlesque upon the Great Frost*:° to *John Bradshaw, Esq.*

A maid compelled to be a gadder°
To abate the extension of her bladder
(Which is an importuning matter)
Was so supported by her water
To ease her knees with a third pillar;   5
That, as she sat, the poor distiller
Looked on the tripod like the famous

Astrologer hight Nostradamus.°
   These stories sound so very oddly
That though men may be pretty godly   10
One should, though, store of mustard° give 'em,
E'er they expect they should believe 'em.
But, to allure your faith a little,
What follows true is to a tittle:
Our country air was, in plain dealing,   15
Some weeks together so congealing
That if, as men are rude in this age,
One spit had in another's visage,
The constable by the back had got him
For he infallibly had shot him.   20
Nay, friend with friend, brother with brother,
Must needs have wounded one another
With kindest words, were they not wary
To make their greetings sideways carry:
For all the words that came from gullets,   25
If long were slugs, if short ones, bullets.
You might have read from mouths (*sans* fable)
Your humble servant, sir in label,
Like those (yet theirs were warmer quarters)
We see in Foxe's *Book of Martyrs*.°   30
   Eyes that were weak and apt to water
Wore spectacles of their own matter,
And noses that to drop were ceased
To such a longitude increased
That whoe'er wrung for ease or losses°   35
Snapped off two handfuls of proboscis . . .

° **Frost** in the Peak district 1682–3. The Rhine froze in 1594, the Thames in 1607, 1684, 1716 etc. 1 **gadder** gad = roam. 8 **Nostradamus** of France, d. 1566. Perhaps he delivered his prophecies on a stool like the Delphic oracle. 11 **mustard** scepticism; pinch of salt. 30 **Martyrs** = enormous account of Christian tortures and martyrdoms, especially suffered by protestants under Queen Mary, with many bloodthirsty and unreliable details, illustrated. Proper title *Acts and Monuments*; Latin ed. 1559, English 1563, still popular in 20th century. Foxe was a puritan priest, d. 1587. 35 **losses** doubtful. Cut off nose to spite face? To wring someone else's nose is to insult him.

See how like twilight slumber falls

See how like twilight slumber falls
To obscure the glory of those balls°

And, as she sleeps,
See how light creeps
Through the chinks and beautifies   5
The rayey fringe of her fair eyes.

Observe love's feuds, how fast they fly
To every heart from her closed eye.
What then will she,
When waking, be?   10
A glowing light for all to admire,
Such as would set the world on fire.

Then seal her eyelids, gentle sleep,
Whiles cares of her mine open keep;
Lock up, I say,   15
Those doors of day
Which with the morn for lustre strive,
That I may look on her, and live.

2 balls   eyeballs.

ANNE KILLIGREW

Father (Henry K.) chaplain to Duke of York (future
James II, 1685) and she became maid of honour to the
duchess, together with Sedley's daughter Catherine (James's
mistress) and the future Countess of Winchelsea, a landscape poetess. Her father, her uncles Thomas and Sir William,
and her cousin Thomas the younger, were all minor dramatists.
She was a painter as well as a poet—work includes landscapes,
portraits of James and the duchess, and a self-portrait. Unmarried when she died of smallpox at 25. Dryden wrote a
famous ode *To the pious memory of the accomplished young
lady:* 'Unmixed with foreign filth, and undefiled, Her wit was
more than man, her innocence a child.' *Poems* 1686 repr.
R. Morton, Gainesville, Fla. 1967.

from Chloris' charms dissolved by Eudora

... Press on till thou descry
Among the trees, sad, ghastly, wan,
Thin as the shadow of a man,
 One that does ever cry,
She is not! and she ne'er will be!   5
Despair and death, come swallow me!
 Leave him, and keep thy way;
 No more thou now canst stray:
  Thy feet do stand
  In sorrow's land,   10
 Its kingdom's every way.

Here gloomy light will show,
Reared like a castle to the sky,
A horrid cliff there standing nigh,
 Shading a creek below,   15
In which recess there lies a cave
Dreadful as hell, still as the grave:
 Sea-monsters there abide

[407]

The coming of the tide;
   No noise is near   20
    To make them fear;
God-sleep might there reside . . .

On the soft and gentle motions of Eudora

Divine Thalia,° strike the harmonious lute,
But with a stroke so gentle as may suit
The silent gliding of the hours,
Or yet the calmer growth of flowers,
The ascending or the falling dew,   5
Which none can see though all find true:
For thus alone
Can be shown
How downy, how smooth
Eudora doth move,   10
How silken her actions appear;
The air of her face
Of a gentler grace
Than those that do strike the ear;
Her address so sweet,   15
So modestly meet
That 'tis not the loud though tuneable string
Can show forth so soft, so noiseless a thing!
O, this to express, from thy hand must fall
Than music's self something more musical.   20

1 **Thalia**   muse of comedy.

EPHELIA

Nothing known except *Female poems on several occasions. Written by Ephelia* 1679. The 2nd ed. 1682 includes poems by other authors.

To Philocles, inviting him to friendship

Best of thy sex! if sacred friendship° can
Dwell in the bosom of inconstant man,
As cold and clear as ice, as snow unstained,
With love's loose crime's unsullied, unprofaned;

Or you a woman with that name dare trust,   5
And think to friendship's ties we can be just:
In a strict league together we'll combine
And let our friendship's bright example shine.

We will forget the difference of sex,
Nor shall the world's rude censure us perplex.   10
Think me all man: my soul is masculine
And capable of as great things as thine.

I can be generous, just and brave,
Secret and silent as the grave;
And if I cannot yield relief,   15
I'll sympathise in all thy grief.

I will not have a thought from thee I'll hide;
In all my actions thou shalt be my guide;
In every joy of mine thou shalt have share
And I will bear a part in all thy care.   20

Why do I vainly talk of what we'll do?
We'll mix our souls, you shall be me, I you,
And both so one it shall be hard to say
Which is Philocles, which Ephelia.

Our ties shall be as strong as the chains of fate;   **25**
Conquerors and kings our joys shall emulate;
Forgotten friendship, held at first divine,
To its native purity we will refine.

1 friendship   see Philips *Friendship*.

JANE BARKER

Poetical recreations 1688. *Love intrigues, or the history of the amours of Bosvit and Galesia as related to Lucasia in St. Germain's Garden: a novel, written by a young lady* 1713 and others; *The Christian pilgrimage* 1718.

Parting with ———

Although thou now put'st me in doubt
  By going I know not where,
Yet know my soul will beat about
Nor rest till she have found thee out
  And tend upon thee there.   5

Look to your actions then, for she
  So strict a watch will keep
That if you give one thought from me
She'll swear it is flat felony,
  Though't be when you're asleep.   10

But if a sigh or glance or smile
  Should to my rival 'scape,
She'll cry out, Robbery! and, Spoil!
But if a kiss thy lips should soil
  Then, Murder! and, A rape!   15

All this a metaphor may seem,
  Or mad philosophy,
To the unthinking world who deem
That but a fancy or a dream
  Which souls do really hear and see.   20

Coming from ——— in a dark night

Farewell, O eyes which I ne'er saw before,
And 'tis my interest ne'er to see ye more:

Though the deprivation of your light
    I'm sure will make it doubly night,
Yet rather I'll lose my way in the dark than stay,   5
For here I'm sure my soul will lose her way.

O 'tis not dark enough—I wish it were!
Some rays are still on my eyes' atmosphere
    Which give sufficient light, I find,
        Still to continue me stark blind: 10
For to eyes that's dazzled with too radiant light,
Darkness proves best restorative of the sight.

In commendation of the female sex

In vain would man his mighty patent show,
That reason makes him lord of all below:
If woman did not moderate his rule
He'd be a tyrant, or a softly fool;
For, ere love's documents inform his breast,   5
He's but a thoughtless kind of household beast.
Houses, alas! there no such thing would be—
He'd live beneath the umbrage of a tree,
Or else usurp some free-born native's cave
And so inhabit, whilst alive, a grave;   10
Or o'er the world this lordly brute would rove—
Were he not taught and civilised by love.

Poetical recreations 1688

MRS. APHRA BEHN

Daughter of a barber called John Amis in Kent but went as
a child to central America with the newly appointed lieutenant-
general of Surinam and his family. He died on the voyage
out but his family and Aphra settled there. She became acquainted with the native royalty of Guiana and so gained
local colour for her novel *Oroonoko or the history of a royal
slave* (c.1678, one of the first statements of sympathy for
slaves, and of benevolent humanism). Returned to England
1658, married wealthy London merchant of Dutch extraction
called Behn. Gained entreé to the court and amused Charles
II. When her husband died she worked as a spy in Antwerp
during the war with Holland. While there promised to marry
one of several Dutch suitors; they arranged to meet in
London but he died of fever in Amsterdam and she was
shipwrecked off Dunkirk. On return, became the first professional woman writer in England: nearly 20 plays in the
70s and 80s, notably *The rover* (about exiled cavaliers) and
The city heiress (bawdy documentary); numerous pamphlets
and panegyrics, half-a-dozen novels and *Poems upon several
occasions, with a voyage to the island of love* 1684. Wide
circle of friends and admirers including Dryden, Otway,
Southern, Ravenscroft (his mistress?). *Works* ed. M. Summers
6 vols. 1915 (with care). *Selected writings . . . with a critical
portrait* ed. R. Phelps 1950. See V. Sackville-West *Aphra
Behn* 1927; W. and C. Jerrold *5 queer women* 1929; G.
Woodcock *The incomparable Aphra* 1948; E. Hahn *Aphra
Behn* 1951.

An ode to Love°

Dull Love, no more thy senseless arrows prize—
    Damn thy gay quiver! break thy bow!
'Tis only young Lysander's eyes
    That all the arts of wounding know.

A pox of foolish politics in love!   5
  A wise delay in war the foe may harm
By lazy siege, while you to conquest move:
  His fiercer beauties vanquish by a storm.

Some wounded god, to be revenged on thee,
  The charming youth formed in a lucky hour,   10
Dressed him in all that fond divinity
  That has out-rivalled thee, a god, in power.

Or else, while thou supinely laid
Basking beneath some myrtle shade
  In careless sleep, or tired with play,   15
When all thy shafts did scattered lie,
The unguarded spoils he bore away
And armed himself with the artillery.

The sweetness from thy eyes he took,
  The charming dimples from thy mouth,   20
That wondrous softness when you spoke
  And all thy everlasting youth.

Thy bow, thy quiver and thy darts,
  Even of thy painted wings has rifled thee,
To bear him from his conquered broken hearts   25
  To the next fair and yielding she.

° **Love** Cupid.

from *A voyage to the Island of Love*

. . . A thousand gloomy walks the bower contains,
  Sacred all to mighty loves;
A thousand winding turns where pleasure reigns,
Obscured from day by twining boughs above,
  Where love invents a thousand plays,   5
  Where lovers act ten thousand joys.
  Nature has taught each little bird
  A soft example to afford:
  They bill and look, and sing and love,
  And charm the air and charm the grove;   10
Whilst, underneath, the ravished swain is lying
  Gazing, sighing, pressing, dying;
  Still with new desire warmed,
Still with new joy, new rapture charmed.

Amongst the green, soft rivulets do pass 15
In winding streams half hid in flowers and grass
Who purl and murmur as they glide along,
And mix their music with the shepherd's pipe and song
   Which echoes through the sacred bower repeat,
Where everything arrives that's ravishing and sweet. 20

   The virgin here shows no disdain
   Nor does the shepherd sigh in vain—
This knows no cruelty, nor that no pain;
No youth complains upon his rigorous fair,
No injured maid upon her perjured dear: 25
'Tis only love, fond love finds entrance here.
   The notes of birds, the murmuring boughs
   When gentle winds glide through the glades,
   Soft sighs of love and oft-breathed vows,
The tender whisperings of the yielding maids, 30
   Dashing fountains, purling springs,
The short-breathed cries from faint resistance sent
   (Cries which no aid desires, or brings),
The soft effects of fear and languishment;
   The little struggling of the fair, 35
The trembling force of the young conqueror,
   The tender arguments he brings,
The pretty nonsense with which she assails—
Which as she speaks she hopes it naught prevails
But, yielding, owns her love above her reasonings— 40
Is all is heard; silence and shade the rest;
Which best with love, which best with joys consist,
   All which young echoes through the bower does sing
Where everything is heard that's sweet and ravishing.

Recesses dark and grottoes all conspire 45
   To favour love and soft desire;
   Shades, springs and fountains' flowery beds
   To joys invites, to pleasure leads,
To pleasure which all human thought exceeds.
   Heaven, earth and sea, here all combine 50
   To propagate love's great design
And render the appointments all divine.
After long toil, 'tis here the lover reaps
Transporting softnesses beyond his hopes;
'Tis here fair eyes, all languishing, impart 55
The secrets of the fond inclining heart;
Fine hands and arms for tender pressings made
In love's dear business always are employed.

The soft enchantments of the tongue
That does all other eloquence control   60
  Is breathed with broken sighs among
  Into the ravished shepherd's soul,
Whilst all is taken, all is given
  That can complete a lover's heaven;
And *io paeans!*° through the woods do ring   65
From new-fletched° god in songs all ravishing.

65 **paeans** see Flatman *New Year's Day.* 66 **new-fletched** newly
fledged with wings.

The disappointment°

One day the amorous Lysander,
By an impatient passion swayed,
Surprised fair Chloris, that loved maid,
Who could defend herself no longer.
All things did with his love conspire: 5
The gilded planet of the day
In his gay chariot drawn by fire
Was now descending to the sea
And left no light to guide the world
But what from Chloris' brighter eyes was hurled.   10

In a lone thicket, made for love,
Silent as yielding maid's consent,
She with a charming languishment
Permits his force, yet gently strove:
Her hands his bosom softly meet   15
But not to put him back designed,
Rather to draw him on inclined
Whilst he lay trembling at her feet.
Resistance 'tis too late to show;
She wants° the power to say, Ah! what d'you do?   20

Her bright eyes, sweet and yet severe,
Where love and shame confusedly strive,
Fresh vigour to Lysander give;
And whispering softly in his ear
She cried, 'Cease! cease your vain desire   25
Or I'll call out! what would you do?
My dearer honour, even to you,
I cannot—must not—give: retire!
Or take that life, whose chiefest part
I gave you with the conquest of my heart.   30

But he, as much unused to fear
As he was capable of love,
The blessèd minutes to improve,
Kisses her lips, her neck, her hair:
Each touch her new desires alarms;   35
His burning trembling hand he pressed
Upon her melting snowy breast
While she lay panting in his arms;
All her unguarded beauties lie
The spoils and trophies of the enemy.   40

And now without respect or fear
He seeks the object of his vows;
His love no modesty allows:
By swift degrees advancing there,
His daring hand that altar seized   45
Where gods of love do sacrifice,
That awful throne, that paradise
Where rage is tamed and anger pleased,
That living fountain from whose trills
The melted soul° in liquid drops distils.   50

Her balmy lips, encountering his,
Their bodies as their souls they joined,
Where both in transports unconfined
Extend themselves upon the moss.
Chloris half-dead and breathless lay,   55
Her eyes appeared like humid light
Such as divides the day and night,
Or falling stars° whose fires decay;
And now no signs of life she shows
But what in short-breathed sighs returns and goes.   60

He saw how at her length she lay,
He saw her rising bosom bare,
Her loose thin robes° through which appear
A shape designed for love and play:
Abandoned by her pride and shame   65
She does her softest sweets dispense,
Offering her virgin innocence
A victim to love's sacred flame—
Whilst the o'er-ravished shepherd lies
Unable to perform the sacrifice.°   70

Ready to taste a thousand joys
The too-transported hapless swain
Found the vast pleasure turned to pain—
Pleasure which too much love destroys!

The willing garment by he laid   75
And, heaven all open to his view,
Mad to possess, himself he threw
On the defenceless lovely maid;
But O what envious gods conspire
To snatch his power yet leave him the desire!   80

Nature's support, without whose aid
She can no human being give,
Itself now wants the art to live:
Faintness its slackened nerves invade.
In vain the enragèd youth essayed   85
To call his fleeting vigour back;
No motion 'twill from motion take;
Excess of love his love betrayed;
In vain he toils, in vain commands:
The insensible fell weeping in his hands.   90

In this so amorous cruel strife,
Where love and fate were too severe,
The poor Lysander, in despair,
Renounced his reason with his life;
Now all the brisk and active fire   95
That should the nobler part inflame
Served to increase his rage and shame
And left no spark for new desire;
Not all her naked charms could move,
Or calm that rage that had debauched his love.   100

Chloris, returning from the trance
Which love and soft desire had bred,
Her timorous hand she gently laid
(Or guided by design or chance)
Upon that fabulous Priapus,°   105
That potent rod (as poets feign);
But never did young shepherdess
Gathering of fern upon the plain
More nimbly draw her fingers back,
Finding beneath the verdant leaves a snake,   110

Than Chloris her fair hand withdrew
Finding that god of her desires
Disarmed of all his powerful fires
And cold as flowers bathed in the morning dew.
Who can the nymph's confusion guess?   115
The blood forsook the kinder° place
And strewed with blushes all her face,
Which both disdain and shame expressed;

And from Lysander's arms she fled,
Leaving him fainting on the gloomy bed.   120

Like lightning through the grove she hies,
Or Daphne° from the Delphic god;
No print upon the grassy road
She leaves to instruct pursuing eyes;
The wind that wantoned in her hair   125
And with her ruffled garments played
Discovered° in the flying maid
All that the gods ere made of fair:
So Venus, when her love° was slain,
With fear and haste flew o'er the fatal plain.   130

The nymph's resentments none but I
Can well imagine and condole;
But none can guess Lysander's soul
But those who swayed his destiny.
His silent griefs swell up to storms   135
And not one god his fury spares:
He cursed his birth, his fate, his stars—
But ne'er the shepherdess's charms
Whose soft bewitching influence
Had damned him to the hell of impotence.   140

° **disappointment** cf. Rochester *Imperfect enjoyment*. 20 **wants** lacks.
50 **soul** cf. Cleveland *State of love*; in this case soul = vaginal secre-
tion. 58 **stars** cf. Herbert *Ode*; Lovelace *Snail*. 63 **robes** see Lovelace
Strive not. 70 **sacrifice** cf. Donne *Elegy VIII*. 105 **Priapus** god of the
phallus. 116 **kinder** kind could still mean nature; sex; soft. 122 **Daphne**
see Carew *Rapture*. 127 **Discovered** uncovered. 129 **love** Adonis, who
rejected the advances of Venus and was eventually gored by a boar.

SIR CHARLES SEDLEY

Family of Kent squires. Wadham College, Oxford: no degree. Married in 1657 Catherine Savage (their daughter Catherine became the favourite mistress of James II, who created her Duchess of Dorchester; and mother of the 3rd wife of Sheffield). After the Restoration, M.P. for New Romney. Notorious for profligacy and literary interests: Lisideius in Dryden's *Essay of dramatic poetry*; Charles II called him 'Apollo's viceroy'. Some plays, notably *Bellamira or the mistress* 1687. Fractured skull by falling off roof of tennis-court in Haymarket 1680. *Works* ed. V. de S. Pinto 2 vols. 1928 and a life by him 1927.

On the happy Corydon and Phyllis

Young Corydon and Phyllis
 Sat in a lovely grove
Contriving crowns of lilies,
 Repeating tales of love
And something else, but what I dare not name.   5

But as they were a-playing
 She ogled so the swain,
It saved her plainly saying,
 Let's kiss to ease our pain
And something else, *etc.*   10

A thousand times he kissed her,
 Laying her on the green;
But as he further pressed her
 A pretty leg was seen *etc.*

So many beauties viewing   15
 His ardour still increased
And, greater joys pursuing,
 He wandered o'er her breast *etc.*

A last effort she trying
  His passion to withstand,
Cried (but 'twas faintly crying),
  Pray take away your hand! *etc.*

Young Corydon grown bolder
  The minutes would improve:
This is the time, he told her,
  To show you how I love *etc.*

The nymph seemed almost dying,
  Dissolved in amorous heat,
She kissed, and told him, sighing,
  My dear, your love is great! *etc.*

But Phyllis did recover
  Much sooner than the swain;
She, blushing, asked her lover,
  Shall we not kiss again? *etc.*

Thus love his revels keeping
  Till nature at a stand,
From talk they fell to sleeping,
  Holding each other's hand
And something else but what I dare not name.

Advice to the old beaux°

Scrape no more your hairless chins,
  Old beaux, in hopes to please:
You should repent your former sins,
  Not study their increase.
Young awkward fops may shock our sight
But you offend both day and night.

In vain the coachman turns about
  And whips the dappled greys—
When the old ogler looks out
  We turn away our face.
True love and youth will ever charm
But both affected cannot warm.

Summer fruits we highly prize,
  They kindly cool the blood;
But winter berries we despise
  And leave 'em in the wood;

On the bush they may look well
But, gathered, lose both taste and smell.

That you languish, that you die,
   Alas! is but too true;
Yet tax not us with cruelty
   Who daily pity you;
Nature henceforth alone accuse:
In vain we grant if she refuse.

                                            20

° **Title** disparity of age, rank, and specialisation of sexual practice, common in this period. An increase in marriages of convenience would produce more old husbands married to young wives, and intensified competition for young mistresses; but I do not know how the situation had changed from that of 1600. But from 1660 onwards a higher premium was put, for 50 years or so, on youth, virginity, proved potency. Is this the obverse of permissiveness?

CAPTAIN ALEXANDER RADCLIFFE

Gray's Inn. *Ovid travestie* and *Bacchinalia coelestia: a poem in praise of Punch* 1680; *The ramble: an anti-heroic poem; together with some terrestial hymns and carnal ejaculations* 1682. Was an army captain in 1696.

from The ramble: an anti-heroic poem

While duns° were knocking at my door
I lay in bed with reeking° whore
With back so weak and p————° so sore,
        You'd wonder.

I roused my doe° and laced her gown,   5
I pinned her whisk° and dropped a crown,°
She pissed and then I drove her down
        Like thunder.

From chamber then I went to dinner,
I drank small° beer like mournful sinner;   10
And still I thought the devil in her
        Clitoris.°

I sat at Muskats in the dark,
I heard a tradesman and a spark,°
An attorney and a lawyer's clerk   15
        Tell stories.

From thence I went, with muffled face,
To the Duke's° House and took a place
In which I spewed, may't please his grace°
        Or highness.   20

Should I been hanged I could not choose
But laugh at whores that drop from stews°
Seeing that Mistress Margaret ————
        So fine is.

When play was done, I called a link;°   25
I heard some paltry pieces clink
Within my pockets—how d'ye think
        I employed 'em?

Why sir, I went to Mistress Spering
Where some were cursing, others swearing,   30
Never a barrel better herring,°
        per fidem.

    •   •   •

At last I made the Watch-men° drunk,
Examined here and there a punk°
And then away to bed I slunk   35
        To hide it.

God save the Queen—but as for you
Who will these dangers not eschew,
I'd have you all go home and spew
        As I did.   40

1 **duns** debt collectors. 2 **reeking** sweaty. 3 **p——** printed so at
the time. There seems to be no rationale of typographical modesty.
5 **doe** girl, chick. 6 **whisk** neckerchief, shawl. **crown** 5 shillings.
10 **small beer** watered beer, usual drink for poor people, children, etc.
(they would not drink water). 12 **Clitoris** first recorded use 1615. 14
spark fop of dubious rank = the 'mod' of c.1967. Muskats presumably
a coffe-house or pub. 18 **Duke's** Dorset Garden Theatre, patronised by
the Duke of York. Wren designed it for Davenant's company, on the
river. Opened 1671. Betterton (see Otway) lived and acted there. Became famous for opera, beginning with Davenant's *Macbeth* and Shadwell's *Tempest*. In the 80s it declined and was eventually used as a
circus and menagerie. See Dryden Vol. I. 19 **grace** i.e. the duke. 22
stews brothel. Theatres were hunting-grounds for prostitutes. 25 **link**
man with a torch to light him through the streets. 31 **herring** vulva. 33
Watch-men night constables. 34 **punk** whore.

TOM DURFEY(?)

Born in Exeter. Grandfather a Huguenot who immigrated
1628. Father married a gentlewoman of the Marmion family.
Stammered except when singing. Prolific writer of popular
songs and satires, purveyor of scandal and dirty stories. Much
favoured by Charles II and James II and their courts; mourned
by Steele and Addison. His songs set by Purcell, Blow and
other friends. *New collection of songs and poems* 1683,
superseded by *Wit and mirth or pills to purge melancholy* 1684
and frequent reprints (sometimes called *Songs compleat*). His
authorship of all the poems is quite uncertain; most are
adaptations of folk poetry. 3-part dramatisation of *Don
Quixote* 1694–96 attacked by Jeremy Collier in his *Short
view of the immorality and profaneness of the English stage;*
Durfey replied with a comedy called *The campaigners, or the
pleasant adventures at Brussels, with a familiar preface upon
a late reformer of the stage, ending with a satirical fable of
the dog and the otter.* See *Spectator* no. 37 (1711); *Tatler*
nos. 1, 4, 11, 43, 126, 214 (1709–10). A selection of songs
ed. C. L. Day, Cambridge Mass. 1939; *Wit and mirth* vols. 1–6
repr. 1870, and that repr. by Day in 3 vols. New York 1959.

The mountebank° song

Sung by Dr. Leverigo, and his merry andrew Pinkanello,
in Farewell to Folly. Set by Mr. Leveridge.

Here are people and sports of all sizes and sorts,
Coached damsel with squire and mob in the mire,
Tarpaulins,° trugmallions,° lords, ladies, sow, babies and
  loobies° in scores,
Some howling, some bawling, some leering, some fleering,
Some loving, some shoving,   5
With legions of furbelowed° whores.
To the tavern some go
And some to a show,

See poppets for moppets,° jack-puddens° for cuddens,°
Rope-dancing, mares prancing,   10
Boats flying, quacks lying,
Pickpockets, pick-plackets, beasts, butchers and beaux,
Fops prattling, dies rattling,
Rooks° shamming, puts° damning,
Whores painted, masks tainted in tallyman's° furbelowed   15
   clothes.
The mob's joys would you know
To yon music-house go,
See tailors and sailors,
Whores oily in doily,°
Hear music makes you sick,   20
Cows skipping, clowns tripping,
Some joking, some smoking like spigot and tap;
Short measure, strange pleasure,
Thus billing and swilling
Some yearly get fairly for fairings, pig, pork and a clap.°   25

° **mountebank** seller of quack medicines who attracted crowds at fairs
by acrobatics, juggling etc., attended by a clown called a merry andrew.
Rochester pretended to be one during a period of banishment from the
court. 3 **Tarpaulins** tars, sailors. **trugmallions** trulls, whores; or cata-
mites. **loobies** louts or idiots. 6 **furbelowed** flounced, gaudily dressed.
9 **poppets . . . moppets** girls, dolls. **jack-puddens** merry andrews.
cuddens idiots. 14 **rooks** sharpers. **puts** bumpkins. 15 **tallyman**
clothier. 19 **doily** light wool. 25 **clap** venereal disease.

A gentle breeze

A gentle breeze from the Lavinian Sea
Was gliding o'er the coast of Sicily
When, lulled with soft repose, a prostrate maid
Upon her bended arm had raised her head;
Her soul was all tranquile and smooth with rest   5
Like the harmonious slumbers of the blest;
Wrapped up in silence, innocent she lay
And pressed the flowers with touch as soft as they.

My thoughts in gentlest sounds she did impart,
Heightened by all the graces of that art;   10
And as she sung I grasped her yielding thighs
Till broken accents faltered into sighs;
I kissed and wished and foraged all her store,
Yet, wallowing in my pleasure. I was poor:

No kind relief my agonies could ease,   15
I groaned and cursed religious cruelties.

The trembling nymph all o'er confusion lay,
Her melting looks in sweet disorder play;
Her colour varies and her breath's oppressed
And all her faculties are dispossessed.   20
At last impetuously her pulses move,
She gives a mighty loose to stifled love;
Then murmurs in a soft complaint, and cries,
Alas! and thus in soft convulsions dies.°

24 **dies** has orgasm.

The bee-hive°

My mistress is a hive of bees in yonder flowery garden,
To her they come with loaden thighs to ease them of
    their burden;
As under the bee-hive lieth the wax, and under the wax is
    honey,
So under her waist her belly is placed, and under that her
    cunny.

My mistress is a mine of gold: would that it were her   5
    pleasure
To let me dig within her mould and roll among her
    treasure;
As under the moss the mould doth lie, and under the
    mould is money, *etc.*

My mistress is a morn of May which drops of dew down
    'stilleth:
Where'er she goes to sport and play, the dew down sweetly
    trilleth;
As under the sun the mist doth lie, so under the mist is   10
    sunny, *etc.*

My mistress is a pleasant spring that yieldeth store of
    water sweet
That doth refresh each withered thing lies trodden under
    feet;
Her belly is both white and soft, and downy as any
    bunny,
That many gallánts wish full oft to play but with her
    cunny.

My mistress hath the magic sprays, of late she takes such   15
    wondrous pain
That she can pleasing spirits° raise, and also lay them
    down again;
Such power hath my tripping doe,° my little pretty bunny,
That many would their lives forego to play but with her
    cunny.

° **bee-hive**   see Carew *Rapture*; Cleveland *Fuscara*; Kynaston *Sugar and sweetness*. **16 spirits** cf. the use of soul to mean semen. **19 doe** cf. Radcliffe *Ramble*.

A new dialogue, set by Mr. Henry Purcell, sung by a boy and girl at the playhouse

He   Celemene, pray tell me,
      Pray, pray tell me Celemene,
      When those pretty pretty pretty eyes I see
      Why my heart beats beats beats beats in my breast,
      Why, why it will not, it will not, why why it will not   5
        let me rest?
      Why this trembling, why this trembling too all o'er?
      Pain I never, pains I never never never felt before;
      And when thus I touch, when thus I touch your hand,
      Why I wish, I wish I wish I was a man?
She How should I know more than you?   10
      Yet would be a woman too:
      When you wash yourself and play,
      I methinks could look all day.
      Nay, just now, nay just now am pleased, am pleased
        so well
      Should you, should you kiss, I won't tell,   15
      Should you, should you kiss me, I won't tell;
      No, no, I won't tell, no no I won't tell, no no I
        won't tell,
      Should you kiss me I won't tell.
He   Though I could do that all day
      And desire no better play,   20
      Sure, sure in love there's something more
      Which makes Mamma so big, so big before?
She Once by chance I heard it named—
      Don't ask what, don't ask what for I'm ashamed.
      Stay but till you're past fifteen,   25

  Then you'll know, then then you'll know what 'tis
   I mean,
  Then you'll know what, then you'll know what 'tis
   I mean.
He However, lose not present bliss
  But now we're alone, let's kiss;
  But now we're alone let's kiss, let's kiss.   30
She My breasts do so heave, so heave, so heave.
He My heart does so pant, pant, pant.
Both There's something, something, something more we
   want,
  There's something, something, something more we
   want.

Early in the dawning
A song. Set by Mr. Leveridge

Early in the dawning of a winter's morn,
Brother Dick and I went forth into the barn
 To get ourselves a heat
 By thrashing of the wheat
From the stack, from the stack, from the stack, the stack. 5
 The straws they flew about
 And the flails they kept a rout
With a thwack, thwack, thwack, thwack, thwack!

Margery came in then with an earthen pot
Full of pudding that was piping hot: 10
 I caught her by the neck fast
 And thanked her for my breakfast
With a smack,° with a smack, with a smack, a smack.
 Then up went her tail
 And down went the flail   15
With a thwack, thwack, thwack, thwack, thwack!

Dick, thrashing on, cried out, Fie, for shame!
Must I beat the bush while you catch the game?
 Sow your wild oats
 And mind not her wild notes   20
Of alack! of alack! of alack! alack!
 Faith, I did the job
 While the flail bore a bob°
With a thwack, thwack, thwack, thwack, thwack!

She shook off the straws and did nothing ail,   25
Swearing there was no defence against a flail,
   But quietly lay still
   And bid me fill, fill, fill
Her sack, her sack, her sack, sack.
   But 'twas all in vain   30
   For I had spilt my grain
With a thwack, thwack, thwack, thwack, thwack!

13 smack kiss. **23 bore a bob** carried a weight on the end.

A new song made in honour of his grace the Duke of Marlborough° and the general officers upon the glorious success of this last campaign. Set by Mr. J. Wheldon.

Beat the drum! beat beat the drum!
Let martial trumpets sound!
The jolly bowl prepare
With fragrant roses crowned:
The grand leviathan° of France is tumbling down,   5
Tumbling down, is tumbling tumbling down!
Laurel wreaths for glorious pains,
Once more great Marlborough, great Marlborough gains.
Thus whilst conquered, whilst conquered Flanders falls,
Proud Orleans from Turin's walls   10
Is like a vapour gone;
The monsieur's mauled by sea and land,
Then take six bumpers° in a hand
To each brave British son
They, they the work have done,   15
They, they the work have done.

° **Marlborough** John Churchill, first duke, son of Winston Churchill, an ardent royalist. Professional soldier, victor of several campaigns, mainly against France, in the War of the Spanish Succession 1702–13. In 1704 relieved allies in Vienna by brilliant strategic movements and victory at Blenheim on the Danube. In 1706 allies took Turin and Marlborough took the Low Countries from the French. His palace, Blenheim, designed by Vanbrugh the architect-dramatist. Charming, dishonest, and treacherous; the first general to impose British force on the continent in modern terms. This is also one of the first poems expressing British patriotism. **5 leviathan** monster in *Job* xli and Psalm civ; used by Hobbes as nickname for the all-powerful state. **13 bumpers** tankards, toasts.

from Don Quixote

Sleep, sleep, poor youth

Sleep, sleep, poor youth! sleep, sleep in peace,
   Relieved from love and mortal care;
Whilst we, that pine in life's disease,
   Uncertain blessed, less happy are.
Couched in the dark and silent grave,   5
   No ills of fate thou now canst fear;
In vain would tyrant power enslave,
   Or scornful beauty severe.

Wars that do fatal storms disperse
   Far from thy happy mansion keep;   10
Earthquakes that shake the universe
   Can't rock thee into sounder sleep.
With all the charms of peace possessed,
   Secure from life's tomentor, pain,
Sleep, and indulge thyself with rest,   15
   Nor dream thou e'er shall rise again.

Past is the fear of future doubt,
   The sun is from the dial gone,
The sands are sunk, the glass is out,
   The folly of the farce is done.   20

THE REVEREND SAMUEL WESLEY
THE ELDER

Born of clerical family at Winterborn Whitchurch, Dorset. Dorchester grammar school; seminary in London (with Defoe) to train for nonconformist ministry; but walked to Oxford and worked his way through Exeter College, publishing *Maggots, or poems on several subjects never before handled,* while there, 1685. Holy Orders, chaplain in man-o'-war; curate in London. Married, his wife Susanna having also abandoned her father's nonconformity. In 1690, rector of South Ormsby, Lincs. Helped Dunton edit *Athenian gazette,* an early newspaper, 1691–97. 1695 rector of Epworth, Lincs. but in debt. 1697 barn fell down; 1702 rectory burnt down; 1704 flax burnt; 1705 gaoled for debt in Lincoln Castle; 1709 the rebuilt rectory burnt down, and MS. of work on *Job* destroyed; 1716 rectory haunted. Gout, palsy. 1731 thrown from wagon and maimed. Of his 19 children, 10 survived infancy including Samuel the younger, a poet; Mehetabel, a poetess who married a plumber; John, the evangelist, Methodist leader, and hymn-writer; and Charles the hymn-writer who founded Methodism while at Oxford.

The boys and the bubble

See where 'tis fallen, among a ring of boys,
Who from it blow them worlds of gaudy joys,
Fine soon-ripe bubbles, *à la mode* and gay,
Dressed in the glories of the blooming day;
Bright as court-madam though they hardly be,   5
Perhaps as tender, or as frail,° as she.
Created both by breath, both upwards borne,
Proud in the beauties of the rainbow morn;
And thus, when sailing through the heavier skies,
By breath 'twas made and lived, by breath it dies   10
And that same blast on which itself it rears
Dashes the airy jewel into tears.

6 frail   easily cracked.

from To my gingerbread mistress

Dear miss, not with a lie to cheat ye,
I love you so that I could eat ye.
'Tis not that gold that does adorn
Your bosom like the rising morn
When, dropping dry from watery bed,   5
Sol shakes his carrot-loggerhead;
'Tis not your gold I mean to woo:
Alas, 'tis you and only you!

      •   •   •

'Tis not the rose of lip-like hue,
Nor virgin plum's celestial blue,   10
Nor all the nuts that plundered be
From the sad squirrel's granary,
Nor pears long crammed in faithful store
As yellow as the golden ore,
Nor crumpling° sweet with cheeks divine   15
(Yet not so fair, my dear, as thine),
Nor custards stuck with plums and flies,
Nor heart-reviving pudding-pies
(Though queasy stomachs them contemn)
Baked on thy own dear granny's wem.°   20

      •   •   •

Nor mellow ducks in claret stewed
When atoms were in altitude.°

      •   •   •

I'll say't, my love, and say't again,
'Twas none of those that caused my pain:
'Twas first thy goggling egg-like eyes   25
Like those in Mahomet's paradise° . . .

15 **crumpling** presumably crumpet or muffin. 20 **wem** 'A Scotch oven.
A traveller eating some cake on the road in Scotland, complained
'twas not well baked. 'Twas replied, that was impossible, for't had
been all night baking upon the hostess's warm wem' [Wesley's note].
Wem = vulva. 22 **altitude** 'Willis in his book *de fermentatione*, gives
that account of putrefaction of bodies; he says the blood, etc., ferments,
and the particles are highly agitated—(and a great deal more which,
if you ha'nt enough for your money, you shall have in the next edition)'.
[Wesley] 26 **paradise** 'Among the other pleasures in the heaven of his
own building, Mahomet's Alcoran promises the Mussalman bedfellows
with eyes as big as eggs; esteemed as great a piece of beauty, it seems,
by the Asiatics, as great lips by most of the Africans'. [Wesley]

THOMAS DUFFETT

London milliner who took to writing plays. His *Mock-Tempest* was staged at the Theatre Royal in 1675 in rivalry with the version of the *Tempest* by Dryden and Davenant, (revised by Shadwell) at the Dorset Gardens.

from The Mock-Tempest, or The Enchanted Castle

[Quakero, son of Alonso; Miranda]

Quakero . . . I will declare before her. Umph-er-hm-er. Most finest, most delicate and most lusciousest creature, whose face is more delicious than a pot of ale with sugar and nutmeg, after a long exercise—
Miranda Ha!
Quakero The favour of whose breath is more comfortable than the hot steam of a Sunday's dinner—
Miranda O-oo!
Quakero Whose paps are whiter than two Norfolk   5
dumplings stuffed with plums, and softer than quaking-puddings—
Miranda Why, did you ever feel my bubbies?
Quakero Nay assuredly, but I hope I shall. Whose soft palms are pleasanter than a warm cloth to my sweaty back, or a hot trencher to an aching belly—
Miranda O rare!
Quakero Whose legs are smoother than my chin on a Saturday night, and sleeker than thy elbows—
Miranda O my honour, my honour, my father says you   10
must not touch my honour, pray!
Quakero Nay sister, far far be it from me to soil thy honour. Thy nature is more inviting than a christening-bowl of warm red wine decked round with lemon-peel.
Miranda O my dear! O! O! O! I can no longer forbear.
 [*Embraces him*]
Quakero Ah, sister mine! Now I am even like unto that

little creature called a cat, when his back is stroked he
longeth to play with his tail.
Miranda   And what are I like, then, tell me what I are
like?
Quakero   Why, thou art like a pretty little mouse,   15
verily . . .

THOMAS FLATMAN

Winchester; New College, Oxford; Inner Temple. London career as minor poet and major painter of portrait miniatures. Acquainted with Walton, Cotton, Katherine Philips. Married 1672 and had a family. *Poems and songs* 1674. Ed. Saintsbury. *Life and uncollected poems* ed. F. A. Child, Philadelphia 1921. See his self-portrait in Victoria and Albert museum; J. M. Murry *Countries of the mind* 1931.

An appeal to cats in the business of love: a song

Ye cats that at midnight spit at each other,
Who best feel the pangs of a passionate lover,
I appeal to your scratches and your tattered fur
If the business of love be no more than to purr?
Old Lady Grimalkin° with her gooseberry eyes   5
Knew something when a kitten—for why? she was wise;
You find by experience the love-fit's soon o'er:
Puss-puss! lasts not long but turns to Cat-whore!
    Men ride many miles,
    Cats tread many tiles,   10
  Both hazard their necks in the fray;
    Only cats, when they fall
    From a house or a wall,
  Keep their feet, mount their tails, and away!

5 **Grimalkin** an old she-cat of the kind witches have. Cf. T. S. Eliot *Old Possum.*

On Mrs. E. Montague's blushing in the cross-bath°

Amidst the nymphs, the glory of the flood,
    Thus once the beauteous Aegle stood:
So sweet a tincture, ere the sun appears,

The bashful ruddy morning wears;
Thus through a crystal wave the coral glows,   5
And such a blush sits on the virgin rose.

Ye envied waters that with safety may
    Around her snowy bosom play,
Cherish with gentle heat that noble breast
    Which so much innocence has blessed,   10
Such innocence as hitherto ne'er knew
What mischief Venus or her son could do.

    Then from this hallowed place
Let the profane and wanton eye withdraw:
For virtue clad in scarlet strikes an awe   15
From the tribunal of a lovely face.

° **cross-bath** public baths where men sat in cross-shaped structure in
centre, women in niches round the walls. Baths were places of assigna-
tion and gossip, popular with bluestockings (and some with whores).

A song on New Year's Day before the King,
Carolus II. Set by Dr. Blow, 1682

My trembling song, awake! arise!
    And early tell thy tuneful tale:
Tell thy great master that the night is gone,
    The feeble phantoms disappear
    And now the New Year's welcome sun°   5
        O'erspreads the eastern skies:
He smiles on every hill, he smiles on every vale;
        His glories fill our hemisphere.
        Tell him Apollo° greets him well
    And with his fellow-wanderers agrees   10
    To reward all his labours and lengthen his days
In spite of the politic follies of hell
        And vain contrivance of the destinies.
Tell him, a crown of thorns° no more
        Shall his sacred temples gore,   15
For all the rigours of his life are o'er.
        Wondrous prince! designed to show
What noble minds can bravely undergo,
        You are our wonder, you our love!
        Earth from beneath, heaven from above   20
Call loud for songs of triumph and of praise,

Their voices and their souls they raise:
   Io paean!° do we sing,
  Long live, long live the King!
Rise, mighty monarch, and ascend the throne,   25
   'Tis yet once more your own,
For Lucifer° and all his legions are o'erthrown:
Son of the morning, first-born star of light,
   How wert thou tumbled headlong down
Into the dungeons of eternal night!   30
While the loyal stars of the celestial choir,
   Surrounded with immortal beams,
   Mingle their unpolluted flames
   Their just Creator to admire:
   With awful reverence they adore him,   35
Cover their faces and fall down before him
   And night and day for ever sing,
Hosanna!° Hallelujah! to the almighty King.

5 **sun** the year, the sun, the king, and his continuing reign after the Restoration. See Waller *To the King*. 9 **Apollo** god of the sun and poetry. 14 **thorns** Charles II's exile, with a glance at his father as martyr or even as sacrificed god. 23 **Io paean** Hail, Apollo! from Greek song of triumph and thanksgiving. 27 **Lucifer** Satan, who rebelled against God; hence Cromwell: 'How art thou fallen from heaven, O Lucifer, son of the morning! How art thou cut down to the ground, which didst weaken the nations! For thou hast said in thine heart . . . I will exalt my throne above the stars of God . . .' *Isaiah* xiv. 38 **Hosanna** Save! Hallelujah = Praise the Lord!

Nudus redibo°

Naked I came, when I began to be
A man among the sons of misery,
Tender, unarmed, helpless and quite forlorn
E'er since 'twas my hard fortune to be born;
And when the space of a few weary days   5
Shall be expired, then must I go my ways:
Naked I shall return, and nothing have,
Nothing wherewith to bribe my hungry grave.
   Then what's the proudest monarch's glittering robe,
Or what's he, more than I, that ruled the globe?   10
Since we must all without distinction die,
And slumber both stark naked, he and I.

° **Nudus redibo** naked I will return. *Job* i.21.

COMMENTARY 11

Restoration and Revolution
1660–1688

Religion: Hymns and Visions

The Restoration was not inhabited exclusively by kings, rakes and whores. Traherne wrote in it the most mystical poetry in English since *The dream of the Rood*, Bunyan the most concrete allegories since *Everyman*. Can explanations be given of the copresence of virtue and vice?

The most important literary development of the age was popularisation. We can say that one wave of this kind had washed over the country in the 16th century with the invention of printing: it gave status to the vernacular and by providing books made it possible to establish a lot of grammar schools. That wave culminated in the Authorised Version of 1611: God spoke English. Now in the Restoration period the press was founded: L'Estrange's *Intelligencer*, *News* and *Observator* in the '80s were the first of the new quotidian journals. The point about the press is its frequency. There is probably a link between the day-to-dayness—the *journess*—of journalism—and the mundane qualities of language which we have increasingly remarked in this anthology; and again with the concreteness of puritan religion.

The literary link is Wesley. He is in the previous section as a writer of burlesque; but he helped to edit another early paper, *The Athenian gazette* (well worth study for its advertisements); and he was the father of John and Charles Wesley, the Methodist hymn-writers and evangelists. Journalism and dissenting religion are both concerned to reach, and attract the participation of, congregations; both live off advertising. For two centuries, the chief literary experience of the plebeians was listening to the Bible, singing hymns, and singing songs. Hymns were the nexus—as carols are still for children—between the world of literate authority, submitted to, and the world of vulgar activity. God or his minions write hymns; but you sing them. This is an important subject, worth pursuing from its representatives here, Tate and Mason. Both assert the popular nature of their writing by their lives: Tate was a hack Shakespearean adaptor (see Commentary 10) and miscellaneous journalist. When children parody Tate's carol as 'While shepherds washed their socks by night' they are being true to the author of *A poetical history of the French disease* and *A poem upon tea*, and also to Tate the industrious anthologist. Mason was a mad evangelist. They differ in this, though: Tate may stand as the last of the long line of translators of the psalms (though metrical psalms have remained more popular with Presbyterians—authority?); while Mason is the first of the inventing hymn-writers. In what sense, then, were they hymns that Donne and, for example, Wotton wrote to God in their sickness?

From a literary point of view, Tate is a sort of easy Marvell—'watery ligaments' is in the micro-bizarre line of section 5. Wanley is also a Marvell, by intellect as well as imagery:

> What if this flesh of mine be made the prey
> Of scaly pirates, cannibals at sea:
> Shall living sepulchres give up their dead—
> Or is not flesh made fish then perishèd?

That wit pokes at the tottering hierarchy of the cosmos. Wanley, writing mostly in the tradition of George Herbert's graced devotion—'Then will I rise and dress me, Lord, for thee'—Wanley nevertheless *thinks*. This is the symptom of his lateness. He thinks with that conscious gaze at things that belongs to Locke's successors. His materials, and Bunyan's snail and Tate's ice, are inherently emblematic; and they write homilectically, preach on the emblems; but the things themselves now have a harder edge, and a value of their own which is independent of any homily that can be extracted from them. We are entering the 18th century where poets see the world's outlines etched, and write nature poetry.

The same is true of the arch-mystic, Traherne. *Shadows in the water* is the apotheosis of Marvell's topsy-turvy vision; *Wonder* of Vaughan's white-eyed world; but *Dreams* is actually about cognition, an essay on human understanding: 'O what a thing is thought!' There is an intolerable splendour about Traherne; we haven't got used to him yet and don't know what to say. In that line, he pushes us back to the historical centre, thought as a thing; or word being regenerated into flesh. This is why so often they relate to Herbert in the same way that Hopkins does, exerting violence to get that good: 'Thou that didst speak them down canst speak us dead'. They demanded 'language welted with emphatic reech', thing-y, folky, rough against metre and syntax, so you get—most obviously in Taylor, free in America from the Latin centuries of English—lines like

> Whose words outstrut the sky) vaunts he hath rife

How did it die? How did it happen that Traherne, Wanley and Taylor remained unprinted for so long? Where did Dryden and Pope find the impudence to despise Tate, Shadwell, Flecknoe? Was Johnson ignorant of Vaughan and Norris? Perhaps the causes were those that made Blake rebel; for Traherne can write like Blake, or rather see, like him, the world not smeared with trade:

> The state of innocence
> And bliss, not trades and poverties,
> Did fill my sense.

The motto is his in *The demonstration*, 'Only extremes and heights are known . . incredibles alone May be by demonstration to us shown'. That is the empiricism of the mystic; it is equivalent to Blake's proverb 'The road of excess leads to the palace of wisdom'.

MRS. ANNE WHARTON

Born at Ditchley (cf. Rochester), daughter and co-heiress of Sir Henry Lee by his wife Anne Danvers. Married Thomas (later marquis of) Wharton in 1673, bringing a dowry of £10,000 and £2,500 p.a. Childless and unhappy; wanted to leave her husband in 1682 but a friend dissuaded her. Wharton remarried after her death, and helped to depose James II. His biographer said of Anne: 'a woman of wit and virtue, yet her person was not so agreeable to him as was necessary to secure his constancy . . . this lady's temper was reserved, severe and the very reverse of gaiety and gallantry.' Lely painted a portrait of her. In 1688 was published *The idea of Christian love*, 'being a translation, at the instance of Mr. Waller, of a Latin sermon upon *John* xiii. 34, 35, preached by Mr. Edward Young, prebend of Salisbury. With a large paraphrase on Mr. Waller's poem of *Divine love*. To which are added some copies of verses from that excellent poetess Mrs. Wharton, with others to her.' She was the Chloris of Waller's poems.

Verses on the snuff of a candle, made in sickness

See there the taper's dim and doleful light
  In gloomy waves silently rolls about
And represents to my dim weary sight
  My light of life, almost as near burnt out.

Ah, health! best part and substance of our joy   5
  (For without thee 'tis nothing but a shade),
Why dost thou partially thyself employ
  Whilst thy proud foes as partially invade?

What we, who ne'er enjoy, so fondly seek,
  Those who possess thee still almost despise: 10
To gain immortal glory, raise the weak,
  Taught by their former want thy worth to prize.

Dear melancholy muse! my constant guide,
  Charm this coy health back to my fainting heart,
Or I'll accuse thee of vainglorious pride   15
  And swear thou dost but feign the moving art.

But why do I upbraid thee, gentle muse,
  Who for all sorrows mak'st me some amends?
Alas! our sickly minds sometimes abuse
  Our best physicians, and our dearest friends.   20

JOHN BUNYAN

Born in village near Bedford where father's family had been certainly since 12th century. Father a tinker, married 3 times; John was 1st child of 2nd marriage; his mother also native of the village. No school but taught to read and write at home. At 15 his mother died; father remarried two months later; Bunyan joined the parliamentary army. In later 1640s, out of the army, married a pious woman and went through long period of conversion trauma (see *Grace abounding to the chief of sinners* 1666); this was consummated 1653 when he joined a nonconformist group in Bedford and began preaching. Wife died c.1656, leaving 4 children of whom the eldest, a girl, was blind. Bunyan ill. Itinerant preaching and concentrated Bible reading. Remarried 1659, two more children. In 1660 arrested for unlicensed preaching and kept in Bedford gaol 12 years, till the Declaration of Indulgence. Wrote several books in prison, notably *Grace abounding* and (1665) *The holy city*; a shorter term of imprisonment in the '70's produced *Pilgrim's progress* 1678 (2nd part 1684); *Mr. Badman* 1680. Spent his last years as a pastor. Chilled riding from Reading to London and died there in a friend's house. *A Book for boys and girls, or country rhymes for children* 1686 (18th-century reprints called *Divine emblems*; see Quarles) ed. E. S. Buchanan 1928. See *Pilgrim's progress* ed. G. B. Harrison 1941 with Blake's illustrations.

Upon the snail°

She goes but softly, but she goeth sure;
    She stumbles not as stronger creatures do:
Her journey's shorter, so she may endure
    Better than they which do much further go.

She makes no noise, but stilly seizeth on   5
    The flower or herb appointed for her food,
The which she quietly doth feed upon,
    While others range, and gare,° but find no good.

And though she doth but very softly go,
    However 'tis not fast, nor slow, but sure;   10
And certainly they that do travel so,
    The prize they do aim at, they do procure.

A book for boys and girls 1686

° **snail** cf. Lovelace; and Thom Gunn *Considering the snail.* 8 **gare**
stare about, gawp.

NAHUM TATE

Son of Faithful Teate, an Irish cleric driven to England after betraying some rebels. Trinity College, Dublin, then an adapting dramatist in London, e.g. 1681 *The Sicilian usurper* = *Richard II*; the version of *Lear* with a happy ending, acted by Betterton, which Dr. Johnson commends; *Injured love* = Webster's *White devil*. Wide range of verse journalism includes *Poems* 1677; Part II of *Absalom and Achitophel* with Dryden 1682, and translating for him; *Syphilis: a poetical history of the French disease* (trans. Fracastoro) 1686; a famous and long-used metrical version of the *Psalms* with N. Brady ('Tate and Brady') 1696; *Panacea: a poem upon tea* 1700; and several anthologies. Probably the author of the carol *While shepherds watched their flocks by night*. Died hiding from creditors in Southwark. Pope refers to 'the mild limbo of our father Tate' in the *Dunciad*. See H. F. Scott-Thomas, 'N.T. and the 17th century' *English literary history* I 1934.

Sliding on skates in very hard frost

How well these frozen floods now represent
Those crystal waters of the firmament:°
Though hurricanes should rage, they could not now
So much as curl the solid water's brow;
Proud fleets, whose stubborn cables scarce withstood   5
The impetuous shock of the unstable flood,
In watery ligaments are restrained
More strict than when in binding ooze detained;
But though their services at present fail,
Ourselves, without the aid of tide or gale,   10
On keels of polished steel securely sail:
From every creek to every point we rove
And in our lawless passage swifter move
Than fish beneath us or than fowl above.

2 firmament sky.

On sight of some martyrs' sepulchres

Here lies dust confusèdly hurled,
But dust that once shall judge the world.
Blest saints! when the quick flames enlarged
Your souls and from dull flesh discharged,
The ambitious fires strove to convey   5
Your spirits on their triumphant way:
But winged with glory they aspired
And left the flames behind them tired.

THE REVEREND JOHN MASON

Clerical family in Northamptonshire. Clare, Cambridge.
Holy orders, living in Buckinghamshire. Married, several
children. *Spiritual songs or Songs of praise* 1683—One of
the first hymn-writers to work from the congregation's point
of view; influenced Pope, the Wesleys, Isaac Watts. But became depressive and extravagant millenarian, especially after
wife died in 1687. Conducted a wild evangelistic group in a
field outside Water Stratford. Headaches, hallucinations, hy-
persensitive to noise. Succeeding rector exhumed his body to
prove his death to crazed followers.

A general song of praise to Almighty God

How shall I sing that majesty
  Which angels do admire?
Let dust in dust and silence lie:
  Sing, sing ye heavenly choir!

Thousand of thousands stand around 5
  Thy throne, O God most high:
Ten thousand times ten thousand sound
  Thy praise: but who am I?

Thy brightness unto them appears,
  Whilst I thy footsteps trace; 10
A sound of God comes to my ears,
  But they behold thy face.

They sing because thou art their sun:
  Lord, send a beam on me,
For where heaven is but once begun 15
  There hallelujahs be.

Enlighten with faith's light my heart,
  Inflame it with love's fire;
Then shall I sing and bear a part
  With that celestial choir. 20

[448]

I shall, I fear, be dark and cold
   With all my fire and light;
Yet, when thou dost accept their gold,
   Lord, treasure up my mite.

How great a being, Lord, is thine,   25
   Which doth all beings keep;
Thy knowledge is the only line
   To sound so vast a deep;

Thou art a sea without a shore,
   A sun without a sphere;   30
Thy time is now and evermore;
   Thy place is everywhere.

How good art thou, whose goodness is
   Our parent, nurse and guide;
Whose streams do water paradise   35
   And all the earth beside.

Thine upper and thy nether springs
   Make both thy worlds to thrive;
Under thy warm and sheltering wings
   Thou keep'st two broods alive.   40

THE REVEREND
THOMAS TRAHERNE

Welsh origin (cf. Herbert, Vaughan); Herefordshire; Brasenose College, Oxford; Holy Orders; chaplain to Sir Orlando Bridgman; died at 37. His *Christian ethics* 1675 and *Serious and pathetical contemplation of the mercies of God* (anon. 1699) contained a few poems, and his brother Philip had intended to publish more, but work remained unknown till MSS. discovered 1886. *Poetical works* first published 1903, with more (*Poems of felicity*) in 1910; poetic prose *Centuries of meditations* 1908. His study of *Magnanimity and chastity* published 1942 ed. J. R. Slater. *Poetical works* ed. G. I. Wade 1932 and biographical study 1944. *Centuries, poems and Thanksgivings* ed. H. M. Margoliouth 2 vols. Oxford 1958; *Poems, Centuries and three Thanksgivings* ed. Anne Ridler, Oxford 1966. See K. W. Salter *T.T., mystic and poet* 1964; L. L. Martz *The paradise within* 1964.

Wonder

How like an angel° came I down!
　　How bright are all things here!
When first among his works I did appear,
　　O how their glory did me crown!
The world resembled his eternity　　　　　　　　　　5
　　In which my soul did walk;
　　And everything that I did see
　　　　Did with me talk.

The skies in their magnificence,
　　The lovely lively air,　　　　　　　　　　　　　　10
O how divine, how soft, how sweet, how fair!
　　The stars did entertain my sense
And all the works of God so bright and pure,
　　　So rich and great, did seem
　　As if they ever must endure　　　　　　　　　　15
　　　　In my esteem.

A native health and innocence
  Within my bones did grow,
And while my God did all his glories show
  I felt a vigour in my sense   20
That was all spirit: I within did flow
    With seas of life like wine;
  I nothing in the world did know
      But 'twas divine.

Harsh rugged objects were concealed,   25
    Oppressions, tears and cries,
Sins, griefs, complaints, dissensions, weeping eyes
  Were hid, and only things revealed
Which heavenly spirits and the angels prize.
    The state of innocence   30
  And bliss, not trades and poverties,
      Did fill my sense.

The streets seemed paved with golden stones,
    The boys and girls all mine—
To me how did their lovely faces shine!   35
  The sons of men all holy ones
In joy and beauty then appeared to me;
    And everything I found
  (While like an angel I did see)
      Adorned the ground.   40

Rich diamonds and pearl and gold
  Might everywhere be seen;
Rare colours, yellow, blue, red, white and green
  Mine eyes on every side behold.
All that I saw, a wonder did appear;   45
    Amazement was my bliss;
  That and my wealth met everywhere:
      No joy to this!

Cursed ill-devised proprieties,°
    With envy, avarice   50
And fraud (those fiends that spoil even paradise)
  Were not the object of mine eyes;
Nor hedges, ditches, limits, narrow bounds—
    I dreamt not aught of those,
  But in surveying all men's grounds   55
      I found repose.

For property its self was mine,
    And hedges, ornaments;
Walls, houses, coffers and their rich conténts
  To make me rich combine;   60

Clothes, costly jewels, laces I esteemed
   My wealth by others worn;
For me they all to wear them seemed
   When I was born.

1 angel see Vaughan *Retreat* etc. **49 proprieties** laws of ownership.

Shadows in the water

In unexperienced infancy
Many a sweet mistake doth lie:
Mistake, though false, intending true;
A seeming-somewhat-more-than view
   That doth instruct the mind
   In things that lie behind,   5
And many secrets to us show
Which afterwards we come to know.

Thus did I by the water's brink
Another world beneath me think;
And, while the lofty spacious skies,   10
Reversèd there, abused mine eyes,
   I fancied other feet
   Came mine to touch or meet:
As by some puddle I did play   15
Another world within it lay.

Beneath the water, people, drowned
Yet with another heaven crowned,
In spacious regions seemed to go
As freely moving to and fro;   20
   In bright and open space
   I saw their very face;
Eyes, hands and feet they had like mine;
Another sun did with them shine.

'Twas strange that people there should walk   25
And yet I could not hear them talk;
That through a little watery chink
Which one dry ox or horse might drink,
   We other worlds should see
   Yet not admitted be;   30
And other confines there behold,
Of light and darkness, heat and cold.

I called them oft, but called in vain:
No speeches we could entertain;
Yet did I there expect to find　　　　　35
Some other world, to please my mind.
　　I plainly saw by these
　　A new antipodes,
Whom, though they were so plainly seen,
A film kept off that stood between.　　　40

By walking men's reversèd feet
I chanced another world to meet:
Though it did not to view exceed
A phantasm, 'tis a world indeed,
　　Where skies beneath us shine,　　　45
　　And earth, by art divine,
Another face presents below,
Where people's feet against ours go.

Within the regions of the air,
Compassed about with heavens fair,　　　50
Great tracts of land there may be found
Enriched with fields and fertile ground,
　　Where many numerous hosts,
　　In those far distant coasts,
For other great and glorious ends　　　55
Inhabit—my yet unknown friends.

O ye that stand upon the brink
(Whom I so near me, through the chink,
With wonder see), what faces there,
Whose feet, whose bodies, do ye wear?　　　60
　　I my companions see
　　In you—another me;
They seemèd others, but are we;
Our second selves those shadows be.

Look how far off those lower skies　　　65
Extend themselves! scarce with mine eyes
I can them reach. O ye my friends!
What secret borders on those ends?
　　Are lofty heavens hurled
　　'Bout your inferior world?　　　70
Are ye the representatives
Of other people's distant lives?

Of all the playmates which I knew
That here I do the image view

In other selves, what can it mean   75
But that below the purling stream
     Some unknown joys there be
     Laid up in store for me,
To which I shall, when that thin skin
Is broken, be admitted in?   80

from The demonstration

The highest things are easiest to be shown,
And only capable of being known.
     A mist involves the eye
   While in the middle it doth live;
   And till the ends of things are seen,   5
The way's uncertain that doth stand between:
     As in the air we see the clouds
     Like winding-sheets or shrouds,
   Which, though they nearer are, obscure
The sun which, higher far, is far more pure.   10

Its very brightness makes it near the eye,
Though many thousand leagues beyond the sky;
     Its beams by violence
   Invade and ravish distant sense.
   Only extremes and heights are known,   15
No certainty where no perfection's shown.
     Extremities of blessedness
     Compel us to confess
   A God indeed, whose excellence
In all his works must needs exceed all sense.   20

And, for this cause, incredibles alone
May be by demonstration to us shown.
     Those things that are most bright
   Sun-like appear in their own light,
   And nothing's truly seen that's mean: 25
Be it a sand, an acorn, or a bean,
   It must be clothed with endless glory
     Before its perfect story
   (Be the spirit ne'er so clear)
Can in its causes° and its ends appear . . .   30

30 causes   see Carew *Ask me no more.*

Dreams

'Tis strange! I saw the skies,
I saw the hills before mine eyes,
  The sparrow fly,
The lands that did about me lie,
The real sun, that heavenly eye.   5
Can closed eyes even in the darkest night
See through their lids and be informed with sight?

  The people were to me
As true as those by day I see;
  As true the air;   10
The earth as sweet, as fresh, as fair
As that which did by day repair
Unto my waking sense: can all the sky,
Can all the world, within my brain-pan lie?

  What sacred secret's this   15
Which seems to intimate my bliss?
  What is there in
The narrow confines of my skin
That is alive and feels within
When I am dead? Can magnitude possess   20
An active memory, yet not be less?

  May all that I can see,
Awake, by night within me be?
  My childhood knew
No difference, but all was true,   25
As real all as what I view;
The world itself was there: 'twas wondrous strange
That heaven and earth should so their place exchange.

  Till that which vulgar sense
Doth falsely call experience   30
  Distinguished things,
The ribands and the gaudy wings
Of birds, the virtues and the sins,
That represented were in dreams by night
As really my senses did delight,   35

  Or grieve, as those I saw
By day; things terrible did awe
  My soul with fear;
The apparitions seemed as near

As things could be, and things they were: 40
Yet were they all by fancy in me wrought
And all their being founded in a thought.

O what a thing is thought!
Which seems a dream, yea, seemeth nought,
Yet doth the mind   45
Affect as much as what we find
Most near and true. Sure, men are blind
And can't the forcible reality
Of things that secret are within them see.

Thought! Surely thoughts are true?   50
They please as much as things can do—
Nay, things are dead
And in themselves are severèd
From souls, nor can they fill the head
Without our thoughts. Thoughts are the real things   55
From whence all joy, from whence all sorrow springs.

The preparative

My body being dead, my limbs unknown—
Before I skilled to prize
Those living stars, my eyes,
Before my tongue or cheeks were to me shown,
Before I knew my hands were mine   5
Or that my sinews did my members join,
When neither nostril, foot nor ear
As yet was seen or felt or did appear—
I was within
A house I knew not, newly clothed with skin.   10

Then was my soul my only all to me,
A living endless eye
Just bounded with the sky,
Whose power, whose act, whose essence was to see.
I was an inward sphere of light   15
Or an interminable orb of sight,
An endless and a living day,
A vital sun that round about did ray
All life, all sense,
A naked simple pure intelligence.   20

I then no thirst nor hunger did perceive,
No dull necessity,

No want was known to me;
Without disturbance then I did receive
   The fair ideas° of all things,   25
And had the honey even without the stings.
   A meditated inward eye
Gazing at quiet did within me lie
      And everything
Delighted me that was their heavenly king.   30

For sight inherits beauty, hearing sounds,
   The nostrils sweet perfumes;
   All tastes have hidden rooms
Within the tongue; and feeling feeling wounds
   With pleasure and delight. But I   35
Forgot the rest and was all sight or eye
   Unbodied and devoid of care,
Just as in heaven the holy angels are;
      For simple sense
Is lord of all created excellence.   40

Being thus prepared for all felicity,
   Nor prepossessed with dross,
   Nor stiffly glued to gross
And dull materials that might ruin me,
   Nor fettered by an iron fate   45
With vain affections in my earthly state
   To anything that might seduce
My sense, or else bereave it of its use,
      I was as free
As if there were no sin nor misery.   50

Pure empty powers, that did nothing loathe,
   Did like the fairest glass
   Or spotless polished brass
Themselves soon in their object's image clothe:
   Divine impressions, when they came,   55
Did quickly enter and my soul inflame.
   'Tis not the object but the light
That maketh heaven: 'tis a purer sight.
      Felicity
Appears to none but them that purely see.   60

A disentangled and a naked sense,
   A mind that's unpossessed,
   A disengagèd breast,
An empty and a quick intelligence
   Acquainted with the golden mean,   65
An even spirit, pure and serene,

Is that where beauty, excellence
And pleasure keep their court of residence.
     My soul, retire!
Get free! and so thou shalt even all admire.   70

25 ideas Descartes (some of whose concerns and analogies are rather similar to Traherne's) held that knowledge of external things is constructed by the mind, not the senses (*Discourse on method* 1637). Locke held that our mind is initially a *tabula rasa*; we build up ideas of things by sense perceptions and the mind's reflection on them, its 'inner sense' (*Essay concerning human understanding* 1690). But Traherne is as much a Christian Platonist.

THE REVEREND
NATHANIEL WANLEY

Father a Leicester mercer. Trinity College, Cambridge. Rector of Beeby, Leics. Married in 1655 the daughter of coroner and town clerk of Coventry; 5 children. In 1662 to a Coventry parish from which the incumbent, John Bryan, had resigned in order to become a dissenting minister; but Bryan also attended Wanley's services as a friend. Poems in MS. till ed. L. C. Martin, Oxford 1928. A credulous prose compilation, *The wonders of the little world, or a general history of man* 1678.

The resurrection

Can death be faithful, or the grave be just?
Or shall my tomb restore my scattered dust?
Shall every hair find out its proper pore.
And crumbled bones be joinèd as before?
Shall long-unpractised pulses learn to beat   5
Victorious rottenness a loud retreat,
Or, eyes eclipsèd in a tedious night,
May they once hope to re-salute the light?
What if this flesh of mine be made the prey
Of scaly pirates, cannibals at sea: 10
Shall living sepulchres give up their dead—
Or is not flesh made fish then perishèd?
What if the working of a subtle flame
By an unkind embrace dissolve this frame
To ashes, and the whistling winds convey   15
Each atom to a quite contráry way?
Shall the small pilgrims that, perhaps, may pass
From grass to flesh and thence from flesh to grass,
Travel until they meet, and then embrace
So strictly as to grow the former face?   20
My God, I know thy powerful word did frame
Out of pure nothing all that hath a name,
From the bright angels bathing in full streams

Of deathless joys, to motes that dance in beams:
And shall I doubt that such a word can call   25
Flesh out of dust, that out of less made all?
No, no! I am resolved that when poor I
Shall slumbering in our mother's bosom lie,
The circling worms shall loose their fast embrace,
And kinder turfs that cover me give place,   30
The bands of death shall burst at the shrill sound
Of heaven's summons, and I shall be found.
Then will I rise and dress me, Lord, for thee
Who didst by death undress thee, Lord, for me.

Felled at a word?

John xviii.6. 'As soon then as he had said unto them,
I am he; they went backward, and fell to the ground'.

Felled at a word? Struck prostrate on the ground?
What, was a thunderbolt lapped in the sound?
Spoke he in anger? did he frowning say,
How dare audacious traitors think to lay
Their rebel hands on their Creator high,   5
Or ashes in their Maker's face to fly?
Say, did he threaten? did the listening ear
Taste in his language any cause of fear?
Did he reprove them? did he strongly dart
Conviction by those words into each heart?   10
No: not a word of anger, but confession;
No mixture of a threat, but all concession.
Great God! thy mighty power teach us to dread:
Thou that didst speak them down canst speak us dead.

THE REVEREND EDWARD TAYLOR

Born in Coventry or nearby in Leicestershire (cf. Wanley); schoolteacher, nonconformist, emigrated to America in his early 20s and arrived Boston in July 1668 with letters of introduction to Increase Mather (later president of Harvard and statesman; father of Cotton Mather the witch-hunter of Salem). Harvard. In 1671 to Westfield, a frontier settlement on the far side of the Connecticut River, as pastor and doctor; stayed there all his life. Married, 7 children but none survived him; wife died 1689. In 1692 remarried a Hartford girl; 6 children. Had a copy of Anne Bradstreet's poems in his library. The large MS. of his 'Poetical works' written 1671–1725, discovered 1937 in the Yale Library, ed T. H. Johnson 1939. *Poems* ed. D. E. Stanford, New Haven 1960.

Lord, dub my tongue

Meditation. *Canticles* i.12: 'While the king sits at his table, my spikenard sends forth the smell thereof'.

Lord, dub° my tongue with a new tier of words
  More comprehensive far than my dull speech,
That I may dress thy excellency, Lord,
  In language welted° with emphatic reech.°
  Thou art my king: my heart thy table make,   5
  And sit thereat until my spicknard wake.

My garden knot° drawn out most curiously
  By thy brave hand, set° with the bravest slips
Of spicknard—lavender that thence may fly
  Their wealthy spirits° from their trunks and tips—   10
  That spicknard oil, and oil of spike most sweet,
  May muskify thy palace with their reek.

Then sit at thy round table with delight
  And feast in me until my spicknard bloom;
And crown thy head with odour-oil rich bright;   15

And crowd thy chamber with her sweet perfume.
The spicknard in my knot then flourish will,
And fringe thy locks with odour it doth 'still.

And when thou at thy circuit table sit'st
   Thine ordinances, Lord, to greet poor hearts,   20
Such influences from thyself thou slip'st
   And make their spicknard its sweet smell impart:
     So make my lavender to spring, and scent;
     In such attire her spirits ever tent.°

And as thou at thy table sit'st to feast   25
   Thy guests thereat, thy supper, Lord, well dressed,
Let my sweet spicknard breathe most sweet, at least
   Those odours that advance thy glory best;
     And make mine heart thine alabaster box°
     Of my rich spicknard to perfume thy locks.   30

If this thou grant (and grant thou this, I pray)
   And sit, my King, at thy rich table thus,
Then my choice spicknard shall its smell display
   That sweetens me and on thee sweet doth rush;
     My songs of praise too, sweetened with this fume,   35
     Shall scale thine ears in spicknardisic tune.

Preparatory meditations: 2nd series; written 1696

1 **dub** dress. Tier = tire, suit of clothes. 4 **welted** a welt is a flanged seam or a fancy border. **reech** reek = smoke, incense—cf. spikenard in line 6. 7 **knot** see Carew *Rapture*. 8 **set . . . slips** planted with cuttings. 10 **spirits** scent. 24 **tent** dressed ? upheld ? 29 **box** from the story of Mary Magadalene in *Mark* xiv; cf. Crashaw *Weeper*.

Upon a wasp chilled with cold

The bear that breathes the northern blast
Did numb, torpedo-like,° a wasp,
Whose stiffened limbs encramped lay bathing
In Sol's warm breath and shine, as saving,
Which with her legs she chafes and stands   5
Rubbing her legs, shanks, thighs and hands.
Her petty toes and fingers' ends
Nipped with this breath she out extends
Unto the sun, in great desire
To warm her digits at that fire;   10
Doth hold her temples in this state

Where pulse doth beat and head doth ache;
Doth turn, and stretch her body small,
Doth comb her velvet capital
As if her little brain-pan were   15
A volume of choice precepts clear;
As if her satin jacket hot
Contained apothecary's shop
Of nature's receipts, that prevails
To remedy all her sad ails;   20
As if her velvet helmet high
Did turret rationality;
She fans her wing up to the wind
As if her petticoats were lined
With reason's fleece, and hoises sails   25
And humming flies in thankful gales
Unto her dun curled palace hall,
Her warm thanks offering for all.
    Lord, clear my misted sight that I
May hence view thy divinity,   30
Some sparks whereof thou up doth hasp
Within this little downy wasp,
In whose small corportation we
A school and a schoolmaster see,
Where we may learn, and easily find   35
A nimble spirit's bravely mind,
Her work in every limb; and lace
It up neat with a vital grace,
Acting each part though ne'er so small
Here of this fustian animal: 40
Till I enravished climb into
The Godhead on this lather° do;
Where all my pipes inspired upraise
An heavenly music furred° with praise.

2 torpedo stingray. 42 lather ladder. 44 furred adorned.

Did ever lord such noble house maintain

Meditation. *John* vi.51. 'I am the living bread'.

Did ever lord such noble house maintain
    As my Lord doth? or such a noble table?
'Twould break the back of king's, nay, monarch's brain

To do it—pish! the world's estate's° not able.
I'll bet a boast with any that this bread   5
I eat excels whatever Caesar had.

Take earth's brightest darlings, in whose mouth all flakes
  Of luscious sweets she hath do crowd their head:
Their spiced cups, sweetmeats, and sugar-cakes
  Are but dry sawdust to this living bread;   10
  I'll pawn my part in Christ, this daintiest meat
  Is gall and wormwood unto what I eat.

The boasting spagyrist° (insipid phlegm
  Whose words outstrut the sky) vaunts he hath rife°
The water, tincture,° lozenge, gold and gem   15
  Of life itself; but here's the bread of life.
  I'll lay my life, his *aurum vitae*° red
  Is to my bread of life worse than deadhead.°

The daintiest dish of earthly cookery
  Is but to fat the body up in print;°   20
This bread of life doth feed the soul, whereby
  It's made the temple of Jehovah in't.
  I'll venture heaven upon't that low or high
  That eat his living bread shall never die.

This bread of life so excellent I see   25
  That holy angels doubtless would, if they
Were prone unto base envy, envy it me.
  But O! come, taste how sweet it is! I say,
  I'll wage° my soul and all therein uplaid
  This is the sweetest bread that e'er God made.   30

What wonder's here, that bread of life should come
  To feed dead dust? dry dust eat living bread?
Yet wonder more by far may all and some
  That my dull heart's so dumpish when thus fed.
  Lord, pardon this, and feed me all my days   35
  With living bread to thy eternal praise.

1st series 1684

---

4 **estate** entire class holding some power, e.g. peers, the church. 13
spagyrist alchemist. See Benlowes *Might souls converse*. 14 **rife** rifled,
plundered. 15 **tincture** alchemical essence, or medical solution; lozenge
similarly. 17 **aurum vitae** gold of life. Powdered gold was used as a
medicine. Red often means golden. 18 **deadhead** chemist's word for
dregs; or skull. 20 **in print** luxuriously tight and exact; or, like a big
pat of butter. 29 **wage** wager.

I, *kenning through astronomy*

Meditation. *John* vi.51. 'I am the living bread'.

I, kenning° through astronomy, divine
  The world's bright battlement, wherein I spy
A golden path my pencil cannot line
  From that bright throne unto my threshold lie;
    And while my puzzled thoughts about it pore,   5
    I find the bread of life in't at my door.

When that this bird of paradise, put in
  This wicker cage (my corpse) to tweedle praise,
Had pecked the fruit forbade; and so did fling
  Away its food; and lost its golden days: 10
    It fell into celestial famine sore
    And never could attain a morsel more.

Alas! alas! poor bird, what wilt thou do?
  The creatures' field no food for souls e'er gave;
And if thou knock at angels' doors, they show   15
  An empty barrel: they no soul-bread have.
    Alas! poor bird, the world's white loaf is done
    And cannot yield thee here the smallest crumb.

In this sad state, God's tender bowels run
  Out streams of grace; and he, to end all strife,   20
The purest wheat in heaven, his dear dear Son,
  Grinds, and kneads up into this bread of life;
    Which bread of life from heaven down came and stands
    Dished on thy table up by angels' hands.

Did God mould up this bread in heaven, and bake   25
  Which from his table came and to thine goeth?
Doth he bespeak thee thus: This soul-bread take;
  Come, eat thy fill of this thy God's white loaf?
    It's food too fine for angels, yet come, take
    And eat thy fill. It's heaven's sugar-cake.   30

What grace is this knead in this loaf? This thing°
  Souls are but pretty things it to admire.
Ye angels, help! this fill would to the brim
  Heaven's whelmed-down crystal meal bowl—yea and
    higher.
    This bread of life dropped in thy mouth doth cry   35
    Eat, eat me, soul! and thou shalt never die.

                          1st series 1684

1 **kenning** looking. 31 **thing** an error in the text.

THE REVEREND JOHN NORRIS

Sometimes called John Norris of Bemerton. Son of ardently anti-puritan Wiltshire priest. Winchester; Exeter College, Oxford. Archbishop Bancroft made him a fellow of All Souls' during one of the usual disputes in that college and he began writing as a mystical Christian Platonist. In 1684 published *Poems*, and was ordained and corresponded with Henry More. *The theory and regulation of love, a moral essay* 1688; 1689 gained a living in Somerset, so able to marry. 1692 rector of Bemerton, near Salisbury (where George Herbert had been rector). Philosophical works in the early 18th century. His two sons became priests and his daughter married one. *Poems* ed. A. B. Grosart 1871. See F. J. Powicke *Dissertation on J. N.* 1894.

Canticle°

'Twas my Belovèd spake,
I know his charming voice. I heard him say:
Rise up my love, my fairest one awake,
    Awake and come away!

The winter all is past   5
And stormy winds that with such rudeness blew;
The heavens are no longer overcast
    But try to look like you.

The flowers their sweets display,
The birds in short preludiums tune their throat,   10
The turtle in low murmurs does essay
    Her melancholy note.

The fruitful vineyards make
An odorous smell, the fig looks fresh and gay:
Arise my love, my fairest one awake,   15
    Awake and come away!

° **canticle**   see *Solomon's Song*.

The meditation

It must be done, my soul; but 'tis a strange,
  A dismal and mysterious change
When thou shalt leave this tenement of clay
And to an unknown somewhere wing away;
When time shall be eternity, and thou   5
Shalt be thou know'st not what and live thou know'st
    not how.

Amazing state! No wonder that we dread
  To think of death or view the dead.
Thou art all wrapped up in clouds as if to thee
Our very knowledge had antipathy.   10
Death could not a more sad retínue find:
Sickness and pain before and darkness all behind.

Some courteous ghost, tell this great secrecy,
  What 'tis you are, and we must be?
You warn us of approaching death, and why   15
May we not know from you what 'tis to die?
But you, having shot the gulf, delight to see
Succeeding souls plunge in with like uncertainty.

When life's close knot, by writ from destiny,
  Disease shall cut or age untie;   20
When, after some delay, some dying strife,
The soul stands shivering on the ridge of life:
With what a dreadful curiosity
Does she launch out into the sea of vast eternity?

So when the spacious globe was deluged o'er,   25
  And lower holds could save no more,
On the utmost bough the astonished sinners stood
And viewed the advances of the encroaching flood;
O'ertopped at length by the element's increase,
With horror they resigned to the untried abyss.   30

RICHARD FLECKNOE

Said to be an Irish priest, who travelled to Rome to study art in 1645, and to Constantinople, Portugal, Brazil. Published some plays in the '50s, and travel-books later. Not known why Dryden made Shadwell his son in *Mac Flecknoe*.

Stillborn Silence

Stillborn Silence, thou that art
Floodgate of the deeper heart;
Offspring of a heavenly kind,
Frost o' the mouth and thaw o' the mind;
Secrecy's confidant, and he   5
Who makes religion mystery;
Admiration's speaking'st tongue—
Leave the desert shades among
Reverend hermits' hallowed cells,
Where retired'st Devotion dwells: 10
With thy enthusiasms come,
Seize our tongues, and strike us dumb.

Miscellanea, or poems of all sorts, with divers other pieces
1653

READING LIST

The biographical notes that introduce each poet indicate where to start reading about individuals. This list is for readers who want to put down test drills of their own at various spots in the 17th century as a period. Place of publication London or New York or both unless specified.

Reference : History : Historical topics : Geography : Religion : History of ideas : Visual art : Music : Domestic arts : Biography : Literary history : Some literary topics : Good anthologies : Classical literature : Examples of continental literature.

Reference

Most literary puzzles are solved by reference to:

Shorter Oxford English Dictionary. 1 or 2 vols. 3rd ed. 1944 corrected 1959. If you have to use another dictionary, choose it for historical coverage and examples, not for modernity or definitions. See W. Empson, *Structure of complex words* 1951.

J. S. Farmer ed. *Slang and its analogues past and present: a dictionary*. 7 vols. 1890 repr. 3 vols. 1965. Fuller and bolder than its modern alternative, Eric Partridge ed. *A dictionary of slang and unconventional English* 1937 5th ed. 2 vols. 1961.

Brewer's dictionary of phrase and fable. 1952 ed. Provided most of the footnotes in this anthology.

Dr. Smith's classical dictionary, officially *A classical dictionary of Greek and Roman biography, mythology and geography* ed. Sir William Smith, Rev. G. E. Marindin 1894. Profusely and quaintly illustrated.

A concordance to the Bible (e.g. 'Cruden's') and a commentary or both together on smaller scales (e.g. *The Bible reader's encyclopaedia and concordance* ed. W. M. Clow 1932 etc.); a student's Bible, e.g. *The Oxford Annotated Bible*. Concordances to Shakespeare and to Milton are also available and useful but not essential.

S. A. Allibone ed. *Critical dictionary of English literature and British and American authors.* Supplement by J. F. Kirk. 5 vols. Philadelphia 1859–91. Historical critical comments on major authors, and some biography.

Grainger's index to poetry ed. W. F. Bernhardt 1904, eds. to 1974, cross-references a very large number of authors, titles, first lines, and anthologies, so constituting the canon of popularity.

History

The sequence of major events and the role of leading characters should be given priority. See any decent schoolbook, e.g. G. T. Warner, C. H. K. Martin and D. E. Muir, *The new groundwork of British history* 1943 etc.

G. P. V. Akrigg, *Jacobean pageant or the court of King James I* 1962. Illustrated.

S. L. Bethell. *The cultural revolution of the 17th century.* 1951.

V. H. H. Green. *Renaissance and reformation: a survey of European history between 1450 and 1660.* 1952 rev. 1964.

C. Hill. *The century of revolution 1603–1714.* 1961.

Philemon Holland. *The history of the world.* 2 vols. 1601 et seq. Based on the *Natural history* of Pliny the elder, a Roman scientist who was killed while observing the eruption of Vesuvius which destroyed Pompeii A.D. 79.

J. P. Kenyon. *The Stuarts: a study in English kingship.* 1956. Illustrated.

P. Laslett. *The world we have lost.* 1965. The first historical sociology.

J. Leasor. *The plague and the fire.* 1962.

S. Lee and C. T. Onions ed. *Shakespeare's England: an account of the life and manners of his age.* 2 vols. Oxford 1916.

D. Mathew. *The Jacobean age.* 1938.

Wallace Notestein. *The English people on the eve of colonization.* 1954.

Lawrence Stone. *The crisis of the aristocracy 1558–1641.* 1965, abr. 1967.

Philip A. M. Taylor ed. *The origins of the English civil war: conspiracy, crusade, or class conflict?* Boston 1960.

G. M. Trevelyan. *England under the Stuarts.* 1904. Whig.

L. B. Wright. *Middle-class culture in Elizabethan England.* Chapel Hill 1935.

Historical topics

Here are a few works, not excerpted in these volumes, on some topics:

Kingship: Shakespeare *Richard II, I & II Henry IV;* Milton *The tenure of kings and magistrates* 1649; Sir Robert Filmer *Patriarcha* ed. P. Laslett 1949.

Witchcraft: Thomas Dekker, John Ford et al. *The witch of Edmonton* 1623; James I *Demonology* 1597 (ed. G. B. Harrison).

Family and marriage: Milton *Doctrine and discipline of divorce* 1643 (see Book I, chapters 1–7); A. Nicholas *Discourse of marriage and wiving* 1615; Philip Stubbs 'A crystal gloss for Christian women' in his *Anatomy of abuses.*

Court, city, country: Thomas Heywood *A woman killed with kindness* 1603; Thomas Dekker *The honest whore* 1604–08; Jonson *Volpone or the fox* 1607; *The alchemist* 1610; *The devil is an ass* 1616; Philip Massinger *A new way to pay old debts;* Thomas Middleton *Women beware women* c.1621.

Geography

For the world, look at a contemporary atlas and hang up a print of part of it. E.g. Gerard Mercator, *Historia mundi or Mercator's atlas* trans. W. Saltonstall 1635 et seq. (original 1595); or Abraham Ortelius, *Theatrum orbis terrarum,* Antwerp 1570, published as *The theatre of the world* in 1608. Emblematic pictures as well as maps.

For localities see a contemporary travel book, e.g.:

Tom D'Urfey (see his poems), *Colin's walk through London and Westminster.* 1690.

Richard Flecknoe (see his poems), *Relation of 10 years' travels in Europe, Asia, Africk and (south) America.* 1654? 1665.

Thomas Harriot (see Chapman's poems). *Brief and true report of Virginia.* 1588, ed. R. G. Adams, Ann Arbor 1931, 1951; and repr. in S. Lorent, *The new world,* 1946.

Peter Heylyn. *Cosmography.* 1652 et seq. Easier to manage than Hakluyt and Purchas.

George Sandy's (see his poetry and Drayton's). *Relation of a journey* (to the middle east). 1610.

Religion

There is no substitute for attending Roman Catholic and Anglican services and the meeting of a dissenters' sect (as 'low' as possible); nor for reading the Prayer Book and the Bible, especially *Genesis, Job, Psalms, Song of Solomon, John, Romans, Revelation.* A painless way in is to look up a Biblical topic or figure in Réau (see art section below), pursue its illustrators and then return to the Bible account. Jonson's *Alchemist* and *Bartholomew Fair* contain caricatures of puritans.

John Donne, *Sermons: selected* by L. P. Smith, Oxford 1919; or L. P. Smith ed. *The golden grove: selected passages from the sermons and writings of Jeremy Taylor,* Oxford 1930. Donne was a friend of several of the earlier poets in this anthology, notably Carew; and Taylor of some of the later, notably Katherine Philips.

Mary Douglas ed. *Witchcraft confessions and accusations.* 1970.

F. M. Powicke. *The reformation in England.* 1941.

Keith Thomas. *Religion and the decline of magic.* 1971.

History of ideas

Katharine M. Briggs. *Pale Hecate's team . . . witchcraft and magic . . .* 1962.

E. Cassirer. *The Platonic renaissance in England.* Trans. J. Pettegrove. 1954.

H. K. Haydn. *The counter-renaissance.* 1950.

B. Willey. *The 17th-century background: studies of the thought of the age in relation to poetry and religion.* 1934.

James Winny ed. *The frame of order: an outline of Elizabethan belief taken from treatises of the late 16th century.* 1957.

Visual art

Attend first to small-scale design of the period come across casually—title-pages, emblems, maps, tombs. Then look quickly at some of the great masters and great buildings; finally study one or two minor artists or topics in depth on your own. Relate all to the poets and their materials.

Painting. The great renaissance painters who most directly influenced our period were the north Italians, Correggio (c.1494–1534), e.g. *Assumption of the Virgin;* Titian (c.1477–

1576), who also has an *Assumption* (Venice); and Jacopo Tintoretto (1518–94)—see his *Presentation of the Virgin* (Venice). The Spanish masters of the next generation are useful for displaying the variousness of technique and subject available to the 17th century: El Greco (1545–1614) for tense religious passion; Caravaggio (1569–1609) for *chiaroscuro* and body; Velasquez (1599–1660) for military and state paintings and for the most courtly treatment of erotic mythology, e.g. his *Venus and Cupid* (National Gallery); and Murillo (1617–82) for religious sentiment of Victorian sweetness. Of French painters, the contemporary Poussin (1594–1665) is most important to us for his many mythological and Biblical subjects treated with the coolest sensuality; see especially his Burghley House *Assumption* to compare with the Italians (note cupids as attendant baby angels and fertility objects); *Diana and Endymion* (Detroit) and *Triumph of Neptune and Amphitrite* (Philadelphia) for many members of the pantheon; Louvre *Childhood of Bacchus* or National Gallery *Bacchanal;* and *Childhood of Zeus* (Dulwich) in which the baby god sucks a goat in such a way that the heads, breasts and genitals of god, man, woman and goat are equated. But the most important painting for us is contemporary Flemish and Dutch, above all Rubens (1577–1640) and Rembrandt (1609–69). Rubens painted for James I and Charles I and for George Villiers, 1st Duke of Buckingham (their favourite, James' lover, Charles' tutor): see his *Apotheosis of James I* and other paintings in the Banqueting Hall, Whitehall; *Apotheosis of Buckingham* (National Gallery); and, for general views of the period, *Henri IV receiving the portrait of Marie de Medici* (Louvre), which includes Zeus and Hera, Eros, cupids, Hymen, the king in armour, the girl's face and a landscape; and *Judgement of Paris* (National Gallery). With Rembrandt it would be best to start with his Biblical pieces (e.g. several illustrating the story of Samson) and his realistic nudes. The best English painters were Dutch. Van Dyck (1599–1641) was a pupil of Rubens but worked mainly in England—royal portraits, portrait of Lovelace, double portrait of Carew and the dramatist Killigrew (at Windsor), a *Cupid and Psyche;* his pupil William Dobson (1610–46) whose work includes a portrait of Newcastle; and Sir Peter Lely who came from Holland in 1641; his work includes illustrations to Lovelace's *Lucasta,* many royal portraits including children of Charles I and mistress of Charles II (Duchess of Cleveland), Fanshawe and his son, Davenant, Pepys, Cotton and his family, and some scenes of voluptuous exhaustion useful for defining restoration sensuality (e.g.

Nymphs at a fountain, Dulwich). Of the poets themselves, Flatman was a distinguished miniaturist and Joseph Beaumont, Crashaw, Butler, George Daniel and Flecknoe were proficient artists.

Buildings. Visit National Gallery and National Portrait Gallery. While in London see: Banqueting Hall, Whitehall, by Inigo Jones, ceiling by Rubens (Charles I was executed from a window); Queen's House by Jones and Hospital by Christopher Wren down the river at Greenwich; those of Wren's City churches which survived the blitz (e.g. St. Stephen Walbrook and St. Paul's, which contains Donne's funeral effigy, ordered by Henry King when prebendary of London from Nicholas Stone, the finest sculptor of the period); Wren's palace at Hampton Court, with staircase mural by Verrior (Pope sneers at Verrior and Laguerre in *Use of Riches*; Laguerre painted the chapel ceiling of Chatsworth, Derbyshire, seat of the dukes of Devonshire since 1688). While in the north visit Welbeck Abbey in Nottinghamshire, seat of the Duke and Duchess of Newcastle (related to the dukes of Devonshire and not far away); this house contains miniatures by Samuel Cooper (a good small-scale artist to study on one's own) and a portrait of the Earl of Strafford (see Shirley's poem) by Van Dyck. At Oxford see Wren's Sheldonian Theatre; at Cambridge, his library at Trinity and chapel at Pembroke. In the south, go to Wilton House, near Salisbury and near Bemerton (the parish of George Herbert and John Norris), seat of the Herbert-Pembroke families; the part rebuilt by Inigo Jones contains a double-cube room in which is a family group of Herberts by Van Dyck, a portrait of Colonel Hutchinson by Robert Walker (another good minor for private study) and a portrait of his mother by Rembrandt. In Paris, wander about at Versailles, and see some of these artists at the Louvre. In Rome, start with Bernini and his sculpture of St. Teresa in mystic ecstasy in the church of S. Maria della Vittoria; *Triumph of the Name of Jesus* and *Apotheosis of St. Ignatius Loyola* by Baciccio in the church called Il Gesù; and Caracci's *Mythologies and allegories of love* in the Palazzo Farnese.

Books. See standard illustrated editions of the major artists and architects mentioned above; and consult some of the following:

E. Auerbach. *Tudor artists.* 1954. *Nicholas Hilliard.* 1961. Tudor miniaturist.

C. H. Collins Baker and W. G. Constable. *English painting of the 16th and 17th centuries.* Florence and Paris 1930.

E. F. Caritt ed. *Calendar of British taste*. 1949.

K. A. Esdaile. *English church monuments 1510–1840*. 1946.

E. H. Gombrich. *Norm and form: studies in the art of the renaissance*. 1966.

J. A. Gotch. *Inigo Jones*. 1928.

Arnold Hauser. *Mannerism: the crisis of the renaissance and the origin of modern art*. Trans. E. Mosbacher. 2 vols. 1965.

René Huyghe ed. *Larousse encyclopaedia of renaissance and baroque art*. 1944.

Henry Peacham the younger. *The complete gentleman*. 1622, rev. 1634, 1661; ed. G. S. Gordon 1906. Contemporary line on classical art.

Louis Réau. *Iconographie de l'art chrétien*. 3 vols. Paris 1955–59. Important guide to pictures that illustrate Biblical subjects.

H. Wölfflin. *Renaissance and baroque*. Trans. K. Simon. 1964.

Music

Work from John Playford, *Brief introduction to the skill of music for song and viol* 1654: Playford was the chief to cash in on the popularity of music with all classes and the development of printing for it from c.1590. See B. Pattison *Music of the English renaissance* (1948) and J. Hollander *The untuning of the sky* (Princeton 1961). Examine a lute (chief accompaniment for most of the songs in this anthology), virginals and (from about 1660) a spinet. Listen to or perform music by the following composers (most at that time also the top executants): William Byrd c.1542–1623: organ, harpsichord, virginals; anthems and masses. John Dowland 1562–1626: lute songs. Thomas Campion d. 1620: music and words for lute. Orlando Gibbons 1583–1625: madrigals, the most important form for some years either side of 1600; from c.1625 Italian influence shifted the emphasis from interwoven, contrapuntal part-music to solos, melody and expressiveness. Henry Lawes 1595–1662: central to any study because of his concern for the words; wrote music for *Comus* and for songs by Cartwright, Herrick, Waller and others; see *Airs and dialogues* 1653, 1655, 1658 or selections ed. Playford as *Select airs* 1669. The rise of chamber and orchestral music and of opera at the Restoration is represented by the greatest musician of the period, Henry Purcell c.1657–95; *Dido and Aeneas*, an opera commissioned for a girls' boarding-school with words by Nahum Tate, 1680; set music to *Lillibulero*, an anti-Irish and anti-papist song written by Anne Wharton's husband which instantly became a hit and was used as propaganda music in World War II; music also for several of Shadwell's plays including *Timon,* and for Dryden, Durfey, etc. See G. M. Hopkins' poem to him.

Domestic arts

B. S. Allen. *Tides in English taste 1619–1800: a background for the study of literature.* 2 vols. Cambridge Mass. 1937.

Barnabe Googe. *Four books of husbandry.* 1577, rev. Gervase Markham as *The whole art of husbandry* 1631.

Alan Macfarlane. *The family life of Ralph Josselin, a 17th-century clergyman: an essay in historical anthropology.* Cambridge 1970.

C. L. Powell. *English domestic relations 1487–1653.* 1917.

M. and C. H. B. Quennell. *History of everyday things in England.* Vol. 2 1500–1732. 1933.

G. Rattray Taylor. *Sex in history.* 1953 rev. 1959.

Hannah Woolley. *The gentlewoman's companion, or a guide to the female sex.* 1675.

Biography

John Aubrey. *Brief lives and other selected writings* ed. A. Powell, 1949. Aubrey (1626–97) left MS. gossip for his projected 'Lives of eminent persons', much of which was used by the less compassionate Anthony à Wood in his biographical dictionary of Oxford writers and bishops called *Athenae oxoniensis* (1691–92). Aubrey's *Miscellanies* (1696) are mostly folklore and ghost-stories. There is a portrait drawing of him by William Faithorne in the Ashmolean, Oxford.

E. W. Blight. *Sir Kenelm Digby and his Venetia.* 1932. A fine stand-off literary figure to start on. Digby was a pirate, also a patron of the arts; see Van Dyck, and miniature portrait by Isaac Oliver. See also R. T. Petersson, *Sir Kenelm Digby, the ornament of England, 1603–55,* 1956.

Gervase Huxley. *Endymion Porter: the life of a courtier 1587–1649.* 1959. See Davenant in this anthology, and portrait of Porter by Cornelius Johnson c.1628 at Althorp, Lincs.

Dorothy Osborne (1627–95). *Letters to Sir William Temple,* ed. G. C. Moore Smith. Oxford 1928. A refreshing change from Pepys and Evelyn (though see any ed. of their diaries which has a good index, and see portraits of Pepys and his wife by John Hales and of Evelyn by Robert Walker.)

D. Nichol Smith ed. *Characters from the histories and memoirs of the 17th century.* Oxford 1918.

Izaak Walton. *Lives* (of Donne, Herbert, Wotton, et al.) 1640; see *Complete Walton* ed. G. L. Keynes 1929.

For further background see the diaries of Evelyn and Pepys c.1660, and the prose of poets in this anthology, especially Wotton, Bacon, Dekker, Burton, Nashe, Sir Thomas Browne, Duchess of Newcastle (autobiography), Jane Barker (novels), Bunyan, Wesley.

Literary history

K. M. P. Burton. *Restoration literature.* 1958.

J. M. Cohen. *History of western literature.* 1956.

P. Cruttwell. *The Shakespearean moment and its place in the poetry of the 17th century.* 1954.

M. S. Day. *History of English literature to 1660;* and *1660–1837.* Separate vols. 1963. Doubleday college course guides.

Boris Ford gen. ed. *Pelican guide to English literature 3* (From Donne to Marvell) 1956 etc.

C. J. Friedrich. *The age of the baroque 1610–60.* 1952.

R. Garnett and E. Gosse. *English literature: an illustrated record.* 4 vols. 1903. Unsurpassed.

Josephine Miles. *Eras and modes in English poetry.* 1957 2nd ed. Berkeley and L. A. 1964.

Lowry Nelson. *Baroque lyric poetry.* New Haven 1963.

Allardyce Nicoll. *Stuart masques and the Restoration stage.* 1968.

Wylie Sypher. *Four stages of renaissance style: transformations in art and literature 1400–1700.* 1955.

G. W. Whiting. *Milton's literary milieu.* Chapel Hill 1939.

Some literary topics

J. B. Broadbent. *Poetic love.* 1964.

Denis de Rougemont. *Passion and society* trans. M. Belgion. 1940 rev. 1956.

H. N. Fairchild. *Religious trends in English poetry.* Vols. 1, 2, 3. 1939, 1942, 1949.

Henry Green. *Shakespeare and the emblem writers.* 1870.

W. R. Keast ed. *17th-century English poetry: modern essays in criticism.* 1962. Includes the standard essays on metaphysical poetry but limited to that.

Peter V. Marinelli. *Pastoral*. 1971. Critical Idiom series.

L. L. Martz. *The poetry of meditation: a study in English religious literature of the 17th century*. 1954 rev. 1962.

H. M. Richmond. *The school of love: the evolution of the Stuart love lyric*. Princeton 1964.

M. M. Ross. *Poetry and dogma: the transfiguration of eucharistic symbols in 17th-century English poetry*. New Brunswick 1954. More businesslike than chat about dissociation of sensibility.

Stanley N. Stewart. *The enclosed garden: the tradition and the image in 17th-century poetry*. Madison 1966.

J. H. Wilson. *The court wits of the Restoration*. Princeton 1948.

Good anthologies

A. B. ed. *Covent Garden drollery*. 1672. One version ed. M. Summers 1927, another G. Thorn-Drury 1928.

K. Allot gen. ed. *The Pelican book of English prose*. Vol. 1 1550–1620 ed. K. Muir; vol. 2 1620–1700 ed. P. Ure. 1956.

Anon. ed. *Academy of compliments*. 1640 etc. to beyond the Restoration.

N. Ault ed. *Elizabethan lyrics*. 1925 rev. 1949. *17th-century lyrics*. 1928 rev. 1950. *Treasury of unfamiliar lyrics*. 1938.

R. C. Bald ed. *17th-century English poetry*. 1959.

Edmund Blunden and Bernard Mellor ed. *Wayside poems of the 17th-century*. Hong Kong 1963.

A. Chalmers ed. *Works of the English poets*. 21 vols. 1810.

J. Cotgrave ed. *Wit's interpreter*. 1655, 1662, 1671.

J. P. Cutts and F. Kermode ed. *17th-century songs now first printed from a Bodleian MS.* (Mus. 6.1.) Reading 1956.

Helen Gardner ed. *The metaphysical poets*. 1957 etc. Penguin.

H. J. C. Grierson ed. *Metaphysical lyrics and poems of the 17th-century: Donne to Butler*. Oxford 1921.

H. J. C. Grierson and G. Bullough ed. *Oxford book of 17th-century verse*. Oxford 1934.

J. W. Hebel and H. H. Hudson ed. *Poetry of the English renaissance 1509–1660*. 1932.

E. A. J. Honigman ed. *A book of masques in honour of A. Nicoll*. Cambridge 1967.

H. Kenner ed. *17th-century poetry: the schools of Donne and Jonson*. 1964.

F. Kermode ed. *English pastoral poetry from the beginnings to Marvell*. 1952.

W. Kerr ed. *Restoration verse 1660–1715*. 1930.

H. Love ed. *The Penguin book of Restoration verse*. 1968.

L. B. Marshall ed. *Rare poems of the 17th-century*. Cambridge 1936.

J. A. Mazzeo gen. ed. *The Borzoi anthology of 17th-century English literature*. 5 vols. 1967. *17th-century English poetry* vol. ed. Miriam K. Starkman.

P. Quennell ed. *Aspects of 17th-century verse*. 1933.

V. de Sola Pinto and A. E. Rodway ed. *The common muse: an anthology of popular British ballad poetry*. 1957. N.B.: For real folk poems, which are undatable and mostly pre-17th-century, see J. Reeves, *The idiom of the people* (1958) and *The everlasting circle*.

H. E. Rollins ed. *Cavalier and puritan: ballads of the great rebellion*. 1923.

Helen C. White, Ruth C. Wallerstein, Ricardo Quintana, A. B. Chambers ed. *17th-century verse and prose* vol. (i) 1600–60. 1951 rev. 1971.

John Williams ed. *English renaissance poetry: a collection of shorter poems from Skelton to Jonson*. 1963. Anchor.

Classical literature

Use Betty Radice, *Who's who in the ancient world* 1971 and G. Highet, *The classical tradition: Greek and Roman influences on western literature* (Oxford 1949) along with the classical dictionary cited above; or write your own paraphrases of literal translations of a few poems from the following: the *Greek anthology* (a collection of short poems starting about 400 B.C. and covering over 1000 years); Theocritus, one of the 'Alexandrian' poets of the 3rd century B.C., native of Syracuse, wrote *Idylls* (i.e. pastorals: see especially *Lament for Daphnis*); Catullus (c.84–c.54 B.C.), love poems to Lesbia, much influenced by Greek; Horace (65–8 B.C.), *Odes;* Tibullus (c.60–19 B.C.), *Elegies* (in the sense of love poems): Propertius (c.50–c.16 B.C.), love poems; Ovid (43 B.C.–A.D. 18), *Amores, Metamorphoses, Fasti;* Ausonius (c.310–c.390 A.D.), Roman consul and a Christian, lived at Bordeaux—*Idylls*.

Examples of continental literature

G. Saintsbury. *A short history of French literature*. 6th ed. Oxford 1901.

J. H. Whitfield. *A short history of Italian literature*. 1960.

Use those as guides and construct your own comparisons by study from among the following:

Francesco Petrarca (Petrarch, 1304–74) Italian poet and scholar. *Sonnetti, trionfi, etc.* 1470. Cf. lyrics in the Sidney and Spenser tradition, and Ayres. Anna Hume trans. *The triumphs of love, chastity, death* Edinburgh 1644.

Giovanni Pico della Mirandola (Pico, 1463–94) Italian humanist. *Commento sopra una canzona de amore da H. Benivieni* 1496. Trans. Stanley as *A Platonic discourse on love* 1651. Links our poets with Marsilio Ficino (Ficino, 1433–99), who translated all Plato into Latin and constructed a Platonic theology.

Pierre de Ronsard (Ronsard, 1524–85) French; member of 'La Pléiade'. *Odes, Amours, Hymnes* 1550–55. Cf. Drummond and other earlier lyric poets.

Joachim Du Bellay (Du Bellay, 1522–60) French; chief theorist of 'La Pléiade,' defender of the vernacular. *L'Olive* (first French sonnet sequence) 1549–50. Start with *Contre les petrarquistes*.

Philippe Desportes (1547–1606) French poet. *Diane* 1573. Seems more 'English' than Ronsard and Du Bellay; also anti-Petrarchan.

Michel de Montaigne (1533–92), French savant. *Essais* (including, of special importance, *L'apologie de Raimond Sebonde*) 1580, et seq. Trans. J. Florio 1603, Cotton 1685. Cf. Bacon's *Essays;* and Cowley's.

Guillaume de Saluste, seigneur du Bartas (Du Bartas, 1544–90) French. *La semaine, ou création du monde* 1578; *La second semaine* 1584. Trans. Sylvester 1605–07.

Agrippa d'Aubigné (1551–1630). *Les tragiques* 1616: heroic maledictions on the wars of religion.

Luis Vas de Camoens (Camoens, 1524–80) Portuguese. *Os Lusiads* (epic) 1572. Trans. Fanshawe 1655.

Torquato Tasso (1544–95) Italian. *Gerusalemme liberata* (epic) 1581. Trans. Fairfax 1600. *Aminta* (pastoral drama) 1581. Trans. Henry Reynolds 1628; cf. Randolph *Amyntas* 1638.

Gian Battista Guarini (Guarini, 1537–1612) Italian. *Il pastor fido* (pastoral drama) 1590. Trans. Fanshawe 1647; cf. J. Fletcher, *Faithful shepherdess* c.1610.

Giambattista Marino (Marino, 1569–1625) Italian. *Rime* 1602. Cf. Crashaw, Sherburne, Stanley. *La Strage degli innocenti* 1633. Trans. Crashaw 1646. See M. Praz 'Stanley, Sherburne and Ayres as translators and innovators,' *Modern Language Rev.* XX 1925.

Luis de Gongora y Argote (Gongora, 1561–1627). Spanish. *Obras en verso.* Madrid 1627. Cf. Stanley, *Poems* 1651.

Jakob Boehme (1575–1624) German mystic. *The high and deep searching out of the threefold life of man* trans. John Sparrow 1650.

Blaise Pascal (1623–62). French mystic. *Pensées* 1670. Trans. J. Walker 1688.

Not much comparative work has been done on the six following French poets who were all writing in the 17th century but before the English revolution.

François de Malherbe (Malherbe, 1555–1628) Neo-classicist. Odes on state occasions from 1600.

Vincent Voiture (1598–1648) Favourite protégé of the '*précieux*' salon of the Marquise de Rambouillet.

Isaac de Benserade (1613–91), also a French society poet, and a writer of masques.

Jean-François Sarasin (c.1610–54) Light lyric poet.

Théophile de Viau (1590–1626), '*précieux*' dramatist, 'libertin' lyricist.

Antoine-Girard de Saint-Amant (Saint-Amant, 1594–1661), another *libertin. Albion,* a satire on English puritans; *Rome ridicule,* a burlesque, 1643.

Jean de la Fontaine (La Fontaine, 1621–95), interesting not only for the famous *Fables choisies* of 1668 but also *Contes et nouvelles en vers* (1664) and the prose *Amours de Psyché et de Cupidon,* 1673.

The following are most important for the Restoration period. Many English royalists had had direct experience of French life and literature in exile.

Pierre Corneille (1606–84), dramatist. *Horace* 1639, part trans. Katherine Philips 1667, completed by Denham 1669; trans. Cotton 1671; etc.

Jean Racine (1639–99), dramatist. *Bérénice* 1670, cf. Otway, *Titus and Berenice* 1677; etc.

Jean-Baptiste Molière (1622–73), dramatist. *L'école des maris* 1661, cf. Otway, *Soldier's fortune* 1681; *L'avare* 1668, cf. Shadwell, *The Miser* 1672; *Le malade imaginaire* 1673, cf. Aphra Behn, *Sir Patient Fancy* 1678.

Jean Regnault de Segrais (1656–1710), a comical follower of Molière and writer of pastoral poetry.

Paul Scarron (1610–60), comic poet. *Le Virgile travestie,* Paris 1648–50, cf. Cotton, *Scarronides* 1665 and Radcliffe, *Ovid travestie* 1680.

Nicholas Boileau-Despréaux (Boileau, 1636–1711), critic and satirist. *Satires* 1666, cf. Rochester, *Satire against mankind;* Butler, *Satires;* Sheffield, *Essay on satire.*

INDEX TO AUTHORS BY SECTION